INDIA'S SOCIAL SECTOR AND SDGs

This book explores the intersectional perspective of sustainable social development in key sectors, such as education and skill development, health and nutrition, gender concerns, food security and agriculture in India. It delves into contemporary concerns of poverty, employment and inclusive growth, and social marginalisation and inequality. The volume brings together the contributions of various stakeholders from academia, research organisations, NGOs and policymakers to address social-sector issues and sustainable development goals (SDGs) in the Indian context. It reflects on policies, strategies and performance in the context of Constitutional goals and the commitment to global SDGs and examines the character and contours of social development in the country.

Comprehensive and topical, this volume will be useful to scholars, researchers, policymakers and practitioners of development studies, political studies, sociology and development economics.

Rangachar Govinda is Distinguished Professor at the Council for Social Development and former Vice-Chancellor of the National Institute of Educational Planning and Administration, New Delhi, India. He was the J. P. Naik National Fellow for Studies in Education and Culture, Indian Council for Social Science Research. He has been a visiting professor at the Institute of Education, University of London, and the International Institute for Educational Planning, Paris. His areas of interest include primary education, decentralised management, leadership development, policy analysis, human rights and democracy.

Poornima M. is Assistant Professor at the Council for Social Development, New Delhi, India. She holds a doctorate from the Centre for the Study of Law and Governance, Jawaharlal Nehru University. She has completed about four to five research and evaluation studies and is currently heading an ICSSR-sponsored research study on "Reviving Government Schools". Her research interests include governance, elementary education, public sector reforms, local government, public policies and gender issues.

INDIA'S SOCIAL SECTOR AND SDGs

Problems and Prospects

Edited by Rangachar Govinda and Poornima M.

LONDON AND NEW YORK

First published 2020
by Routledge
2 Park Square, Milton Park, Abingdon, Oxon OX14 4RN

and by Routledge
52 Vanderbilt Avenue, New York, NY 10017

Routledge is an imprint of the Taylor & Francis Group, an informa business

© 2020 selection and editorial matter, Council for Social Development, New Delhi, India; individual chapters, the contributors

The right of Rangachar Govinda and Poornima M. to be identified as the authors of the editorial material, and of the authors for their individual chapters, has been asserted in accordance with sections 77 and 78 of the Copyright, Designs and Patents Act 1988.

All rights reserved. No part of this book may be reprinted or reproduced or utilised in any form or by any electronic, mechanical, or other means, now known or hereafter invented, including photocopying and recording, or in any information storage or retrieval system, without permission in writing from the publishers.

Trademark notice: Product or corporate names may be trademarks or registered trademarks, and are used only for identification and explanation without intent to infringe.

British Library Cataloguing-in-Publication Data
A catalogue record for this book is available from the British Library

Library of Congress Cataloging-in-Publication Data
Names: Govinda, R., editor. | M., Poornima, editor.
Title: India's social sector and SDGs : problems and prospects / edited by Rangachar Govinda and Poornima M.
Identifiers: LCCN 2019019687 (print) | LCCN 2019021638 (ebook)
Subjects: LCSH: Social planning—India. | India—Social policy. | India—Social conditions.
Classification: LCC HN683.5 (ebook) | LCC HN683.5 .I5398 2020 (print) | DDC 306.0954—dc23
LC record available at https://lccn.loc.gov/2019019687

ISBN: 978-1-138-36151-5 (hbk)
ISBN: 978-0-367-34180-0 (pbk)
ISBN: 978-0-367-34182-4 (ebk)

Typeset in Bembo
by Apex CoVantage, LLC

 Printed in the United Kingdom by Henry Ling Limited

CONTENTS

Foreword viii
Preface x
List of figures xii
List of tables xiv
List of abbreviations xvii
List of contributors xxiii

PART I
Introduction 1

1 Social-sector development in India: an overview 3
  Rangachar Govinda

PART II
SDGs: process and outcome 63

2 Reflections on sustainable development goals from the perspective of developing countries: transformative change or business as usual? 65
  Mitu Sengupta

PART III
Education and skill development — 77

3 School education in India and SDGs: issues and challenges — 79
Preet Rustagi, Swati Dutta and Deeksha Tayal

4 Knowledge, skills and sustainable development: role of higher education — 97
N. V. Varghese

5 Challenges beyond schooling: skilling youth to realise the goal of vocational education and training in India — 112
Santosh Mehrotra and Vinay Swarup Mehrotra

PART IV
Health, nutrition and food security — 127

6 Achieving sustainable development goal 3 in the Indian context: the policy-action incoherence — 129
T. Sundararaman and Alok Ranjan

7 Public health policies: generating revenues or relief? — 142
Imrana Qadeer

8 Macro-masking of micro realities: access to food and nutrition among tribals — 167
Nitin Tagade and R. S. Deshpande

9 Food security and sustainable agriculture in India — 182
Mondira Bhattacharya and Ankita Goyal

PART V
Gender equality — 201

10 Gender and sustainable development goals — 203
Suneeta Dhar

11 Women's work participation and maternity protection conundrum in India: call for high-priority interventions — 228
Lakshmi Lingam

PART VI
Poverty, employment and inequality   **247**

12 Are we really concerned about employment? Some
    reflections on India's current macroeconomic policy regime   249
    Praveen Jha

13 Exploring the relationship between economic growth,
    employment and education in Indian states   264
    Mona Khare

14 Elite dominance and rising inequality in India   283
    Zoya Hasan

15 Thinking *samata* at the SDG moment   296
    Manoranjan Mohanty

PART VII
Conclusion   **313**

16 Making India's development inclusive: centrality of
    education and health   315
    Muchkund Dubey

Index   *328*

FOREWORD

This is an authoritative book on India's pursuit of social development goals in the context of SDGs ... a collection of global goals set by the United Nations General Assembly in 2015 for the year 2030. There was an age when social and environmental issues lay largely in the local domain. In a trade-dominated economy; however, social outcomes emerge through different strands working out in a larger stage.

Significantly, this book comes with an Indian perspective. Its reasoning is therefore different from what is called the Washington Consensus, a set of policy prescriptions supported by prominent global economic institutions. It does not take the position that India was ahead of East Asian countries in the 1960s but somehow fell behind later. The fact is that South Korea was ahead of India then and continues to be so even now. However, the authors make more compelling comparisons with China with respect to various social development indicators.

The contributors to this volume constantly come across interdependencies between different development objectives and with larger socio-economic processes. Such intersections need levels of coordination, since instruments lie outside the sector. But the Planning Commission has been abolished, and the danger of isolation in silos is real, so the authors wistfully look to the Niti Aayog, which, as an institution, unfortunately does not have the powers to allocate resources or evaluate outcomes systematically.

On the issue of gender and demographics, it has been established that girls going to colleges end up marrying and consequently bearing their first child later. Nutrition and gender priorities cannot be overempathised, and insensitive nationalists need to understand that strong soldiers cannot be born of weak mothers.

The authors underline the fact that the much-heralded demographic dividend has the potential to turn into a national nightmare because frustrated youth are a powerful disruptive force if not integrated into benign socio-economic processes.

Skill development is not simply a set of certificates that are to be handed out; rather, it is a certification that needs to be integrated with growth and innovation.

The authors look deeply into the crucial areas of poverty and nutrition, much to the satisfaction of this economist, who has been tirelessly campaigning over the last two decades that the Alagh Poverty Line constructed in 1979 for rural and urban areas on the basis of nutritional requirements must change to a more comprehensive view of "desired outcomes". They are with Louis Dumont in the understanding that India is the only civilisation in which exploitation of man by man is justified (*Homo Hierarchicus: The Caste System and Its Implications*). This volume is a testimony to the argument that poverty reduction is not enough and that reduction of inequality between classes and countries has to be achieved for a sustainable future. As Gandhi famously said, "There is enough for everybody's need but not for everybody's greed". So we called him the Mahatma – but shot him. He wanted sustainable villages, abolition of hunger and self-reliant communities of workers with advanced decentralised techniques. Clearly he was a man ahead of his times. To rediscover him in this millennium read this deeply engaging treatise.

Yoginder K. Alagh
Camp Gurugram
7 March 2019

PREFACE

There is increasing realisation that, in a country as diverse as India, sustainable development can be achieved only through broad-based social policies well supported by financial resources. Exclusive focus on economic growth even while supported by legislative measures cannot lead to enduring transformation in the quality of life of the people and in the way government functions. What would be the character and contours of such an approach for development in general and for addressing social development concerns in particular is the subject matter of this volume. The volume discusses policy issues, prospects and strategies to address in the social sector in India in the context of globally endorsed sustainable development goals (SDGs). The volume, consisting of scholarly papers placed under four thematic sections, critically examines the progress made in India's social sector and highlights key concerns to be focused on in its development journey.

Papers in the volume were originally presented in "Indian Perspectives on Social Sector Issues and Sustainable Development Goals (SDGs): Policies, Prospects and Future Directions", a seminar organised by the Council for Social Development in July 2016. The papers have been since revised and updated based on the rich discussions during the seminar.

Working on this volume and bringing it out in the current form has been an enriching experience and we are grateful to the authors and the Council for Social Development for giving us this opportunity. We would like to especially thank Prof. Muchkund Dubey for entrusting us with the task of organising the Durgabhai Deshmukh National Seminar in 2016, which eventually resulted in this edited volume. Our sincere thanks are due to the late Ms Anita Kaul, then director of CSD, for her encouragement and support. We acknowledge the continued support of Prof. Ashok Pankaj, current director of the CSD. The edited volume benefitted immensely from the contributions of various people who participated in the seminar. The partial financial contribution made by UNESCO in conducting the seminar is acknowledged with thanks; in particular, we would like to thank Mr Shigeru Aoyagi, director and UNESCO representative to Bhutan, India, Maldives and Sri Lanka.

We would like to thank Ramandeep Kaur, Taarika Singh and Antora Borah, the research associates of CSD, and Ajay Kumar Samariya, Consultant of CSD for their research and secretarial assistance. We owe special thanks to the Routledge team, in particular Mr Shashank Sinha and Antara Ray Chaudhury, for their patience and support in preparing the manuscript. Thanks are also due to the peer-reviewers for their feedback and insightful suggestions.

FIGURES

1.1	HDI over the years: China and India	18
1.2	SPI: status of Indian states	20
1.3	No. of physicians per 1,000 people	25
1.4	Education and health as a percentage of social service expenditure	27
1.5	Expenditure on education and health as a percentage of total public expenditure	28
1.6	Expenditure as percentage of GDP	28
1.7	Social-sector (social services and rural development) expenditure by centre and states, 1987–2016	30
1.8	Current health expenditure per capita $US, 2015	31
1.9	Aggregate expenditure on health as percentage of GDP	31
1.10	Health Expenditure as percentage of total government expenditure	32
3.1	Adult literacy rate by gender and location (%)	80
3.2	Youth literacy rate by gender and location (%)	81
3.3	Net attendance ratio across educational levels by location and monthly per capita consumption expenditure (MPCE) quintile	83
3.4	Percentage of children 3–6 years attending pre-primary school by location and gender	85
3.5	Percentage of children 3–6 years attending pre-primary school by gender and MPCE class	85
3.6	Percentage distribution of students by type of institutions attended by level of education	86
3.7	Percentage distribution of students by type of institutions attended by level of education in rural areas across social group	87

3.8	Percentage distribution of students by type of institutions attended by level of education in urban areas across social group	87
3.9	Component of household educational expenditure per student (%)	88
3.10	Proportion of dropout children (class X and below) by consumption expenditure quintile across social groups	92
6.1	Sustainable development goal 3 and its targets	137
8.1	Poverty in India (%), 2011–12	169
8.2	Differences in poverty among tribal and non-tribal population (2011–12)	170
8.3	Proportion of undernourished children below 5 years in Maharashtra (%), 2005–06	173
8.4	Proportion of underweight children below 5 years in Maharashtra (%), 2012–13	173
9.1	Per capita net availability of cereals and pulses (g/day)	186
9.2	Public distribution of food grains as a percentage of procurement	187
9.3	Area under organic cultivation (MHa)	194
9.4	Area under coarse cereals (000 Ha)	196
9.5	Area under pulses (000 Ha)	196
11.1	Percentage distribution of male and female workers 15–49 years by education level and social group (2009–10)	233
11.2	Total fertility rate by background characteristics (NFHS-4)	234
11.3	Hypothesised relations between poverty, stunting, child development and school achievement	238
12.1	Sectoral growth rates (at 2004–05 prices) since the early 1990s	250
12.2	Sectoral growth rates (at 2011–12 prices) since 2011–12	252
12.3	ASI estimates of registered manufacturing employment	254
12.4	Employment in organised sector manufacturing (100,000 persons)	255
13.1	Framework for virtuous circle of EG/HD growth	266
13.2	LTGRs for NSDP at factor cost (1993–94 to 2011–12)	267

TABLES

1.1	Sustainable development goals (SDGs)	6
1.2	MDGs and targets – summary of progress achieved by India	8
1.3	HDI and its components	18
1.4	State of social development: key indicators	22
1.5	Health and gender indicators for Bangladesh, India and Sri Lanka	25
1.6	Trends in social services expenditure by the general government (centre and states)	26
1.7	Changing share of states in total social-sector expenditure (actuals in %)	27
3.1	Youth literacy rate across social and religious groups (%)	82
3.2	Net attendance ratio by gender, location, social and religious groups across levels of schools (%)	82
3.3	Provision of free education	88
3.4	Component of educational expenditure with and without free education (%)	89
3.5	Educational expenditure per student by levels of school (per academic year) with and without free education (in INR)	89
3.6	Educational expenditure per student by levels of school and category of institution (per academic year) with and without free education (in INR)	90
3.7	Educational expenditure per student by school level and type of institution (per academic year) with and without free education (in INR) in rural and urban areas	90
3.8	Estimated percentage of children among dropouts according to class completed before dropping out across social groups	91
3.9	Percentage of out of school children in terms of dropout, never enrolled and never attended	91

3.10	Reasons for dropout (class X and below) among social groups (%)	93
3.11	Comparison – availability of school facilities between 2010 and 2018 (%)	94
4.1	Labour force participation rates (%)	99
4.2	Employed by gender and level of education, 2011–12 (%)	100
4.3	Distribution of employed by caste and level of education, 2011–12 (%)	101
4.4	Unemployment rate by education, 2011–12	102
4.5	Unemployment rates among social groups (rural and urban)	102
4.6	Wage differentials by levels of education	103
8.1	Poverty and malnutrition in districts with ST population above state average	168
8.2	Classification of states across the levels of GSDP and underweight	172
8.3	Food insecurity in the study area	174
8.4	Prevalence of undernutrition across study regions (%)	175
8.5	Basic socio-economic features	176
8.6	Linear regression results related to undernutrition	177
9.1	Crop yields and growth rates	183
9.2	Crop yield comparisons (2016–17) Kg/Ha	184
9.3	Official poverty estimates in India: percentage and number of poor (Tendulkar methodology)	185
9.4	Fractions of population living in households with per capita calorie consumption below stipulated norms	185
9.5	Nutritional status	186
9.6	Growth of food grains, procurement and public distribution (%)	187
9.7	Growth rate of ICDS in India (%)	188
9.8	Midday meal statistics	189
9.9	Access to safe drinking water (%)	190
9.10	Number per 1,000 households in India by some "improved" and "unimproved" principal source of drinking water (1993–2012)	190
9.11	Number per 1,000 households in India by some important characteristics of principal source of drinking water (1993–2012)	191
9.12	Number per 1,000 households in India by some important characteristics of bathroom and sanitation facilities (1993–2012)	191
9.13	Selected indicators of human development	192
9.14	Farm area treated with chemicals and FYM	193
9.15	Coarse cereal statistics	196
9.16	Pulses statistics	197
9.17	Area under crops as percentage of gross cropped area (triennium ending 2014)	197
9.18	Budgetary allocations (percentage of GDP)	197

11.1	Labour force participation rates of women and men by number of children in the household	235
13.1	Net state domestic product growth (base year: 2004–05)	267
13.2	Growth rate and employment quality, 2011–12	272
13.3	Growth and education attainment index, 2011–12	273
13.4	Relationships: growth, education, employment, inequality	274
13.5	Relationship between growth rate and education Gini (2011–12)	275

ABBREVIATIONS

ACCORD	Action for Community Organisation Rehabilitation and Development
ADB	Asian Development Bank
AICTE	All India Council for Technical Education
AIDS	Acquired Immunodeficiency Syndrome
AIIMS	All India Institute of Medical Sciences
ANC	Antenatal Care
ANM	Auxiliary Nurses & Midwives
API	Active Pharmaceutical Ingredients
APL	Above Poverty Line
APWAPS	Asia-Pacific Women's Alliance for Peace and Security
ASER	Annual Status of Education Report
ASI	Annual Survey of Industries
ASSOCHAM	Associated Chambers of Commerce and Industry of India
AWCs	Aanganwadi Centres
AWID	Association of Women in Development
AYS	Average Years of Schooling
BAIF	Bhartiya Agro Industrial Foundation
BE	Budget Estimates
BJP	Bharatiya Janata Party
BMI	Body Mass Index
BPfA	Beijing Declaration and Platform for Action
BPL	Below Poverty Line
CAGR	Compound Annual Growth Rate
CAW	Crime against Women
CBSE	Central Board of Secondary Education
CCT	Conditional Cash Transfer

CEDAW	Convention on the Elimination of all Forms of Discrimination Against Women
CELAC	Community of Latin American and Caribbean States
CESR	Centre for Economic and Social Rights
CII	Confederation of Indian Industries
CPRHE	Centre for Policy Research in Higher Education
CSOs	Civil Society Organisations
CSR	Corporate Social Responsibility
CSSTE	Centrally Sponsored Scheme on Teacher Education
CSW	Commission on the Status of Women
CV	Coefficient of Variation
DAWN	Development Alternatives with Women for a New Era
DDUGJY	Deen Dayal Upadhyaya Gram Jyoti Yojana
DGET	Directorate General of Employment and Training
DHS	District Health Surveys
DIET	District Institute for Education and Training
DIPP	Department of Industrial Policy and Promotion
DLHS	District Level Household & Facility Survey
DPEP	District Primary Education Programme
DS	Developed States
DTP	Diptheria, Tetanus, Pertussis
EAI	Education Assessment Index
EC	Economic Census
ECCD	Early Childhood Care and Development
ECCE	Early Childhood Care and Education
EFA	Education for All
EG	Economic Growth
EGS	Education Guarantee Scheme
EPWRF	Economic and Political Weekly Research Foundation
EQ	Employment Quality
EQI	Employment Quality Index
EQF	European Qualifications Framework
ES	Educational Status
ESD	Education for Sustainable Development
ESI	Education Status Index
FCI	Food Corporation of India
FCRA	Foreign Contributions Regulation Act
FDI	Foreign Direct Investment
FIPB	Financial Investment Promotion Board
FYM	Farm Yard Manure
FYP	Five Year Plan
GDP	Gross Domestic Product
GER	Gross Enrolment Ratio
GHI	Global Hunger Index

GMR	Global Monitoring Report
GNI	Gross National Income
GoI	Government of India
GR	Growth Rate
GSDP	Gross State Domestic Products
GST	Goods and Services Tax
GVA	Gross Value Added
Ha	Hector
HC	Human Capital
HD	Human Development
HDI	Human Development Index
HIV	Human Immunodeficiency Virus
HLEG	High Level Expert Group
HLPF	High-level Political Forum
HMIS	Health Management and Information Systems
HPHM	High Poverty and High Malnutrition
HPLM	High Poverty and Low Malnutrition
HSR	Health Sector Reforms
IAMR	Institute of Applied Manpower and Research
IBEF	India Brand Equity Foundation
ICCPR	International Covenant on Civil and Political Rights
ICDS	Integrated Child Development Scheme
ICESCR	International Covenant on Economic, Social, and Cultural Rights
ICMR	Indian Council of Medical Research
ICT	Information and Communication Technology
IFC	International Finance Corporation
IGMSY	Indira Gandhi Matritva Sahyog Yojana
IIFCL	India Infrastructure Finance Corporation Limited
IIP	Index of Industrial Production (IIP)
IIPDF	India Infrastructure Project Development Funds
IISD	International Institute for Sustainable Development
ILO	International Labour Organisation
IMF	International Monetary Fund
INC	Indian Nursing Council
IPA	Indian Pharmaceutical Alliance
IPO	Initial Public Offerings
ITIs	Industrial Training Institutes
IUCN	International Union for Conservation of Nature
IVFA	India Value Fund Advisors
JSY	Janani Suraksha Yojana
KALIA	Krushak Assistance for Livelihood and Income Augmentation
Kg	Kilogram
LDS	Less Developed States
LEED	Local Economic and Employment Development

LGBTIQ	Lesbian, gay, bisexual, transgender, intersex and queer
LPG	Liquefied Petroleum Gas
LPHM	Low Poverty and High Malnutrition
LPLM	Low Poverty and Low Malnutrition
LTGR	Long Term Rate of Growth
MBP	Maternal Benefits programme
MDGs	Millennium Development Goals
MDI	Multi-Dimensional Index
MDM	Mid-Day Meal
MGNREGA	Mahatma Gandhi National Rural Employment Guarantee Act
MHRD	Ministry of Human Resource Development
MMR	Maternal Mortality Rate
MMU	Mobile Medical Units
MNC	Multinational Corporation
MOHFW	Ministry of Health & Family Welfare
MoI	Means of Implementation
MoSDE	Ministry of Skill Development and Entrepreneurship
MPCE	Monthly Per Capita Consumption Expenditure
MP	Member of Parliament
MSDE	Ministry of Skill Development & Entrepreneurship
MSDP	Multi Sector Development Program
MSJE	Ministry of Social Justice and Empowerment
MSMEs	Micro, Small and Medium Enterprises
MWCD	Ministry of Women and Child Development
MWR	Main Workers
NAC	National Advisory Council
NAWO	National Alliance of Women
NCD	Non-Communicable Disease
NCEUS	National Commission for Enterprises in the Unorganised Sector
NCOF	National Centre of Organic Farming
NCTE	National Council for Teacher Education
NCW	National Commission for Women
NDA	National Democratic Alliance
NFHS	National Family Health Survey
NGOs	Non-Government Organisations
NHA	National Health Action
NHEQF	National Higher Education Qualification Framework
NHM	National Health Mission
NHP	National Health Policy
NHSRC	National Health Systems Resource Centre
NITI	National Institution for Transforming India
NMP	National Manufacturing Policy
NOSs	National Occupational Standards
NPA	Non-Performing Assets

Abbreviations

NREGA	National Rural Employment Guarantee Act
NREP	National Rural Employment Programme
NRHM	National Rural Health Mission
NSAP	National Social Assistance Programme
NSDA	National Skill Development Agency
NSDC	National Skill Development Corporation
NSDP	Net State Domestic Product
NSQF	National Skills Qualification Framework
NSSO	National Sample Survey Organisation
NTCP	National Tuberculosis Control Programme
NTFPs	Non-Timber Forest Produce
NUEPA	National University of Educational Planning and Administration
NYAY	Nyuntam Aay Yojana
OAEs	Own Account Enterprises
OBCs	Other Backward Castes
OBHE	Observatory of Borderless Higher Education
OECD	Organisation for Economic Co-operation and Development
OOPE	Out-of-Pocket Expenditure
PCNSDP	Per Capita Net State Domestic Product
PDS	Public Distribution System
PG	Post-Graduates
Ph.D	Doctor of Philosophy
PMKVY	Pradhan Mantri Kaushal Vikas Yojana
PMMVY	Pradhan Mantri Matru Vandana Yojana
PPP	Public-Private Partnership
PUCL	People's Union for Civil Liberties
QF	Qualification Frameworks
R&D	Research and Development
RBI	Reserve Bank of India
RCH	Reproductive and Child Health
RLEGP	Rural Landless Employment Guarantee Programme
RMPs	Registered Medical Practitioners
RMSA	Rashtriya Madhyamik Shiksha Abhiyan
RPL	Recognition of Prior Learning
Rs.	Rupees
RSBY	Rashtriya Swasthya Bima Yojana
RSoC	Rapid Survey on Children
RSW	Regular Salaried Workers
RTAs	Regional Trade Agreements
RTE	Right to Education
SBAs	Skilled Birth Attendants
SCs	Schedule Castes
SDGs	Sustainable Development Goals
SEP	Secondary Education Population

SEWA	Self Employed Women's Association
SNA	System of National Accounts
SPI	Social Progress Index
SRI	System of Rice Intensification
SSA	Sarva Shiksha Abhiyan
SSC	Sector Skill Councils
STs	Schedule Tribes
TBAs	Traditional Birth Attendants
TFR	Total Fertility Rate
THE	Total Health Expenditure
TRIPS	Trade-Related Aspects of Intellectual Property Rights
TSP	Training Service Provider
TVET	Technical and Vocational Education and Training
UGC	University Grants Commission
UHC	Universal Health Coverage
UK	United Kingdom
UN	United Nations
UNCTAD	United Nations Conference on Trade and Development
UNDP	United Nations Development Programme
UNESCAP	United Nations Economic and Social Commission for Asia and the Pacific
UNIFEM	United Nations Development Fund for Women
UPA	United Progressive Alliance
UPBEP	Uttar Pradesh Basic Education Programme
URAs	Uruguay Round Agreements
US	United States
UTs	Union Territories
VAW	Violence Against Women
VET	Vocational Education and Training
VGF	Viability Gap Funding
VHSNC	Village Health Sanitation and Nutrition Committee
WCED	World Commission on Environment and Development
WEF	World Economic Forum
WEP	World Employment Programme
WHO	World Health Organization
WMG	Women's Major Group
WTO	World Trade Organisation
WWF	World Wildlife Fund

CONTRIBUTORS

Mondira Bhattacharya is an assistant professor (senior grade) at the Council for Social Development, India. She completed an MA and a MPhil in geography with specialisation in agricultural geography and her PhD in agricultural economics from the Centre for the Study of Regional Development (CSRD), Jawaharlal Nehru University (JNU), New Delhi. She pursued interdisciplinary social science research in current and relevant topics especially in the field of agriculture and rural development.

R. S. Deshpande is Honorary Visiting Professor, Institute for Social and Economic Change (ISEC), Bangalore, India. He was formerly Rajiv Gandhi National Fellow, Indian Council of Social Science Research (ICSSR); before that, he was director of ISEC. He has authored seventeen books and more than 140 research papers published in national and international journals. He has been a visiting professor at the University of Ottawa, Canada; Saskatchewan Institute of Policy Planning, Regina, Canada; University of France, Paris; and the Lund University, Sweden. He was the founder and director of the Dr B. R. Ambedkar School of Economics at Bengaluru.

Suneeta Dhar is a feminist development professional with four decades of work on women's rights, ending violence against women and safer cities for women/girls. She has worked with UNIFEM at both the South Asia and the New York office. She is senior advisor, Jagori and member, SANGAT Feminist Network. She has served on expert committees of NCW (2016) and the Supreme Court on Widow's Rights (2017). Dhar has an MA (social work) from TISS, Mumbai, and is a recipient of Fulbright and Advocacy Institute fellowships.

Muchkund Dubey is the president of the Council for Social Development, New Delhi (CSD), and a former professor at Jawaharlal Nehru University. He studied economics at Oxford University and New York University and has a DLitt degree (honoris causa) from the University of Calcutta. He had an illustrious career in the Indian Foreign Service, serving as, among other positions, India's high commissioner to Bangladesh and the permanent representative to UN organisations in Geneva. He retired from the Indian Foreign Service after occupying the post of foreign secretary to the Government of India.

Swati Dutta is Associate Fellow at the Institute for Human Development, New Delhi, India. She has extensive research experience, especially in developing innovative quantitative tools to understand development issues. She is a trained economist with the specialisation in Econometrics and its application in various development issues. She has more than ten years of research experience in the fields of financial inclusion, poverty, human development, child deprivation, gender inequality, education, labour market and social protection.

Ankita Goyal is an assistant professor at the Council for Social Development, New Delhi, India. She has a PhD in economics and her specialisation covers agriculture and food security and issues related to land and rural development. She has earlier worked as a consultant with the Ministry of Panchayati Raj, Government of India. She has various national and international research publications to her credit and has co authored a book, *Socio-economic Impact Assessment of BT Cotton in India*.

Zoya Hasan is Distinguished Professor at the Council for Social Development, New Delhi, India. She has been a former professor of political Science and the dean of the School of Social Sciences, Jawaharlal Nehru University, New Delhi, and a former member of the National Commission for Minorities. She has undertaken extensive research on the social and educational aspects of Indian Muslims and Muslim women. Her areas of interest are in Indian government and politics, the state party system, political mobilisation, minority rights and gender studies.

Praveen Jha is a professor of economics at the Centre for Economic Studies and Planning (CESP) and an adjunct professor at the Centre for Informal Sector and Labour Studies (CISLS), Jawaharlal Nehru University, New Delhi, India. His major areas of research and teaching include political economy of development, with particular reference to labour, agriculture, natural resources, public finance, education, and history of economic thought. His most recent books include *Labour in Contemporary India* (2016) and (co-edited with Sam Moyo and Paris Yeros) *Reclaiming Africa: Scramble and Resistance in the 21st Century* (2019).

Mona Khare is a professor at the Department of Educational Finance & Centre for Policy Research in Higher Education, National University of Educational Planning and Administration, New Delhi, India.

Lakshmi Lingam is a professor at the Tata Institute of Social Sciences (TISS), Mumbai, India. She is a well-known gender specialist with long years of teaching, researching and publishing in the areas of women's health; women's work and employment; empowerment; migration, globalisation, social movements and public policies. She has several national and international publications and research awards to her credit.

Santosh Mehrotra is a professor of economics at the Centre for Informal Sector and Labour Studies, Jawaharlal Nehru University, India. He spent fifteen years with the UN in research positions, as the head of UNICEF's global research programme, Innocenti Research Centre, Florence, and as the chief economist, Global Human Development Report, New York. He returned to India to head the Development Policy Division of Planning Commission, Government of India, and was also the director general of the National Institute of Labour Economics Research, Planning Commission.

Vinay Swarup Mehrotra is a professor at PSS, Central Institute of Vocational Education (PSSCIVE), a constituent unit of NCERT at Bhopal, India. He is the head of the Department of Agriculture and Animal Husbandry, Curriculum Development and Evaluation Centre, Centre for International Relations and National Skill Qualification Cell at PSSCIVE. He is the coordinator of the UNEVOC Network Centre at PSSCIVE, Bhopal.

Manoranjan Mohanty is Distinguished Professor at the Council for Social Development, New Delhi, India. A political scientist and China scholar whose writings have focused on theoretical and empirical dimensions of social movements, human rights, the development experience and the regional role of India and China. He is also the chairperson of Development Research Institute, Bhubaneswar and Honorary Fellow of Institute of Chinese Studies (ICS) Delhi. He was also formerly the director of Developing Countries Research Centre, professor of political science at Delhi University and chairperson and director of ICS.

Imrana Qadeer is Distinguished Professor at the Council for Social Development, New Delhi, India, since 2012 and a public health expert. Previously she was a professor at the Centre of Social Medicine and Community Health, Jawaharlal Nehru University, where she taught for thirty-five years. She was also a J. P. Naik Senior Fellow at the Centre for Women's Development Studies. Her areas of interest include organisational issues in health services in South Asia with a special focus on India, social epidemiology and political economy of health, nutrition, women's health and research methodology for interdisciplinary research.

Alok Ranjan is a senior research fellow at the Indian Council of Medical Research and is presently pursuing his PhD in public health from Tata Institute of Social Sciences, Mumbai. His main area of interest is health system research.

Preet Rustagi was a professor at the Institute for Human Development (IHD), New Delhi, India. Her areas of research included employment and institutions, gender development indicators, crimes against women, women's equality and empowerment, urban poverty, children's education and work, child wellbeing and deprivations and food security.

Mitu Sengupta is a Full Professor in the Department of Politics and Public Administration at Ryerson University, Toronto, Canada. She has a PhD in political science from the University of Toronto and an MA and BA (honours) in political science from McGill University. Her more recent work focuses on normative concerns in international development and international relations, such as the quest to create universal development goals (like the UN Sustainable Development Goals) and fair climate change and trade agreements.

T. Sundararaman, was formerly head of the National Health Systems Resource Center, New Delhi, India, and currently teaches at the Tata Institute of Social Sciences, Mumbai. His major public health contributions have been to the design and implementation of the National Rural Health Mission and earlier of the Mitanin program and health systems strengthening in Chhattisgarh. He has also been one of the founders and leading activists of the People's Health Movements.

Nitin Tagade is Assistant Professor at the Department of Economics, Savitribai Phule Pune University, Pune, India. He obtained PhD from the Institute for Social and Economic Change, Bangalore, and worked as an assistant professor at the Indian Institute of Dalit Studies, New Delhi. His work has been mainly in the areas of development economics, inequality and economics of discrimination. He has published several articles in journals and edited books, concerning the issues of food security, poverty, inequality, employment and land policy.

Deeksha Tayal is a senior researcher at the Institute for Human Development, New Delhi, India. She is a development economist focusing on issues and problems that confront women and children, including labour force participation, discrimination and gender inequality, deprivation, violence etc. She has more than twelve years of experience spanning research in industry and academic arenas, covering areas such as unpaid work of women, WASH and gender responsive provisioning, gender and climate change, child poverty and multiple deprivations, labour force participation and violence against women.

N. V. Varghese is the vice-chancellor of the National Institute of Educational Plannning and Administration and the director of the Centre for Policy Research in Higher Education (CPRHE), New Delhi, India. He holds a doctoral degree in economics with specialisation in educational planning. He was the head of Governance and Management in Education at the International Institute for Educational Planning (IIEP/UNESCO), Paris, till October 2013 and head of its Training and Education Programmes from 2001 to 2006.

PART I
Introduction

1

SOCIAL-SECTOR DEVELOPMENT IN INDIA

An overview

Rangachar Govinda

The context

Improving the quality of life and human wellbeing, individually and collectively, form the *raison d'être* for all developmental policies and action. That this should be the guiding principle for designing development strategies at national and global levels has never been contested. But the ground reality has been slow to change in practical terms. Persistence of poverty and galloping inequalities tend to indicate that, in critical decision-making bodies, the economistic point of view of singularly focusing on economic growth wins over the protagonists of a more holistic perspective that underscore improvement in quality of life. This unmitigated duality in policy perspective is also exemplified by the development strategies and actions pursued over the years in India.

Where are we in India after several decades of development planning? None can deny that the situation has vastly improved on several social development indicators. From a situation when not even one of five Indians could read and write, we have now around 75 per cent capable of doing that; this has been achieved in spite of a galloping population. And although not even one out of two children ever got enrolled in primary school in the 1950s, we have now reached near-universal enrolment. In 1960, average life expectancy at birth was 41 years; in 2015, it was 68 years (Government of India 2016a, p. 2). While change in almost every sector is clearly visible, the questions continue: Is the level of improvement adequate? What is the quality of change? Is it sustainable over time? Have we been able to overcome social and economic inequalities such that the change and improvement is equitable? Overall, has the quality of life significantly improved for all?

It is indeed a paradox that India is among the fastest growing large economies of the world; the intellectual springboard for engineering the global knowledge revolution as leaders in information and communication technology (ICT). Yet, India has the largest number of illiterate citizens in the world and the largest number of out-of-school children. The level of child malnutrition is so steep that it is comparable only to sub-Saharan Africa; overall, with its HDI rank in the world continuing to remain around 130, the record of human development is hardly creditable. India remains home to one-quarter of the world's undernourished population, over a third of the world's underweight children, and nearly a third of the world's food-insecure people (United Nations 2015). As Amartya Sen wrote:

> We live in a world of unprecedented opulence, of a kind that would have been hard even to imagine a century or two ago.... And yet we also live in a world with remarkable deprivation, destitution and oppression. There are many new problems as well as old ones, including persistence of poverty and unfulfilled elementary needs.... Overcoming these problems is a central part of the exercise of development.
>
> *(Sen 1999, p. xi)*

Even though Sen wrote this nearly two decades ago, it aptly captures the current situation in India. News reports keep showing that more Indians are joining the global club of HNI (the ultra-rich), constituting the top-most echelons of global wealth; on the same page, one can never miss reading reports of extreme destitution and financial distress pushing people to take their own lives. Inequality is so visible and increasing that one has to wonder what is happening to the wealth being created through the high rate of economic growth – is it sustainable without adequate attention to social wellbeing of the people of the country?

As if anticipating the emergence of such a problem in its developmental journey, the Indian Constitution directs the state to strive to minimise the inequalities in income; to endeavour to eliminate inequalities in status, facilities and opportunities; and to secure that the citizens – men and women equally – have the right to an adequate means of livelihood and that the operation of the economic system does not result in the concentration of wealth and means of production to the common detriment. Furthermore, the Indian Constitution also directs that the state will, among its primary duties, promote with special care the educational and economic interests of the weaker sections of the people (in particular, those of the scheduled castes and the scheduled tribes), protect them from social injustice and all forms of exploitation, and regard the raising of the level of nutrition and the standard of living of its people and the improvement of public health. These principles clearly pointed to the need to look beyond indicators of economic growth. Many experts within the country have repeatedly cautioned to avoid dichotomy between economic growth and social progress. For example, as early as 1964, Durgabhai Deshmukh said:

> Achieving progressive economic development in terms of growth of average per capita income only is not enough.... The progress in terms of wellbeing and prosperity among the large masses of people has also to be kept in view.
>
> *(cited by Mohanty 2015)*

Have we heeded this advice?

As we complete nearly seven decades of these Constitutional commitments, and as the economic growth indicators surge ahead, the situation seems to be quite disturbing with respect to several social development indicators. There is a sense of urgency today as never before that we engage in a comprehensive re-examination of the policies and strategies being adopted in the country to pursue social development goals. The chapters in this volume represent one such exercise to reflect on the development strategies adopted and the state of social progress and improvement in quality of life achieved in the country. In this exercise, the recently adopted sustainable development goals (SDGs) framework has been used as a broad canvas for examining social development concerns in India within the global context.

Sustainable development goals (SDGs): global vision and framework for development

Concern for persistent inequality and issues of health, education and livelihood are not unique to development efforts in India. These issues have also found prominent reference in all discourses and declarations at the international level, placing improvement in the quality of life at the centre-stage of development. Emergence of the Human Development Index (HDI) in the 1990s seemed to offer us new metrics to measure the progress of countries in improving quality of life in a holistic sense. Though HDI reports are published annually, assigning global rank to each country on this count, it is difficult to clearly discern the impact of the exercise on development planning practices on the ground. Towards the latter half of the 1990s, the UNESCO Commission on Culture and Development highlighted the following:

> In spite of four decades of development efforts, poverty remains high. Although the proportion of poor people has diminished significantly on all continents except Africa, absolute numbers have increased.... Over a billion people have been largely bypassed by the globalisation process. Involuntary poverty and exclusion are unmitigated evils. All development efforts aim at eradicating them and enabling all people to develop their full potential. Yet, all too often in the process of development, it is the poor who shoulder the heaviest burden.
>
> (Cuéllar. 1996, p. 30)

In the background of such persisting poverty and unmet basic needs of personal and social development, the world community adopted millennium development goals (MDGs) at the beginning of this millennium under the auspices of the UN. Through this, all countries pledged to halve the proportion of people living in extreme poverty, to reduce child and maternal mortality, to provide clean water and basic education for all, to reverse the spread of HIV/AIDS and to reach many other development goals that are vital for our future. Emphasising the need to look ahead by focusing on the future generations, the declaration adopted at the Special UN

Session on Children in 2002 pledged to break the cycle of poverty within a single generation, uniting UN members in the conviction that investments in children and the realisation of their rights are among the most effective ways to eradicate poverty. The summit called for immediate action to eliminate the worst forms of child labour and reaffirmed that each girl and boy is born free and equal in dignity and rights; therefore, all forms of discrimination affecting children must end.

These were indeed profound thoughts and solemn commitments. But increasing inequality across and within the countries – both developed and developing – threatens to derail the achievements made through the implementation of poverty reduction strategies pursued under MDGs. As Zygmunt Bauman (2011) points out, the inflammable mixture of growing social inequality and the rising volume of human suffering marginalised as "collateral" is becoming one of the most cataclysmic problems of our time. The poor have become the "aliens inside", who are deprived of the rights enjoyed by other members of the social order. Coupled with this realisation is the increasing evidence of damage to human existence through climate change triggered by unsustainable patterns of production and consumption across the globe. It is in this context that the international community has evolved

TABLE 1.1 Sustainable development goals (SDGs)

GOAL 1. End poverty in all its forms everywhere
GOAL 2: End hunger, achieve food security and improved nutrition, and promote sustainable agriculture
GOAL 3: Ensure healthy lives and promote wellbeing for all at all ages
GOAL 4: Ensure inclusive and equitable quality education and promote life-long learning opportunities for all
GOAL 5: Achieve gender equality and empower all women and girls
GOAL 6: Ensure availability and sustainable management of water and sanitation for all
GOAL 7: Ensure access to affordable, reliable, sustainable, and modern energy for all
GOAL 8: Promote sustained, inclusive and sustainable economic growth, full and productive employment and decent work for all
GOAL 9: Build resilient infrastructure, promote inclusive and sustainable industrialisation and foster innovation
GOAL 10: Reduce inequality within and among countries
GOAL 11: Make cities and human settlements inclusive, safe, resilient and sustainable
GOAL 12: Ensure sustainable consumption and production patterns
GOAL 13: Take urgent action to combat climate change and its impacts
GOAL 14: Conserve and sustainably use the oceans, seas and marine resources for sustainable development
GOAL 15: Protect, restore and promote sustainable use of terrestrial ecosystems, sustainably manage forests, combat desertification, and halt and reverse land degradation and halt biodiversity loss
GOAL 16: Promote peaceful and inclusive societies for sustainable development, provide access to justice for all and build effective, accountable and inclusive institutions at all levels
GOAL 17: Strengthen the means of implementation and revitalise the global partnership for sustainable development

a new agenda for pursuing global development under the banner of SDGs. The SDG framework adopted by the UN as a post-2015 development agenda consists of seventeen goals and 169 targets/strategies for implementation.

Social development and the SDG framework

The SDGs as a package continue to address the unfinished agenda of the MDGs and expand them to respond to new and emerging challenges through convergence of multiple strategies. In particular, it attempts to bring together concerns of environmental conservation and development on a common platform in the spirit of what the World Conservation Strategy had argued back in 1980: Conservation, like development, is for people; development aims to achieve human goals largely through use of the biosphere, but conservation aims to achieve them by ensuring that such use can continue. Conservation's concern for maintenance and sustainability is a rational response to the nature of living resources (renewability and destructibility) and an ethical imperative, expressed in the belief that "we have not inherited the earth from our parents; we have borrowed it from our children" (IUCN-UNEP-WWF 1980).[1] The Earth Summit of 2012, often referred to as Rio+20, set the stage for evolving a comprehensive development agenda that combines economic development, social progress and environmental sustainability in a common frame leading to the emergence of the sustainable development goals (United Nations 2012). Though the SDGs themselves are subject to continual scrutiny (see Chapter 2, this volume), for India they provide a contemporary canvas with specific objectives to pursue the national development agenda in coherence with its commitment at the global level.

The SDGs are quite comprehensive, covering a range of concerns which can be broadly grouped as representing sustainability concerns in three dimensions – economic, social and environmental. All the goals have to be seen as forming a holistic compact and should not be pursued in an isolated manner. However, a review of the accompanying targets indicate that some goals are quite technical, focusing on climate change concerns while several have more bearing on social development concerns. In particular, goals 1–5, 8, 10, 11 and 16 and their targets (poverty eradication, hunger, nutrition and sustainable food production, health, education, gender, equality, cities and peace) are viewed as significantly focused on social objectives (Cutter et al. 2015). But this is a broad classification based only on the words and phraseology in different goals. We have to recognise that SDGs constitute an integrated framework with strong interconnections and overlaps. Also the goals and targets have to be recontextualised in each country in order to be integrated with national development efforts.

Moving from MDGs to SDGs

The HDI annually declared for each country by UNDP presents an overall aggregate picture of development in human wellbeing and social progress. But

TABLE 1.2 MDGs and targets – summary of progress achieved by India[2]

MDG 1: ERADICATE EXTREME POVERTY AND HUNGER	
TARGET 1: Halve, between 1990 and 2015, the proportion of people whose income is less than one dollar a day	On-track
TARGET 2: Halve, between 1990 and 2015, the proportion of people who suffer from hunger	Slow or almost off-track
MDG 2: ACHIEVE UNIVERSAL PRIMARY EDUCATION	
TARGET 3: Ensure that, by 2015, children everywhere, boys and girls alike, will be able to complete a full course of primary schooling	Moderately on-track
MDG 3: PROMOTE GENDER EQUALITY AND EMPOWER WOMEN	
TARGET 4: Eliminate gender disparity in primary and secondary education, preferably by 2005, and in all levels of education no later than 2015	On-track
MDG 4: REDUCE CHILD MORTALITY	
TARGET 5: Reduce by two-thirds, between 1990 and 2015, the Under-Five Morality Rate	Moderately on-track because of the sharp decline in recent years
MDG 5: IMPROVE MATERNAL HEALTH	
TARGET 6: Reduce by three quarters, between 1990 and 2015, the maternal mortality ratio	Slow or off-track
MDG 6: COMBAT HIV/AIDS, MALARIA AND OTHER DISEASES	
TARGET 7: Have halted by 2015 and begun to reverse the spread of HIV/AIDS	On-track as trend reversal in HIV prevalence has been achieved
TARGET 8: Have halted by 2015 and begun to reverse the incidence of malaria and other major diseases	Moderately on-track as trend reversal has been achieved for Annual Parasite Incidence of Malaria and for prevalence of TB
MDG 7: ENSURE ENVIRONMENTAL SUSTAINABILITY	
TARGET 9: Integrate the principle of sustainable development into country policies and programmes and reverse the loss of environmental resources.	Moderately on-track
TARGET 10: Halve, by 2015, the proportion of people without sustainable access to safe drinking water and basic sanitation	On-track for the indicator of drinking water but slow for the indicator of sanitation
TARGET 11: By 2020, to have achieved a significant improvement in the lives of at least 100 million slum dwellers	The pattern not statistically discernible
MDG 8: DEVELOP A GLOBAL PARTNERSHIP FOR DEVELOPMENT	
TARGET 12: In cooperation with the private sector, make available the benefits of new technologies, especially information and communications	On-track

assessment of effort made and the cumulative changes achieved over a period of time require a disaggregated view of various component factors. The MDGs pursued over fifteen years, beginning in 2000 provided such a picture for eight critical areas of human development. Evaluation of the MDGs in 2015 showed that India made considerable progress on certain MDGs, including halving the poverty rate, reducing the incidence of HIV/AIDS and achieving gender parity in primary school enrolment. India has also shown positive results in increasing access to clean drinking water and reducing maternal mortality. However, the country still lags behind in the targets of achieving universal primary school completion, empowering women through wage employment and political participation, reducing infant mortality and improving access to sanitation.

As we commit ourselves again to the SDG framework, which promises to end poverty, address inequality and create a just society in a sustainable way, it is vital that we re-examine our approach to dealing with issues of the social sector. This is important to address the persistence of deep-rooted inequalities, explicit as well as implicit, that have fostered discrimination across space and time with negative consequences on overall development, particularly affecting the wellbeing of the poor and the marginalised sections of society.

As it was with MDGs, a long-term, fifteen-year timeframe has been set to pursue the goals and targets under the SDGs. Such an extended timeframe has the advantage of allowing the national governments to be flexible in setting short-term targets, designing strategies and applying mid-course corrections to meet the goals. It also facilitates smooth integration of the global goals and targets with national policies and programmes. The impact of MDGs on the development thinking in India was quite evident from the way planning process was envisioned and pursued post-2000. For example, the Tenth Five Year Plan document made explicit reference to MDGs and set clearly monitorable targets to be achieved which corresponded with the MDGs: (a) 5 per cent reduction in poverty by 2007, 15 per cent by 2012; (b) all children in school by 2003, all children to complete five years of schooling by 2007; (c) reduction of IMR to forty-five per thousand live births by 2007, to twenty-eight by 2012; (d) reduction in MMR to two per thousand live births by 2007, to one by 2012; and (e) sustained access to potable drinking water for all villages (Government of India 2002). Implementing a long-term vision stretched over a decade and half also poses institutional challenges as it demands stable organisational arrangement for monitoring the progress towards goals and applying necessary adjustments in programmes and strategies.

The MDGs had set clear quantitative targets to be achieved on a universal basis by every country with respect to each of the eight goals and specified an overall time frame of fifteen years. Specifying measurable targets for several of the social-sector goals might have appeared undue trivialisation of profound concerns of well-being. Nevertheless, it offered clear-cut objectives and indicated the directions in which to proceed. The SDG framework is more indicative of the direction and largely leaves it to national leadership in each country to set physical targets and time frames with respect to each SDG and monitor the progress. Has India set quantitative targets and timelines for each of the seventeen goals and the corresponding targets? For monitoring the progress towards MDGs the then–Planning Commission functioned as the institutional anchor, collating and coordinating the data from different sources. With the Planning Commission playing the lead role, most of the MDG concerns got reflected in the Five Year Plans and mid-term assessment documents – no special effort was to be made to generate and collate data. But with the closure of the Planning Commission, no alternative institutional arrangement has emerged with similar expertise and comprehensive development data. Nor is there any medium-term or long-term development plan prepared that could reflect SDG concerns and allow for periodic assessment and monitoring. This change may not affect assessment of economic growth parameters but is likely to impact regular assessment and monitoring of progress towards social development commitments made under the SDGs. Also, as the responsibility for planning largely lies with the respective government ministries, it is necessary to guard against the strong possibility that the individual SDGs will be pursued, assessed and reported as unconnected silos.

Social-sector policies in India: a brief retrospect

India in the 1950s, liberated from colonial control and entering the era of constitutional democracy was undoubtedly vibrant, enthusiastic and emotional as the country moved forward. But the development reality in terms of economic and social conditions was least favourable for any quick action. The policymakers were heavily preoccupied with creating physical and social infrastructure and establishing institutions of governance and management. This is clearly evident from the emphasis laid on industrial and agricultural development in the initial Five-Year Plans. In the social sector, the focus was on opening schools, dispensaries and hospitals and ensuring adequate access to institutional facilities. In the input-output model of planning, social-sector concerns were viewed as items of social "consumption" and broadly grouped under "social services" for financial allocation. Evaluation studies in the 1960s did reveal that mere infrastructure creation may not guarantee effective utilisation of the facilities. For instance, the Third Five Year Plan observed that, in spite of availability of a primary school in the neighbourhood, many children did not get enrolled and many, having been enrolled, dropped out without completing five years of schooling. But the plan perspective and strategy did not see any radical shift. With two major wars and political turbulence in the post-Nehru period, coupled with severe food shortage verging on famine and difficult foreign exchange situation, the 1960s hardly offered any leeway for planners to change the framework.

The dominant political rhetoric of poverty alleviation in the mid-1970s was accompanied by a major shift in the policy and planning perspective with respect to social-sector concerns. This period, which could broadly be called the "welfare benefit" phase, was exemplified by the launch of the Minimum Needs Programme. Whatever the political considerations might have been, the programme ushered in a new perspective on the obligation of the state in meeting social development concerns of the masses and explicitly introduced the vocabulary of "development with social justice" in the planning framework. The Minimum Needs Programme specifically covered eight vital areas of social development: (a) rural health, (b) rural water supply, (c) rural electrification, (d) adult education, (e) nutrition, (f) environmental improvement of urban slums and (g) houses for landless labourers. It was recognised that, even with expanded employment opportunities, the poor would not be able to buy for themselves all the essential goods and services for achieving a minimum standard of living. There was a need to supplement the measures for providing greater employment opportunities and investment in social sectors, such as education, health, nutrition, drinking water, housing, communications and electricity. It is in this perspective that the Minimum Needs Programme emphasised that neither growth nor social consumption can be sustained, much less accelerated, without being mutually supportive. The provision of free or subsidised services through public agencies was expected to improve the consumption levels of those living below the poverty line and thereby improve the productive efficiency of both the rural and urban workers. This integration of social consumption programmes with economic development initiatives was considered necessary to accelerate growth and to ensure the achievement of plan objectives. It was also considered that the benefits of social services could not reach the poorest without conscious efforts to that end (Government of India n.d.a).[3] Besides the Minimum Needs Programme, the Sixth Five Year Plan identified several other thrust areas that specifically targeted the poor and the marginalised. In fact, the Sixth Five Year Plan also launched the first National Rural Employment Programme, which could be viewed as a precursor to the Mahatma Gandhi National Rural Employment Guarantee Scheme (MGNREGS) and recommended the states to adopt the Maharashtra model of implementation. Although these initiatives were criticised by some as unaffordable populist programmes, they significantly changed the way social-sector initiatives were to be viewed within the planning establishment. Although economic liberalisation began in the 1980s, the decade did not witness much change in the perspective on social sectors.

With the rolling out of structural reform processes in 1990s under severe fiscal constraints and precarious balance-of-payment crisis, the language and vocabulary of social-sector development underwent a transformation even though the contents remained practically unchanged. What were called incentives in the 1960s and welfare benefits for the masses in the 1970s came to be referred to as "subsidies to the poor". The contours of programmes in the social sector during this "early reform phase" did not witness any major shift, as they largely fit the framework of "social safety net".[4] However, the way the programmes were to be financed and implemented began to change substantively. Sectors which were hitherto fully financed by state revenue were opened up for external financial assistance through the World Bank and other multilateral entities. Areas which were treated fully as state obligations got diluted and began to be heavily dependent on private enterprise, seriously jeopardising the interest of the poor and the marginalised. Public-private partnerships (PPP) entered the planning parlance irrevocably. The social justice rhetoric was practically abandoned and replaced by a new vocabulary of globalisation. These were well illustrated by the developments in health and education sectors.

Despite slow progress, primary education had always been considered a core responsibility of the state and to be fully financed by domestic resources. This principle was abandoned with the launch of the World Bank funded basic education projects, such as Uttar Pradesh Basic Education Programme (UPBEP) and, subsequently, the District Primary Education Programme (DPEP) in several states of India. Even though borrowings and grants from the World Bank and other sources were described as means of raising additional resources for the education sector, cost-cutting measures replaced funding and gave way to the substitution of professional teachers with para-teachers; Education Guarantee Scheme (EGS) centres and alternative schools began to replace primary schools (Govinda and Mathew 2018). Similarly, promotion of private enterprise in the health sector contributed to further deterioration of primary services by the government which were already under severe strain because of underfunding. The pro-private health sector policies during this period also laid the foundation for the emergence of a health care market providing premium services at high cost. Interestingly, the Minimum Needs Programme continued through this period of reform, but the rhetoric of social justice was subdued, and benefits provided to the poor were broadly treated as subsidies. The focus was on reducing subsidies in line with structural adjustment policies and strengthening of fiscal responsibility and budget management practices.

The post-2000 period presents a complex picture with respect to policy-making in social sectors. On the one hand, liberalisation policies adopted in the 1990s were further reinforced with more market-orientated reforms in all areas of the government's work. On the other hand, this phase also experienced intense civil society activism and proactive intervention from the judiciary for recasting social development initiatives from the rights perspective. The last two decades have indeed witnessed adoption of a series of social legislations in several sectors, including employment, food security and education transforming, which were till then considered as welfare benefits and subsidies into justiciable legal entitlements. It is not that the Indian State had a change of heart and decided to embrace a rights framework for public provisioning in the social sector. Each of these was invariably preceded by a long story of intense public advocacy campaigns and prolonged legal battle. These have been well documented and commented upon by several scholars, and we do not intend to engage in a detailed discussion here.

It is, however, pertinent to illustrate the difficult journey involved in moving from a benefit and subsidy framework to a rights framework, from welfare schemes to the legal entitlement of citizens and from government largesse to state obligation. For instance, the Food Security Act of 2010 was preceded by a more than decade-long public campaign advocating right to food as a fundamental requirement coupled with an equally long battle through a Supreme Court case, the *People's Union for Civil Liberties (PUCL) v. Government of India*. What was most significant about this court adjudication was not the legal interpretation given to Article 21 in the Constitution declaring a "right to food" as fundamental but the judiciary's proactive engagement with the issue of starvation and malnutrition across the country. The court judgement was not based on ideological conviction or taken out of the chapter on economic and social rights. Instead, it was convincingly derived from the painstaking empirical work carried out by the (court-appointed) food commissioners to gauge the magnitude of starvation and malnutrition in the face of food surplus, wastage and destruction on account of mismanagement of the procurement and distribution system. The MGNREGA has had a long history of multiple schemes providing employment opportunities for rural poor beginning with the Schemes of National Rural Employment Programme (NREP) and Rural Landless Employment Guarantee Programme (RLEGP) during the Sixth Five Year Plan. Several state governments, including the well-documented Maharashtra Employment Guarantee Act, 1977, had launched schemes for the rural poor. But the transformation of these benefit schemes to legal entitlements through NREGA in 2005 could not have happened without the intense civil society campaign which, in fact, was revived in an overlapping manner with the Right to Food and Right to Information campaigns.

The Right to Education (RTE) legislation came through a somewhat different trajectory and was perhaps more radical in nature as it involved a Constitutional Amendment leading to the inclusion of education in the Fundamental Rights chapter as Article 21a. RTE legislation adopted by the Parliament in 2009 was in pursuance of Article 21a of the Constitution. It is pertinent to recall that inclusion of elementary education as a fundamental right was a subject of serious debate in the Constituent Assembly that prepared the Constitution. The idea was not pursued further at that time on the ground that the state was not financially equipped to implement education as a justiciable right. The demand got revived after more than four decades, and the trigger was the Supreme Court judgement in *Unnikrishnan vs. Andhra Pradesh* (1993). The court held that Article 45 in Part IV of the Constitution must be read in "harmonious construction" with Article 21 (Right to Life) in Part III since Right to Life is meaningless if it lacks access to knowledge. Through this the status of fundamental right was accorded to "free and compulsory education" of all children up to 14 years of age. This was followed by public campaigning but not a forceful movement to amend the Constitution, culminating in the insertion of 21a in the fundamental rights chapter of the Constitution. It took another eight years before the corresponding legislation making the Article enforceable was passed by the Parliament (adopted in August 2009 but notified in April 2010), determining the boundaries and contents of the entitlement of the children under the right.

Indeed, the first decade of the millennium has to be marked as a watershed period in the history of independent India. It is within a small window of a few years that a slew of social legislations were adopted. One cannot lose sight of the fact that this was also the period when neoliberal policies and programmes got deeply entrenched with increased accommodation of private enterprise in public provisioning under the framework of a PPP. It would be naive to assume that public campaigning and judicial action, however forceful, could have independently brought about such a radical shift in the stance of the Indian State with respect to social-sector initiatives. Nor was it merely fortuitous that the events happened during this short period. We have to recognise that it could not have materialised without the covert play of favourable dynamics within the ruling political dispensation.

Whatever the motive and external pressure might have been, the willingness of the ruling class to do a balancing act by opening legal entitlement channels in the social sector while pursuing policies of economic liberalisation was unquestionably remarkable. Perhaps the combination of factors that worked in favour of adopting social legislations was the recognition of unprecedented increase in inequality and the call within the establishment for making economic growth more inclusive as evidenced by generous use of the phrase "growth with equity and social justice" in all policy and plan documents of the period.

Is this change irreversible, and does it signify that the state in India is decisively embracing the rights approach to social-sector provisions? There cannot be a categorical response. Parliamentary resolutions and *Gazette* notifications do not by themselves represent the full acceptance of the rights perspective. Legislations can be reversed or diluted by the political leadership. More importantly, the delivery of legal entitlements in the social sector requires proactive and protective measures by the government even in case of a fundamental right, such as the RTE. The real value of such legislations, therefore, will continue to be circumscribed by the nature of schemes and programmes designed and designated for their implementation and, most significantly, the financial resources allocated for the purpose.

The implementation challenge

India has undoubtedly made huge progress in terms of policy perspective with respect to social sectors focusing on basic necessities and treating several of them not merely as welfare measures but as legal entitlements of the citizens. But the real value of these policies lies in the action on the ground contributing to tangible improvement in the quality of the lives of the citizens. Over the past seven decades, several programmes and schemes have been designed and implemented by both central and state governments. Currently several centrally sponsored programmes are operational across the country. However, in the federal governance arrangement, social-sector operations are largely within the purview of state governments. Therefore, even for the centrally funded programmes, the implementation responsibility lies with the state government. Additionally, funding for several of the central programmes is conditional as they require counterpart contributions from the state governments. For instance, funding of SSA (which has now been made part of Samagra Shiksha) is shared between the centre and the state governments on a 65:35 basis. Apart from contributing to Centrally Sponsored Schemes, some state governments implement state-specific schemes/programmes in different areas. Several state governments offer free education for girls even beyond elementary level, which is guaranteed by RTE.

Several of the schemes/programmes have been sustained and expanded over time, while some have been transformed by and adapted to the changing policy considerations. Social-sector programmes are spread across different ministries of the central government even though the bulk of the programmes are with Ministry of Human Resource Development (MHRD), Ministry of Health, Ministry of Women and Child Development (MWCD) and Ministry of Social Justice and Empowerment (MSJE). While some programmes and schemes are universal in nature, the majority of the programmes focus on impacting the lives of the poorer sections of society. Some programmes are also specially targeted to tackle issues arising out of existing social inequalities with particular reference to scheduled castes (SCs), scheduled tribes (STs) and minorities. Recognising the need for continuity and sustained action, most of the large programmes have continued over the years. In some cases they have been restructured to include new elements and dimensions but maintain continuity of operation in the field level. For instance, the Integrated Child Development Scheme (ICDS), launched more than four decades ago, has continued with minor changes in terms of basic goals and processes. The Public Distribution System (PDS) for providing food support to the poor has been in operation for a long time and has been made part of the Food Security Mission. Sarva Shiksha Abhiyan (SSA) has been there for nearly two decades and is officially considered as the vehicle for implementing RTE.

The trend during the last two decades has been to reduce multiplicity of schemes by creating umbrella programmes that subsume these efforts. National Health Mission, Food Security Mission and Sarva Shiksha Abhiyan are illustrative of this trend. In fact, the schemes are currently being further merged and integrated for operational purposes. The MHRD, Government of India, has recently created the framework for merging the operations under the three major schemes related to school education – SSA, Rashtriya Madhyamik Shiksha Abhiyaan (RMSA) and Centrally Sponsored Scheme on Teacher Education (CSSTE) – under one integrated scheme, Samagra Shiksha. This is conceived as an integrated programme covering all aspects of school education with a view to giving greater intra-sector flexibility and promoting convergence of management and operations at the field level. With such merging, the number of centrally assisted and centrally sponsored schemes has been brought down significantly. The official website of the Department of School Education and Literacy of the Government of India lists only four schemes under elementary education and four under adult education.

Historically, planning and allocation of resources for various schemes used to be done for a five-year cycle as part of the Five Year Plan by the Planning Commission based on the demands and proposals made by different ministries. The planning exercise under the auspices of the Planning Commission as a necessity involved assessing the performance of the programmes/schemes in terms of physical targets achieved and utilisation of allocated resources. However, with the abandonment of the five-year planning process and conversion of the Planning Commission into the National Institution for Transforming India (NITI) Aayog (official think-tank for the Government of India), action on the ground and its monitoring and evaluation are largely entrusted to respective ministries and state governments.

Over the years, there have been a number of evaluation studies of almost every programme/scheme, particularly the large ones that have been in operation for more than five years. We do not propose to engage in a review of this aspect. However, it is pertinent to observe that development programmes in the social sector have to be designed and pursued from a long-term view. Impact of quality of life of the people cannot be seen in instantaneous fashion as with infrastructure development programmes. The focus of evaluation within the planning establishment has unfortunately been unduly focused on measuring project targets in physical and financial terms but not on development goals in a holistic way. For instance, successive reports would highlight establishment of health centres, ICDS centres, primary schools and so on. But do people get real access to health facilities, nutritional support and quality education? And what is the quality of service made available in these facilities? It is these factors that help determine improvement in the quality of life. For this to happen, the programmes at the operational level need constant support and monitoring. Further, effective implementation of social development programmes is human intensive, and it is essential that the knowledge and skills among the field functionaries are constantly nurtured and upgraded through capacity-building activities. Unfortunately, this has remained a major challenge in the social-sector implementation process. Another challenge faced in implementation is that most of the programmes in the social sector are interconnected and overlapping. But it is not uncommon to find programmes from different ministries doing similar and closely related activities in an unconnected and parallel manner with same target individuals and families.

The issue is not only one of coordination but also one of achieving true convergence. For example, the directives contained in a recent circular from the MHRD – on the new scheme of Samagra Shiksha – demands that the state plans should clearly indicate the areas of convergence with schemes of other ministries and state governments, such as Integrated Child Development Scheme (ICDS) of MoWCD (for preschool education), Ministry of Social Justice and Empowerment (for CWSN and residential facilities for children), Ministry of Tribal Affairs (residential facilities for ST children), Pradhan Mantri Kaushal Vikas Yojana (PMKVY) of Ministry of Skill Development and Entrepreneurship (MoSDE) (for vocational education), National Rural Drinking Water Programme and Swachh Bharat Mission (for providing and maintaining of toilets and drinking water facilities), MGNREGS of Ministry of Rural Development (for construction of play fields and compound walls for government run schools), Multi Sector Development Program (MSDP) of the Ministry of Minority Affairs (for infrastructural development in minority dominated areas) and Khelo India of Ministry of Youth Affairs and Sports (for Sport and Physical Education).[5] Indeed, the challenge is too huge for the administrators functioning at the grassroots level. While recognition of the need for convergence by the government is a commendable step, can this be achieved through mere directives and circulars? Is it fair to expect lower-level functionaries to plan and manage convergence when there is no structure or system in place? It requires a structural change in the planning and budget allocation processes from the top – central and state levels – and a reform in the mechanism of governance of the social sector to make it more participatory.

Have the programmes and schemes delivered? It is difficult to give a conclusive answer. Performance in the social sector has to be examined with respect to the current state of progress as reflected in various aspects of quality of life. There can be no absolute measure of progress. Satisfaction with the progress is relative to our expected level of performance, or it could be viewed in comparison to the situation prevalent in other countries. One could also assess the performance against what could have been achieved over the years. The last point may seem theoretical, but in essence it refers to a central question – could we have done better if the delivery was effective and efficient and the level of financing was sufficient?

In the following two sub-sections we highlight some of these issues examining the state of social development in India in comparison to selected countries and the level of investment in social-sector development programmes over the years.

State of social development in India: a macro view

Development is not an instantaneous phenomenon, and measuring progress cannot be anchored merely in the current state of affairs. Progress towards social development goals have to be viewed on a time scale and as a multi-dimensional exercise. But social progress cannot be fully divorced from economic growth indicators; nor can one ignore the context-specific nature of social development concerns in a country. Finding an inclusive framework for assessing development has indeed remained a huge challenge both in theoretical and in practical terms. Reflecting on the possibility and scope of such an exercise, the Commission on the Measurement of Economic Performance and Social Progress points out:

> Research has shown that it is possible to collect meaningful and reliable data on subjective wellbeing. Subjective Wellbeing encompasses three different aspects: cognitive evaluations of one's life, positive emotions (joy, pride) and negative ones (pain, anger, worry). While these aspects of subjective wellbeing have different determinants, in all cases these determinants go well beyond people's income and material conditions. . . . All these aspects of subjective wellbeing should be measured separately to derive a more comprehensive measure of people's quality of life and to allow a better understanding of its determinants (including people's objective conditions).
>
> *(Stiglitz et al., n.d.)*

Such an inclusive measure of development is still in the stage of proposition and would require significant effort by national statistical offices to collect necessary data to develop an index or indices of social development. Within this context, HDI and SPI are two macro-level measures that look beyond economic growth and capture social progress and wellbeing in different countries. In this section we present a comparative view of India and some select countries. In fact, relevant information has been generated with respect to both the indicators for several states in India. The data in the following section gives a summary view of the state of progress but has to be corroborated with in-depth qualitative analysis of the policies, programmes and their impact on the quality of life of the people – as will be done in various chapters included in the volume.

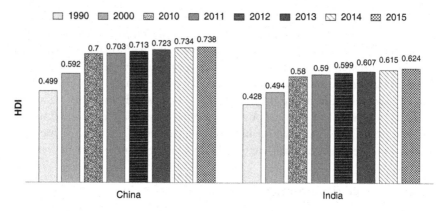

FIGURE 1.1 HDI over the years: China and India

HDI as a measure of social development in India

With a global rank of around 130 for many years, India's human development record is quite disappointing. The Human Development Report (HDR) classifies India as a Medium HD country. With an HDI of 0.624, it is far below in comparison to all other countries in the BRICs grouping. What should worry us even more is the pace of improvement. In 1990, both China and India had HDIs <0.5, with China marginally higher. But by 2010, China had made a big jump in HDI value, reaching 0.7 while India continued to languish with an HDI of 0.58. Even among the South Asian countries, some of the poorer neighbours fare better than India. For instance, with respect to life expectancy, which indicates progress in health dimension, India is ahead of only Pakistan and Afghanistan among the eight South Asian countries. Sri Lanka leads the table with figures for the HDI and various components far higher than those of India, despite suffering from the long-drawn internal conflict (Table 1.3).

TABLE 1.3 HDI and its components

Countries		HDI	Life expectancy at birth	Mean years of schooling	GNI per capita	HDI rank
South Asia	Sri Lanka	0.766	75.0	10.9	10,789	72
	Maldives	0.701	77.0	6.2	10,383	105
	India	0.624	68.3	6.3	5,663	131
	Bhutan	0.607	69.9	3.1	7,081	132
	Bangladesh	0.579	72.0	5.2	3,341	140
	Nepal	0.558	70.0	4.1	2,337	144
	Pakistan	0.550	66.4	5.1	5,031	148
	Afghanistan	0.479	60.7	3.6	1,871	169

Source: UNDP, 2016.

Social progress index

Another summary index that has emerged in recent years is the Social Progress Index (SPI) developed by the Social Progress Imperative and computed every year beginning 2014.[6] The exercise views social progress as

> the capacity of a society to meet the basic human needs of its citizens, establish the building blocks that allow citizens and communities to enhance and sustain the quality of their lives, and create the conditions for all individuals to reach their full potential.
>
> *(Porter et al. 2017)*

The three broad dimensions covered under SPI include basic human needs, foundation of wellbeing or access to improved living conditions, and access to opportunity measured through fifty indicators. SPI tries to measure social progress without taking into account economic aspects and focuses on the outcome rather than the input.

According to the 2017 SPI report, India's SPI of 58.39 ranks ninety-third among 128 countries. In terms of meeting basic human needs, the performance of India has been good in the indicators of shelter, water and sanitation and personal safety. However, India seems to be lagging behind in the indicators of nutrition and basic medical care. An area of serious concern with respect to health care is the infant mortality rate of India, which stands at 37.9. Even the low-income neighbouring countries of Nepal and Bangladesh have performed better in this indicator.

Some of the Indian states have shown remarkable achievement in terms of social progress in spite of having low or moderate levels of economic development (Kapoor 2017). For instance, development in Kerala and in Gujarat gives a contrasting picture. While the performance of Gujarat in terms of GDP seems to be good, with a net SDP of $120.91 billion US in 2014–15, the performance in case of social progress is moderate, with a score of 57.4. On the other hand, while Kerala's net SDP is $59.7 billion US in 2014–15, the score in social progress is 67.75 in 2016 (Ibid.).

On the whole, eight states fall in the "very high" category of social progress – with Kerala, Himachal Pradesh and Tamil Nadu occupying the first three positions. The progress of Tamil Nadu seems to be balanced, as the state shows good performance in both economic and social indicators. Tamil Nadu is thus on the path of inclusive development, because of both the policies and implementation measures adopted by the state in almost all the areas, such as health care, education and the economy. At the other end of the spectrum is a mixed group of seven states with low SPI, belonging to low- and middle-level income categories. Some of them have serious problems, particularly in the health sector. For instance, prevalence of anaemia, infant mortality rate and maternal mortality rate in Uttar Pradesh is one of the highest in the country.

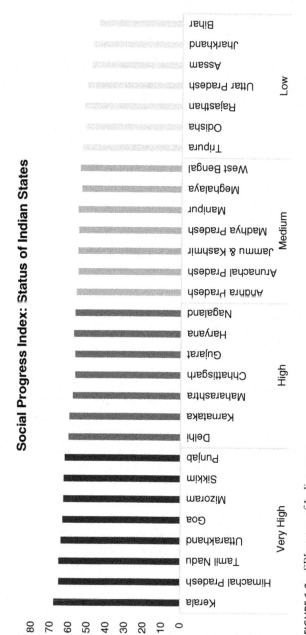

FIGURE 1.2 SPI: status of Indian states

Source: Kapoor (2017).

Key social indicators

During the twenty-seven years since HDRs emerged on the global scene, even though the relative ranking for India has not significantly changed, its HDI value has gone up. In 1990, when the first HDR was published, India had a HDI of 0.428 (0.624 in 2015). The HDI for China was also below 0.5 in 1990, but the improvement over the years was substantial enough to move the country to a higher group with respect to human development (see Figure 1.1). In contrast, the growth for India has remained sluggish over the decades. While this and the discussion on SPI give a summary picture of the relative state of India in social development, it is necessary to disaggregate and examine the component factors that, taken together, characterise the state of social development in the country. Figures in Table 1.4 derived from the data compiled mainly from the 2016 HDR present such an overview of the components contributing to progress in social indicators.

The key indicators appear impressive when seen with respect to positive change achieved over seventy years. But as it stands, India is still far from reasonably satisfactory levels in almost every aspect of social development. Besides the fact that India failed to reach the adult literacy target set by Dakar EFA goals, it is of serious concern that around 10 per cent in the age group 15–24 are still non-literate and around 20 per cent of children leave primary education without completing even five years of schooling. Only about 47 per cent (with a wide gender gap) in the age group 25+ have got at least some secondary education. Relatively low average levels of education in the adult population are likely to negatively impact economic growth, particularly as we move into knowledge-intensive production systems.

The situation with respect to health, nutrition and gender equality is most disturbing as even a poorer neighbour, Bangladesh, has performed better. And India's indicators are far below those of Sri Lanka. Neither of these two neighbours has experienced the kind of upswing in the economy as India has consistently done for the last twenty years. In fact, both Bangladesh and Sri Lanka have undergone catastrophic events in the form of internal conflicts and natural disasters during the last few decades. Equally disturbing are the indicators of poverty and inequality in income and human development components. What is not captured in the quantitative indicators is the deep division emerging within Indian society of unequal access to quality education and health facilities based on economic and social considerations. The issue is also one of the flawed priorities in education development. While India is emerging as one of the top destinations for medical tourism, we have failed to train an adequate number of health functionaries. Figure 1.3 shows how China has made consistent progress over time in this regard, while India continues to stagnate at about the same level as it began a decade ago, resulting in poor and inadequate public health care facilities while the private health industry flourishes with high-cost and high-end services for the rich and foreign medical tourists.

TABLE 1.4 State of social development: key indicators

Key indicators		Values	Key indicators		Values
Education			**Health and nutrition**		
Adult Literacy Rate (per cent Ages 15+) Census Data, 2011		74.04	Mortality Rates per 1,000 Live Births, HDR, 2016	Infant (2016**)	34
Youth Literacy (per cent Ages 15–24), UIS Data, 2015	Male	92.87		Under 5	47
	Female	87.21		Female (2014)	145
Gross Enrolment Ratio (per cent), U-DISE, 2015–16	Primary	99.21		Male (2014)	217
	Upper Primary	92.81	Infants Lacking Immunisation (per cent 1 Year Olds) HDR, 2016	DTP (2014)	10
	Secondary	80.01		Measles (2014)	17
	Higher Secondary	56.16	Child Malnutrition – Stunting (Height for Age) (per cent Under Age 5), NFHS-4, 2015–16		38.4
Annual Average Drop-Out Rate at Primary Level, U-DISE 2014–15		4.13	Life Expectancy at Birth, World Bank Data, 2016	Female	70.16
Pupil Teacher Ratio at Primary Level (per cent), UIS Data, 2015		31.5		Male	67.09
Population with at Least Some Secondary Education (per cent ages 25+), HDR, 2016		48.7	Deaths Due to: (per 100,000 people), WHO, 2017	Malaria (2017)	7.0
				Tuberculosis (2014)	26.0
			Physicians (per 1,000 People), World Bank Data, 2016		0.75
Gender equality			**Poverty and employment**		
Gender Development Index (2015)	Value	0.819	Multi-Dimensional Poverty Index^^^	Year and Survey	2005–06D
Gender Inequality Index (2015)	Value	0.530		Index	0.282
	Rank	125	Multi-Dimensional Poverty (Head Count) (per cent)		55.3

Maternal Mortality Ratio (Deaths per 100,000 Live Births) (2015)		174	Intensity of Deprivation (per cent)	51.1
Share of Seats in Parliament (per cent Held by Women) (2015)		12.21	Contribution of Deprivation in Dimension to Overall Poverty (per cent)	Education	22.7
Population with at Least Some Secondary Education (per cent ages 25+), 2005–15	Female	35.33		Health	32.5
	Male	61.40		Living Standards	44.8
Labour Force Participation Rate (per cent Ages 15+), 2015	Female	26.80	Population Below Income Poverty Line (per cent), Planning Commission, 2014		21.9
	Male	79.11	Employment to Population Ratio (per cent Ages 15+), World Band Data, 2015		51.9
Security			Labour Force Participation Rate (per cent Ages 15+), World Band Data, 2017		51.89
Internally Displaced Persons, 2015		61,2000	Employment in Agriculture (per cent Total Employment), World Bank Data, 2017		42.73
Orphaned Children (in 1,000s), 2014		29,600	Employment in Services (per cent Total Employment), World Bank Data, 2017		33.47
Homicide Rate per 100,000 People, 2010–14		3.2	Unemployment Rate (per cent of Labour Force), World Bank Data, 2015		3.5
Suicide Rate per 100,000 People, 2012	Male	25.8	Youth Unemployment Rate (per cent ages 15–24), World Bank Data, 2015		9.7
	Female	16.4	Youth Not in School or Employment (per cent ages 15–24), World Bank Data, 2015		27.2
Violence Against Women Ever Experienced, 2005–15	Intimate Partner	37.2	Vulnerable Employment as per cent of Total Employment, World Bank Data, 2015		77.49
	Non-Intimate Partner	0.3	Working Poor at PPP $3.10 a Day as per cent of Total Employment, 2004–2013		52.9
Depth of Food Deficit (Kilocalories per Person per Day), World Bank Data, 2016		109	Poverty Gap at $1.90 a Day, (Mean Shortfall in Income from Poverty Line), Word Bank, 2011		4.3

(Continued)

TABLE 1.4 (Continued)

Key indicators	Values	Key indicators		Values
Food Subsidy Released 2014–15 (Rs. in Millions), Economic Survey, 2017–18	1,131,711.6	Child Labour (per cent Ages 5–14), ILO, 2011		10.13
Inequality				
Coefficient of Human Inequality, 2015	26.5	Income Inequality (Gini Coefficient)		35.2
Inequality-Adjusted HDI (IHDI) (per cent), 2015	0.454	Income Inequality: Income Share of, 2015#	Bottom 50 per cent	14.7
Inequality in Life Expectancy (per cent), 2010–15	24.0		Middle 40 per cent	29.2
Inequality in Education (per cent), 2015	39.4		Top 10 per cent	56.1
Inequality in Income (per cent), 2015	16.1		Top 1 per cent	21.3

Source: UNDP 2016; UIS Data 2015, U-DISE 2015 and 2015–16; World Bank Data 2016, GOI 2013; # Chancel and Piketty 2017; * GOI 2018; ** National Institution for Transforming India (NITI Aayog 2016), Government of India; World Bank Data available at https://data.worldbank.org/indicator/SPDYN.LE00.MA.IN; and Unicef.org available at https://data.unicef.org/topic/maternal-health/maternal-mortality/; National Family Health Survey 4; UNESCO 2015 and www.youthpolicy.org/factsheets/country/india/; World Health Organization 2017.

Note: ^^^ D indicates data from demographic and health surveys; M, Multiple Indicator Cluster Surveys (MICSes).

TABLE 1.5 Health and gender indicators for Bangladesh, India and Sri Lanka

Key indicators		Bangladesh	India	Sri Lanka
Mortality Rates per 1,000 Live Births	Infant, 2015	30.7	37.9	8.4
	Female, 2014	107	145	75
	Male, 2014	152	217	201
Child Malnutrition – Stunting (Moderate to Severe) (% Under Age 5), 2010–15		36.1	38.7	14.7
Life Expectancy at Birth, 2015	Female	73.3	69.9	78.4
	Male	70.7	66.9	71.7
Gender Development Index, 2015	Value	0.927	0.819	0.934
Gender Inequality Index, 2015	Value	0.520	0.530	0.386
	Rank	119	125	87
Maternal Mortality Ratio (Deaths per 100,000 Live Births), 2015		176	174	30
Share of Seats in Parliament (% Held by Women), 2015		20.00	12.21	4.89
Population with at Least Some Secondary Education (% Ages 25+), 2005–15	Female	42.01	35.33	80.18
	Male	44.26	61.40	80.55
Labour Force Participation Rate (% Ages 15+), 2015	Female	43.13	26.80	30.23
	Male	80.98	79.11	75.64

Source: HDR 2016.

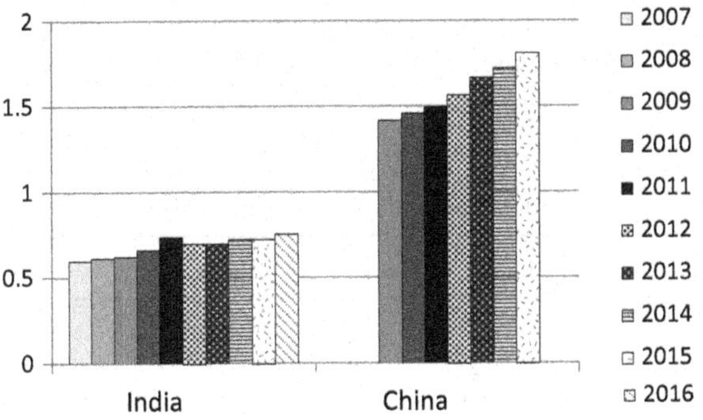

FIGURE 1.3 No. of physicians per 1,000 people

Financing social development

India has witnessed unprecedented level of economic transformation during the last three decades, transforming itself from a state of economic crisis in 1990s to one of the fastest-growing large-size economies in the world. It is not uncommon to find India being bracketed with China as the new engines of global economic growth. With the fast growth of the economy, it is natural to expect that more resources were available for improving the quality of life of the people at large. But India continues to be several notches below China in human development and social sectors. With India's indicators scoring lower even in comparison to some of its poorer neighbours, pertinent questions include how much is India spending on social-sector development and whether the investment is adequate to positively impact the quality of life of the common people.

Assessing the level of expenditure on social sector is a complex task involving spending in multiple sectors – education, health, nutrition, gender equality, livelihood and so on. Government expenditure on each of them tends to be through different ministries and departments, making the task even more complex. Nevertheless, education and health are considered the core components of social-sector spending almost everywhere in India. There is no standard norm to examine if the quantum of expenditure in these areas is adequate. One can also infer this from the changing pattern of expenditure to examine if the government has increased the allocation of resources for these sectors as the economy grows. Another reference could be to compare India's level of expenditure with those of other countries placed in similar conditions. In this section we will present data to illuminate India's effort in the social sector from these perspectives.

How much is India spending on social sector?

The amount of public resources to be spent on the social sector is essentially a political decision as the leadership deals with contending demands from different sectors ranging from defence to education, health, rural development and so on. Also, as noted earlier, social-sector expenditure in India is shared by both central and state governments. Figures in Table 1.6 gives a picture of how this issue has been addressed in recent years.

TABLE 1.6 Trends in social services expenditure by the general government (centre and states)

Items		2012–13	2013–14	2014–15	2015–16	2016–17 RE	2017–18 BE
							(' in trillion)
Total expenditure		26.95	30.00	32.85	33.78	40.60	43.96
Expenditure on social services		6.58	7.46	7.68	7.90	9.84	10.94
I1	Education	3.13	3.48	3.54	3.31	3.95	4.41
I2	Health	1.26	1.39	1.49	1.52	2.26	2.25
I3	Others	2.20	2.59	2.65	3.07	3.63	4.27

Source: Economic Survey 2018, Government of India 2018; Budget Documents of Union and State Governments, Reserve Bank of India.

Notes: Social services include education, sports, art and culture; medical and public health, family welfare water supply and sanitation; housing; urban development; welfare of SCs, STs and OBCs, labour and labour welfare; social security and welfare, nutrition, relief on account of natural calamities etc. Expenditure on "Education" pertains to expenditure on "Education, Sports, Arts and Culture"; expenditure on "Health" includes expenditure on "Medical and Public Health", "Family Welfare" and "Water Supply and Sanitation"; GDP data, 2011–12, is as per the new base year 2011–12. GDP for 2016–17 and 2017–18 are provisional estimates and advance estimates respectively; Data pertains to Union Government and twenty-six states.

Being a joint responsibility of the central and state governments, policy changes at the national level and increased spending priority for the social sector by the central government may not be adequate to impact the reality in terms of delivery of services. This is particularly important as the major share of expenditure in the social sector is borne by the state governments. As the figures in Table 1.7 indicate, state share in more than 80 per cent in all major components and fluctuations in the allocations in individual states could lead to substantial variations in actual supply of services. Seetha Prabhu (2001), studying the impact of economic reform on social-sector development, found that although the central government increased its allocation to the social sector in the reform period, the states decreased their allocations. She specifically investigated the situation in Maharashtra and Tamil

TABLE 1.7 Changing share of states in total social-sector expenditure (actuals in %)

S. No.	Major heads	1998–99	2013–14
1	Education, Art and Culture	88.1	80.73
2	Medical and Public Health, Water and Sanitation	89.3	79.52
3	Family Welfare	85.9	48.60
4	Housing	44.6	49.32
5	Urban Development	93.1	95.69
6	Labour and Employment	60.4	64.16
7	Social Security and Welfare	89.2	96.74
8	Others*	21.2	40.00
9	Social and Community Services (1 to 8)	82.3	79.00
10	Rural Development	64.2	50.00
11	Total (9 + 10)	80.0	75.48

Source: Indian Public Finance Statistics (IPFS), 2015–16, Government of India; figures computed by CBGA.

Note: *For combined figures of centre and states, expenditure on "Others" is a summation of expenditure on "Others", "Scientific Services & Research" and "Broadcasting". But for the states, the "Broadcasting" head does not exist. Hence, the states' expenditure under "Others" is the summation of expenditure on "Others" and "Scientific Services & Research".

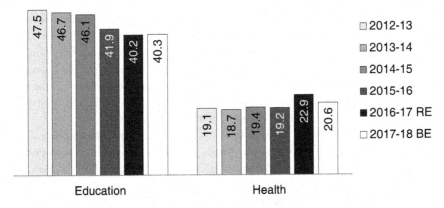

FIGURE 1.4 Education and health as a percentage of social service expenditure

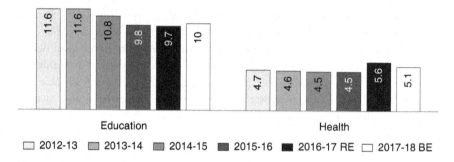

FIGURE 1.5 Expenditure on education and health as a percentage of total public expenditure
Source: GoI, Economic Suvey 2017-18.

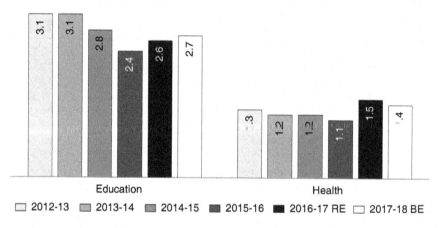

FIGURE 1.6 Expenditure as percentage of GDP

Nadu and concluded that they made no special effort during the reform period to change the level or pattern of social-sector spending.

Even though the aggregate expenditure on social sector shows a substantial increase in the last two years, the ratio of social sector to total expenditure has been around 24–25 per cent and accounts for about 6.6 per cent of the GDP. Education and health are the major components of the social-sector expenditure. Surprisingly, even though the overall allocation in budget shows an increase for social service, share of education component in social service has seen a steep decrease in the last few years, and the share of health has remained more or less the same, notwithstanding the recent announcements of major schemes in the sector.

Assessment of the share of education and health in overall expenditure during the recent years also shows similar trends. Both as a proportion of total public expenditure and as that of GDP, share of education decreased while the share of health sector has only marginally risen.

As mentioned earlier, the country has witnessed enormous change in its economic fortune over the last three decades. How has this impacted expenditure for social sectors?

Analysis of the budgets and expenditure pattern during the 1990s by Mooij and Dev (2004) revealed a mixed picture of priority accorded to social sector. They observed that, throughout the 1990s, social sector expenditure in terms of percentage of GDP was lower than it was in the late 1980s. However, beginning from 1995 to 1996, a higher percentage of government expenditure went to the social sector than when the reforms started or during the last years preceding the reforms. But as Figure 1.7 shows, the increasing trend lasted for less than five years, and the figures fell sharply beginning in 2000. Although we find an upwards trend in recent years, it is still below the level of expenditure observed in late 1980s before the reforms began. What should be a matter of concern is that the allocations for social sector has remained range bound around 24–27 per cent of the aggregate public expenditure and around 6 per cent of the GDP for the last thirty years despite significant uptrend in economic growth during the last two decades. In other words, it seems that passing through financial crisis, followed by austerity under structural adjustment policies and surging economic growth subsequently has had no impact on the relative priority attached to social sector.

Debate on whether economic reforms have dented the financial provisions for social sector development is likely to continue with the data on allocations remaining inconclusive. However a more pertinent issue to examine is the following: Does India spend adequately on social sector development? Ideally this should be based on empirical assessment of the requirement and deciding the basic benchmarks for public provisions to be made available for all on a universal basis. At the global level, the specification of social protection floor[7] by the International Labour Organisation (ILO) offers a basic benchmark for assessing the provisions (ILO 2012). In fact, legislative measures in India such as the Right to Education Act, Food Security Act and MGNREGA specify certain basic level provisions to be made by the government. Government will be compelled by this to allocate adequate finances to meet these legally binding provisions. For instance, the RTE Act clearly specifies the basic facilities that every school should be equipped with. However, DISE data for various years clearly shows that only a small proportion of government schools satisfy all the specifications. Unfortunately, financial adequacy gets intermixed with efficiency of implementation and becomes difficult to draw any categorical conclusions.

A second basis for assessing the adequacy is to compare with norms specified within the country with regard to allocations for different social sectors. For instance, successive governments have invariably made commitment to increase spending for education and bring it to the level of 6 per cent of GDP. But public spending on education in India has barely touched 4 per cent of GDP and has remained around 10–12 per cent of aggregate public expenditure in the last seventy years. Such statements therefore have remained only aspirational as there is no legal basis to compel the government to spend the resources at that level. In fact, legally mandating a minimum level of spending on a particular sector is a practice adopted in some countries. For example, Indonesia has made a clear commitment by passing

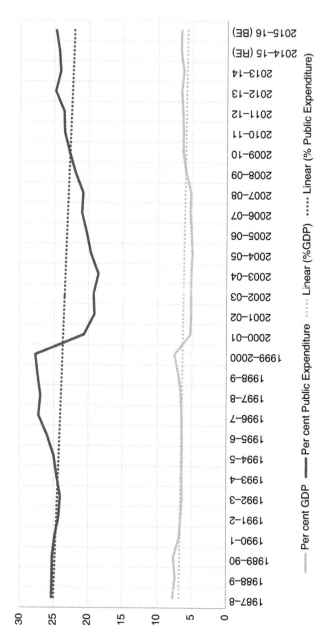

FIGURE 1.7 Social-sector (social services and rural development) expenditure by centre and states, 1987–2016

Source: Indian Pubic Finance Statistics; Mooji and Dev (2004) for years 1987–2000 and computed by CBGA for years 2001–16.

Notes: 1 *Social Sector Expenditure* includes Social Services – "Education, Art and Culture", "Medical and Public Health, Water and Sanitation", "Family Welfare", "Housing", "Urban Development", "Labour and Employment", "Social Security and Welfare" and the category "Others". The category "Others" includes expenditure on "Scientific Services and Research" and "Broadcasting"; 2 GDP figures are at current market prices; 3 Aggregate Public Expenditure is the sum of "Non-Developmental Expenditure", "Developmental Expenditure" and "Loans and Advances" as reported in the reports of IPFS.

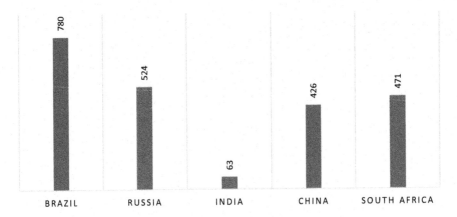

FIGURE 1.8 Current health expenditure per capita $US, 2015

Source: World Health Statistics 2018, WHO, 2018.

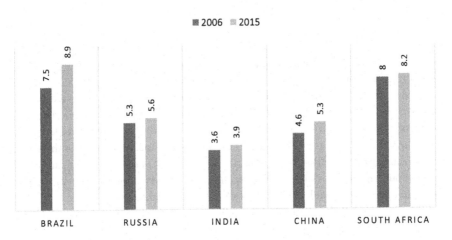

FIGURE 1.9 Aggregate expenditure on health as percentage of GDP

a constitutional mandate to allocate at least 20 per cent of the total government budget to education (the "20 per cent rule") (The World Bank 2007, p. 18).[8]

We could also examine the level of spending in comparison to what other countries are spending. There is no universally accepted definition of what constitutes social-sector expenditure. Available data sets from OECD and ADB refer to components of expenditure on "social protection" keeping in view the "social protection floor" formulated by ILO (ILO 2012). ILO presents financial data separately for "social protection" and "health care". The definition of social protection adopted by the Asian Development Bank consists of three components – Social Insurance, Social Assistance and Labour Market Programmes. Together they cover most of the items of expenditure in the social sector including health and some aspects of education and training. Yet they do not fully match all the items that are counted in

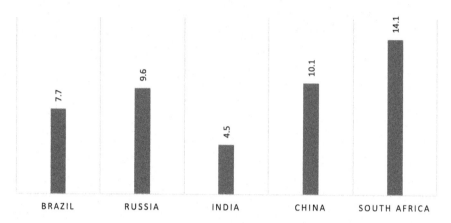

FIGURE 1.10 Health Expenditure as percentage of total government expenditure
Source: World Health Statistics, WHO, 2018; and GoI, Economic Survey, 2018.

"social services" in the Indian accounting system. Notwithstanding these issues of data compatibility for comparison, Indian expenditure on social sector primarily consisting of health and education continues to remain woefully below peers (Singh and Mate 2018). On average, countries in Latin America spend 5 per cent of the GDP and 17.6 per cent of the public expenditure on education. Corresponding figures for Europe and North America are 5.1 per cent and 11.8 per cent, respectively; and the figures are 4.1 per cent and 18.5 for South East Asia. Brazil and South Africa, which are part of the BRICS grouping, spend 6 per cent of their GDP on education. Even countries of Sub-Saharan Africa spend more on education, with an average of 4.1 per cent of GDP and 16.9 per cent of public expenditure.

Under spending in comparison to other countries become even more glaring in health sector expenditure. World Health statistics show that among the BRICS countries, India is at the bottom in all indicators, share of GDP, share of public expenditure and per capita expenditure on health. An extremely low level of per capita expenditure is indeed a matter of serious concern. Analysis of the composition of the expenditure is even more disturbing. The world average for share of government expenditure in current health expenditure is 52 per cent, while for India the figure is as low as 25.6 per cent. Corresponding figures for China, Russia, Brazil, South Africa and Sri Lanka are 59.8, 61, 42.8, 53.6 and 53.7 per cent, respectively. The World Health Organisation warns that relying on people paying for health services out-of-pocket at the time of use could push them to crisis condition with catastrophic impact. The world average for out-of-pocket expenditure as share of current health expenditure is 32 per cent. Again in this case India is far behind at 65.1 per cent and is one among a group of very few countries, several of them war-torn, with a figure above 65 per cent. Corresponding figures for China, Brazil and South Africa are 32.4, 28.3 and 7.7, respectively. Even Sri Lanka, which has faced conflict situation for a prolonged period, fares much better at 38.4 per cent.

Social development and SDGs in India: problems and prospects

In the preceding section of this chapter we have presented a macro overview of policies, programme and financing of social development initiatives in India. Besides giving a glimpse of the changing nature of policies and programmes, we attempted to compare the status of India with that of other countries with the help of quantitative indicators in the context of globally formulated SDGs. Even though the quantitative indicators may not capture the full picture, the analysis clearly points to the inability of the country to make a significant mark in provision of quality social services to the people in general and to the poorer sections of the population in particular. This is so despite the claim of substantial reduction in income poverty levels in the post-reform period. The central question to be addressed is why we are in this state and what needs to be done to move ahead in areas of critical concern for social development such as education, health, gender, employment and inequality. This requires deeper analysis and assessment of the state of affairs in each of these sectors. Various chapters included in the volume engage in such critical analysis of the situation in different aspects of social sector development.

The seventeen goals in the SDG framework cover a wide range of concerns that are cross-cutting and comprehensive. Even though each SDG is identified with a specific area of concern, targets listed under different SDGs substantially overlap and intersect each other. The chapters included in the volume also carry this spirit and invariably deal with intersecting concerns. For instance, Varghese (chapter 4) deals with higher education and employment, while Lingam (chapter 11) examines the theme of maternity benefits in an intersectional perspective combined with concerns of nutrition and female work force participation. Taken together, chapters in the volume attempt to cover various SDGs that have been identified with social development concerns. With this consideration in view, the remaining chapters in the volume have been grouped under different sections. The introductory chapter is followed by a chapter exclusively on SDGs highlighting the process of SDG formulation as well as a critical assessment in the context of developing countries. Thereafter, thematic chapters have been grouped into four sections: (a) education and skill development; (b) health, nutrition and food security; (c) gender equality; and (d) poverty, unemployment and inequality. The final chapter (Dubey) articulates the need for pursuing inclusive development goals and strategies with education and health as the basic building blocks.

Will India meet the expectations embodied in the SDGs by 2030? While it is not possible to offer a clear response to this question, several chapters in the volume examine the requirements and implications of pursuing SDGs in the Indian context. It is equally important to ask ourselves, "Should and can SDGs guide India in its progress towards social development?" As noted earlier the SDGs framework has also been the subject of critical examination. Sengupta[9] (in the following chapter) argues that

> they (SDGs) are remarkably comprehensive in scope, deserve considerable praise for making some clear advances over the MDGs. Nonetheless, they

miss a valuable opportunity to address structural causes of poverty and systemic roots of inequality, both nationally and globally. This shortcoming, in turn, limits the SDGs' ability to successfully address systemic concerns in health and other social sectors.

She raises some critical concerns that are of direct relevance to India. For instance, she questions the appropriateness of income-based measure of poverty (indicated in SDG1) as it fails to capture many of the hardships that constitute poverty in the real world, such as chronic undernourishment, illiteracy, and lack of access to safe drinking water.

Lumping together civil society organisations (CSOs) and corporate actors is also a matter of concern as it ignores the profound differences in their orientation, interests and accountability. This is indeed a very important issue in India as in official considerations there is an emerging trend of obfuscating the difference between for-profit and not-for-profit organisations in both education and health sectors, particularly when they are promoted by corporate entities. It is further argued that the SDGs are marred by a weak accountability structure that undermines its otherwise persuasive language on universalism and partnership. Given that the SDGs do not sufficiently challenge the prevailing paradigm of neoliberal economic development, they cannot justifiably be regarded as "transformative". While there are very important observations that cannot be easily countered, we cannot dismiss SDGs as totally inconsequential. For India, the value, perhaps, lies in reminding the policymakers the commitments made as signatory, the direction in which we have to move steadfast, and the enormous effort needed to bridge the gap between the current status and the targets to be achieved by 2030 for enhancing the wellbeing and quality of life of the people. In this subsection, we examine some of the critical issues confronting social development in India in the context of the SDGs, suitably drawing upon the various chapters in the volume.

Education and skill development

The Education Goal – SDG-4 takes an overarching view of the tasks to be done by 2030 in the education sector as a whole. Unlike the Education MDG, which focused only on primary schooling, SDG-4 encompasses all levels of education from a lifelong perspective and calls for ensuring inclusive and equitable education for all. Explicit reference is made to youth and adult education with particular focus on skill development (Target 4.4).

Rustagi and others (chapter 3) on school education and by Varghese (chapter 4) on higher education describe the enormous expansion of educational infrastructure at all levels in recent years. If it is only about creating access to education, India is well on its way to reach the goal. But we are still seriously falling short with respect to ensuring sustained participation and acquisition of learning. As we move up the ladder, participation levels keep falling. Around one out of five children joining the school does not complete even five years of education; it becomes nearly one out of three by the time we move up to eight years, which marks the compulsory education level. Unfortunately the situation is not significantly improving in recent years. This is clearly evident from the fact that even now around 10 per cent of youth aged 15–24 are non-literate. With a gross enrolment rate of around 76 per cent and net enrolment rate of around 58 per cent, universal participation in secondary education seems to be a formidable mountain to climb. Even though higher education has witnessed massive expansion in recent years, the participation levels are still far from satisfactory in comparison to global averages. Besides this issue of participation, four other critical problems confronting the education system require attention.

As Rustagi *et al.* point out,

> The single greatest challenge facing the school education sector of India is inequity in the provisioning and utilisation of educational opportunities across social and economic groups. This is being prominently faced by children from marginalised households, namely Dalit, Adivasi, and Muslim.

Net attendance ratio drops sharply at secondary level and becomes worse at the higher secondary level as only 18 per cent of the children from the poorest income quintile are going to higher secondary level in rural areas and 23 per cent in urban areas, while the corresponding figures are 66 per cent and 53 per cent for the top quintile. This inequity is getting accentuated by the emergence of a multi-layered system of schooling deeply fragmented and segmented to the disadvantage of the marginalised (Govinda and Bandopadhyay, forthcoming). It is necessary that we avoid excessive attention to elite institutions such as CBSE affiliated schools, IITs, IIMs and not-yet-created world class universities which cater to a small proportion of the population and invest our effort and resources to build a more inclusive system of robust quality serving. The problem of inequality within the education system is further compounded by vast regional disparities. As Varghese highlights educational inequalities are persisting in India and are much higher than those in most of the less developed countries. Further educational opportunities are unevenly distributed among regions and social groups as the states, such as Odisha, Madhya Pradesh, Bihar and Uttar Pradesh, which have relatively higher concentration of the poor and the marginalised also have higher educational inequalities.

Besides the fact that the sector is perpetually underfunded, expansion in secondary as well as tertiary levels is increasingly dependent on private providers, allowing for free play of market forces and commercialisation. Increase in enrolment has happened mainly in some selected states with higher levels of private self-financing institutions. For example, the share of private unaided colleges is 81.8 per cent in Andhra Pradesh, and it has a density of forty-eight institutions per 100,000 people. The same is the case with Karnataka with 64.9 per cent and Puducherry with 61.3 per cent unaided institutions. The states which have predominantly public universities and colleges have a lower density of institutions (Varghese, in this volume). This overdependence on private provision coupled with promotion of loans in place of grants and scholarships has raised legitimate apprehension that the state has begun to abdicate its responsibility towards higher education. Such promotion of private provision is also considered to be widening inequalities in access to higher education and consequently to employment opportunities.

Another issue that has come for sustained scrutiny in recent times is the unsatisfactory quality of education, in general and poor learning outcomes, in particular. This has indeed eroded the credibility of the system as a whole. However, it is important to recognise that quality of learning is directly dependent on teachers and their capabilities. Unfortunately, very little has been done over the years to strengthen this aspect. Quality of teacher education institutions which has a major role in this regard remains neglected. In fact, with more than 90 per cent of teacher education institutions belonging to private self-financing category, the government has little control or capacity to influence the quality of teacher education. Professional development of teachers is also thwarted by the fact that a large proportion of them continue to function on annual contract basis which restricts their ability to access long-term continuing education programmes and also negatively impacts their motivation to acquire or upgrade knowledge and skills as teachers. This is a phenomenon one can observe across the spectrum from primary to university level.

Linking education with employment through vocational education and skill development programmes has been an old proposition that has remained elusive. Target 4.4 of the SDGs exhorts nations to substantially increase the number of youth and adults who have relevant skills, including technical and vocational skills, for employment, decent jobs and entrepreneurship. The sector got significant boost a decade ago when the government of India launched a major programme for imparting skill to around 500 million young persons in the country under a mission mode and subsequent formulation of a National Skill Qualifications Framework. While a separate ministry has been established and considerable budgetary allocations have been made, the issue continues to bother. For instance, while around 12.8 million enter the workforce every year, the existing capacity to provide skills training is limited to around 3.1 million. The problem is further compounded by the negative image and low aspirational value attached to vocational education and training (VET) and the lack of coordinated efforts to integrate VET with general education for meeting the labour market needs (Mehrotra and Mehrotra, chapter 5). Also, workers in the unorganised sector who constitute a major part of the employed need a system for recognition of prior learning so that they get an opportunity to obtain relevant certification of their competencies acquired through informal learning and enter the formal education system, thus becoming lifelong learners. At present the non-formal VET system is fragmented and largely uncoordinated.

Health and nutrition

The centrality of health for achieving goals of human development and wellbeing needs no special emphasis. Health touches our lives as nothing else does. Indeed, providing health for all or universal health coverage (UHC) has been a long-standing goal in all countries including India. But it is well recognised that health goals cannot be pursued in isolation without meeting the basic needs of food and nutrition. Viewed from this angle, the goals and targets under SDG 2 (hunger, nutrition and food security) and SDG 3 (health needs) are closely interwoven. Thus, UHC demands that the two SDGs and targets therein are pursued together as intersecting components of human development. Four chapters in the volume devoted to health, nutrition and food security raise several critical issues confronting the country.

The SDGs call for achieving universal health coverage, including financial risk protection, access to quality essential health care services and to safe, effective, quality and affordable essential medicines and vaccines for all. They also expect that by 2030, we totally end hunger and ensure access by all people, in particular the poor and people in vulnerable situations, including infants, to safe, nutritious and sufficient food all year round; and end all forms of malnutrition, including achieving, by 2025, the internationally agreed-on targets for stunting and wasting in children aged 5 and under. They also call for addressing the nutritional needs of adolescent girls, pregnant and lactating women and older persons. Will we meet these goals? From the state of progress in which we are this appears to be truly utopian.

As the NITI Aayog documents accept, even the modest goals set by the Twelfth Five Year Plan remained unfulfilled with respect to creating institutional infrastructure and development of human resources to meet the needs of health sector particularly affecting rural areas (Government of India, n.d.b Appraisal Document of Twelfth Five Year Plan, 2012–17). Despite visible improvements in some of the health indicators, there are significant shortfalls especially in maternal and child health with serious supply side gaps persisting in the health-sector provisions. Qadeer (chapter 7 in this volume) attributes this to a drastic shift in the official approach towards a business model of health care. Imposing limits on assured services and inserting the notion of affordability is indicative of state's shrinking commitment to public health provision. India's approach is very different from the experience of many other middle-income countries like Brazil and South Africa that have undertaken health-sector reforms, but have managed to protect or revive their basic health service sectors by investing higher proportions of their GDP.

India's commitment to the principle of UHC is not in question. But the scepticism about its ability to achieve the SDG goals and targets arise out of clearly visible large gaps observed between policy pronouncements and policy actions. Even within the policy regime conflicting perspectives are promoted characterised as "structured policy incoherence" by Sundararaman and Ranjan (chapter 6 in this volume). Furthermore, policy goals have invariably been defeated by conflicting financial propositions. Universal health coverage (UHC), based as it is on principles of justice and equity, calls for making a comprehensive list of health care services available to all. However, in practice it has remained a shallow basket as there has been very limited movement beyond the traditional reproductive and child health (RCH) area. This may partly be because of inadequacy of funds. But it is also because essential health packages are defined based on computations of cost-effectiveness and affordability. UHC also implies that a set of common core facilities made available as public provision would be such that it is used by all irrespective of social and economic considerations. But, government seems to have accepted as inevitable a system of two-tier care – one for those with means and a voice and the other for the voiceless and indigent, even though one might find it morally and ethically reprehensible. This approach expresses itself in shifting of responsibility to families and civil society through cash transfers and voucher systems, and state-funded insurances provided through private entities (Qadeer).

The central issue is not whether such a shift is inherently inimical to building a robust public health system. Private players in health sector in India who have occupied significant space over the years cannot be wished away. Rather the issue to be addressed is whether such involvement of private entrepreneurs in health sector is distorting the structure and delivery of public health system to the disadvantage of common citizens at large. It is in this context that Sundararaman and Ranjan point out that tax concessions and facilitation provided to private health care establishments, the introduction of publicly financed health insurance programmes and the promotion of medical tourism have together created a favourable climate for the growth of the corporate health care industry but has negatively impacted public services in the sector. First, this has led to an internal brain drain of health professionals from public services to the corporate segment, further depleting the staff position in government health establishments which are already understaffed. Second, it has also resulted in reinforcing the discriminatory multi-tier system essentially based on affordability. While private investment in the health sector is increasing, there has been a modest growth in funds for strengthening public services. Some efforts have been made in recent years to strengthen the network of sub-centres and primary health centres. But will this suffice to meet the stupendous challenge involved in reaching the SDG targets by 2030?

As noted earlier, progress in provision of health facilities has to be seen in conjunction with our efforts and outcomes in the area of hunger, food and nutrition. Unfortunately, India faces a huge uphill task to move forward in these areas. Global ranking with respect to fighting hunger places India closer to the bottom among 119 countries in the world and lower than most of our neighbours in the region (Bread for the World Institute 2016). It is estimated that average per capita food consumption in developing countries is 2,683 KCAL per capita per day. The corresponding figure for India is 2,354, which is lower than the figures for Bangladesh, Nepal and Pakistan. In China, it is as high as 3,044 KCAL per capita per day, which is higher than the world average of 2,795 KCAL per capita per day (IFPRI 2018). Can the Food Security Act 2013 take us to the goal of zero hunger by 2030? This would require very intensive and focused effort as the pace at which we have progressed in recent years is not quite encouraging and also depends on our success in dealing with the problem of under-nutrition.

As highlighted in the national strategy paper on nutrition, under-nutrition levels in India have remained persistently high – especially in utero, in the early years of life, in adolescent girls and in women across the life cycle, particularly in disadvantaged/excluded community groups and those living in areas or conditions of high nutritional vulnerability and multiple deprivations (Government of India, n.d.c). Child under-nutrition rates have been declining at a relatively accelerated pace particularly during the last ten years. Yet developments are below the rate needed to meet the global nutrition targets. And, despite the progress, child under nutrition rates in India are among the highest in the world, with nearly one-half of all children under three years of age being either under-weight or stunted. India is still the home to over 40 million stunted[10] children and 17 million wasted[11] children under age 5 (Raykar et al. 2015). Child under-nutrition is a primary cause for reduced school attendance; it negatively impacts cognitive development; and constricts realisation of full potential causing immeasurable loss to the individual and the society.

As the strategy paper elaborates, under-nutrition is perpetuated as an intergeneration cycle. The girl child goes on to become an undernourished and anaemic adolescent girl, often deprived of adequate health care and nutritional support, educational opportunities, denied her right to be a child – married too early, with early child-bearing and inadequate inter-pregnancy recoupment. This perpetuates a vicious cycle of under-nutrition and morbidity that erodes human capital through irreversible and intergenerational effects on cognitive and physical development. The National Family Health Survey (NFHS) 4 findings reveal that around 26.8 per cent of currently married women aged 20–24 years were married before attaining the age of 18 years (IIPS and ICF 2017).

The problem is accentuated by multiple deprivations related to poverty, social exclusion and gender discrimination. Nutrition vulnerabilities are compounded by differentials in socio-economic status and vary by vulnerable community groups such as SC, ST, minorities and others. For instance, an empirical study by Tagade and Deshpande (chapter 8 in this volume) in Maharashtra revealed that tribal population in the state experience high levels of food insecurity and under-nutrition compared to non-tribals. The calorie value of their daily food consumption is significantly lower than the national average as well as non-tribals in the same geographical locations. The study also reported significantly higher proportion of under-nutrition cases among the ST population.

It is somewhat a paradox that despite consistent reduction in poverty levels, under-nutrition in India refuses to budge. A study of sixty-three countries, including India, attempted to understand the importance of economic growth in reducing under-nutrition, by analysing the relationship between child nutrition and variables related to economic growth, food availability, women's education, women's status, and access to safe water. The study found that increase in per capita national income translated into improvements in child nutritional status only if the economic gains facilitated public and private investments that could improve conditions related to diet and disease (Smith and Haddad 2002). The finding is particularly significant for India, as there is evidence that the relationship between economic growth and stunting reduction in India is not as strong as in many other countries.

Addressing the challenge of persisting under-nutrition demands actions in multiple sectors and at multiple levels, in close coordination with initiatives in the health sector. There have been several long standing programmes in India, such as ICDS, which is by design significantly nutrition-specific to meet the needs of maternal care and child development or a dietary/nutrition supplement scheme, e.g. the Mid-Day Meal Scheme (MDMS) meant for young children in the school-going age. These have been in operation for several decades. While one cannot undermine their contribution over the years in reducing the prevalence of under-nutrition, they have remained largely static and rigid in their framework and operations. There is a need to re-examine them in a more fundamental fashion with respect to content, structure and operations, learning from numerous empirical studies available on the subject and arrive at alternate innovative designs that are variable and context specific in place of pan-Indian models.

With the wide geographical coverage achieved, ICDS has the best potential to influence maternal health and nutritional status of children in the country. However, the programme's outreach within the community at the grassroots level remains quite weak. The Rapid Survey on Children (RSoC) conducted by MWCD, reported that among all the women who had a live birth in the three years preceding the survey, 70 per cent registered their pregnancy in an Anganwadi Centre (AWC) (Government of India 2014). However, proportion of women ultimately receiving ante natal check-ups (ANC) at AWCs was much lower (22 per cent). Similarly, only 49 per cent children under three years received supplementary nutrition under ICDS, indicating limited uptake, even though more than 90 per cent of centres surveyed reported providing supplementary food. The corresponding figures for the age group 3–6 years were 44 per cent. The RSoC also points to the need for better parental education as only 10 per cent mothers of children (newborn to seventy-one months) were aware of all six services available from AWCs and about 6 per cent did not have awareness of any service. There is an urgent need to increase investment in the programme not only for improving the infrastructure and inputs but also the professional status and capabilities of the women managing the AWCs.

With multiple actors involved in implementing programmes of health and nutrition, creating an effective mechanism for governance and oversight is critical to achieving convergence of actions. The National Health Mission (NHM) framework designates Village Health Sanitation and Nutrition Committee (VHSNC) as the forum for grass root level action to address the various issues related to health. They are expected to ensure convergence of various initiatives at the village level by involving accredited social health activists (ASHA), auxiliary nurse midwives (ANM) and Anganwadi workers (AWWs) in programmes of capacity building in the areas of sanitation, drinking water, health and hygiene, the prevention and identification of malnutrition and safe water storage. But in reality, many AWCs are largely left to work in isolation within the hierarchy of an indifferent bureaucracy with meagre support and guidance. With a view to strengthening community engagement, the High-Level Expert Group (HLEG) recommended for recasting the VHSNCs into participatory Health Councils which would organise annual Health Assemblies at different levels (district, state and nation) to enable community review of health plans and their performance as well as indicate corrective measures at the systemic level based on ground level experiences (Government of India 2011). It would also be beneficial to strengthen the role of *Panchayati Raj* Institutions and urban local bodies in order to motivate local self-governments to own, promote, monitor and sustain health and nutritional initiatives in a convergent manner.

There is an urgent need to enhance the availability of health personnel particularly in rural areas. Between 2007 and 2011, rural sub-centres grew by 2 per cent, primary health centres by 6 per cent, community health centres by 16 per cent and district hospitals by 45 per cent. Yet shortfalls remain. In 2011 the gap between staff positioned and required was 52 per cent for ANMs, 72 per cent for doctors, 88 per cent for specialists and 58 per cent for pharmacists (Bhattacharya and Goyal, chapter 9, this volume). Unless there is a concerted effort to strengthen health education facilities in the public sector, it is unlikely that the shortage will be made up and the goals of health for all or a malnutrition free India will materialise.

Health and nutrition concerns cannot be met without food security which involves ensuring that all people, at all times, have physical and economic access to sufficient, safe and nutritious food to meet their dietary needs and food preferences for an active and healthy life. Having achieved food self-sufficiency and becoming a net exporter, India has been for too long engrossed in streamlining the public distribution system. But for food security to be fully met we have also to engage with more fundamental issues related to agriculture and food production. Such engagement could contribute to health and nutrition through multiple pathways: increasing incomes of farming households, diversifying production of crops, strengthening agricultural diversity and productivity, promoting sustainable agricultural practices and designing careful price and subsidy policies that do not discourage the production and consumption of nutrient-rich crops (Raykar et al. 2015). As the conditions vary widely across the country, active association of state governments in designing such initiatives is critically important.

Finally, as a G20 document exhorts, we should prioritise the health and wellbeing of the most vulnerable and marginalised within their own local contexts, rather than aiming for the "lowest hanging fruit" as a way of demonstrating more rapid success in meeting targets (Boutillier et al. 2017). This should also be the key criterion for monitoring the performance of our health initiatives and measuring their success. Government should identify marginalised populations based on the criteria of health (access and outcomes) as well as wealth (health as human capital), and show leadership in developing health strategies for these populations. All the dimensions of marginality (availability, accessibility and affordability) should be taken into consideration while designing appropriate policies and programmes.

Gender equality and empowerment of women

Recent decades have seen commitment to "gender equality" emerging as an integral component of all global development agenda. This indeed has been the result of a long drawn public campaigning by civil society organisations, women's groups and academia across the world, including India. Women's groups have imprinted upon the worlds' consciousness the need to develop enabling policy frameworks (that are pro-women) and fast-track their implementation to ensure significant changes in the lives of women and marginalised populations. They have also raised critical questions of how equality, inclusion and participation would be embedded in a world that is structured around grave inequalities and exclusions (Dhar, this volume).

Gender equality and women's empowerment got firmly placed as areas for priority action in global discourses and action plans when the UN Millennium Declaration set it as one of the eight MDGs. In fact, the UN held a special session of the General Assembly, titled "Women 2000: Gender equality, development and peace for the twenty-first century". Building on the progress made towards the MDGs, a more comprehensive vision was set under SDGs:

> The achievement of full human potential and of sustainable development is not possible if one half of humanity continues to be denied its full human rights and opportunities. Women and girls must enjoy equal access to quality education, economic resources and political participation as well as equal opportunities with men and boys for employment, leadership and decision making at all levels.
>
> *(United Nations n.d.)*

SDG 5 encompasses a multi-dimensional approach to gender equality with a wide range of targets that include ending discrimination and violence against women, including trafficking and sexual (and other types of) exploitation; ending child, early and forced marriage and female genital mutilation; recognising unpaid care and domestic work; promoting women's participation and opportunities for leadership; ensuring universal access to sexual health and reproductive rights; enabling ownership of land and other property, including natural resources; and providing access to intermediate technology.[12]

India has been a signatory to these and several other global declarations and conventions related to gender equality. In fact, Indian policy documents, beginning with "Towards Equality", a pioneering report on the status of women, have consistently, albeit somewhat ritualistically, accorded a prominent place to the subject (Government of India 1974). Every Five-Year Plan document and various policy pronouncements in different sectors have invariably devoted substantial importance to highlight the need for creating a society underscored by gender equality. There has been progress in creating relative parity in some areas such as primary education. But India has yet to traverse a long way on the road to gender equality. India was placed 108th out of 144 countries in the Global Gender Gap Report of 2017, significantly lagging behind its neighbours, such as China and Bangladesh (World Economic Forum 2017). It ranked 127th among 189 countries on the Gender Inequality Index, below South Asian neighbours Bhutan and Nepal (UNDP 2018).

We have to recognise that policy commitments, progressive legislations and launch of national campaigns and programmes can only create necessary conditions. The ground reality in India significantly contrasts with the rhetoric of the policies and legislations, and the goals and targets set by the programmes. The key challenge for India is to understand more deeply why, despite constitutional guarantees on women's equality and rights and the adoption of several policies and programmatic directions over the years, patriarchal mind-sets and misogyny continue to persist and limit women's freedom, voices and dignity (Dhar, chapter 10).

Discrimination and violence against women have, in recent years, come to the centre stage of national discourse leading to the adoption of progressive policy and legislative measures. These steps, in fact, largely reconfirm the comprehensive commitments made by the country under Convention on the Elimination of all Forms of Discrimination Against Women (CEDAW), described as an "international bill of rights for women", and several other international instruments. But perceptible change in the ground reality is not easy to find. Besides inefficient implementation and insufficient institutional mechanisms, the low rates of prosecution and conviction seem to undermine the drive to reduce violence against women and girls. One has also to contend with the perception that the perpetrators of discrimination and violence against women often enjoy political patronage and immunity under the pretext of tradition and culture. The state has to be proactive in creating and implementing measures for the elimination of structural barriers that impede women's human rights. Tackling such deep-seated problems requires a transformative vision and an approach that views women as autonomous and equal citizens, with rights to bodily integrity and the right to assert their sexualities, freedoms and voice (Dhar).

It is also well established that women's labour force participation and access to decent work are critical requirement for giving women equal rights to economic resources and access to full and productive employment as explicitly specified in the SDGs. Unfortunately, this has been thoroughly neglected over a long period of time. In fact, recent data show a significantly declining trend in the participation of women in the labour force. Women face a host of barriers to realising their economic rights. They are largely employed in the informal sector that is marked by insecure and precarious work conditions with little or no access to social protection. Further, inflexible gender norms impact their employment opportunities and mobility patterns. Labour markets also provide fewer and lower-paying work options for women (Dhar). This unfavourable condition tends to perpetuate itself as women receive fewer years of schooling than men in all segments of the workforce and the educational attainments of female workers continue to be at low levels. In 2009–10, amongst women workers, 34.4 per cent (rural and urban) were illiterate. Despite considerable improvement since 2004–05, a little less than half the female ST (48.2 per cent) and SC (45.6 per cent) workers remained illiterate in 2009–10, the highest rates for any group (Lingam, chapter 11, this volume). The skill-building projects also seem to get trapped by gender stereotype. Technical and vocational skill-building courses are attended more by men than by women while women's participation is higher in literacy-linked programmes (Govinda 2017).

Problems of women working in vulnerable conditions continue to be a major concern as data on the nature of work show that 81 per cent of women workers are engaged in vulnerable employment placing them perpetually at the risk of falling into economic distress (ILO 2018); they are either self-employed or contributing family workers, which are also the two employment groups often characterised by higher poverty rates and limited social protection. This figure is much higher than the average for Asia-Pacific Region which is 63 per cent for women and 56 per cent for men (UN ESCAP 2015). It should also be recognised that current poverty measures do not adequately capture women's vulnerability to poverty. Because of prevalent social norms that restrict their right to work, child care demands and gender-based wage and work disparities in labour markets, women either have lower income than men or remain without an income of their own. For many women, poverty and vulnerability prompt them to seek some form of work often at the expense of their health, child care, rest and leisure. It has been observed that working-women have lower levels of maternal health care utilisation and higher levels of anaemia and poor health (Lingam).

Maternity protection is recognised as an essential prerequisite for women's rights and gender equality. Article 42 of the Constitution of India stipulates that state shall make provision for securing just and humane conditions of work and for maternity relief. This is not merely a subject concerning women's rights. Neglect of maternal care directly impinges on the child and the whole family as well. Responsive care, provided by a care-giver, is an essential component contributing to cognitive development, emotional wellbeing and health, not to mention the safety and protection of young children. But the overall Indian maternal mortality figure of 167 per 100,000 live births (2011–13) tells us the story of neglect of women during the critically important period of pregnancy and childbirth. Maternity benefits, which encompass several provisions including leave, wage compensation, nursing breaks as well as strictures against discrimination of women on account of reproduction, is an important tool that levels the playing field for women in the labour market. Maternity benefit schemes in India have been in existence for over five decades, yet the vast majority of Indian women do not get any maternity entitlements as the legislation does not apply to the unorganised sector (Lingam). There has been some progress in recent years to extend selected benefits to women in the unorganised sectors. It is perhaps too early to determine how it will impact the indicators on maternal health and child nutrition.

Even though the subject finds place in every policy document, achieving the goals of gender equality and empowerment of women is proving to be the toughest of all SDGs. It is urgent that the country – government as well as civil society organisations, significantly step up efforts. Four areas need immediate attention of policymakers as well as activists. The first is related to improving the level of participation of women in leadership positions. The SDG stipulates that we ensure women's full and effective participation and equal opportunities for leadership at all levels of decision-making in political, economic and public life. India's position in this regard is abysmally low with only 12 per cent representation in the parliament and 9 per cent in the state/UT bodies. It is time that building on the gains made by creating electoral gender quota in *panchayati raj* institutions, we move forward on the stalled agenda for electoral quota in national and state level legislatures as this has the potential to structurally transform the political landscape and institutions of public governance across the country.

Second, values of gender equality and empowerment of women has to be more pervasive characterising the larger ambience of socio-political life in the country. Policy and legislative measures for protection of women against violence and discrimination even when accompanied by stringent punitive action will have limited deterrent value if the issues get mired in procedural delays and judicial wrangles in the absence of supportive environment. They also often conflict with local forces and parallel institutions that function freely under the pretext of culture and tradition, implicit with undercurrent of caste and religious identity. Third, we have to recognise that such social transformation agenda can be realised only by increasing the space for women's voices in public policy-making, by adopting a rights-based framework and ensuring that lived realities rather than theoretical assumptions inform the processes of policy and action. This in turn demands that we, more proactively, strengthen the role of autonomous women's organisations which have been found to be the most effective means of tackling social and cultural norms that work against the value of equality and non-discrimination.

Finally, we have to recognise the phenomenon of clustered deprivations. Women and girls at the intersection of different forms of discrimination tend to fare worse across multiple dimensions of wellbeing – in other words, they face multidimensional and clustered forms of deprivation. Poverty, for example, is a strong correlate of poor educational outcomes; it is also one of the main drivers of child marriage. These three forms of deprivation will often cluster and reinforce each other (UN Women 2018, p. 139). Empirical analysis in India show that a young woman aged 20–24 from a poor, rural household is 5.1 times as likely as one from a rich urban household to marry before the age of 18; significantly more likely that she has never attended school; high likelihood of her becoming an adolescent mother; not likely to have access to money for her own use; and may not have much role in decisions related to spending the money. Further, the likelihood of being poor is greater if she is landless and from a scheduled caste and her low level of education and status in the social hierarchy will almost guarantee that if she works for pay, it will be under exploitative working conditions (Roy et al. 2008, pp. 72–73, cited in UN Women 2018).

The lesson for policy-making is clear. Merely reacting to events and issues in an isolated manner is inadequate. There is an urgent need to be innovative in designing multi-sectoral integrated approaches. Broad-based partnerships that break boundaries are a critical ingredient in driving successful innovations for women's empowerment as they can leverage broader reach and resources – both financial and human, to yield wider larger-scale results (Malhotra et al. 2009). There are no adversaries in this effort. Different players from the government, private sector, civil society, trade unions and academic institutions leading innovations have to come on a common platform as no single sector has the unique pathway to implement the transformative agenda.

Poverty, Unemployment, Inequality

Poverty eradication has been a goal pursued by all countries. This was the central concern of the MDGs. The dynamic interaction and organic linkage between poverty levels, employment opportunities and inequality in the society needs no special explanation. SDGs and the accompanying targets make special mention of all the three. We will reflect on the problems and prospects of pursuing the three goals in India drawing upon four chapters included in this volume and other relevant sources. There has been more contestation than consensus on determining when a person would qualify to be designated as "poor". The issue becomes quite complicated if we consider "poverty in all its forms everywhere"; when we go beyond the basic form of income poverty and examine it under the rubric of capability poverty as formulated by Amartya Sen; and when we locate it in the broader social political context and link it with the concept of human wellbeing. The SDG benchmark for measuring poverty has, in fact, come for serious questioning (Sengupta, chapter 2, this volume). However, it is worthwhile to examine the problem of achieving the ambitious target of ending poverty of all forms and specifically extreme poverty in India using the global benchmark as well as the Indian definition of the poverty line.

For many decades, poverty eradication remained the favourite phrase of the political leadership in India. But in recent times the catchword is GDP growth rate. GDP growth rate has become the principal means of judging how beautiful we are both as an economy and as a society. It is all around us. You can't smell it or touch it. But it is the background noise of the modern world. It is the fodder of headlines, business channels and political debate (Pilling 2018, p. 1). There is no denying the fact that the Indian economy has registered a fast rate of growth during the last couple of decades and that in global assessment, poverty reduction has also been quite substantial during this period. But we should not lose sight of the fact that despite rapid growth India is one of the poorest countries in the world (Dreze and Sen 2011). India is indeed a study in contrasts. India has the largest number of poor in the world. In terms of per capita GDP India is ranked 20th from the bottom among 126 countries with a per capita income of less than $2,000 US. In terms of people living in extreme poverty, India accounts for 33 per cent of the extreme poor in the world which refers to people living with income less than $1.25 US per day. In absolute numbers, these constituted around 394 million people in 2010 (Olinto et al. 2013).

If the official poverty line defined by the government (which works out to around an income of Rs.32 per day per person) is taken to indicate extreme poverty, one out of every five persons in India belongs to this category, accounting for nearly 300 million people (Patnaik 2013; Nayyar and Nayyar 2016; Mehta and Venkatraman 2000).[13] In several states (Arunachal Pradesh, Chhattisgarh, Jharkhand and

Odisha) the corresponding figure is around one out of three persons (RBI 2013).[14] Further disaggregation shows that more than 40 per cent ST and nearly 30 per cent SC are BPL compared to the general population of 21.9 per cent.[15] Further, as the World Development Report, 2015, points out, individuals living in poverty have also to contend with social and psychological consequences in the form of depletion of cognitive resources. Poverty may also generate an internal frame, or a way of interpreting the world and poor people's role in it. Poor people may feel incompetent and disrespected, without hope that their lives can improve. If these kinds of frames prevent them from taking advantage of economic opportunities, then the poor could also miss chances to escape poverty because of a deficit of aspirations. Further, this cognitive depletion induced by scarcity is not limited to poor farmers in India or to people living under some absolute poverty line (The World Bank 2015, p. 83). A large number of families who are around and above the poverty line also suffer the wretchedness of deprivation in their lives, particularly during periods of crisis related to health or natural calamities. Poverty cannot be treated as a binary of below poverty line (BPL) and above poverty line (APL). Placed in such a challenging position, it demands gigantic efforts for India to succeed in eliminating poverty in all its forms and everywhere by 2030.

Poverty eradication/alleviation is not only a desirable social cause but has also been a politically attractive public policy. Successive governments at the centre and the states have launched a plethora of schemes and programmes with the avowed objective of liberating the poor from the miseries of poverty they are trapped in. Of the various initiatives, the MGNREGS has been hailed by the government as well as social activists as an outstanding effort with the potential to deeply impact the lives and livelihood of the rural poor. The scheme purports to provide a legal guarantee for at least 100 days of paid employment in every financial year to adult members of any household willing to do unskilled manual work at the statutory minimum wage fixed by the state government, failing which the government would transfer the equivalent amount to the household. The scheme is demand based and no restriction is placed on the income level of the household.

Would this scheme be the harbinger of poverty free life for the rural households in India? That is perhaps a far cry if we consider the empirical data generated in a recent evaluation by the Ministry of Rural Development. The performance of MGNREGA in terms of full realisation of the entitled one hundred days of work per year appears to be very low. The evaluation report reveals that only 13.8 per cent received employment, for an average, of more than 80 days while only 7.9 per cent received on an average sixty-one to eighty days of work. Just more than 50 per cent got employment for an average of twenty-one to sixty days (TNS India 2015). There were 26 per cent of the households who got employment for less than twenty days (p. 40). The national average of employment per household has been forty-seven days, forty-two days and 46.2 days for the years 2010–11, 2011–12 and 2012–13, respectively (p. 34). The main reason for not having a full period of one hundred days was lack of funds and/or work in local area. The daily wage paid ranged from Rs.167 to Rs.240 linked to consumer price index of agricultural labour across different states. The situation may have improved during recent years. Yet with an average of fifty days of labour in a year and an average daily wage of Rs.200, the total accruing to a BPL household through the scheme works out to be around Rs.10,000 per year. For a household steeped in extreme poverty this could at best be able to save them from absolute immiseration. This is not to totally deny the value of the scheme alleviating rural poverty.

The scheme, indeed, has several collateral positives. As Chandrasekhar and Ghosh (2014, p. 28) point out, because of the wage and work norms that are defined in the Act, it has the potential to stabilise rural wages at levels that are at least close to the legal minimum wage and even to increase them beyond it in some cases, to reduce the extremely exploitative working conditions that prevail in rural labour markets in many parts of India and to provide work on relatively equal terms to women and workers from scheduled castes and tribes who are routinely discriminated against in rural labour markets. Yet one cannot dismiss the value of the scheme for the rural poor; the outreach and coverage achieved does not warrant any euphoria on its contribution to eliminating poverty or guaranteeing employment. What is on offer, after all, is only informal unskilled wage labour, not full employment and decent work as specified under the SDGs. The excitement has perhaps been overdone on both sides. The high hopes of radical change in power relations, or of dramatic poverty reduction, have not materialised; nor did the doomsday predictions of financial bankruptcy or economic chaos (Dreze and Sen 2014, p. 200).

The SDG framework has set a very ambitious target of achieving full and productive employment and decent work for all women and men, including for young people and persons with disabilities, and equal pay for work of equal value by 2030. Will India be able to reach this level of employment and decent work? While the new millennium witnessed increased income levels, employment generation has been sluggish. Analysing economic growth and employment patterns in the post-reform period, Chandrasekhar and Ghosh highlight that the income growth process has not been accompanied by large increases in employment, other than in a few sectors, such as construction. In fact, aggregate recorded employment has declined for women over this period, mostly because of declining self-employment and less engagement in casual labour. The standard notion that higher growth has generated more demand for labour and thereby led to higher wage rates is complicated by the lack of increase in aggregate employment (see Chandrasekhar and Ghosh 2014; Jha and Negre n.d,). Examining the relationship between economic growth and employment, Khare (chapter 13, this volume) found that high growth states do not necessarily have low unemployment. Out of the first eight high growth states only two, namely Himachal Pradesh and Maharashtra are in the lowest unemployment quadrant. This certainly is an issue of grave concern. But what is even more worrisome is the fact that quality of employment is poor in low growing states. Problems of "underemployment" and "disguised unemployment" are pervasive and have tended to worsen when we audit the large scale data systems for the reform era (Jha 2016). In fact between 2001 and 2011 census the proportion of "marginal" workers went up in comparison to the proportion of "main" workers. In general, employment challenge and informality seem to have aggravated and deepened during the last two decades. How do we tackle this disconnect between economic growth and generation of employment and decent work for all?

The reform advocates would argue that this is only temporary and reform measures will trigger growth in employment. Not everyone agrees with this. Jha (Chapter 12 in this volume) argues for revisiting the overall economic policies in general and the industrial policy in particular. He points out that India's policy obsession almost entirely with "big players" needs to be revisited. The context and prospects of India's industrial landscape, particularly from the point of employment, are organically connected with the unorganised segments and MSMEs. The country needs, first and foremost, a robust industrial policy for them, embedded in an overall macro-economic policy regime. As per recent estimates, MSMEs contribute approximately 8 per cent of the country's GDP, 45 per cent of the manufacturing output and 40 per cent of the country's exports, and the sector is the second largest provider of employment in the country, after agriculture. Thus it is quite evident that a policy conducive towards MSMEs will play a critical role in India's broad based industrialisation and employment engendering drive.

A second issue to be addressed in the context of SDG commitments is that of quality of employment. This is an area that is truly daunting for India as around 92 per cent of the employed are informal workers. 50 per cent of the total workers are self-employed while 30 per cent are casual, 18 per cent are regular workers. Regular formal workers are only 8 per cent of the total workers. Aggravating the situation further is the generally low levels of education and professional and vocational skills of workers. Disadvantaged social groups like SCs and STs are not employed in productive sectors but are more in casual employment. There is considerable segmentation in labour market by sector, location, region, gender, caste, religion, and tribe (Dev 2016). Jha points out that deteriorating quality of employment as reflected in growing informalisation and high incidence of vulnerable self-employment demands an urgent rethink on the overall policy regime. Such a rethink must include "labour" as a partner instead of viewing it as a hindrance to economic and social progress.

Compared to the issues of poverty and unemployment, concern for rising inequality is a relatively recent entry into global declarations on development. It was first highlighted in the Report on the World Social Situation 2005 and subsequently the Report in 2013 was titled "Inequality Matters". The issue since then gained further importance and found place in the SDGs as an independent goal. Target 10.1 of the SDGs aspires to "progressively achieve and sustain income growth of the bottom 40 per cent of the population at a rate higher than the national average" by 2030. While this specific attention to the bottom 40 per cent is welcome, the formulation refuses to engage with the problem of undue concentration of wealth at the narrow top or on the need for redistribution measures within the country. Globalisation enthusiasts in India as elsewhere would like to explain away rising inequality in income and wealth as a short-term phenomenon and that people should show forbearance in the interests of greater and long term good.

However, others consider this to be too serious to ignore as mere unintended collateral damage (Bauman 2011). Within the Indian context the issue of rising inequality is even more complex as income and wealth inequality combines with the structural fault lines of caste and gender that are deeply embedded in the Indian society. It is the mutual reinforcement of severe inequalities of different kinds that creates an extremely oppressive social system, where those at the bottom of these multiple layers of disadvantage live in conditions of extreme disempowerment (Dreze and Sen 2014, p. 213).

India in the new millennium is emerging as a deeply divided nation. While a handful of people at the top, the HNWIs as they are referred to, have never had it so good, millions of families are struggling to make both ends meet. Indian media almost celebrates an Indian replacing a Chinese as the richest man in Asia whilst barely mentioning the millions of Indians who still live on the edge of destitution and experience a sense of hopelessness in life. Income inequality in India has reached historically high levels. In 2014, the share of national income accruing to India's top 1 per cent of earners was 22 per cent, while the share of the top 10 per cent was around 56 per cent. Since the beginning of deregulation policies in the 1980s, the top 0.1 per cent earners have captured more growth than all of those in the bottom 50 per cent combined. The middle 40 per cent have also seen relatively little growth in their incomes (Alvaredo et al. 2017, p. 123).

Empirical studies in India also point to the same observation. Examining employment and inequality in India, Kundu and Mohanan analysed the trend and performance of economic growth in the context of changing macroeconomic scenario over the past three and a half decades. They found that the high growth in income and other economic indicators have been associated with increase in regional and social inequality. There has been systematic reduction in poverty but inequality in consumption expenditure has gone up both in rural and more significantly urban areas (Kundu and Mohanan n.d.). Are our policymakers addressing this rising inequality as a problem? It is difficult to give an affirmative answer as this contradiction is only apparent to those who see both sides of life – great concentration of wealth coexisting with the highest concentration of poverty (Dorling 2014, p. 107). The Governments in general have been eager to promote a singular perspective and fail to see both sides.

In fact, the inequality situation demands urgent attention of policymakers on multiple fronts as income and wealth inequalities get further intensified through inadequate investment and inappropriate institutional arrangements in areas of health and education. Tackling the problem of rising inequality demands us to address the issue of relative poverty which manifests itself through several concomitant deprivations. As Khare emphasises, creating more regular and stable jobs may not help reduce inequalities until it is simultaneously matched with reducing educational inequalities. As a policy measure the country should aim at a minimum threshold level of compulsory education (secondary level) for all in order to develop skilled and quality human resource. Absence of a common public school system and the downstream impact of privatisation of education with high fee charging schools and colleges could have serious implications which go beyond measurable indicators of income and wealth disparities. The collateral damage they cause is immeasurable and remains invisible immediately. They tend to engender a sense of superiority closely related to that fostered in a segregated society – not least because the most expensive schools could not continue to function as they do without a small number of very highly paid individuals to pay the huge fees (Reich 2014, p. 164).

While the prospect of increasing economic inequality should worry us greatly, its social and political consequences if unheeded, portend more serious threat to the very foundations of Indian democracy. As Mohanty (Chapter 15 in this volume) highlights, inequality is not merely about quantitative or arithmetical differences of possessions, it is about power relationships. Extreme inequality in a society could have bizarre outcomes. It could lead to a situation in which a person or group of people are excluded, dominated and/or humiliated, to the point of becoming non-existent to the rest of the society. They may speak, but their voice is not heard and their words do not matter. They may protest, but their action remains unsupported and ultimately ineffective. They may analyse the central dynamics of power and privilege, but their analysis gets lost in the news cycle and buried by official rhetoric (Guenther 2013 cited in Dorling 2014). Even though this sounds somewhat alarmist and is an observation made in a different context in America, it posts a huge warning for us not to ignore the problem as already evidenced in the country by public expression of increasing social desperation and protest in recent years.

Unfortunately over the years, particularly during the last three decades, growing structural anomalies that have accompanied rising inequality have been left unattended to by the political leadership. This has resulted in the emergence of vested interests influencing policy-making and leading to what Hasan (chapter 14 in this volume) characterises as "elite capture" of the institutions of political governance. Why is the state in India as much as in most other countries disengaged from the problem of inequality even though it could disrupt social harmony and even political stability? Is widening inequality creating a skewed political power structure in the country that favour only a few, disregarding the constitutional commitment of equality and justice? Whatever the answer be, apart from an economic analysis, rising inequality calls for an analysis of political and policy processes that allow certain politically and economically powerful groups to control and manipulate not just economic activities but also democratic processes. The upshot of inequality is elite dominance which in turn has consequences for the operation of democracy and eventually for people's wellbeing. The elite capture of policy space has indeed worsened economic inequality, and undermined the rules and regulations that give the poorest and the most marginalised citizens a fair chance (Hasan).

In order to move forward in addressing the problem of rising inequality, we have to recognise the organic linkage between poverty and inequality and tackle them together. Disconnecting the problem of poverty from that of inequality tends to create artificial binary as the poor and the non-poor, and legitimises characterising the poor as "them" – people who are different from most of us; "they" invariably lack self-discipline and intrinsic motivation; therefore, any attempt to alleviate poverty requires that "they" change their ways (Reich 2014). Obviously, such a premise in policy-making absolves the state from dealing with the problem of inequality arising out of the concentration of disproportionate wealth of the country in a few private hands and in effect, allows the Indian State to abdicate its responsibility towards distributive justice. Secondly, we have to accept that inequality is multidimensional and is shaped by a variety of national, institutional and political contexts but there is no inevitability behind the rise of income inequality. For instance, when countries are compared with one another over the past decades, China grew much faster than India, with a lower level of inequality, and the EU had a more equitable path than the United States but a relatively similar growth rate. This suggests that it is possible to pursue equitable development pathways in a way that does not also limit total growth in the future (Alvaredo et al. 2017, p. 255).[16] In other words, inclusive growth and development need not be mere rhetoric; it can become a reality if we learn lessons from around the world and reorient our policies and priorities.

Moving forward: need for a vision of inclusive development

The vision of India emerging as a global economic power dominates all contemporary debates and discourses on development, mainly impelled by the recent upswing in economic growth. While rapid economic growth that India has been able to register is widely appreciated, it has its critics too. It is like a double-edged sword. On the one hand, it may be viewed as a narrative of liberation, lifting people out of poverty. On the other, it may be viewed as one of alienation, increasing inequality and associated with environmental degradation (IPSP 2018). But as we embark on a reflection on the prospects of achieving SDGs in the social sector, it serves no purpose, and surely stands no logic if we pit economic growth and social progress as adversarial objectives. It is also not worthwhile to speculate on whether India will meet all the social sector goals by 2030 as specified under SDGs. Working towards improved quality of life and human wellbeing is not a matter of choice in development planning; it is indeed the *raison d'être* of development. It is not that India has not made any progress in social sectors over the years. Data clearly indicate substantial progress on several dimensions in the last seven decades. But significant gaps remain and the road yet to be traversed is quite challenging. The issue therefore is: how do we reshape development policies and action in India to achieve speedier progress in social sector goals? We do not propose to engage in a full exploration of the process of such reshaping of the development vision, but will confine to highlighting a few critical steps required for such a process as evidenced by the analysis presented in various chapters of this volume.

There is an increasing feeling that the Indian leadership has been pursuing economic growth with a narrow singular focus often to the detriment of progress in social sectors in a holistic sense. While some at the top of the ladder are benefitting from this approach, a large majority are left behind without access to even basic social protection. It is against this background that Dubey (concluding chapter of the volume) calls for adopting a vision of development that is inclusive. He argues that inclusive development is needed in India not only for imparting speed and sustainability to growth, not only for alleviating a substantial part of the current distress and deprivation but also for the very survival of the nation with all its diversity and plurality – the most defining characteristic of India. For, the centrality of inclusion grows out of the need to weld a diverse people into a modern nation and to overcome the deeply entrenched and long-established injustices and hierarchies in Indian society. Pursuing such a vision of development demands that we view social progress also in a larger canvass of human progress and wellbeing.

As Sen points out, the purpose of development is indeed "expanding the real freedom that people enjoy" and cannot be reduced to a statistic (Sen 1999). The International Panel on Social Progress defines social progress as a compass consisting of key values and principles that include: equal dignity, basic rights, democracy, the rule of law, pluralism, wellbeing, freedom, non-alienation, solidarity, esteem and recognition, cultural goods, environmental values, distributive justice, transparency and accountability. This is not a rejection of the market or the role of economic growth in human progress. But if social progress is not to be halted or even reversed, there is a need for the market to be re-embedded in society with the perspective of inclusive development. The central message underlying these observations is that the pursuit of social sector goals is as essential and intrinsic to development. They cannot be treated as mere instruments for boosting economic growth.

A common thread that we find across chapters on different themes is the state of education and health sectors and their centrality for improving human wellbeing. Broadly defined as human resources development, these are considered foundational for social progress as core components of human wellbeing and also as critical instruments for promoting inclusive development and improving quality of life. The ground reality, however, with respect to the state of these sectors is quite challenging. This indeed is the central argument of the concluding chapter by Dubey which lays out the needed action if further progress is to be made in meeting social sector concerns. As the authors throughout this volume highlight, the government has to enhance attention to these sectors both through increased spending and strengthening the field operations.

Both in education and health, overdependence on private entities for expanding schools and hospitals is a matter of serious concern. This approach coupled with continued underfunding of the sectors is having a significantly negative effect on the quality of services provided through public institutions. Over the years, market instrumentality of loans and insurance has begun to replace public funding even for basic services. In effect, while policy documents refer to universal provision, action on the field is quite contrary to such a proposition. It is in this context that Dubey considers that in India, education and health constitute the biggest constraint to development in general and inclusive development in particular. Most of the development schemes are unlikely to succeed fully in the prevailing conditions of health and education in the country. For example, an uneducated or poorly educated India cannot be "Skilled India". Skills of the required quality can be acquired only on the foundation of good quality basic education.

An issue that has come for considerable attention in recent years is the impact of the changing nature of political and economic institutions on social sector development. Institutions, indeed, are the vital organs in any governance system facilitating translation of development policies into action. Dreze and Sen identify two kinds of institutions: (i) Institutions that are important for growth and development seen together; and (ii) the specific institutional needs of translating the achievements in growth into the broader perspective of development and flourishing of human beings (Dreze and Sen 2014, p. 36). Inclusive development can be realised only if these institutions are inclusive in their structure and functioning. But as Acemoglu and Robinson argue in *Why Nations Fail*, inclusive economic and political institutions do not emerge by themselves. They are the outcome of significant conflict between elites and those wishing to limit the economic and political power of existing elites. Through such struggles, inclusive institutions emerge during critical junctures (Acemoglu and Robinson 2013, p. 332). That critical juncture in India's history happened seven decades ago when the colonial rule was jettisoned and the newly formed nation embraced a constitutional democracy. Acemoglu and Robinson further elaborate that under inclusive institutions, wealth is not concentrated in the hands of a small group that could then use its economic might to increase its political power disproportionately. Contrastingly, extractive institutions enrich a few at the expense of many. Those who benefit from extractive institutions gain wealth and power that in turn help such institutions to persist and self-perpetuate. Are inclusive institutions in India getting weakened and are in the process of becoming extractive? This in fact is the red flag raised by Hasan (in this volume) on the emerging phenomenon of "elite capture" of institutions of democratic governance. It is true that some incursions on the inclusive nature of institutions are happening at various levels. Also, in the vast spread of institutions one may also find local nexuses engaging in extractive practices. But, it is unlikely that the institutions will totally degenerate into extractive ones abandoning the core constitutional values of equality and social justice. However, we cannot take this for granted. The inclusive characteristics of the institutions need to be nurtured and protected. Furthermore, the vastness and diversity as well as varying historical antecedents make the institutional structure in India quite complex defying description in a single unified frame. From national to village level and from policy-making to delivery point, development action encompasses a wide range of institutions involving multiple categories of actors. It involves stupendous efforts to safeguard the institutions from being swayed away from the inclusive path and becoming extractive.

There are several lessons in this regard emerging from past experiences within the country. First lesson relates to improving transparency and accountability in the functioning of state institutions. India has taken a huge step in this direction by enacting the Right to Information Act which obligates public institutions to provide information on demand from any citizen. This undoubtedly has begun creating a culture of transparency in public dealings and providing the basis for holding public institutions accountable for their actions. Use of digital platforms for obligatory sharing of information in public space on a regular basis could be another means of enhancing transparent functioning of institutions. Such open access to information could also have a positive impact on efforts to curb corruption and other types of abuse of official privileges. But these steps only mark the beginning in strengthening transparency and accountability of institutions. As Dreze and Sen point out, agenda for initiating legislative measures in this direction include several subjects such as redressal of grievances, judicial accountability, public procurement, electoral reforms, corporate lobbying, protection of whistle blowers, and people's right to public service. Of course, the much debated *Lokpal* Act is yet to become a reality in the operational sense. A second lesson is about creating and sustaining space for social movements. Democracies across the world have witnessed huge social movements in the recent decades. These have not been campaigns of resistance and revolution but have emerged as valuable means of communicating public opinion on critical issues of concern. India also had its fair share of such intense public campaigns and social movements in recent decades often led by civil society organisations. As discussed earlier in this chapter, such movements and campaigns had a positive impact resulting in several social legislations. We also witnessed spontaneous campaigns for protection of women from violence, following the ghastly incident, the brutal gang rape of a 23-year-old girl of Delhi on December 2012.

In recent years such campaigns and movements have created opportunities for the underprivileged to take leadership role in public life and articulate the need for building and sustaining an inclusive ethos. Further, they offer legitimate space for the civil society organisations to generate an alternate force to counter the emergence of extractive tendencies in the official establishment. Another strategy that has helped in improving institutional accountability is to create direct interface between the citizens and the public authorities in the form of public hearings (*jan sunvayee*). Electronic platforms such as e-choupal have also been used effectively to build such interface. The value of such exercises lies not only in their capacity to influence development action but also in rebuilding citizens' trust in public institutions. As such exercises invariably happen in local contexts, their effectiveness increases if there is greater devolution of power to local self-governments as envisaged under the *panchayati raj* system.

In conclusion, raising the average life expectancy from 42 to 68 years, achieving self-sufficiency in food production, reducing poverty level from 77 per cent to 22 per cent, ensuring universal enrolment of all children in primary schools, raising the level of adult literacy from 18 per cent to 75 per cent, and achieving global recognition in the areas of Space Science and Information Technology and more in a short period of 70 years is undoubtedly remarkable. None would deny that India has significantly progressed in its developmental journey. But, as the Economic Survey 2015–16 assessing the current state of development and economic reforms states, there is still a journey ahead to achieve both dynamism and social justice. Completing this journey will require a further evolution in the underlying economic vision across the political spectrum. Further the Survey invokes Gandhi and goes on to state: "Despite making remarkable progress in bringing down poverty from about 70 per cent at independence to about 22 per cent in 2011–12 (Tendulkar Committee), it can safely be said that "wiping every tear from every eye" is about a lot more than being able to imbibe a few calories. And the Mahatma understood that better, deeper, and earlier than all the Marxists, market messiahs, materialists and behaviouralists. He intuited that it is also about dignity, invulnerability, self-control and freedom, and mental and psychological unburdening. From that perspective, Nehru's exhortation that "so long as there are tears and suffering, so long our work will not be over" is very much true nearly 70 years after independence (Government of India 2016b, p. 173).

Then, how do we move from here in this development journey ahead? An unambiguous implication arising out of not only the statement of the Economic Survey but also from the analysis presented in various chapters in this volume is that our development priorities and perspective have to change. We have to shift our focus from economic growth at any cost to growth that is firmly tethered to social wellbeing. Development policies have to more consistently and sincerely refocus attention on the wellbeing of the bottom 40 per cent of the socio-economic hierarchy. This indeed is the commitment made in the global Declaration adopted at the launch of the SDGs:

> As we embark on this great collective journey, we pledge that no one will be left behind. Recognising that the dignity of the human person is fundamental, we wish to see the Goals and targets met for all nations and peoples and for all segments of society. And we will endeavour to reach the furthest behind first.[17]

The development perspective has to recast itself and embrace the idea of "reach the furthest behind first". How do we ensure that we are on the right path? The best way forward would be to adhere to the profound advice left behind by Gandhi:

> I will give you a talisman. Whenever you are in doubt, or when the self becomes too much with you, apply the following test. Recall the face of the poorest and the weakest man whom you may have seen, and ask yourself, if the step you contemplate is going to be of any use to him. Will he gain anything by it? Will it restore him to a control over his own life and destiny? In other words, will it lead to *swaraj* for the hungry and spiritually starving millions? Then you will find your doubts and yourself melt away.
>
> (Pyarelal 1958, p. 65)

Acknowledgement

The author acknowledges with thanks the comments on an earlier draft of the paper from Praveen Jha, Anjana Mangalgiri, Poornima M. and Mona Sedwal.

Notes

1 IUCN, UNEP and WWF: World Conservation Strategy: Living Resource Conservation for Sustainable Development (Gland 1980) section 1, paragraph 5.
2 Government of India, *Millennium Development Goals: India Country Report 2015*, Social Statistics Division' Central Statistics Office, Ministry of Statistics and Programme Implementation, New Delhi, 2015.
3 Government of India, 6th Five Year Plan, Chapter 14, Planning Commission, New Delhi, available at: http://planningcommission.nic.in/plans/planrel/fiveyr/welcome.html
4 The phrase was popularly promoted by the World Bank at that time to represent social protection measures in order to overcome the impact of economic shocks accompanying structural adjustment policies and other crisis on vulnerable sections of the population.
5 Available at: http://samagra.mhrd.gov.in/docs/letter_240418.pdf [accessed June 20, 2018].
6 The Social Progress Imperative is registered as a non-profit organisation in the United States which functions through a network of partners in government, business, academia, and civil society. Besides the international assessment, an independent exercise for India has been carried out by the Institute for Competitiveness, India in association with NITI Aayog. Even though the broad dimensions and components remained the same, the Indian exercise involved assessment for 54 indicators generating a national report and state level reports for 28 states and Delhi.
7 Social Protection Floors Recommendation, 2012 (No. 202): Recommendation concerning National Floors of Social Protection Adoption: Geneva, 101st ILC session (14 June 2012), International Labour Organization, Geneva, 2012.
8 Indonesian Constitution was amended in 2002 to specify the following: "The state prioritises a budget for education of at least 20 per cent from the national budget and regional budgets to fulfill the needs of providing national education". This was again amended in 2003 to specify that the 20 per cent allocation would exclude "salary of educators and service education expenditure". World Bank, Investing in Indonesia's Education: Allocation, Equity, And Efficiency Of Public Expenditures, Poverty Reduction and Economic Management Unit East Asia and Pacific Region, Jakarta, 2007 (p. 18)
9 Authors (without further details) quoted in this section refer to chapters included in this volume.
10 "Stunting" is an indicator to measure malnutrition, and according to Joint Child Malnutrition Estimates (2019) "stunting is the devastating result of poor nutrition in-utero and early childhood."
11 "Wasting" is an indicator to measure malnutrition, and according to Joint Child Malnutrition Estimates (2019) "Wasting in children is the life-threatening result of poor nutrient intake and/or disease."
12 Stuart and Woodroffe, 2016 quoted by Suneeta Dhar (in this volume).
13 The claim of significant reduction in poverty levels and the approach adopted for measuring poverty has been contested by many experts. See for instance, Utsa Patnaik 2013; Gaurav Nayyar and Rohini Nayyar 2016; Jaya Mehta and Shanta Venkatraman 2000.
14 https://web.archive.org/web/20140407102043/www.rbi.org.in/scripts/Publications-View.aspx?id=15283
15 These estimates are based on Tendulkar Committee which faced severe criticism for fixing the level very low. The revised level, subsequently proposed by Rangarajan Committee marginally increasing the base level, would push the number below poverty line to around 400 million.
16 *World Inequality Report 2018*.
17 Paragraph 4 of Declaration in *Transforming Our World: the 2030 Agenda for Sustainable Development*, UN, New York, available at: https://sustainabledevelopment.un.org/content/documents/21252030%20Agenda%20for%20Sustainable%20Development%20web.pdf

References

Acemoglu, D. and Robinson, A. 2013. *Why Nations Fail: The Origins of Power, Prosperity and Poverty*. London: Profile Books.

Alvaredo, F., Chancel, L., Piketty, T., Saez, E., and Zucman, Gabriel. 2017. *The World Inequality Report 2018,* World Inequality Lab. Available at: https://wir2018.wid.world/files/download/wir2018-full-report-english.pdf

Bauman, Z. 2011. *Collateral Damage: Social Inequalities in a Global Age*. Cambridge: Polity Press.

Boutillier, Z., Kickbusch, I., Mehdi, A., Neupane, S., Sangiorgio, M., Told, M., and Taylor, P. 2017. *SDGs and Health: A Vision for Public Policy*. [Online] Available at: www.g20-insights.org/wp-content/uploads/2017/05/Agenda-2030_SDGS-and-health_Final_19May-1.pdf

Bread for the World Institute. 2016. *2017 Hunger Report: Fragile Environments, Resilient Communities*. Washington: Bread for the World Institute.

Chancel, Lucas and Piketty, Thomas. 2017. "Indian Income Inequality 1922–2015: From British Raj to Billionaire Raj? World Working Paper Series N° 2017/11." *World Inequality Database, World Inequality Lab*. Available at: wid.world/dev/document/chancelpiketty2017widworld/

Chandrasekhar, C. and Ghosh, J. 2014. *Growth, Employment Patterns and Inequality in Asia: A Case Study of India*. Bangkok: ILO Regional Office for Asia and the Pacific.

Cuéllar, Javier Pérez de. 1996. *Our Cultural Diversity: Report of the World Commission on Culture and Development*. 2nd ed. Paris: UNESCO.

Cutter, A., Osborn, D., Romano, J., and Ullah, F. 2015. Sustainable Development Goals and Integration: Achieving a Better Balance Between the Economic, Social and Environmental Dimensions – A Study Commissioned by the German Council for Sustainable Development. [Online] Available at: http://nbsapforum.net/sites/default/files/Stakeholder%20Forum.%202015.%20Sustainable%20Development%20Goals%20and%20Integration_Achieving%20a%20better%20balance%20between%20the%20economic.pdf

Dev, M.S. 2016. *Labour Market Changes, Rural Employment and Poverty in India*. [Online] Available at: www.un.org/esa/socdev/egms/docs/2016/MahendraDev.pdf

Dorling, D. 2014. *Inequality and the 1%*. London: Verso.

Dreze, J. and Sen, A. 2011. Putting Growth in its Place. *Outlook*, 14 November.

Dreze, J. and Sen, A. 2014. *An Uncertain Glory: India and its Contradictions*. London: Penguin Books.

Government of India. 1974. *Towards Equality: Report of the Committee on the Status of Women in India*. New Delhi: Ministry of Education and Social Welfare.

———. 2002. *Tenth Five Year Plan 2002–2007 Volume II: Sectoral Policies and Programmes*. New Delhi: Planning Commission, Government of India.

———. 2011. *High Level Expert Group Report on Universal Health Coverage for India*. New Delhi: Planning Commission.

———. 2013. *Census of India 2011*. New Delhi: Office of the Registrar General & Census Commissioner.

———. 2014. *Rapid Survey on Children (RSOC) 2013–14: National Report*. New Delhi: Ministry of Women and Child Development.

———. 2015. *Millennium Development Goals: India Country Report 2015*. New Delhi: Social Statistics Division, Central Statistics Office, Ministry of Statistics and Programme Implementation, Government of India.

———. 2016a. *SRS Based Abridged Life Tables 2010–2014*. [Online] Available at: www.censusindia.gov.in/Vital_Statistics/SRS_Life_Table/2.Analysis_2010-14.pdf [Accessed September 1, 2018].

———. 2016b. *Economic Survey 2015–16*. New Delhi: Ministry of Finance.

---. 2018. *Economic Survey 2017–18*. New Delhi: Ministry of Finance.
---. n.d.a *6th Five Year Plan, Chapter 14: Minimum Needs Programme*. New Delhi: Planning Commission.
---. n.d.b *Appraisal Document of Twelfth Five Year Plan 2012–17*. New Delhi: NITI Aayog.
---. n.d.c *Nourishing India: National Nutrition Strategy*. New Delhi: NITI Aayog.
Govinda, R. 2017. *The Status of Adult Learning and Education in Asia and the Pacific: Regional Report*. Hamburg: UNESCO.
Govinda, R. and Bandopadhyay, M. forthcoming. "Exclusion and Inequality in Indian Education." In Haque, T. and Reddy, D.N. (eds.). *India Social Development Report 2018: Rising Inequalities in India*. New Delhi: Oxford University Press.
Govinda, R. and Mathew, A. 2018. *Universalisation of Elementary Education in India: Story of Missed Targets and Unkept Promises*. New Delhi: Council for Social Development.
Guenther, L.N. 2013. California Prison Hunger Strikes and the Meaning of Solidarity. [Online] Available at: www.newappsblog.com/2013/07/california-prison-hunger-strikes-and-the-meaning-of-solidarity.html
IFPRI. 2018. *2018 Global Food Policy Report*. Washington: International Food Policy Research Institute.
IIPS and ICF. 2017. *National Family Health Survey (NFHS-4), 2015–16*. Mumbai: International Institute for Population Sciences.
ILO. 2012. *R202-Social Protection Floors Recommendation, 2012 (No.202)*. Geneva: International Labour Organisation.
---. 2018. *World Employment Social Outlook: Trends 2018*. Geneva: International Labour Organisation.
IPSP. 2018. *Rethinking Society for the 21st Century: Report of the International Panel on Social Progress (IPSP)*. Cambridge: Cambridge University Press.
IUCN-UNEP-WWF. 1980. *World Conservation Strategy: Living Resource Conservation for Sustainable Development*. Gland, Switzerland: IUCN.
Jha, P. 2016. *Labour in Contemporary India*. New Delhi: Oxford University Press.
Jha, P. and Negre, M., n.d. *Indian Economy in the Era of Contemporary Globalisation: Some Core Elements of the Balance Sheet*. [Online] Available at: https://myweb.rollins.edu/tlairson/asiabus/indiaeconomy.pdf
Joint Child Malnutrition Estimates. 2019. *Levels and Trends in Child Malnutrition: Key Findings of the 2019 Edition*. UNICEF/WHO/World Bank Group. Available at: https://www.who.int/nutgrowthdb/jme-2019-key-findings.pdf?ua=1
Kapoor, A. 2017. *Social Progress Index: States of India*. Gurugram: Institute of Competitiveness.
Kundu, A. and Mohanan, P. n.d. *Employment and Inequality Outcomes in India*. [Online] Available at: www.oecd.org/employment/emp/42546020.pdf
Malhotra, A., Schulte, J., Patel, P., and Petesch, P. 2009. *Innovation for Women's Empowerment and Gender Equality*. Washington: International Center for Research on Women (ICRW).
Mehta, J. and Venkatraman, S. 2000. "Poverty Statistics: Bermicide's Feast." *Economic and Political Weekly*, 35(27): 2377–2379.
Mohanty, M. 2015. *Reconceptualising Social Development*. In: *Development, Decentralization and Democracy*. New Delhi: Orient Black Swan.
Mooij, J. and Dev, S.M. 2004. "Social Sector Priorities: An Analysis of Budgets and Ependitures in India in the 1990s." *Development Policy Review*, 22(1): 97–120.
Nayyar, G. and Nayyar, R. 2016. "India's 'Poverty of Numbers': Revisiting Measurement Issues." *Economic and Political Weekly*, 51(35): 61–71.
NITI Aayog. 2016. *Infant Mortality Rate (IMR) (Per 1000 Live Births)*. Available at: https://www.niti.gov.in/content/infant-mortality-rate-imr-1000-live-births

Olinto, P., Beegle, K., Sobrado, C., and Uematsu, H. 2013. "The State of the Poor: Where are the Poor, Where is Extreme Poverty Harder to End and What Is the Current Profile of the World's Poor?" *Economic Premise*, October, Issue 125.

Patnaik, U. 2013. "Poverty Trends in India 2004–05 to 2009–10: Updating Poverty Estimates and Comparing Official Figures." *Economic and Political Weekly*, 48(40): 43–58.

Pilling, D. 2018. *The Growth Delusion: The Wealth and Well-Being of Nations*. New Delhi: Bloomsbury.

Porter, M.E., Stern, S. and Green, M. 2017. *Social Progress Index 2017*. Washington: Social Progress Imperative.

Prabhu, S.K. 2001. *Economic Reform and Social Development: A Study of Two Indian States*. New Delhi: Sage.

Pyarelal. 1958. *Mahatma Gandhi: Last Phase, Vol. II*. Ahmedabad: Navajivan Mudranalaya.

Raykar, N., Majumder, M., Laxminarayan, R., and Menon, P. 2015. *India Health Report: Nutrition 2015*. New Delhi: Public Health Foundation of India.

RBI. 2013. *RBI Publications*. Available at: https://web.archive.org/web/20140407102043/www.rbi.org.in/scripts/PublicationsView.aspx?id=15283

Reich, R.B. 2014. "The American Right Focuses on Poverty, not Inequality, to Avoid Blame." *The Guardian*, 23 February, p. 164.

Roy, K.C. Blomqvist, H.C., and Clark, C. 2008. *Institutions and Gender Empowerment in the Global Economy: World Scientific Studies in International Economics*. Singapore: World Scientific Publishing Co.

Sen, A. 1999. *Development as Freedom*. New Delhi: Oxford University Press.

Singh, K. and Mate, K. 2018. *Union Budget 2018–19: An Assessment, RBI*. [Online] Available at: https://rbidocs.rbi.org.in/rdocs/Bulletin/PDFs/01AR_100418D58BFE5F50F748D8B1C918A2D8C6F77E.PDF

Smith, L. and Haddad, L. 2002. "How potent is Economic Growth in reducing Undernutrition: What are the Pathways of Impact? New Cross-Country Evidence." *Economic Development and Cultural Change*, 51(1): 55–76.

Stiglitz, J.E., Sen, A., and Fitoussi, J.P. n.d. *Report by the Commission on the Measurement of Economic Performance and Social Progress*. [Online] Available at: https://ec.europa.eu/eurostat/documents/118025/118123/Fitoussi+Commission+report [Accessed May 30, 2018].

TNS India. 2015. *A Report on Nationwide Evaluation of the Flagship Program of Mahatma Gandhi National Rural Employment Guarantee Act (MGNREGA)*. New Delhi: Ministry of Rural Development.

U-DISE. 2015. *School Education in India 2014–15(Provisional)*. New Delhi: NUEPA and Department of Education and Literacy, MHRD, GOI.

UIS Data. 2015. *UIS.Stat: Data by Theme*. UNESCO Institute for Statistics. Available at: http://data.uis.unesco.org/

UNDP. 2016. *Human Development Report (HDR) 2016: Human Development for Everyone*. New York: UNDP. Available at: https://doi.org/10.18356/b6186701-en

UNDP. 2018. *Human Development Indices and Indicators: 2018 Statistical Update*. Washington: UNDP.

UN ESCAP. 2015. *Time for Equality: The Role of Social Protection in Reducing Inequalities in Asia and the Pacific*. Bangkok: UN ESCAP.

UNESCO. 2015. *Education for All 2000–2015: Achievements and Challenges*. Paris: UNESCO.

United Nations. 2012. *The Future We want: Outcome Document of the United Nations Conference on Sustainable Development, Rio de Janeiro, Brazil 20–22 June 2012*. [Online] Available at: https://sustainabledevelopment.un.org/content/documents/733FutureWeWant.pdf [Accessed August 24, 2018].

———. 2015. *India and the MDGs: Towards a Sustainable Future for All.* [Online] Available at: www.unescap.org/sites/default/files/India_and_the_MDGs_0.pdf

———. n.d. *Transforming our World: The 2030 Agenda for Sustainable Development*, A/RES/70/1. New York: United Nations.

UN Women. 2018. *Turning Promises into Action: Gender Equality in the 2030 Agenda for Sustainable Development.* New York: UN Women. The World Bank. 2007. *Investing in Indonesia's Education: Allocation, Equity and Efficiency of Public Expenditures.* Jakarta: The World Bank Office Jakarta.

———. 2015. *World Development Report 2015: Mind, Society and Behaviour*, Washington: The World Bank.

The World Bank Data. 2016. *World Bank Data.* Available at: https://data.worldbank.org/indicator/SP.DYN.LE00.MA.IN

World Economic Forum. 2017. *The Global Gender Gap Report 2017: Insight Report.* Geneva: World Economic Forum.

World Health Organization. 2017. *World Health Statistics 2017: Monitoring Health for the SDGs.* Geneva: WHO.

PART II
SDGs
Process and outcome

2

REFLECTIONS ON SUSTAINABLE DEVELOPMENT GOALS FROM THE PERSPECTIVE OF DEVELOPING COUNTRIES

Transformative change or business as usual?

Mitu Sengupta

On September 25, 2015, the United Nations (UN) General Assembly adopted resolution A/RES/70/1 – also known as "Transforming Our World: The 2030 Agenda for Sustainable Development". Agenda 2030 is an intergovernmental agreement that is designed to guide global development efforts over the next fifteen years, between 2015 and 2030. Its centrepiece, the Sustainable Development Goals (SDGs), replaces the Millennium Development Goals (MDGs), which held sway between 2000 and 2015. The new goals are designed to build on the MDGs and "complete what they did not achieve". But while there were only eight MDGs, the SDGs are 17 in number, with 169 associated targets, and some 230 indicators. This dramatic jump in the number of goals and targets may appear to be a formula for incoherence, but the governments that have signed on exude much confidence. "On behalf of the peoples we serve, we have adopted a historic decision on a comprehensive, far-reaching and people-centred set of universal and transformative goals and targets", their resolution states (A/RES/70/1). Is the UN's certitude about the merits of its new agenda defensible?

Based on a textual analysis of the new goals and targets, this chapter interrogates the main strengths and weaknesses of the SDGs, specifically from the point of view of developing countries. It also briefly examines the implications borne by the SDGs for social sector development in developing countries, particularly in relation to health. It is argued, in this chapter, that the SDGs, which are remarkably comprehensive in scope, deserve considerable praise for making some clear advances over the MDGs. Nonetheless, they miss a valuable opportunity to address structural causes of poverty and systemic roots of inequality, both nationally and globally. This shortcoming, in turn, limits the SDGs' ability to successfully address systemic concerns in health and other social sectors. It is argued, furthermore, that the SDGs are marred by a weak accountability structure that undermines its otherwise persuasive language on universalism and partnership. Finally, it is argued, given that the SDGs do not sufficiently challenge the prevailing paradigm of neoliberal economic development, they cannot justifiably be regarded as "transformative".

Core strengths

It should be noted, at the outset, that one of the key strengths of the post-2015 framework is that the process for creating the SDGs was far more open and inclusive than the process that gave rise to the MDGs. This has been widely acknowledged (for example, see Gore 2015; Buse and Hawkes 2015). The SDGs have come to reflect *some* preferences of virtually every major "stakeholder" in development, be this the pro-growth global South government, or the conservationist civil society organisations (CSOs) based in the global North. The large sprawl of goals and targets that is viewed as a weakness of the framework by some (see Kenny 2015) may actually be an asset. A shorter slate of goals might have been better for public relations purposes, but it would have meant excluding more asks and endorsing only a limited conceptualisation of "development". The SDGs certainly do well to provide official, global recognition to a wide spectrum of achievements, besides economic growth, that have come to be associated with the term "development". Given that Agenda 2030 was birthed out of an international system in which states jealously guard their sovereignty, it is certainly extraordinary that such a strong common denominator was possible at all.

The SDGs arguably capture the complexity and interconnectedness of sustainable development concerns. They address key challenges, such as combatting climate change and achieving gender equality, not only through comprehensive standalone goals, but in a crosscutting manner throughout the framework. For example, in addition to SDG-8, "achieve gender equality and empower all women and girls", gender equality targets are woven into other goals critical to social sector development, such as SDG-4.8, which seeks to eliminate gender disparities in education. In addition to SDG-3, "ensure healthy lives and promote wellbeing for all at all ages", health-related targets appear under several other goals, such as SDG-2, on ending hunger, SDG-6, on sustainable management of water and sanitation, and SDG-11, on sustainable cities (for a longer list of such crosscutting health targets, see Buse and Hawkes 2015, p. 3). Most significantly, the SDGs go beyond advocating for basic needs, which was the main concern of the MDGs (Fukuda-Parr 2015), to tackling deeper drivers of poverty, such as failing institutions. Through SDG-16, for example, they address governance concerns overlooked by the MDGs, such as improving access to justice, reducing corruption, and increasing representative decision-making. SDG-16.8, notably, commits to increasing developing country participation in the institutions of global governance, which has been a longstanding demand of developing countries. All of this constitutes a commendable message to policymakers, particularly in the social sector, that their work cannot be done in silos; that policy failures in one area can easily infect another; and that a collaborative, "big picture" approach is needed to solve problems, both nationally and globally.

Another striking feature of the SDGs is the presence, under each goal, of means of implementation (MoI) targets that are meant to provide a roadmap for achieving the goal. Because MoIs name specific tasks that need to be accomplished in order to achieve a particular goal – some of which are politically difficult – their insertion into the SDGs platform was controversial, and a persistent source of tension between developed and developing countries during negotiations over how the goals would be worded (see Alas 2015; Muchhala 2014).[1] Developing countries – represented by the Group of 77 (G-77) and China – wanted strong MoIs, with clear resource commitments from developed countries, to be listed under each SDG, while developed countries wanted to limit MoIs only to SDG-17, the "global partnership" goal. It is, therefore, a sizeable gain for developing countries, which lobbied hard to include supportive language in the SDGs on their use of TRIPS flexibilities, that a goal-specific MoI was included under health (SDG-3.b) that advises governments to: "Provide access to affordable essential medicines and vaccines, in accordance with the Doha Declaration which affirms the right of developing countries to use to the full the provisions in the Trade-Related Aspects of Intellectual Property Rights (TRIPS) agreement regarding flexibilities to protect public health and, in particular, provide access to medicines for all". Since improving access to affordable medicines while keeping within the current regime of intellectual property rights has been a struggle in India as well as in other developing countries, the fact that the SDGs openly name what needs to be done to address the problem, not only nationally, but also globally, is an important gain for health advocates worldwide.

Agenda 2030's fairly exhaustive language on human rights should also be recognised as a strength. The commitment to human rights is affirmed in Agenda 2030's preamble, and then reinforced by the proclamation that the SDGs are "grounded in" the Universal Declaration of Human Rights, international human rights treaties, and "other instruments such as the Declaration on the Right to Development". The MDGs, on the other hand, intersected with only a limited section of the international human rights agenda. While they coincided with some provisions of the International Covenant on Economic, Social, and Cultural Rights (ICESCR) – such as the indicators on access to clean water and primary education completion rates – they contained no references to civil and political rights, other than the indicator on the proportion of seats held by women in national parliaments. In contrast, the 17 goals and 169 targets of the SDGs overlap with a much wider range of economic, social, and cultural rights, covering the ICESCR's content not only in the areas of hunger, education, and access to clean water (like the MDGs), but also in relation to decent work, social protection, mental health, and various other areas important to social development.

The SDGs also coincide with some provisions of the International Covenant on Civil and Political Rights (ICCPR), such as equal access to justice for all, the provision of legal identity for all, and public access to information, and contain multiple references to universal access and universal applicability, which have been longstanding rallying points for the human rights community. Language on ensuring universal access appears in many of the goals relevant to social development, such as health (see SDG-3.7 and SDG-3.8), water and sanitation (see SDG-6.1 and SDG-6.2), and safe and affordable housing (SDG-11.1). The SDGs, in this sense, have the potential to empower human rights advocates and activists worldwide by providing justification to the use of rights-based approaches in addressing social sector development concerns. In India and in other developing countries, such as Brazil and South Africa, there has been mounting support, propelled by civil society, for taking on rights-based approaches to health, education, housing, the provision of social security, and other social development issues (on this, see Ruparelia 2013). While support for rights-based approaches has precipitated the enactment of many groundbreaking laws and government schemes by progressive governments – such as India's Right to Education Act (RTE) of 2009 and National Rural Employment Guarantee Act (NREGA) of 2005 – such initiatives have also been vigorously resisted by conservative political alliances. The SDGs can play an important role in this struggle by strengthening the hand of rights advocates, who can legitimately claim that, since the SDGs have been endorsed by every UN Member State, they signal powerful global recognition that human rights principles, such as universal access and universal applicability, should guide the formulation of social sector policies.

Another strength of Agenda 2030 is that the principles of equality and non-discrimination receive explicit recognition. In keeping with the principle of "leave no one behind", which was widely endorsed in global consultations on the post-2015 agenda, the SDGs commit signatories to consider targets achieved only if they are met for all segments of a population, especially those who are subject to discrimination on the grounds prohibited in international human rights law. This is articulated in SDG-17.8's pledge to disaggregate relevant data "by income, gender, age, race, ethnicity, migratory status, disability, geographic location and other characteristics relevant in national context". If governments honour their commitment in this regard, the implications could be profound, especially in relation to the production of data in social development sectors such as education and health, where inequalities abound. It has been pointed out, for example, that key populations vulnerable to HIV in developing countries – men who have sex with men, people who inject drugs, transgender people, and sex workers – are "often hidden due to stigma and criminalization", and "the absence of this data creates a paradox in which invisibility reinforces invisibility" (Davis 2017, p. 1,144). As Davis suggests, the paucity of data on vulnerable populations gets in the way of effective HIV programming, both nationally and globally. The SDGs could play a positive role here, by pushing governments to identify, count, and service hard-to-reach populations, as part of their commitment to "leaving no one behind".

Yet another strength of Agenda 2030, which dovetails nicely with its pledge to "leave no one behind", is that the SDGs commit to "ending", i.e. reaching a statistical zero, on poverty, hunger, preventable child deaths, the abuse of children, and many other key social development goals. This sits in contrast with the MDGs, which aimed to "halve" the proportion of people living on less than $1.25 a day, or "halve" the proportion of people who suffer from hunger, demands that disproportionately burdened the poorest countries (on this, see Easterly 2009). The shift in language from "reducing" to "ending all forms everywhere" is a progressive move not only because it signals global recognition that poverty, hunger, discrimination, and other violations are morally unacceptable, but also because getting to zero requires an honest focus on empowering the poorest and hardest to reach, even in the most affluent countries of the world. While goals such as "end poverty in all its forms everywhere (SDG 1)" and "end all forms of discrimination against all women (SDG 5.1)" are meaningful to the poorest countries on the planet, they are also relevant to its wealthiest states, as are the goals that commit governments to try to attain universal access in areas such as health care and education. Indeed, this brings us to identify a final strength of the SDGs, namely their universal applicability.

That the SDGs are meant for all countries, not only developing countries, is prominently highlighted in Agenda 2030. It was also a point of emphasis in all the major documents, such as the High Level Panel's report (UN 2013), that led up to the final post-2015 draft. The demand for universally applicable goals was, in fact, a consistent feature of the MDG-replacement debates, owing to disgruntlement that none of the MDGs, with the exception of MDG-8, were of relevance to developed countries, especially when taken at their target and indicator levels. This not only imparted the impression that the MDGs were a slate of instructions for developing countries alone, but that the UN was "hark[ing] back to a model of development centred more on charity than a sense of obligation between states, let alone duties to their people" (CESR 2013, p. 1). In this regard, the SDGs represent a course correction. Many, if not most, of the SDGs include targets and indicators that are applicable to all countries. Some targets, such as SDG-3.4, which aims to reduce mortality from non-communicable diseases and promote mental health, are perhaps of even greater relevance to developed countries than they are to developing countries. The inclusion of targets emphasising the universality of sustainable development concerns is significant not only on principled grounds, but also for political reasons. If developed countries view the SDGs as objectives and guidelines that also apply to them, their commitment to the new agenda is likely to be stronger.

Reasons for concern

As argued earlier in this chapter, it is indeed a positive feature of the SDGs that they address key objectives, such as achieving gender equality and ensuring healthy lives, not only through comprehensive standalone goals, but in a crosscutting manner through the structuring of targets and indicators (for example, we see health-related targets under several other goals). There is a practical downside, however, to successfully capturing the theoretical complexity and interconnectedness of sustainable development concerns, which the SDGs arguably do. What policymakers have on hand is a vast forest of goals (17), targets (169) and indicators (230 and counting), that are not properly ranked. Other than SDG-1, which is considered Agenda 2030's flagship goal, no indication is given of one goal being more important than the other. Targets are not ranked either. While this decision makes sense in theory – since all goals and targets may be considered inter-related and, therefore, equally important – it does not translate into the best guide for policymakers, especially those working in the social sector, where funding is rarely plentiful.

Take the health goal, for example, with its 13 targets and 26 indicators, ranging from reducing the global maternal mortality ratio (SDG-3.1), to ensuring universal access to sexual and reproductive health care services (SDG-3.7), to reducing the number of deaths and injuries from road traffic accidents (SDG-3.6). As Buse and Hawkes (2015) suggest, a major strong point of SDG-3 is its breadth of scope and explicit recognition, via targets such as the one on road safety, that some of the most important determinants of health fall outside the realm of health care as narrowly conceived, i.e. as only hospitals and medicines. In this sense, SDG-3 signals the enormity of the task ahead, and the need to focus on preventive as well as curative measures in health. Despite such clear positives, however, SDG-3 presents practical problems. What should one focus on? Where should scarce resources be allocated? Indeed, the sprawl of unranked targets leaves room for governments to cherry-pick from the list, focusing on relatively easy tasks, while neglecting more difficult but urgent priorities. While reporting their progress on the SDGs, it is tempting for governments to highlight what they have already accomplished in an area – the programmes and schemes that are already in place – rather than to break new ground.

The risk that governments will cherry-pick easier targets is compounded by another feature of the SDGs, which, at least in theory, could be seen as a strong point. During SDG negotiations, developing countries repeatedly stressed the need for domestic policy autonomy. Adopting too rigid a structure, it was thought, would be tantamount to a kind of neocolonial imposition from above (for more on this debate, see Muchhala 2014). Developing countries won significant concessions on this point, and respect for domestic policy autonomy is made possible in the SDGs through nationally determinable targets (for example, the "x" percentage in MoI 4.c is scalable, to be determined at the national level), along with language on recognising "national policies and priorities" (example: SDG-12.7), "national circumstances" (SDG-12.c), and "respect(ing) each country's policy space" (SDG-17.15). While the demand for language on respecting domestic policy space is completely understandable, such language also provides governments with wiggle room to evade important responsibilities by claiming that they lack the resources to meet a specific target. This problem could potentially be counteracted through effective mechanisms to hold both national governments and international donors to account (for resourcing critical targets), but as suggested later in this chapter, such accountability mechanisms are largely missing from the SDG-platform. Before we address this point, however, a number of further concerns should be discussed.

One concern relates to the new agenda's flagship poverty goal. While there is a welcome shift in language, from ending only "extreme poverty and hunger" (in MDG-1) to ending "poverty in all its forms everywhere", SDG-1 abides by the same measure of poverty that was used in MDG-1, i.e. the money-metric calculus of $1.25 per day. This income-based measure not only fails to capture many of the hardships that constitute poverty in the real world, such as chronic undernourishment, illiteracy, and lack of access to safe drinking water, it has also been defined ever more narrowly over the years, by replacing the original threshold of $1.00 per person per day in 1985 US dollars (as referenced in the UN Millennium Declaration and MDG-1) with a lower $1.08 per person per day in 1993 US dollars, and then with an even lower $1.25 per person per day in 2005 US dollars (Pogge and Sengupta 2015). Each of these revisions has produced a better looking (and politically convenient poverty) trend, raising concern that definitions and methods involved in developing targets will be changed midstream once again, especially as the 2030 deadline draws closer. SDG-1's ambitious tone is also undermined by the weak MoI targets associated with it, which call for "enhanced development cooperation" but make no reference to structural reforms that are needed to tackle root causes of poverty, such as cancelling the debt of highly indebted poor countries. As Muchhala (2014) indicates, developing countries wanted to insert a reference to debt cancellation in the SDGs, but were defeated during negotiations. In the final document, she points out, the key term "cancel" is weakened to "address", which is "problematic because the word 'cancel' denotes an action, whereas the word 'address' does not . . . entail any action whatsoever".

Some scepticism about the new agenda's stated commitment to inequality reduction, and also to human rights, is also warranted. While the inclusion of a standalone goal on reducing "inequality within and among countries" (SDG-10) is a clear positive, the framing of the first target within this goal does not sufficiently reflect the urgency of reducing inequality: "by 2030, progressively achieve and sustain income growth of the bottom 40 per cent of the population at a rate higher than the national average". By asking that such faster income growth for the poorest 40 per cent should be achieved (and then sustained) sometime before 2030, this target effectively permits countries to *continue to shrink* the income share of the poorest 40 per cent for another 13 years. SDG 10.1 is compatible, then, with an increase in inequality over the whole 2016–30 period (for more on the problematical language of "goals", see Pogge and Sengupta 2016). Another weakness is that inequality reduction is not integrated into other goals in a cross-cutting manner, as it is done for a host of other objectives. There is no reference to inequality outside of SDG-10. Yet another concern in relation to SDG-10 is that it does not sufficiently recognise the need to design economic rules – either national or global – that will keep inequality in check. For example, there is no reference, in the MoI for this goal, to inheritance and progressive income taxes.

The SDGs' language on human rights, though an improvement on how it appears in the MDGs, is not as strong as it could be. For example, community land rights are not recognised, including the rights of indigenous peoples to land, even though a large amount of land in developing countries is held by communities, based on a shared culture or heritage, rather than by individuals. Another omission is the absence of references to important provisions of the ICCPR, such as freedom from arbitrary arrest and detention, and the freedoms of thought, expression, and association. Realising core civil and political rights such as freedom from arbitrary arrest is not only morally imperative, but it is also crucial to the realisation of a host of other rights, and is critical to effective monitoring and accountability. The inclusion of such rights in the new agenda should have been non-negotiable.

Our strongest criticism is reserved, however, for the SDGs' weak accountability structure. This foundational flaw undermines the new agenda's otherwise persuasive language on universalism and partnership. Like the MDGs, the SDGs are goals without commitment. They do not include any clear reference to who is accountable for achieving (or not achieving) them. The concept of a goal implies some definite individual or collective agent whose goal it is. While common goals do not presuppose a single leader, and a group can decide collectively what to aim for and how to get there, this group must have a shared understanding of who is to do what towards implementation. No such shared understanding emerged around the MDGs since governments never agreed on a division of labour towards achieving ambitious targets such as cutting down the prevalence of hunger by half. The MDGs left entirely unspecified who was to do what. So, when we fell behind on the undernourishment target, for example, there was no authoritative way of identifying the party or parties required to make additional efforts to get us back on track. This exclusion of specific responsibilities from the agreement made it easy for governments to sign on, because they were committing themselves to nothing in particular. Should some of the agreed wishes remain unfulfilled, each government could always respond by admonishing others' insufficient efforts. This flaw is repeated in the SDGs. They are goals without agents, and the agreement leaves entirely unspecified who is to do what. A government may claim, for example, that it does not have the resources to tackle a specific problem, blaming foreign donors for failing to meet their obligation to provide the necessary gap-closing aid. Foreign donors, in turn, could refuse to acknowledge any obligation on their part.

The SDGs' accountability gap is perhaps most clearly visible in the new global partnership goal, SDG-17, which is intended to be an improved version of the ineffectual MDG-8, but nonetheless suffers from its key defect. The world's most powerful agents – affluent states, international organisations, multinational enterprises – are shielded from any concrete responsibilities for achieving the SDGs when they should actually be doing the most. In fact, the most serious failure of the new framework is that its anchoring principle of "global partnership for development" is not understood in its original invocation, as that of international cooperation on a range of development issues, principally between governments of developed and developing countries, with developed countries *taking the lead* in providing resources and means of implementation. This invocation, it should be pointed out, is also in line with Agenda 2030's avowal that the SDGs are grounded in the "Declaration on the Right to Development".

Negotiations over the SDGs, however, betrayed a different reality. Any move to adhere to an understanding of "global partnership" was routinely blocked by developed countries (Muchhala and Sengupta 2014, p. 29). For example, in discussions about SDG-12, on sustainable consumption and production, developed countries rejected a clause, suggested by the G-77, that they "take the lead" in providing resources. Instead, they actually demanded equal treatment, implying that there are no significant differences between developed and developing countries (Ibid.). The refusal, by developed countries, to take on any special responsibilities for sustainable development is in keeping with a broader trend. As Martin Khor (2016) points out:

> Principles or even phrases that have long been agreed to as part of global cooperation are now challenged or even made taboo by the developed countries. They had previously been amenable to place on record the need to transfer technology and provide financial resources and special treatment to developing countries. Now it is considered almost too sensitive to propose language on "additional financial resources" and "technology transfer", while big battles have to be waged to reaffirm the long-accepted principles of "common but differentiated responsibility" and "special and differential treatment for developing countries". The developed countries have become less secure in their domination over the global economy and thus they are no longer willing to recognize many of the rights of and concessions to the developing countries that are embedded in the global development system.

This brings us to another important concern. While developed countries have steadily retreated from past commitments, the private sector has taken on a more pronounced role in global development as well in other areas of global governance, including global security. The 2030 Agenda's unmistakable emphasis on securing private sector financing for development, particularly through public-private partnerships, has drawn criticism from many different corners. During SDG negotiations, Brazil and the Community of Latin American and Caribbean States (CELAC) cautioned against excessive reliance on private sector financing for sustainable development. They pointed out that while the UN should be open to catalysing all types of support for sustainable development, this should not lead to an evasion of government responsibility or compensate for unmet commitments in official development assistance. Brazil warned that since outsourcing development cooperation to the private sector involves expanding outside the purview of intergovernmental oversight, the UN's identity as an intergovernmental organisation is brought into question (Muchhala and Sengupta 2014, p. 29).

Civil society has also taken issue with how the term "partnership" is being used by the UN. The authors of a briefing note produced for Global Policy Forum argue that the "notion of partnership is misleading to cover every type of engagement between UN entities and non-state actors. It promotes a false sense of equality. Lumping CSOs and corporate actors ignores the profound differences in their orientation, interests and accountability". They further argue that since private resources are

> procyclical (dependent on the overall economic situation) and generally not made available to support the norm setting, policy and advocacy work of

> the UN, the use of public resources to secure these partnerships can drain depleted public funds at crucial times.
>
> *(Adams and Martens 2016, p. 1)*

In the face of declining public resources on both global and national scales, however, it is unlikely that such criticism will shift any gears on how things are done. The gradual privatisation of global development appears to be here to stay. This point has been made evident time and time again, such as at the Addis Ababa Finance for Development meeting in July 2015, whose outcome, according to Muchhala (2015), only "legitimizes the predominance of private finance through blended finance and public-private partnerships (PPPs)".

Indeed, when viewed through the prisms of accountability and financing, the SDGs are neither "historic" nor "transformative". They do not challenge the dominant trend in relation to global development finance (as described by Khor 2016), and nor do they question the prevailing neoliberal economic paradigm that is, ultimately, the source of this trend. Given the system-affirming nature of the SDGs, it is no surprise, therefore, that they also miss a crucial opportunity to properly question and reform unjust global institutional arrangements. While official and non-governmental development assistance substantially improves the evolution of global poverty and income inequality, it can only very partially mitigate the centrifugal tendencies produced by the ordinary operation of the world economy as presently structured. The SDGs contain only a few references to institutional reforms – such as SDG-16.8, on increasing developing country participation in institutions of global governance – that could diminish the headwinds blowing against the poor, even though such reforms are crucial for the achievement of every goal. For example, SDG-17, on strengthening domestic resource mobilisation, makes no mention of the structural barriers to domestic resource mobilisation in developing countries, such as that of chronic tax evasion and avoidance, which is facilitated by rules that allow multinational corporations operating in developing countries to engage in abusive transfer pricing (for more on this argument, see Pogge and Sengupta 2015, p. 585–586).

In order to conclude this chapter, we might return to the concept of "sustainable development". How are we to achieve sustained economic growth while being cognizant of planetary boundaries? The new agenda provides no clear answer to this key question, and there is a palpable tension between SDG-8, "promote sustained, inclusive and sustainable economic growth", and SDG-13, "take urgent action to combat climate change and its impacts", that reflects how tough it is to integrate human development goals with sustainability goals. As Sen and Anand (1994) have argued, the "safeguarding of future prospects has to be done without giving up the efforts towards rapid human development and the speedy elimination of widespread deprivation of basic human capabilities which characterise the unequal and unjust world in which we live". This is an immense challenge that most developing countries are unlikely to be able to meet on their own, even if private sector financing comes up reliable and plentiful resources. In the absence of concrete commitments of resources, technology transfer, and institutional reform from developed countries, the SDGs may bring upon developing countries a new layer of environment-related obligations that will disproportionately burden the poorest and most vulnerable of the planet. If this happens, the new agenda's much-celebrated language of universalism, partnership, and human rights will be remembered, years on, as little more than diversions that were used to deflect attention from persistent global inequalities, and the refusal, by the most privileged among us, to meet their responsibilities in mitigating these.

Note

1 The MDGs, it should be noted, did not specify any means of implementation. As Deepak Nayyar has observed, the MDGs specified outcomes of development, "but [did] not set out the process which would make it possible to realize the objectives" (2012, 6). This was a strategic move, because the architects of the MDGs chose to focus "on people and the ends of development, around which a common vision could be established, rather than the means to get there, which was fiercely contested" (Fukuda-Parr and Hulme 2011, p. 24). It was also thought that not specifying means would preserve policy autonomy at the national level. According to Nayyar, what actually happened, however, was that "the silence was transformed into an opportunity by orthodoxy . . . Conventional economic thinking and orthodox economic policies simply occupied that vacant space" (2012, p. 9). If Nayyar's argument is accepted, the inclusion of MoIs in the SDGs should indeed be considered a step forward.

References

Adams, Barbara and Martens, Jens. 2016. "Partnerships and the 2030 Agenda." *Global Policy Forum*, May, pp. 1–4. Available at: www.globalpolicywatch.org/wp-content/uploads/2016/05/On-Partnerships-GPF-input-to-discussion.pdf [Accessed August 20, 2016].

Alas, Mirza. 2015. "Post-2015 Development: North-South Divide over Means of Implementation." *Third World Network*, July 2.

Buse, Kent and Hawkes, Sarah. 2015. "Health in the Sustainable Development Goals: Ready for a Paradigm Shift?" *Globalization and Health*, 11(13): online/open access.

Centre for Economic and Social Rights (CESR). 2013. *A Matter of Justice: Securing Human Rights in the Post-2015 Sustainable Development Agenda*, January 11. Available at: http://cesr.org/downloads/matter.of.justice.pdf [Accessed August 9, 2016].

David, Sara L.M. 2017. "The Uncounted: Politics of Data and Visibility in Global Health." *The International Journal of Human Rights,* 21(8): 1144–1163.

Easterly, William. 2009. "How the Millennium Development Goals are Unfair to Africa." *World Development*, 37(1): 26–35.

Fukuda-Parr, Sakiko. 2015. "The 2030 Agenda and the SDGs – A Course Correction?" *Sheffield Political Economy Research Institute (SPERI)*, September 30. Available at: http://speri.dept.shef.ac.uk/2015/09/30/the-2030-agenda-and-the-sdgs-a-course-correction/ [Accessed August 7, 2016].

Fukuda-Parr, Sakiko and Hulme, David. 2011. "International Norm Dynamics and the 'End of Poverty': Understanding the Millennium Development Goals." *Global Governance*, 17: 17–36.

Gore, Charles. 2015. "The Post-2015 Moment: Towards Sustainable Development Goals and A New Global Development Paradigm." *The Journal of International Development,* 27(6): 717–732.

Kenny, Charles. 2015. "MDGs to SDGs: Have We Lost the Plot?" *Centre for Global Development*, May 27. Available at: www.cgdev.org/publication/mdgs-sdgs-have-we-lost-plot [Accessed August 7, 2016].

Khor, Martin. 2016. "UNCTAD's Role Reaffirmed, After Significant Wrangling." *South Views*, No. 128 (August 5).

Muchhala, Bhumika. 2014. "Means of Implementation Nearly Toppled Process of SDGs Agenda." *Third World Network*, July 24. Available at: www.globalpolicy.org/component/content/article/252-the-millenium-development-goals/52671-means-of-implementation-nearly-toppled-process-of-sdgs-agenda.html [Accessed August 20, 2016].

———. 2015. "The Third Financing for Development Conference in Addis Ababa: Failing to Finance Development?" *Third World Network*, July 26.

Muchhala, Bhumika, and Sengupta, Mitu. 2014. "A Déjà vu Agenda or a Development Agenda?" *Economic and Political Weekly*, XLIX: 46(15 November): 28–30.

Nayyar, Deepak. 2012. "The MDGs after 2015: Some Reflections on the Possibilities." *UN System Task Team on the Post-2015 UN Development Agenda*. Available at: www.un.org/millenniumgoals/pdf/deepak_nayyar_Aug.pdf [Accessed August 9, 2016].

Pogge, Thomas and Sengupta, Mitu. 2015. "The Sustainable Development Goals: Nice Idea, Poor Execution." *Washington International Law Journal*, 24(3): 571–587.

———. 2016. "Assessing the Sustainable Development Goals from a Human Rights Perspective." *Journal of International and Comparative Social Policy*, 32(2): 83–97.

Ruparelia, Sanjay. 2013. "India's New Rights Agenda: Genesis, Promises, Risks." *Pacific Affairs*, 86(3): 569–590.

Sen, Amartya, and Anand, Sudhir. 1994. "Sustainable Human Development: Concepts and Priorities. UNDP Human Development Report Office Occasional Papers, September 1. Available at: http://papers.ssrn.com/sol3/papers.cfm?abstract_id=2294664 [Accessed August 13, 2016].

United Nations. 2013. *A New Global Partnership: Report of the High Level Panel on the Post-2015 Development Agenda*. Available at: www.post2015hlp.org/wp-content/uploads/2013/05/UN-Report.pdf [Accessed August 20, 2016].

PART III
Education and skill development

3
SCHOOL EDUCATION IN INDIA AND SDGS

Issues and challenges

Preet Rustagi, Swati Dutta and Deeksha Tayal

Education forms a core element of human development and is being re-emphasised in the context of the post-2015 agenda as one of the goals which impinge on several other SDGs. School education is a foundational input for capability enhancement and improving opportunities, although returns from higher education may exceed those from elementary education. Preschool education as a critical input for preparedness of children for schooling and the successful completion of schooling with quality education are two components specifically mentioned in targets 4.1 and 4.2 of the SDGs. This chapter highlights the current status, issues and challenges for attainment of the SDGs for school education, keeping these two targets in view. The NSSO 71st round (2014–15) unit level data has been used for relevant indicators.

The Right of Children to Free and Compulsory Education Act, 2009, marks India's move forward by adopting a rights-based framework casting a legal obligation on central and state governments. Further, it aims at addressing the issue of exclusion through its various provisions. In order to facilitate involvement of private schools in this process, the Act mandates that unaided private schools set aside at least 25 per cent of their seats at the entry level to students from the weaker sections and disadvantaged groups. Under the RTE Act, the government is mandated to reimburse private schools an amount equal to either the expenditure incurred per child by the state or the actual amount charged by the school, whichever is less (Sarin and Gupta 2013). This provision has further sparked the debate on public and private educational set-up in India. There have been several efforts to achieve universalisation of elementary education, such as the Sarva Shiksha Abhiyan (SSA), Operation Blackboard and District Primary Education Programme (DPEP), among many others. School education has received significant attention through the years, from the Constitution of India to the various National Policies on Education. Inclusion of education in our Constitution as a fundamental right underlines the fact that education is a public good and government has the prime responsibility of ensuring that all children up to the age of 14 have equal access to this facility. However, the single greatest challenge facing the school education sector in India is inequity in the provisioning and utilisation of educational opportunities across social and economic groups. In particular, educational exclusion is being prominently faced by children from marginalised households belonging to Dalit, Adivasi and Muslim communities. SDG 4 also refers to ensuring inclusive and equitable quality education and promoting lifelong learning opportunities for all.

School education in India – literacy, enrolment and attendance

Despite increasing commitments and continuous efforts by the Government of India, a large number of children remain highly vulnerable to missing formal education as they are unable to continue going to school and eventually dropout. There is a strong linkage between socio-economic class and access to education with students from various marginalised groups being excluded from access to education.

Literacy rate[1] is one of the basic indicators that reflect the socio-economic progress of the country. Considered for the adult population, the literacy rate can be lower because of the surviving illiterates, but youth literacy rates pertaining to ages 15–24 is a clear reflection of the current scenario. If this needs to be altered, serious steps need to be taken to ensure that no child slips out of the school education stream and all of them complete basic schooling at least up to the elementary level. The literacy rates among the population ages 15+, i.e. the adult literacy rate, is 78 per cent, with a gender gap of nearly 16 points (males – 86 per cent and females – 70 per cent). The rural scenario continues to record a poorer literacy rate compared to the urban locales (72 per cent and 86 per cent respectively) (Figure 3.1). The gender gap is also much worse in rural locations (19 points), while the gap is 11 points in urban areas. Youth literacy rates (ages 15–24) are also showing a similar pattern (Figure 3.2).

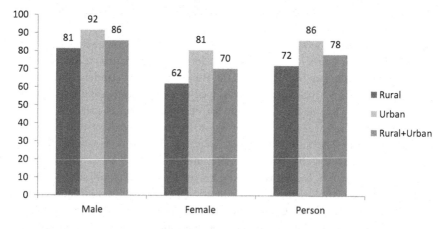

FIGURE 3.1 Adult literacy rate by gender and location (%)

Source: 71st NSSO Unit Level data (2014–15)

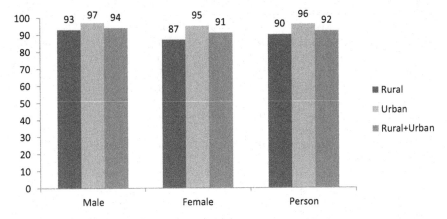

FIGURE 3.2 Youth literacy rate by gender and location (%)
Source: 71st NSSO Unit Level data (2014–15)

Youth literacy rates for Muslims are lower than for any other social group. Muslims in general are worse off in terms of literacy rate. The Sachar committee report highlighted this prominently together with its consequences (Sachar Committee 2006). The committee found that the literacy gap between Muslims and the general average is greater in urban areas and for women. Owing to their socio-economic backwardness, Muslims have not been able to respond to the challenge of improving their educational status, whereas other communities, such as SCs and STs, have been able to reap the benefit in the field of education with active support of the government.

Social group analysis reveals the extremely poor situation among the tribals, with rural tribal girls among the youth (aged 15–24) faring the worst after Muslim girls. In urban areas, it is the SC children who record a lower literacy rate (Table 3.1). The lowest literacy rates are recorded for SC females in urban areas and ST females in rural areas among all ages above 15 (Table 3.1).

School attendance is a more meaningful indicator for education compared to enrolment, since in India many children enrol but do not attend classes regularly. NSSO in its 71st round (2014–15) on education has provided attendance-related information. The net attendance ratios[2] given in Table 3.2 for successive stages of education confirm the declining pattern of school attendance as we go to higher levels of education. The attendance ratio for males is higher than for females in both rural and urban areas. A similar pattern is observed across social groups. However, the net attendance ratio for Muslims is much lower than the all-India average. Although there is not much gender difference at the primary level across social groups, the net attendance ratio for Muslim females is much lower than for their male counterparts at the primary level. Interestingly, the gender gap reduces at higher levels of education, although there is an overall decline in attendance (Table 3.2).

Figure 3.3 shows that 89 per cent of children of primary school going age of the richest fifth of the population attend school both in the rural and urban areas, whereas that proportion drops to 79 per cent for children in the poorest fifth of the

TABLE 3.1 Youth literacy rate across social and religious groups (%)

Youth literacy		ST	SC	OBC	Others	Muslim
Rural	Male	91	92	94	97	91
	Female	80	85	87	93	80
	Person	85	88	90	95	84
Urban	Male	97	96	95	98	92
	Female	92	93	94	97	90
	Person	95	94	96	97	91
Rural + Urban	Male	91	92	94	87	91
	Female	81	87	89	95	80
	Person	86	90	84	94	83
Adult literacy rate						
Rural	Male	68	69	77	85	72
	Female	46	47	53	69	52
	Person	56	59	65	77	62
Urban	Male	89	85	89	94	82
	Female	74	67	75	87	69
	Person	82	76	82	91	77
Rural + Urban	Male	70	73	81	89	76
	Female	49	52	60	76	59
	Person	60	62	69	83	67

Source: 71st NSSO Unit Level data (2014–15)

TABLE 3.2 Net attendance ratio by gender, location, social and religious groups across levels of schools (%)

	Primary	Upper primary	Secondary	Higher secondary
Male				
SC	81	62	46	29
ST	83	62	45	28
OBC	83	63	51	38
Others	86	69	59	47
Muslims	76	52	38	24
Female				
SC	80	57	51	30
ST	82	60	45	27
OBC	82	60	49	36
Others	84	69	56	44
Muslims	69	49	32	21
Persons				
SC	82	59	48	30
ST	83	61	46	28
OBC	82	62	50	37
Others	85	69	58	46
Muslims	72	51	35	22
Rural Male	84	64	51	36
Rural Female	82	61	49	33
Urban Male	85	67	56	45
Urban Female	84	64	59	47
Rural + Urban Persons	83	63	52	38

Source: 71st NSSO Unit Level data (2014–15)

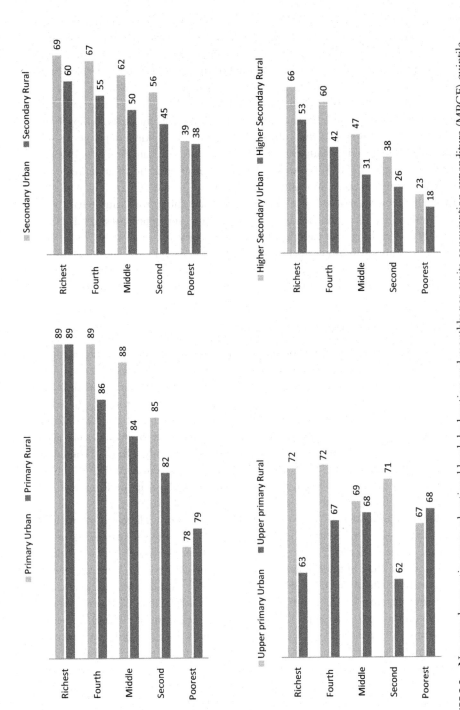

FIGURE 3.3 Net attendance ratio across educational levels by location and monthly per capita consumption expenditure (MPCE) quintile

Source: 71st NSSO Unit Level data (2014–15)

population in rural areas and 78 per cent in urban areas. But as the figure shows, net attendance ratio drops sharply when it comes to secondary school and becomes worse at the higher secondary level. It is noticed that only 18 per cent of the children from the poorest quintile are going to the higher secondary level in rural areas and only 23 per cent in urban areas. This clearly indicates there is no equality of opportunity in accessing education in the real sense. The pressures of socio-economic conditions and the costs involved to get oneself educated often push out the children belonging to the vulnerable sections (for multiple deprivations and other disadvantages, see Ramachandran et al. 2003, Ramachandran 2009; PROBE 1999; Rustagi et al. 2011; Rustagi 2013). The lower educational attainment and current pursuits in education among the Muslims, STs and SCs are a reflection of this. The gender variations and discrimination stemming from patriarchal structures and norms that influence investment decisions and approaches to education are reflected in the gender gaps in educational outcomes (Rustagi 2013). Even with enrolments improving under RTE and gender gaps declining in the new millennium, the problem of children dropping out continues because of different factors, such as cost of schooling and the low levels of preparedness for schooling.

Preparedness of children for schooling

SDG 4 has focused on the preschooling element as a critical aspect for preparedness of children for schooling. The government's universal Integrated Child Development Scheme (ICDS) programme, under which the anganwadi centres are established and operate to cater to both rural and urban poor children; they do perform this function, although in a very weak sense. There are variations in the capabilities across different anganwadis in terms of the educational component provided to children, since all of them cater to the basic nutrition component quite prominently. The early childhood care and development (ECCD)/early childhood care and education (ECCE) literature refers to a holistic development of the child which also helps in disciplining the child towards being prepared for schooling (Sinha and Bhatia 2009).

Among the households which are covered by an anganwadi centre, 38 per cent of children aged 3–6 reported receiving preschool education from the anganwadi centres, whereas another 31 per cent of children went to privately run institutions. Less than one-third of the children in this age group (27 per cent) were not attending preschool education (UNICEF RSOC 2013–14). Among this category of not attending, the share of children from the lowest wealth quintile is 35 per cent; it is 20 per cent among households belonging to the highest wealth quintile. Interestingly, one-half of all children from the lowest wealth index quintile are attending the anganwadis, whereas only 16 per cent of the highest quintile reported sending their children to similar facilities/institutions. The bulk of the highest wealth index quintile (62 per cent) families send their children to privately run institutions (play schools, nurseries etc.).

The NSS data reports that only one-fifth of all children are attending pre-primary school, which excludes informal education, such as that in the anganwadi centres

(Figure 3.4). NSS data also reports that the share of children attending the pre-primary level is 27 per cent in the richest monthly per capita consumption expenditure (MPCE) class, whereas it is only 12 per cent in the lowest MPCE class. Further, the share of females attending the pre-primary level at the lower MPCE class is smaller than for males.

The gender bias in terms of parents/guardians not being interested in sending girls to a preschool facility is reflected here. There is also the fear for her safety given the incidence of crimes against children that occur in the country. The activities that must be pursued for ECCE remain highly inadequate, as most of the

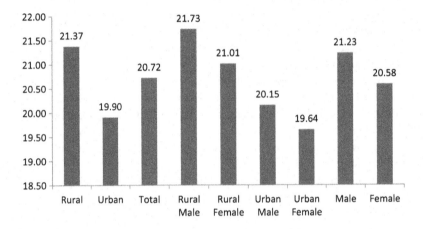

FIGURE 3.4 Percentage of children 3–6 years attending pre-primary school by location and gender

Source: 71st NSSO Unit Level data (2014–15)

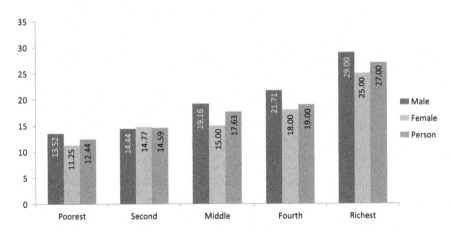

FIGURE 3.5 Percentage of children 3–6 years attending pre-primary school by gender and MPCE class

Source: 71st NSSO Unit Level data (2014–15)

anganwadi centres function as nutritional centres with greater emphasis on this critical aspect, but the focus on education takes a backseat. Even pre-schooling in several parts of the country remains similar, with only the midday meals operational, which attracted the children in the first place.

Type of institution and cost of schooling

Government institutions are generally the least expensive mode of schooling available to the masses. Indeed, the bulk of school education is provided by government institutions. In terms of percentage of students currently attending by type of institutions, more than one-half of them attend government institutions. In rural areas, the government institutions cover almost three-fourths of the students, whereas the urban scenario is different, with private institutions surpassing the government ones (see Figure 3.6).

The percentage of students enrolled in government institutions in rural areas is higher for ST and SC students up to the higher secondary level. However, OBCs and others are enrolled relatively more in private institutions compared to the SCs and STs (Figures 3.7 and 3.8). On the other hand, irrespective of the social groups in urban areas, the majority of the students are attending private institutions from the primary level onwards (Figure 3.8).

Cost of education tends to remain an important variable impeding educational access for a large proportion of the economically poorer sections. The endeavour to make education free and equitable is yet to be attained (Tilak 2009). Even among the free from fee schools, only close to 60 per cent reported this for elementary

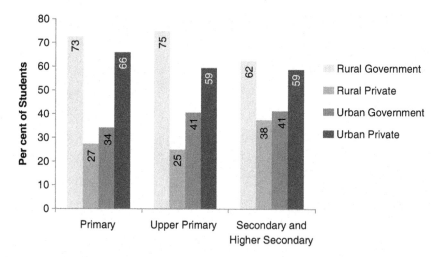

FIGURE 3.6 Percentage distribution of students by type of institutions attended by level of education

Source: 71st NSSO Unit Level data (2014–15)

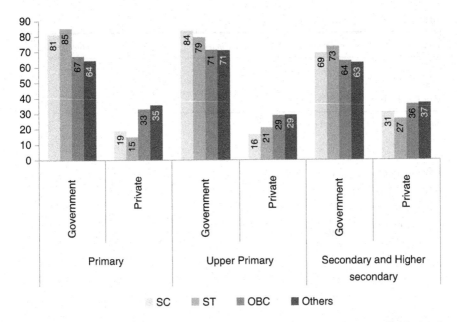

FIGURE 3.7 Percentage distribution of students by type of institutions attended by level of education in rural areas across social group

Source: 71st NSSO Unit Level data (2014–15)

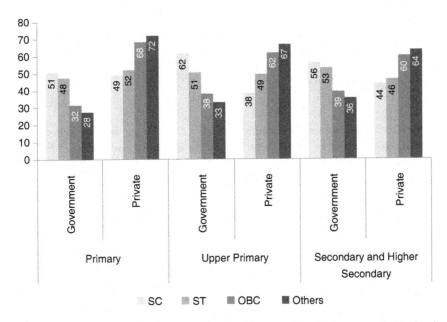

FIGURE 3.8 Percentage distribution of students by type of institutions attended by level of education in urban areas across social group

Source: 71st NSSO Unit Level data (2014–15)

88 Rustagi, Dutta and Tayal

TABLE 3.3 Provision of free education

Location	Primary	Upper primary	Secondary	Higher secondary
Rural	69.89	69.79	49.08	25.51
Urban	29.47	34.01	26.95	15.92
Rural + Urban	59.88	60.43	42.29	22.45

Source: 71st NSSO Unit Level data (2014–15)

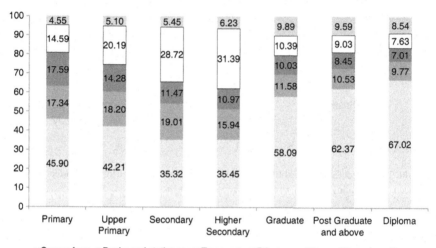

FIGURE 3.9 Component of household educational expenditure per student (%)
Source: 71st NSSO Unit Level data (2014–15)

schools, with the proportion declining to 42 per cent among the secondary school students and further to 23 per cent among the higher secondary levels. For the rural-urban situation, see Table 3.3.

Among the reported costs at the household level irrespective of rural-urban location, the fees continue to constitute a bulk of the expenses, followed by private coaching, books and stationery, transport and other costs (see Figure 3.9). Share of expenditure on private coaching increased from 14 per cent at primary level to 31 per cent at higher secondary level.

The NSS estimates are perhaps conservative estimates of schooling expenditures. An attempt to see the distribution of costs incurred among students who are availing free education compared to those who have to pay the course fees even for school education shows that close to one-half of all expenses are incurred for the fees among the latter, whereas almost similar proportions of costs among the no-fee school students is spent on private coaching. Of course, the actual amount spent is lower among the no-fee school education category (see Table 3.4).

TABLE 3.4 Component of educational expenditure with and without free education (%)

School type	Course fees	Books and stationery	Transport	Private coaching	Other expenditures
	With free education				
Primary	7.93	34.48	8.18	39.42	9.99
Upper primary	7.58	30.84	9.74	42.88	8.95
Secondary	10.13	26.67	10.29	45.96	6.95
Higher secondary	16.16	22.32	12.98	40.65	7.89
	Without free education				
Primary	47.94	16.96	18.63	12.21	4.26
Upper primary	47.13	16.94	15.23	16.11	4.60
Secondary	40.27	17.60	11.79	25.07	5.27
Higher secondary	37.65	15.23	10.71	30.34	6.07

Source: 71st NSSO Unit Level data (2014–15)

TABLE 3.5 Educational expenditure per student by levels of school (per academic year) with and without free education (in INR)

School type	With free education	Without free education
Primary	1044.25	9936.11
Upper primary	1730.32	10976.96
Secondary	3417.49	10505.34
Higher secondary	6099.12	14393.27

Source: 71st NSSO Unit Level data (2014–15)

Among the elementary school students, the average educational expenditure per student incurred is less than Rs.2000, whereas the fee among the other paying students is close to Rs.10,000 per annum (Table 3.5). The variation across government and private institutions and costs incurred per student are provided in Table 3.6. It is shown that education is not free till the elementary level, even in the government schools where there are no tuition fees. There are expenditures incurred on books, stationery, transport etc., and many students now opt for private tuition, even in rural areas, adding to the financial burden of schooling. Moreover, the education-related expenditure rises steadily as the level of education rises. The rural-urban disparity in education expenditure is enormous at the all-schools average but much less for government schools, at least till the upper primary level (Table 3.7). This is due to the fact that a greater proportion of students in urban areas attend private schools, usually a much costlier option than government schools.

The rural government primary school expenditure per student ranges approximately from Rs.1000 without fees to Rs.2000 with fees. The margin of difference increases in urban areas from Rs.1500 (without fees) to Rs.6200 (with fees), even in government schools, whereas the private school expenditure ranges from Rs.3800 to Rs.14000 respectively. This is a mere reflection of the parental paying capacity

TABLE 3.6 Educational expenditure per student by levels of school and category of institution (per academic year) with and without free education (in INR)

Type of institution	Government	Private
Schooling level	**With free education**	
Primary	980	3017
Upper primary	1654	3369
Secondary	3272	5244
Higher secondary	5529	11754
	Without free education	
Primary	2995	10712
Upper primary	3378	12973
Secondary	4611	13845
Higher secondary	7821	18223

Source: 71st NSSO Unit Level data (2014–15)

TABLE 3.7 Educational expenditure per student by school level and type of institution (per academic year) with and without free education (in INR) in rural and urban areas

School type	Rural		Urban	
	Government	Private	Government	Private
	With free education			
Primary	906	2612	1547	3794
Upper primary	1483	3091	2723	3929
Secondary	3056	4322	4352	7461
Higher secondary	5091	8943	7039	20789
	Without free education			
Primary	1958	7944	6197	14009
Upper primary	2575	8992	5964	17144
Secondary	3895	9519	7397	19251
Higher secondary	6665	12771	11472	26164

Source: 71st NSSO Unit Level data (2014–15)

and their pursuit of sending their children to schools which provide quality education. Whether quality is being achieved remains a big challenge.

Dropout

Dropout figures for the social groups of SC and ST at the elementary and higher levels confirm the poor retention of children at school (Table 3.8). At the national level, the dropout rate is highest among girls for classes VI–VIII and IX–X, while boys' dropout rate is slightly more at the primary level. This indicates that boys leave school earlier than girls. The compulsion of early entry into the labour market for

TABLE 3.8 Estimated percentage of children among dropouts according to class completed before dropping out across social groups

	Male			Female			Total		
	I–V	VI–VIII	IX–X	I–V	VI–VIII	IX–X	I–V	VI–VIII	IX–X
ST	39	31	29	34	36	29	37	32	29
SC	26	41	31	29	44	26	28	42	28
OBC	30	38	32	30	40	29	53	39	30
Others	38	31	30	29	41	28	32	42	29
Muslims	34	36	28	37	32	29	36	34	29

Source: 71st NSSO Unit Level data (2014–15)

TABLE 3.9 Percentage of out of school children in terms of dropout, never enrolled and never attended

	Number	Per cent
Total out-of-school children	6064229	
Who never enrolled	2698377	44.50
Total number of children who dropped out	2242003	36.97
Number of children who enrolled but never attended	1123849	18.53

Source: National Sample Survey of Estimation of out-of-school children ages 6–13 in India (2014)

boys from economically weaker sections is in most cases the explanation for such behaviour. Girls, for whom various social barriers are often of greater importance, such as household chores, looking after siblings, devaluation of their education, puberty, early marriage and motherhood,[3] tend to drop out more towards the middle level or later.

For tribal students, the dropout rate is high at I–V levels, whereas for SCs these are high at VI–VIII levels. For Muslims, the dropout rate is high at I–V levels. The dropout rate among ST males is high at I–V levels, whereas for ST girls the dropout rate is high at VI–VIII levels. However, for SC males and SC females, the dropout rate is high at VI–VIII levels. For Muslim females, the dropout rate is high at I–V levels, and for Muslim males, the dropout rate is high at VI–VIII levels.

For all youth 15–24 years old to complete schooling and continue without dropping out, universal enrolment amongst school-age children with no dropouts will have to be ensured. As per the Social & Rural Research Institute and Educational Consultants India LTD 2014 national survey on the estimation of out-of-school children, there are nearly 6.1 million out-of-school children amongst 6–13 years olds, which is only 3 per cent. A major share of these out-of-school children, nearly 4.7 million, are from rural areas. Of all out-of-school children, 45 per cent have never enrolled and another 19 per cent enrolled but never attended. Only 2.2 million children resorted to dropping out, which constitutes 37 per cent (Table 3.9). However, ensuring that even these small proportions of children do not slip out of the system will pose a much bigger challenge together with ensuring that the enrolment of the out-of-school children is encouraged and supported by all possible means if the SDGs are to be met.

Figure 3.10 indicates that a very high proportion of children drop out in the first two expenditure quintiles. It is noticed that in the poorest two expenditure quintile dropouts among STs are high, followed by SCs. In the middle and fourth expenditure quintile, the dropout rate is high among OBCs, followed by others.

There can be a wide variety of reasons that can be attributed to the high dropout rate among tribals as compared to other social categories. The reasons can be external as well as internal. The internal problems need a more focused strategy-based system to combat the problems. The external factors are the problems that need some intervention and a programme-based approach that focuses on the environment and factors that help in alleviating the educational levels that can be achieved by the tribal children. The main reason for dropping out among tribal students is financial constraint (22 per cent) followed by no interest in education (19 per cent) and unable to cope up (15 per cent). For scheduled castes and OBCs main reason for dropping out is financial constraint followed by no interest in schooling (Table 3.10).

The reasons for non-enrolment, dropping out/discontinuation and non-attendance tend to be quite varied. There are both supply and demand factors affecting the situations. Non-availability of schools in terms of proximity is one factor which is hardly relevant for the primary schooling, since schools are now available in close neighbourhood for almost all children, but for higher levels of schooling this remains a factor to contend with. One of the factors for dropping out or discontinuation tends to relate to the low levels of pre-primary education and organised development exposure that children have in our country. Lack of preschool institutions and the varied provisioning from the government anganwadi centres to the school-run

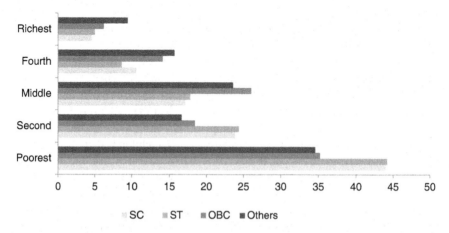

FIGURE 3.10 Proportion of dropout children (class X and below) by consumption expenditure quintile across social groups

Source: 71st NSSO Unit Level data (2014–15)

TABLE 3.10 Reasons for dropout (class X and below) among social groups (%)

	SC	ST	OBC	Others
No interest	21	19	21	16
Financial constraint	26	22	26	23
Domestic activities	14	9	16	14
Economic activities	13	16	15	24
Quality of teacher	1	2	0	0
Unable to cope	6	15	6	5
Completed desired level	1	2	1	3
Others*	14	16	12	15

Source: 71st NSSO Unit Level data (2014–15)

* include marriage; inadequate number of teachers, language, school is far and timing of school

pre-primary classes for 3–6 year olds to the privately run playschools and childcare creches which especially in urban locations cater to very different sets of children.

The other prominent reason relates to cost of schooling, with the children of the poorest sections of society being adversely affected. Even those who attend government schools and are beneficiaries of fee-free schooling often cannot complete ten years of schooling. The economic compulsion of taking up paid work to supplement household incomes influences these children away from continuation in schooling.

Quality of education

In 1990, the World Declaration on Education for All (EFA) committed countries to improving quality of education. The declaration identified quality as a prerequisite for achieving the fundamental goal of equity. It recognised that expanding access alone would be insufficient for education to contribute fully to the development of individuals and society. A decade later, the Dakar Framework for Action declared that access to an education of good quality was the right of every child. It expanded the definition of quality to address desirable characteristics of learners, processes, facilities, learning materials, content, governance and management and learning outcomes. Whereas many countries have made impressive gains in access to education since Dakar, improvement in quality has not always kept pace. A discernible shift in emphasis towards quality and learning is likely to become more central to the post-2015 global framework, since, as the 2013/14 EFA Global Monitoring Report (GMR) showed, 250 million children have not had the chance to learn the basics – and 130 million of them have spent at least four years in school (UNESCO 2015).

In defining quality of education, UNICEF (2000) included several components such as health, well-nourished and motivated learners/students; safe, protective and non-discriminatory environment; processes such as trained teachers who use child centred teaching approaches; content consisting of relevant curricula and materials for acquisition of basic skills; and outcomes that encompasses knowledge, skills that are linked to national education goals. Several dimensions and indicators can figure within these broad set of factors.

Annual Status of Education Reports (ASER), brought out by Pratham give some indications of current trends in some dimensions of quality education in rural India. As per 2014 report, 96.7 per cent of the children in the age group 6–14 years have been found to be enrolled in school in rural India. Comparing the availability of school facilities, the report finds that from 2010, there has been some improvement over the years from 2010 to 2018 (Table 3.11).

However, learning outcomes do not seem to be showing much progress. Reading, the foundation skill was found to be below expected levels. Just 50 per cent of the children enrolled in standard V were found to be able to read the text taught in standard II. In fact there seems to be a decline or stagnation in the reading levels of standard V students, assessed between 2008 and 2014. Even in case of students completing standard II, there is a rising trend (13.4 per cent in 2010 to 32.5 per cent in 2014) in the proportion of children enrolled in government schools who cannot even recognise letters (ASER 2014). A similar declining trend is visible in the proportion of children from standard II and III, who are able to recognise numbers. Increasing deficit in such basic skills during the early schooling levels is a clear indication of poor educational foundation and questions the quality dimension of the system (ASER 2014). Hence, the challenge is not merely to guarantee universal access to education but also to ensure that it is of good quality. This is essential because it is the right of all to have a good quality education and because it will allow maximum economic, social and health benefits from education. Moreover, poor families will not make the sacrifices necessary to send their children to school if it is perceived to be of poor quality (Govinda and Bandyopadhyay 2011). It is necessary to tackle both, the clear exclusion of children being out of school and also the hidden exclusion of children being in school, but receiving a poor quality education (Save the Children Education Global Initiative 2013).

TABLE 3.11 Comparison – availability of school facilities between 2010 and 2018 (%)

Percentage of schools	2010	2014	2016	2018
Complying with pupil-teacher ratio norms	38.9	49.3	**	**
Mid-day meals being served on day of visit	84.6	85.1	87.1	87.1
Having boundary wall	51	58.8	**	**
Having playground	62	65.3	**	**
Drinking water is available	72.7	75.6	74.0	74.8
Having useable toilets	47.2	65.2	68.6	74.2
Having useable girls' toilets	32.9	55.7	61.9	66.4
Having library books	62.6	78.1	**	**
Having computers	15.8	19.6	**	**

Source: Annual Status of Education Report – ASER 2014, ASER 2018

Concluding remarks

Education clearly forms one of the core elements critical for achieving several of the stated goals in the SDGs. Whereas substantial attention and investment have gone into the sector with the enhancing recognition of its significance for human and sustainable development, the challenges of ensuring equity, inclusiveness, gender parity and non-discrimination alongside quality of education are huge. Our analysis shows that although both adult and youth literacy rates of India are impressive, gender gap is a serious issue. Further, both scheduled tribes and Muslims have comparatively low literacy rates among the others. The net attendance ratio for Muslim females is much lower than for their male counterparts at the primary level. Hence, to reach the SDG pertaining to education we first need to reduce gender inequality and give more opportunity to Muslims and scheduled tribe students to maintain the inclusiveness, gender parity and non-discrimination. Further, we need to increase the attendance of pre-primary school, which will be the basis of the foundation for the future. At present only one-fifth of all children are attending pre-primary school, which excludes the anganwadi centres. Dropouts and out-of-school children also pose a major challenge for India to achieve SDGs. To reduce the dropout rates we need to reduce the cost of education, which is supposed to be free up to the elementary level but is not yet.

The possibilities of enhancing availability of facilities and infrastructure is relatively simpler compared to transformating of elements that affect the quality of education such as appropriate and child friendly curriculum and pedagogy, teacher training and motivation, improving student-teacher transactions in school thereby retaining interest of children in schooling which prevents them from dropping out before school completion and even motivate them to continue further higher studies. Efforts that are currently being made such as reducing the applicability of no detention policy from elementary to only primary levels; making examinations and tests for learning assessments mandatory are regressive. How these steps are going to ensure completion of school education, leaving no child behind, being inclusive and providing quality education to all girls and boys seems to pose several challenges, as discussed in this chapter, which are yet to be addressed.

Notes

1 A person who can read and write a simple message in any language with understanding is considered literate in NSS surveys.
2 Net Attendance Ratio is defined as for each education class-group, this is the ratio of the number of persons in the official age-group attending a particular class-group to the total number of persons in the age-group. For primary school age group is 6–10, for upper primary level it is 11–13, secondary level it is 14–15 years and higher secondary level it is 16–17 years.
3 See UNICEF (2014) for further details of reasons and barriers leading to out of school children.

References

ASER Centre/Pratham. 2014. *Annual Status of Education Report 2014*. Delhi: Pratham.

ASER Centre/Pratham. 2018. *Annual Status of Education Report (Rural) 2018 Provisional*. New Delhi: ASER Centre. Available at: http://img.asercentre.org/docs/ASER%20 2018/Release%20Material/aserreport2018.pdf

Govinda, R. and Bandyopadhyay, M. 2011. "Overcoming Exclusion through Quality Schooling: Pathways to Access." *Research Monograph No. 65*. Delhi: National University of Educational Planning and Administration.

PROBE. 1999. *Public Report on Basic Education in India*. New Delhi: Oxford University Press.

Ramachandran, V. 2009. "Right to Education Act: A Comment." *Economic and Political Weekly*, 44(28).

Ramachandran, Vimala, Jandhyala, Kameshwari, and Saihjee, Aarti. 2003. "Through the Life Cycle of Children – Factors that Facilitate/Impede Successful Primary Education Completion." *Economic and Political Weekly*, 38(47).

Rustagi, Preet. 2013. "Education: Achievements and Challenges." In *India Human Development Report 2012–13*, pp. 179–206. New Delhi: Oxford University Press.

Rustagi, Preet, Mishra, Sunil Kumar, and Mehta, Balwant Singh. 2011. "Scheduled Tribe Children in India: Multiple Deprivations and Locational Disadvantage." *IHD-UNICEF Working Paper Series on Children of India: Rights and Opportunities*, No. 8. New Delhi: UNICEF and Institute for Human Development.

Sachar Committee Report. 2006. *High Level Committee to Examine the Socio Economic and Educational Status of the Muslim Community in India*. New Delhi: Government of India.

Sarin, A. and Gupta, S. 2013. *Quotas under RTE. Leading towards an Egalitarian Education System*. Ahmedabad: Indian Institute of Management.

Save the Children Education Global Initiative. 2013. *Ending the Hidden Exclusion: Learning and Equity in Education Post-2015*. London: Save the Children International.

Sinha, Dipa and Bhatia, Vandana. 2009. *Learning from Models of ECCD Provision in India*. Available at: forces.org.in/.../Dipa_Sinha_ECCD_in_India.pdf [Accessed October 24, 2016].

Tilak, Jandhyala B.G. 2009. "Universalizing Elementary Education: A Review of Progress, Policies and Problems." In Rustagi, Preet (ed.). *Concerns, Conflicts and Cohesions: Universalisation of Elementary Education in India*, pp. 33–71. New Delhi: Oxford University Press.

UNESCO. 2015. *EFA Global Monitoring Report: Education for All 2000–2015: Achievement and Challenges*. Paris: UNESCO. Available at: www.unesco.nl/sites/default/files/dossier/gmr_2015.pdf?download=1

UNICEF. 2000. *Defining Quality in Education*. New York: UNICEF.

UNICEF. 2014. *All Children in School By 2015: Global Initiative on Out-of-School Children*. Kathmandu: UNICEF. Available at: http://uis.unesco.org/sites/default/files/documents/out-of-school-children-south-asia-country-study-education-2014-en.pdf

4
KNOWLEDGE, SKILLS AND SUSTAINABLE DEVELOPMENT
Role of higher education

N. V. Varghese

Universities contribute significantly to sustainable development (SD) by linking knowledge generation and knowledge transfer to development concerns of the society. Provision of knowledge as a "public good" is one of the tasks of higher education, and unhindered access to knowledge is a prerequisite for sustainable development (UNESCO 2004). Further, education for sustainable development (ESD) is a means of enabling students to develop the attributes, behaviours and skills needed to work and live to safeguard ecological, social and economic wellbeing. Higher education institutions bear a profound moral responsibility to increase the awareness, knowledge, skills, and values needed to create a just and sustainable future (Cortese 2003).

This chapter focuses on one of the dimensions of the SD, namely the role of higher education in imparting knowledge and skills to promote equity and to create a just and sustainable future. The concern for equity cuts across many other dimensions of SD and certainly has a heavy reliance on economic and social dimensions. While wealth and inheritance were the major sources of income inequalities in traditional societies, employment and earnings from professions form the major sources of inequalities in the present context. Creation of productive employment for all is a necessary condition for reducing inequalities, achieving the sustainable development goals (SDGs) and rebalancing the global economy towards sustainable economic growth path (ILO 2016).

Access to professions is regulated by education and skills. Therefore, access to and success in higher education influence access to jobs and income distribution in the present context. Any inequalities in the distribution of opportunities to pursue higher education will encourage unequal access to jobs and will result in income inequalities. This chapter views equity in access to higher education and skill formation as necessary paths towards better jobs, improved wellbeing and sustainable development.

We are growing unequal

The economic growth and inequalities have been a recurring theme for discourses among development scientists. It can be argued that world showed relatively more tolerance to inequalities in the 1950s and 1960s than in the later decades. The increasing inequality in economic and social development led to a call for "Redistribution with Growth" (Chenery et al. 1974) and had a profound influence in shaping the strategy of development in the 1970s. The World Bank focused on poverty reduction strategies and prioritised investments towards agriculture and rural development. The International Labour Organization (ILO) came up with its flagship initiative of World Employment Programme (WEP). The world leaders agreed on an agenda centred on "employment-oriented strategy of rural development" (Mellor 1975) to address the pressing global problem of poverty when 40 per cent of the population was below poverty line.

Empirical evidence shows that inequalities between countries and between regions within the same country have widened in the recent decades and especially from the turn of this century. Inequalities have, indeed, worsened rapidly in the post-economic crisis period in the developed countries and remained high in the emerging and developing economies. Most economists have now become fairly sceptical about universal laws, similar to Kuznets curves, relating development and income inequality (Pikketty 2006).

It is the changes in the employment patterns that are considered to be contributing to the widening of income inequalities. The decline in medium-skilled jobs and a rising demand for jobs at the lower and upper ends of the skill hierarchy seem to be compelling educated workers to compete for lower-skilled occupations. This has resulted in increasing wage and income inequalities between those who are employed in high-end jobs and others (ILO 2015). In other words, education level and employment status are determining the nature of income distribution and the extent of income inequalities in the present context.

Inequalities in employment

The globalisation process has strengthened the market forces which contributed to widening of economic and social inequalities. Migration of people and jobs plays an important role in widening inequalities. Globalisation is characterised by migration of the highly skilled people to developed countries and migration of low skill jobs to the developing countries. The increase in demand and wages for high-skilled labour in developed countries and an increase in the demand for the low-skilled workers in the developing countries contribute to widening income inequalities between countries (Pérez-Megino and Berumen 2015). Between 1970 and 2000, the average real compensation of the top one hundred CEOs was multiplied by a factor of more than 30, while the average wage of those engaged in lower-end jobs in the U.S. economy increased by about 10 per cent. Although there are social scientists (Dollar and Kraay 2002) who argue that globalisation helped in closing the inequality gap, a growing number of analysts tend to conclude that globalisation has, in fact, accentuated inequality both within and between countries (Firbaugh 2003; Wade 2004).

The global unemployment in 2014 was around 201 million and is expected to increase to 212 million by 2019. If new labour market entrants over the next five years are taken into account, an additional 280 million jobs need to be created by 2019 to close the global employment gap (ILO 2015). A major share of the increase in global unemployment is in the East and South Asia regions which together account for more than 45 per cent of additional job seekers.

Among those employed, a large share is either in the category of vulnerable employment or in informal employment or both. It is estimated that nearly 48 per cent of the employed are in the category of vulnerable employment and that the informality rate is as high as 90 per cent in some of the countries in South and South East Asia. The share of vulnerable employment and high informality rate in employment are a source of major concern since those employed in these categories have neither stability in employment nor social security support systems in their favour (ILO 2014).

Education and employment in India

Income inequalities are widening since globalisation process started in India. The states that are experiencing higher growth rates in India are also witnessing increases (or lower reductions) in inequality. For example, the state of Kerala has shown high growth and an increase in inequality; Maharashtra and Tamil Nadu have experienced moderate growth and higher decreases in inequality (Motiram and Vakulabharanam 2011; Vakulabharanam 2010). Access to employment continues to be one of the reasons for inequalities and a major challenge in India. In the last decade, the economy grew at an annual rate of around 8.0 per cent and jobs at a dismal rate of below 1.0 per cent. This has, certainly contributed to widening disparities in income distribution (Government of India 2006).

According to NSSO, India has a labour force of around 485 million in 2012. The labour force in India increased at an annual average rate of 1.45 per cent between 1999–2000 and 2011–12. However, the labour force participation rates declined over a period of past three decades from 42.9 per cent in 1984 to 39.5 per cent in 2011–12 (Table 4.1). The decline in the overall participation rates is primarily because of the sharp decline in the participation rates of females. While the male participation rates remained stable at around 55.0 per cent the female labour force

TABLE 4.1 Labour force participation rates (%)

Year	Male	Female	Participation rate
1983	55.1	30.0	42.9
1993–94	55.6	29.0	42.8
2002–05	55.9	29.4	43.0
2011–12	55.6	22.5	39.5

Source: NSSO: 2014 (68th round).

participation rates declined sharply from 30.0 per cent in 1984 to 22.5 per cent in 2011–12. It accounts for nearly 25.0 per cent reduction in the participation rates of women.

The decline in female labour force participation rates may be due to an income effect – rising male incomes may lower female participation. Income effect may be more visible at the middle-end jobs than at the low-end jobs and income levels. At low end jobs, economic distress may override income effect considerations. This may be the reason for higher rates of labour force participation among women who are illiterate or having lower levels of education.

Table 4.2 shows education levels of those employed. Of the total labour force of 485 million, 146 million (30 per cent) are illiterate; 40 per cent are with primary; 12 per cent less than secondary; 3 per cent of the workforce has technical education at tertiary level, and another 7.2 per cent has general academic education at tertiary level. More than half of the female workers and nearly one-fourth of the male workers are illiterate. Population of youth (age group of 15 to 29 years) in India is expected to increase steadily to approximately 350 million by 2022 (World Bank 2006). Educational qualification levels of the people in the age group 15 to 29 are expected to improve.

Employment by educational levels of the disadvantaged (Table 4.3), indicate that illiterates account for a good share of the employed among the disadvantaged groups – 46.2 per cent among the ST and 38.8 per cent among SC categories. The disparities in the share of the educated among the disadvantaged and other groups widen at higher levels of education. For example, while the share of the middle level educated in employment is comparable among the social groups, the disparities in their respective shares increases when one moves to secondary, higher secondary and higher education levels.

These trends in education and employment are also a reflection of the nature of jobs which are engaging different categories of people. The share of the disadvantaged groups is higher in the casual labour category while the non-disadvantaged groups have a higher share in the regular employment category. The shares

TABLE 4.2 Employed by gender and level of education, 2011–12 (%)

Educational level	Persons	Male	Female
Illiterate	30.7	23.0	50.8
Literate & below primary	10.9	11.3	9.9
Primary	13.3	13.9	11.9
Middle	16.4	18.5	11.1
Secondary	11.8	13.9	6.4
Higher secondary	6.6	7.8	3.4
Diploma/Certificate	1.4	1.6	0.8
Graduate and above	8.8	10.0	5.7
Total	100.0	100.0	100.0

Source: NSSO 2014 (68th round)

TABLE 4.3 Distribution of employed by caste and level of education, 2011–12 (%)

Educational categories	ST	SC	OBC	Others
Illiterate	46.2	38.8	31.5	17.9
Literate & below primary	13.0	12.2	11.3	8.6
Primary	13.3	15.2	13.1	12.3
Middle	14.0	15.7	17.3	16.5
Secondary	5.9	8.9	12.2	15.4
Higher secondary	3.7	4.4	6.2	9.8
Diploma/Certificate	0.5	0.8	1.5	2.0
Graduate and above	3.2	4.0	6.9	17.4
Total	100.0	100.0	100.0	100.0

Source: NSSO 2014 (68th round)

of females, SC, ST and OBC in casual employment are higher than that in other categories. These job categories are vulnerable jobs and informal in nature with no social protection. Nearly 50 per cent of the Muslim urban male workers and about 60 per cent of urban female workers were engaged in self-employment. Among Hindus in urban areas, about 44 per cent of male workers and about 40 per cent of female workers were engaged in regular wage/salaried employment whereas the access to regular employment for Muslims are 29.8 and 21.9 per cent which is very low compared to other religious communities (Madheswaran and Singhari 2017).

Unemployment of the educated

According to the 68th round of the NSSO, the unemployment rate increases consistently with increasing levels of education for both males and females in rural as well as in urban areas (Table 4.4). There is a declining trend in the rate of unemployment at the PG and above level. In the 1980s and 1990s the relationship between education levels and unemployment rate formed an inverted U-shaped curve indicating increasing unemployment rates with educational levels, reaching a peak at secondary level of education and declining thereafter (Varghese 1989, 1996). However, the peak has now shifted from secondary to university graduate level of education indicating the gravity of the situation faced by the higher education graduates. Surprisingly, the unemployment rates among those with diploma or certificate levels are also high which questions the quality and relevance of training programmes offered by our technical institutions.

The trends in unemployment rates are similar among all social groups. The unemployment rates are consistently high by levels of education for all social groups. The unemployment rates in general and that among the graduates and above in particular are higher among females, disadvantaged groups and among minorities. This pattern is consistent both in the urban and rural areas (Table 4.4). For any given level of education above secondary level, unemployment rates are higher among the SC, OBC and ST than among general categories.

TABLE 4.4 Unemployment rate by education, 2011–12

Education level	Rural			Urban			Total		
	Male	Female	Total	Male	Female	Total	Male	Female	Total
Not literate	0.6	0.7	0.6	0.9	1.0	0.9	0.6	0.8	0.7
Below primary	1.0	1.4	1.1	2.9	2.1	2.8	1.4	1.6	1.4
Primary	1.6	1.1	1.5	1.9	1.9	1.9	1.7	1.2	1.6
Middle	2.2	4.2	2.5	2.3	4.7	2.6	2.2	4.4	2.5
Secondary	2.6	8.8	3.5	2.3	8.3	2.9	2.5	8.7	3.3
Higher secondary	4.3	14.2	5.5	4.9	10.7	5.7	4.5	12.7	5.6
Diploma/Certificate	10.0	25.9	12.6	6.1	11.2	7.0	8.0	18.3	9.7
Graduate	8.0	23.7	10.2	5.8	14.8	7.4	6.6	17.5	8.4
PG and above	10.0	23.2	12.6	4.5	12.4	6.5	6.1	14.9	8.2
Total	2.1	2.9	2.3	3.2	6.6	3.8	2.4	3.7	2.7

Source: NSSO 2014 and Madheswaran and Singhari (2017)

TABLE 4.5 Unemployment rates among social groups (rural and urban)

Social group	Not literate	Literate & up to primary	Middle	Secondary	Higher secondary	Diploma/ Certificate	Graduate	Post-graduate & above
ST	0.1	0.4	1.8	6.2	6.4	5.5	8.9	8.9
SC	0.3	1.6	2.5	2.6	5.0	12	10.5	13.1
OBC	0.4	0.8	2.1	2.7	4.0	10	8.2	8.3
Others	0.4	1.4	2	2.2	4.5	4.7	6.4	6.1
All	0.4	1.1	2	2.7	4.4	8.1	7.6	7.5

Source: Based on *NSSO 2014* (NSS 68th round)

Table 4.6 shows that there exists a positive association between levels of education of the employees and wage levels. The wage differentials between secondary school graduates and tertiary education graduates are the sharpest and it is widening in this century. In 2004–05 and in 2011–12 the wage levels of tertiary graduates were double that of the secondary school graduates. This also reflects the trends we discussed earlier that more educated people in higher end job categories are beneficiaries of increases in wages than those at the lower-end jobs.

This pattern of concentration of less educated in lower end jobs with associated wage structure is a source of inequalities. In fact, the higher educated occupy higher paid jobs and therefore employment opportunities are determined by educational levels. Strategies to increase enrolment and retention of the disadvantaged in higher education, providing technical and professional training could be effective means for enhancing their employability and to contribute to reducing income inequality.

Educational opportunities are unevenly distributed among regions and social groups. Educational inequalities are persisting in India and are noted to be much

TABLE 4.6 Wage differentials by levels of education

Level of schooling	1983	1993–34	2004–05	2011–12
Not literate	1.0	1.0	1.0	1.0
Up to primary	1.4	1.3	1.3	1.1
Up to middle	1.5	1.4	1.3	1.3
Up to secondary and higher secondary	2.3	2.1	2.3	2.1
Tertiary	3.7	3.6	4.6	4.1

Source: Madheswaran and Singhari 2017

higher than those in most of the less developed countries. More importantly, the less developed states in India such as Odisha Madhya Pradesh, Bihar, Uttar Pradesh etc. record higher educational inequality, compared to the developed states (Kundu 2017). In other words, the states which have relatively higher concentration of the poor also have higher educational inequalities.

Massification and continuing inequalities in access to higher education

Higher education in India has been expanding in the past decades. The expansion process accelerated in the 2000s and the country entered into a stage of massification of higher education. The overall growth rate of the sector was the highest at 11.7 per cent during the period between 2001–02 and 2013–14. The GER increased from 5.9 to 21.1 per cent during 1990–2012 period and further to 23.6 per cent in 2014–15. A major share of the expansion was accounted for by state universities and private institutions.

The massive expansion and the public initiatives are also accompanied by widening regional disparities and persisting social disparities. While all states expanded their higher education sector and improved their GERs in the previous decade, the rates of growth varied. While GER increased by three times in states such as Andhra Pradesh and Tamil Nadu and it doubled in many of the major states, the increase was relatively less in other states such as West Bengal. Consequently, the inter-state disparities in enrolment increased over a period of time. The variations in GER in enrolment between states increased from 23.7 percentage points in 2002–03 to 46.6 percentage points in 2012–13 (Varghese 2015).

A close examination of the state level data will indicate that larger gains in GER took place mainly in those states where private institutions accounted for a good share of the total institutions. The states that have a high share of private unaided colleges also have a higher density of higher education institutions. For example, the share of private unaided colleges is 81.8 per cent in Andhra Pradesh, and it has a density of 48 institutions per 100 thousand population. The same is the case with Karnataka with 64.9 per cent and Puducherry with 61.3 per cent unaided institutions. The states which have predominantly public universities and colleges have a lower density of institutions.

Another dimension of the disparities is that among social groups with regard to their access to and enrolment in higher education. The scheduled caste (SC) accounts for 12.2 per cent and the scheduled tribes (ST) 4.5 per cent of the total enrolment in higher education in India. The share of SC in enrolment is higher than the national average in some of the states such as West Bengal (16.4 per cent), Tripura (16.4 per cent), Puducherry (15.9 per cent) and Tamil Nadu (15.6 per cent). The GER varies between 8.3 per cent for rural females and 30.5 per cent for urban females and between 7.7 per cent for the Scheduled Tribe population and around 45 per cent for the Christian population.

Although the share of enrolment of students belonging to the Scheduled Tribes is very low (at 4.5 per cent), some of the states with higher concentration of Scheduled Tribe population have a higher share in enrolment. For example, the students belonging to scheduled tribes account for 94.3 per cent in Mizoram, 83.6 per cent in Nagaland, 77.5 per cent in Arunachal Pradesh and 58.3 per cent in Meghalaya (Table 4.7). This does not reflect any policy shift or targeted intervention strategies adopted by the governments. These states have a very high concentration of tribal population.

Women account for 44.4 per cent of the total higher education enrolments in India in 2011–12. The state of Kerala has the highest share (58.5 per cent) of women in colleges followed by 56.8 per cent in Meghalaya. Interestingly two of the educationally backward states of Assam and Jammu and Kashmir also have more women than men in higher education institutions. There has been progress towards gender equality in enrolment. However, the gender parity index remains at 0.78 at the national level. However, in some of the states where GER is relatively high, the number of girls enrolled is larger than that of the boys resulting in a gender parity index of greater than unity.

The share of women in enrolment is less in diploma courses than in certificate and degree courses. For example, women constitute 30 per cent of enrolment in diploma courses and 32 per cent in PG diploma courses while their share is 46 per cent at under-graduate levels and 45 per cent in post-graduate courses. The share of women in different levels of study programmes is higher in Kerala and Meghalaya than in other states.

The policy towards private institutions has played an important role in the expansion, diversification and persisting inequalities in higher education enrolment in India. From the 1980s onwards privatisation of public institutions and promotion of private higher education institutions became common in India. Privatisation was reflected through cost recovery and self-financing measures in public institutions while capitation fee colleges represented proliferation of private higher education institutions.

Most of the self-financing private colleges, commonly known as "capitation fee colleges" were established in the subject areas of engineering, medicine, and management (Agarwal 2007) and their proliferation took place mostly in the Southern states of Andhra Pradesh, Karnataka, and Tamil Nadu and the Western state of Maharashtra. In the 2000s, many private universities came into existence. Following the passage of the private universities Acts in several state legislatures, the private universities proliferated and between 2002 and 2011 around 178 private universities were established in India.

With the wide-spread expansion of private institutions, the state is indirectly showing symptoms of withdrawing from the sector.

> The most disturbing development pertains to the fact that the state is gradually abdicating its responsibility towards higher education, including planning for higher education, policymaking for higher education, and of course, the funding and delivery of higher education in favour of the private sector, under the guise of private participation, public-private participation and private initiatives.
>
> *(Tilak 2014)*

Expansion of private institutions contributed to widening inequalities in access to education and employment at least in two ways. First, the private institutions contributed to disciplinary distortions since most of them were offering employment friendly courses in engineering, medical and management subject areas. Second, students from well to do families opted for these courses leaving the courses in arts and humanities mostly to students from the disadvantaged households. Since the employment friendly courses were mostly in private institutions they were expensive for the students from disadvantaged groups. In this way one could argue that private higher education institutions helped in widening inequalities in access to employment of graduates.

The private sector is fuelling another trend in higher education in India. A large share of the students from SC and ST families is enrolled in public higher education institutions since they cannot afford study programmes in private higher education institutions. They are enrolled mainly in Arts and humanities study programmes which have a low premium in the labour market. Therefore, weakening of the linkages between education and jobs affect more adversely the disadvantaged groups, especially the SC and ST students, than others.

It is worthwhile to examine the employment and employability implications of these trends as employers continue to complain about lack of employability skills among higher education graduates in India. The issue is important as enrolment in technical and professional courses such as engineering, medical, management and law grew at a faster rate than in other subject areas. More than 50 per cent of the increase in enrolment during the eleventh plan period was experienced in technical and professional study programmes. A recent study (National Employability Report 2014) shows that one third of graduates from the Tier II, III and IV engineering colleges are not employable even after interventional training (Aspiring Minds 2014). Inadequate English language and computer skills have been quoted to be major deterrents for small town employability prospects (Khare 2014). In other words, our technical and professional institutions are not well equipped to develop the skills demanded by employers.

Another trend in the expansion of higher education is the surge in enrolment at the diploma level courses experienced in the past decade. Enrolment in these courses experienced an annual average growth of 70.1 per cent and they improved their share in total enrolment from 1 per cent of the total higher education enrolment in 2005 to 8.8 per cent of the enrolments in 2012–13. Many of these courses leading to diploma or certificate levels are offered in non-university institutions and are in high demand despite the relatively high costs because of the employment prospects of their graduates. In other words, higher education sector needs to take into account expansion of the non-university institutions.

Recent efforts to link education, skills and job market

People in the highest earning brackets in India are mostly professionals and they are more educated than others. Their income levels are high and inequalities among workers in this category seems to be less irrespective of their social background. People belonging to the lowest earning brackets have low educational endowment and compete with each other for jobs that do not necessarily require high level skills. Their wages and earnings levels are low and do not vary significantly across social groups. However, individuals who lie between these two extremes work in formal or quasi-formal enterprises and have education qualifications of heterogeneous quality. In other words, the widening inequalities are more among those in the middle range occupations where the type of education and the nature of skills possessed by the individuals play an important role in recruitment and placement.

There are major skill deficiencies in our work force. In the new and emerging knowledge sectors the skill sets required in the labour market include professional and social skills of varying categories. Our technical institutions-engineering colleges and polytechnics – are not sufficiently equipped to offer the type of skills demanded in the new economy even though there was a jump in the allocations to higher education in the eleventh five year plan and that nearly one-thirds of the enhanced allocations were earmarked for technical education (Mehrotra 2016).

One of the major challenges of higher education in India is in linking it with employment and employability. India recently established a Ministry of Skill Development & Entrepreneurship (MSDE) and launched Pradhan Mantri Kaushal Vikas Yojana (PMKVY) programme. This skill-India programme is an outcome-based skill training scheme for the youth to make them employable. Another important step taken in the recent past is to develop Qualification Frameworks (QF). The global move towards qualification frameworks (QF) is to link education with employment. The QFs focus on learning outcomes and classify qualifications according to a set of criteria (using descriptors) applicable to specified levels of learning outcomes (Tuk 2007). A qualification framework is designed to provide: (a) quality assured nationally recognised and consistent training standards; (b) recognition and credit for all acquisition of knowledge and skills. It is a way of structuring existing and new qualifications (OECD 2006).

India has developed a National Skills Qualification Framework (NSQF) which defines competence as proven ability to use acquired knowledge, skills and personal and social abilities to do a job well. Learning outcomes represent what a learner knows, understands and able to do after completion of a learning process which will be expressed in terms of knowledge, skills and competence. The NSQF organises qualifications according to a series of levels of knowledge, skills and aptitude. These levels are defined in terms of learning outcomes regardless of the modes (formal or informal) of acquiring them. It is a nationally integrated education and competency-based skills framework with provisions for multiple pathways including mobility between technical and general education. It also provides for entry to labour market and to exit the labour market to acquire more skills and re-enter labour market again after acquiring higher level qualifications. It is expected that NSQF will provide principles for recognising skill proficiency and competencies at different levels leading to international equivalency, multiple entry and exit, recognition of prior learning and opportunities for lifelong learning.

The NSQF assures quality in higher education in terms of awarding credits and allowing transfer of credits, re-routing the Indian education system with more flexibility in terms of entry and exit points, timeline mobility, etc., give value to every form of education level, and allow comparability among all qualifications inter- as well as intra-country. Importantly, the transparency will help widen the horizon for both employers to identify skills as well as learners to choose from the category of work the qualification can serve.

The framework comprises 10 levels of which each level represents a distinct set of knowledge, complexity and autonomy that is required to represent the competence of that particular level. Level one represents the lowest complexity and level 10 the highest complexity. The NSQF levels are not related directly to years of study. They are defined by the extent of demands made on the learner to acquire professional knowledge, professional skills, core skill and responsibility. The individuals can move to higher levels as they acquire new skills and learning.

Each level of the NSQF is associated with a set of descriptors made of outcome statements in five domains: (a) process, (b) professional knowledge, (c) professional skill, (d) core skill and (e) responsibility. The level descriptors are broadly defined and every qualification is not expected to have all of the characteristics set out in the level descriptor. Each qualification at the NSQF level may be defined in terms of curriculum, notional contact hours, duration of studies, workload, trainer quality and the type of institution attended. Standardisation of course contents, syllabus, notional learning time and credit values will become necessary. It is expected to develop a qualification register (NSQF Register) indicating all qualifications aligned to NSQF levels.

The UGC is in the process of developing a National Higher Education Qualification Framework (NHEQF) whereby the levels of 6 and above in the NSQF will be brought under the post-secondary levels of education. The effort is to link the skills and higher education curriculum and student assessment. The major challenge lies in linking the skills indicated by the NSQF with the teaching-learning process in higher education institutions.

At present not more than 10 per cent of the youth has received any vocational training. Nearly 12.8 million enter workforce every year and the existing skill development capacity can accommodate only 3.1 million (IAMR 2012; Mehrotra 2016). Further, nearly 93 per cent of the workforce is in unorganised sectors and nearly 83 per cent of the new entrants in the workforce have no opportunity for skill training. All these data indicate the massive demand for higher education and skill training in the years to come. This implies a further fast paced expansion of the higher education sector.

It is difficult to envisage a situation where higher education institutions will remain solely as skill imparting institutions. Higher education institutions need to be focusing on research and education on the one hand and employable skills on the other. Based on the major functions involved, one may imagine a diversified institutional structure of higher education in India. Higher education institutions in India can be broadly divided into three categories – degree awarding institutions and institutions/universities, Institutions offering degree level courses and non-university professional training institutions. Degree awarding institutions and universities can be categorised into (a) research universities focusing mainly on research and postgraduate teaching (master's and above), (b) professional universities offering professional and technical courses and are authorised to award degrees, (c) teaching universities focusing more on teaching than on research and (d) open universities.

The second category of higher education institutions can be institutions offering degree level courses in general and professional subjects but without any degree awarding authority. The affiliated colleges in India may come under this category. These are institutions offering courses leading to degrees in professional and vocational study programmes. They offer more practical and vocationally-oriented courses which may lead to a bachelor's degree or its equivalent. The BVoc courses in the regular colleges, vocational colleges, hotel management institutions, fashion schools etc. belong to this category.

The third category of institutions may be those offering more of technical training than academic training. They are authorised to award diplomas which are not equivalent to degrees. The polytechnics, teacher training institutes, nursing institutions etc. belong to this category. The polytechnics offer the multi-purpose technician course and vocational training courses which are recognised by AICTE. The Teacher Training Institutes such as DIETs which are recognised by NCTE and the diploma level nursing institutes recognised by Indian Nursing Council (INC) also belong to this category.

Concluding observations

This chapter started from the premise that inequalities are inconsistent with the objectives of SD and how employment distributed among population will determine the extent of inequalities existing in a society. It is argued in the paper that education plays an influential role in improving access to jobs and income distribution in India.

The paper analysed education and employment pattern in India and showed that the relationship between levels of education and quality of employment is positive. Higher level educated people receive better paid employment. The earnings are also positively related to levels of education. In fact the earning differentials are the highest between secondary and higher education graduates than any other levels of education.

The rate of unemployment is positively associated with levels of education. This is a trend different from that existed in the 1980s and 1990s when unemployment rate and levels of education represented an inverted U-shape curve where the peak used to be secondary level of education. It seems that over a period of time the peak of the curve has shifted from secondary to higher education levels indicating a positive association between levels of education and unemployment rate in a period of massification of higher education. In other words, unemployment is slowly but steadily spreading to higher levels of education.

The enrolments in higher education in India is pre-dominantly at the under graduate level. Unemployment is high among general education graduates and less among technical and professional graduates. Therefore, there is a need to enhance employability skills of our higher education graduates including those graduating from technical and professional subject areas. The Skill India programme and the move towards QFs attempt to link learning outcomes and competencies demanded on the job. India has already developed the NSQF and is in the process of developing a national higher education qualification framework (NHEQF). These are efforts that attempt to link higher education with skills and jobs.

Skill development, no doubt, is an important function of education and training institutions if they are to remain relevant to production and useful to graduates. However, skill formation cannot be the sole purpose of higher education. Higher education institutions need to be focusing on research and education on the one hand and on employable skills on the other. This may imply a more diversified system of post-secondary level of education (Varghese 2014). There is a need to organise higher education institutions according to varying focus on research, teaching and employability skills.

Based on the requirements of knowledge production and skill formation, the paper proposes a diversified structure of higher education where research universities, professional universities, teaching universities, open universities and institutions offering study programmes in skill oriented subject areas may co-exist to meet the varying requirements of society. There is a need to expand higher education, but a good share of the expansion may be in the non-university sector focusing more on imparting employable skills than on research and knowledge production.

References

Agarwal, Pawan. 2007. *Private Higher Education in India: Status and Prospects*. London: Observatory of Borderless Higher Education (OBHE).

Aspiring Minds. 2014. *National Employability Report: Engineers – Annual Report 2014*. Gurgaon: Aspiring Minds. Available at: www.aspiringminds.com/sites/default/files/National%20 Employability%20Report%20-%20Engineers,%20Annual%20Report%202014.pdf

Chenery, Hollis, Ahluwalia, Montek S.A, Bell, C.L.G., Duloy, John H., and Jolly, Richard. 1974. *Redistribution with Growth*. London: Oxford University press.

Cortese, A.D. 2003. "The Critical Role of Higher Education in Creating a Sustainable Future." *Planning for Higher Education*, 31: 15–22.

Dollar, D. and Kraay, A. 2002. "Spreading the Wealth." *Foreign Affairs*, 81: 120–133.

Firebaugh, G. 2003. *The New Geography of Global Income Inequality*. Cambridge, MA: Harvard University Press.

Government of India. 2006. *Towards Faster and More Inclusive Growth: An Approach to the 11th Five Year Plan (2007–2012)*. New Delhi: Planning Commission.

IAMR. 2012. *A Proposed National Qualification Framework for Vocational Education for India*. New Delhi: Institute of Applied Manpower Research.

ILO. 2014. *Global Employment Trends 2014: Risk of a Jobless Recovery?* Geneva: International Labor Organization.

———. 2015. *World Employment and Social Outlook: Trends 2015*. Geneva: International Labor Organization.

———. 2016. *World Employment and Social Outlook: Trends 2016*. Geneva: International Labor Organization.

Khare, M. 2014. "Employment, Employability and Higher Education in India: The Missing Links." *Higher Education for the Future*, 1(1): 39–62.

Kundu, Amitab. 2017. 'Economic and Educational Inequalities in India within a Global Perspective: Focus on Access and Outcome Indicators for Different Socio-Religious Groups' In Varghese, N.V, Sabarwal, Nidhi, and Malish, M. eds., *India Higher Education Report 2016: Equity*. New Delhi: Sage.

Madheswaran, S. and Singhari, S. 2017. "Disparities in Outcome: Graduate Labour Market in India." In Varghese, N.V., Sabarwal, Nidhi, and Malish, M. (eds.). *India Higher Education Report 2016: Equity*. New Delhi: Sage.

Mehrotra, Santosh. 2016. "Employment of Tertiary-level Graduates in India." In Varghese, N.V. and Malik, Garima (eds.). *India Higher Education Report* 2015, pp. 177–196. New Delhi: Routledge.

Mellor, J.W. 1975. "Employment-oriented Strategy of Rural Development." In Ephraim, Raymond and Brainard, Lawrence J. (eds.). *Problems of Rural Development: Case Studies and Multi-Disciplinary Perspectives*. Brill (Netherlands): Leiden, pp. 131–139.

Motiram, S. and Vakulabharanam, V. 2011. "Poverty and Inequality in the Age of Economic Liberalization." In Nachane, D. (ed.). *India Development Report 2011*. New Delhi: Oxford University Press.

NSSO. 2014. *Employment and Unemployment Situation in India* (NSS 68th round). New Delhi: Ministry of Statistics and Programme Implementation.

OECD. 2006. *Moving Mountains: The Role of National Qualifications Systems in Promoting Lifelong Learning*. Paris: Organization for Economic cooperation and Development.

Pérez-Megino, L.P. and Berumen, S.A. 2015. "Globalization and Inequalities in Developed Economies: Kuznets was Not Right." *Neumann Business Review*, 1(2): 23–36.

Piketty, Thomas. 2006. "The Kuznets Curve: Yesterday and Tomorrow." In Banerjee, Abhijit, Bénabou, Roland and Mookherjee, Dilip (eds.). *Understanding Poverty*. Oxford Scholarship Online: September 2006. doi: 10.1093/0195305191.001.0001.

Tilak, J.B.G. 2014. "Private Higher Education in India." *Economic and Political Weekly*, 49(40): 32–38.

Tuk, Ron. 2007. *Introductory Guide to National Qualifications Frameworks: Conceptual and Practical Issues for Policy Makers*. Geneva: Skills and Employability Department, International Labour Office (ILO).

UNESCO. 2004. "Higher Education for Sustainable Development." *Education for Sustainable Development Information Brief*. Paris: UNESCO.

Vakulabharanam, V. 2010. "Does Class Matter? Class Structure and Worsening Inequality in India." *Economic and Political Weekly,* 45(29): 67–76.

Varghese, N.V. 1989. "Higher Education and Employment: Some New Evidence and their Implications." *Perspectives in Education,* 5(2): 71–80.

———. 1996. "Higher Education and Employment of the Educated in India." *Productivity,* 37(3): 444–450.

———. 2014. *Diversification of Post-Secondary Education.* Paris: IIEP/UNESCO.

———. 2015. *Challenges of Massification of Higher Education in India,* CPRHE Research Papers 1. New Delhi: CPRHE/NUEPA.

Wade, R.H. 2004. "Is Globalization Reducing Poverty and Inequality?" *World Development,* 32: 567–589.

World Bank. 2006. *India's Employment Challenge: Creating Jobs, Helping Workers.* Washington: World Bank.

5

CHALLENGES BEYOND SCHOOLING

Skilling youth to realise the goal of vocational education and training in India

Santosh Mehrotra and Vinay Swarup Mehrotra

In India, skill acquisition takes place through two basic structural streams – a small formal one and a large informal or non-formal one. The formal structure includes: (i) higher technical education imparted through professional colleges in courses that last one year (certificate course), two years (diploma course) or a three-four year degree courses, (ii) vocational education in schools at the secondary and higher secondary stage, (iii) vocational training in Industrial Training Institutes (ITIs) (these were earlier with the Ministry of Labour and Employment (MoL&E), but are now managed by the Ministry of Skill Development and Entrepreneurship (MSDE)), and (iv) apprenticeship training. Institutional training outside the school is mainly provided through a network of 13350 Industrial Training Institutes spread across India with a total seating capacity of 2.847 million in 126 trades. However, the current annual skilling capacity in India is inadequate to match the skill demand, with many initiatives un-aligned and suffering from lack of coordination (Mehrotra 2014; MSDE Expert Group Report 2016; MSDE National Skills Policy 2015). The Institution-based vocational education and training (VET) system has been slow to respond to industry's changing skills needs. The major reason has been the outdated curricula, infrastructure, and lack of trained VET teachers and instructors. The 68th round of National Sample Survey (NSS) conducted during July 2011 to June 2012, reports that among persons of age 15 years and above, only 2.4 per cent had technical degrees or diplomas or certificates. Among persons of age 15–59 years, about 2.2 per cent reported to have received formal vocational training and 8.6 per cent reported to have received non-formal vocational training (NSSO 2015). The situation is further complicated by the large number of states and UTs having different demographic situations and skill training needs, hence different skilling needs and challenges.

About 5 million persons enter the labour market every year after 2012 (Mehrotra 2014). But this number will increase to 12 million youth between 15 and 29 years of age who are expected to enter India's labour force every year for the next two decades.[1] These youth have many more years of education than the agricultural workers who are leaving rural areas for urban jobs. While the latter being poorly educated can only be accommodated in construction work or traditional service activities in urban areas, the youth will look for modern service sector jobs as well as employment in organised industry. With the current and expected economic growth, this challenge is going to only increase further, since more than 75 per cent of new job opportunities are expected to be "skill-based". Mehrotra et al. (2013) estimated that the capacity for skill training that needs to be established by 2022 will be 200 million and not 500 million for vocational skills, which was projected in the National Skill Development Policy 2009 (MoL & E 2009) nor 400 million as projected by the National Policy on Skill Development and Entrepreneurship 2015 (MSDE 2015).[2]

India is expected to become the world's youngest country by 2020, with an average age of 29 years, and accounting for 28 per cent of world's workforce, turning the population burden of the past into a demographic dividend (UN Habitat 2013). Youth[3] unemployment and youth skills development are the major agenda of the government of India. The Sustainable Development Goals (SDGs), as defined in "Transforming Our World – the 2030 Agenda for Sustainable Development" adopted by the UN Sustainable Development Summit on 25 September, 2015 aims to realise inclusive and equitable economic, social and environmentally sound sustainable development. The government of India is in the process of preparing a 15 year Perspective Plan which includes a 7 year strategy and a 3 year Action Plan. The terminal year of 2030 for the Perspective Plan was chosen because India stands in respect of the various targets included in SDG 4 (education). Target 4.1 of SDG 4 exhorts that by 2030, all girls and boys complete quality primary and secondary education, along with relevant learning outcomes. India achieved 97 per cent net enrolment rate at the primary level in 2007 (UDISE 2010). Primary school enrolment has increased significantly and has led to rising demand for secondary schooling. Currently the gross enrolment ratio at the upper primary level for 11 to 14 year old children is at about 95 per cent. In addition, there has been a rapid expansion of lower secondary education (defined in India as grades 9 and 10). The gross enrolment rate in these grades has increased from 58 per cent in 2010 to 85 per cent in 2015, a very sharp increase within a matter of five years.

Universalisation of lower secondary and higher secondary education is assured at this pace of enrolment growth, well before 2030. There is already gender parity at secondary level of enrolment in India, which is very unusual for India's level of per capita income. However, gender inequity in education, which is characterised by lack of access to and availability of gender sensitive educational infrastructure, materials and training programmes, as well as a high dropout rate amongst secondary school aged girls, is still a matter of concern and much efforts need to be directed to reduce the gender disparities in education. This is especially the case in skill development. One result of poor access to skilling for girls in India is the low female labour force participation rate, which has been falling for over two decades (Mehrotra and Parida 2017; Mehrotra and Sinha 2017).

The major drivers of skills demand, which include economic growth, expansion of primary and secondary education, urbanisation, demographic changes and global competitiveness call for higher-order competencies and employability skills that can use new technologies and perform complex tasks efficiently. The education system in India has not done well in responding to society's demands for learning, as learning levels of children completing schooling remain very low (ASER 2014). In addition, there have been enormous challenges of skilling youth. The key obstacles and challenges have been the negative image and low aspirational value of vocational education and training (VET) and the lack of coordinated efforts to integrate VET with general education for meeting the 21st Century skill demand for current and future labour market needs. The current formal education system does not focus on training young people in employability skills[4] that can provide them with employment opportunities.

Determining the supply and demand of skilled manpower in the labour market to bridge the gap between the two is a major challenge. We define skills of three kinds: cognitive ones (reading, writing, and numeracy); employability skills (teamwork, computing skills, and communication skills); and vocational skills (trade or occupation related). Poor quality education and training deny young people employment opportunities as well as the resultant earnings and improved quality of life. The demands of employers, at least in the formal economy are, such that they now expect learners to acquire relevant 21st Century skills (for example, critical thinking, problem solving, and creativity) before entering the workforce (Ertmer and Newby 2013). The main skill development areas for low-skilled employees should, therefore, be generic skills, which include occupational health and safety, and information technology skills, whereas for highly skilled employees, the focus is on productivity and competence-building skill areas (e.g. technical and management skills, entrepreneurship development), and to the extent that they are undertaken at all, green skills. This applies to both manufacturing and service firms (OECD 2013).

This chapter is organised as follows: Section 1 examines India's National Policy on Skill Development 2015. It goes on to discuss the National Skills Qualification Framework (NSQF) which provides the overarching design for the rest of the country in VET. Section 2 discusses the skilling efforts taken by the government that goes into integrating the academic skills with vocational skills. Section 3 reflects on the targets under SDG 4 that discusses vocational education and deliberates on the importance of integrating soft skills and vocational skills into VET in achieving SDG targets. Section 4 discusses the new private sector trainers that have emerged in recent years, on account of government funding of a new institution, the National Skill Development Corporation (NSDC). Section 5 offers some sustainable solutions to address the challenges in skill development, which includes bringing changes in work based skills.

National policy on skill development

The Government of India framed the National Policy for Skill Development and Entrepreneurship 2015 to meet the challenges of skilling at scale with speed, standard (quality) and sustainability. It aims to provide an umbrella framework to all skilling activities and align them to common standards and labour market demands. It also aims to bridge the existing skill gaps, promote industry engagement, operationalise a quality assurance framework, leverage technology and promote apprenticeship training. In the entrepreneurship domain, the policy seeks to promote entrepreneurial culture through advocacy and integration of entrepreneurship education as part of the formal education. The policy encourages companies to spend at least 25 per cent of corporate social responsibility (CSR) funds on skill development, seeks to introduce fee paying model along with skill vouchers, and suggests setting up a credit guarantee fund for skill development to meet the specific needs of the learners.

The non-formal and the informal training sector accounts for almost 90 per cent of the skills training in India, as the skills needs of out-of-school youth, early school leavers, and adults are best addressed by informal sector training providers. According to the National Policy on Skill Development and Entrepreneurship 2015, all formal and non-formal skill training programmes will have to align with the NSQF by December 2018. This is an extremely ambitious agenda, both in its timeline as well as in the assumption that competent vocational trainers would be available to train people as per the National Occupational Standards (NOSs) set by the Sector Skill Councils (SSCs).

SSCs are autonomous bodies, incorporated either as Societies under the Societies Registration Act, 1890 or under Section 25 as Company, under the Company's Act, 1956 with the objective of bringing about necessary connectivity between the education and training providers and industry for development of NOSs and conducting training and assessment of students/trainees (Mehrotra 2016). The process so far has been understandably slow amongst the various stakeholders including SSCs, as there is little understanding about Qualification Packs (QPs) and NOSs. A National Quality Assurance Framework (NQAF) has been developed to improve the consistency of outcomes linked to certification and consequently improve the status of skills training. The QAF for certification and assessment aims at setting minimum standards and providing guidance for effective, valid, reliable, fair and transparent assessment within the context of the NSQF. NOSs developed by the SSCs are examined and reviewed by the National Skills Qualifications Committee (NSQC) and thereafter conferred the status of "National Standards".

Skilling is being increasingly integrated in higher education with community colleges under All India Council for Technical Education (AICTE) and University Grants Commission (UGC) and degree colleges affiliated to universities offering NSQF-aligned[5] vocational courses and bachelor of vocational education (BVoc) degrees. These courses are being aligned to a credit framework to provide horizontal and vertical mobility, which was not available to trainees in technical and vocational education and training (TVET) hitherto. Community colleges have been set up to provide aspirants with opportunities to avail of higher education and to bring them at par with appropriate NSQF levels through bridge courses. Community colleges are located to facilitate easy access to underprivileged students and such colleges could either be established as affiliated colleges of universities or as entirely autonomous institutions. Community colleges serve as a crucial point of access to higher education, especially for those who otherwise would not be able to go for it because of several reasons. There are 248 community colleges and 187 BVoc degree institutions approved by the University Grants Commission (UGC) for offering skill based vocational courses. The UGC has set a target of covering 37,500 learners in 500 institutions between 2014–15 and 2018–19 in community colleges.

Aligning skilling efforts to sustainable development: new framework and new institutions

Development cannot be sustainable from a jobs and labour market perspective unless non-agricultural jobs grow in India. In the fastest growing large economy in the world, jobs will grow, but since with GDP growth the product and technology mix will also diversify, it is critical that the labour force is not only educated but also vocationally trained. India is one of the youngest nations in the world, with more than 54 per cent of the total population below 25 years of age (MSD & E 2015). The share of youth in total population will be around 32 per cent in 2030. The government projects the labour force to increase by 88 to 113 million people between 2010 and 2020, mainly through the entrance of the young into the labour force who tend to be better educated. Mehrotra and Parida (2017) consider this estimate to be much too high for new entrants, since the Government of India seems to believe that the rate of increase of new entrants to the labour force will be same as in the very unusual period of 1999–2000 to 2004–05, when 12 million joined the labour force every year: never before nor ever since has such a large increase materialised. In fact, the rate of increase, as estimated by Mehrotra and Parida (2017) should be no more than 2–3 million per annum between 2011–12 and 2019–20, and the government's Labour Bureau Annual Surveys (2011–12 to 2015–6) have proven their estimate to be correct, as only 2.5 million have been joining the labour force per annum since 2011–12.

Formal VET delivery systems tend to be largely school-based and driven by a rigid supply-side curriculum and rote learning methods. In most of the cases, linkages of schools with the Industry, necessary for providing on-the-job training and specialised training was lacking, which generally resulted in lack of adequate practical skills required by the employers. To promote lifelong learning, the government is now promoting skill development programmes outside schools.

There are 21 central government ministries that offer skill development courses through various schemes and programmes, which are being brought onto the NSQF platform, but the problems of coordination across ministries of central government still remains as there are different norms with regard to the eligibility criteria, duration of training, learning outcomes[6] and monitoring and tracking mechanism. Government is introducing new regulations, additional compliance requirements and a range of programmes that require an appropriate response from the VET providers and industry. The actions of government are driving changes in the knowledge and skill requirements of most industry sectors. Most of the schemes and projects of VET, however, aims at achieving certain numerical targets of number of youth trained, and not the aspirations of individuals or labour market needs. It results in beneficiaries dropping out of the vocational courses or not benefiting appropriately from the training. A high participation rate in educational programmes along with the motivation of individuals, as well as subsequent utilisation of the acquired skills in working life can be expected only if educational activities are designed in a way that they meet not only the needs of the labour market but also of individual participants (Pilz 2016).

A problem that all South Asian TVET systems, including India face is the lack of articulation between lower and higher level TVET institutions (Mehrotra 2016a). Schools have not been able to meet the needs of highly skilled workers, even in advanced countries, as opportunities for specialised and hi-tech training are very few because of lack of industries around the schools and also the syllabi are too broad to meet the requirements for handling advanced and new technologies (Mehrotra 2012). Integration of long separated tracks of academic and vocational education is taking place under the NSQF. Since the introduction of the NSQF, vocational subjects have been introduced from secondary stage (Grades 9 and 10) in most of the states/union territories for the first time in India's history. It was earlier available only at the senior/higher secondary level (Grades 11 and 12). The curriculum is oriented to measure the amount of the knowledge and skills of learners through outcome based or competency based education and training. The learning outcomes are aligned to nationally recognised occupational standards, which encompasses the cognitive and vocational skills. The qualifications obtained in schools, as well as in ITIs are now being linked to formal educational qualification at appropriate level through learning outcomes and suitable bridge courses for providing academic equivalence and vertical mobility. The existing vocational courses in ITIs and Polytechnics are being aligned to the emerging competencies in the market and the requirements of the NSQF.

Towards achieving the TVET goal and targets of the SDGs

The Target 4.3 of SDG 2030 calls upon nations to ensure access to women and men to affordable quality technical, vocational and tertiary education, including University. Similarly, the Target 4.4 exhorts nations to substantially increase the number of youth and adults who have relevant skills, including technical and vocational skills, for employment, decent jobs and entrepreneurship. Despite significant improvements in increasing primary school enrolment in India, such improvements have not necessarily been followed by an equivalent transition to secondary education, vocational training, non-formal education or entry into the labour market, especially for girls and young women. The number of young people joining the labour force in India every year is presently roughly 5 million, but expected to increase sharply to 12 million per annum by the year 2030. Therefore, the number to be skilled has to increase accordingly. Greater awareness on the importance of TVET in addressing skill needs of the youth and adults is to be generated to meet target 4.4 of SDG. In addition, indicators for measuring the success of the TVET programmes in terms of placement and entrepreneurial growth will have to be developed to meet the global agenda of linking TVET with job market and entrepreneurial activities.

Capacity development programmes to promote life-long learning and sustainable development through VET are needed for translating SDG Goal 4 into action and for achieving the specific targets of equitable, inclusive and quality education. UNESCO's recommendations concerning TVET provides for an integrated and holistic approach to promoting education and training that develops a broad spectrum of knowledge, skills and competencies for work and life. Sustainable economic growth will pave the way for societies to create the conditions that allow people to have quality jobs. The SDG 4 targets for 2030 call for ensuring the completion of primary and secondary education, and guaranteeing equal access to opportunities for access to quality technical and vocational education for everyone. VET, therefore, should aim at ensuring substantial increase in the number of youth and adults who have relevant skills, including technical and vocational skills for employment, decent jobs and entrepreneurship. It should aim at eliminating gender disparities and ensure equal access to all levels of education and vocational training for the vulnerable, including persons with disabilities, indigenous peoples and children in vulnerable situations. Introduction of VET programmes that integrate various kinds of soft skills and vocational skills with skills for environmental responsibility (e.g. waste management), economic responsibility (e.g. financial accountability), and social responsibility (e.g. gender neutrality, dignity of labour and health) will have to be introduced to promote quality VET at all levels.

Private sector participation to meet skill demands of the workplace

A radical change in the skill development landscape is taking place in India with the involvement of private players and a paradigm shift from fully public funded to private funded programmes under the NSQF. The 12th Five Year Plan (2012–2017) document observes that the skill development programmes in the past are run mainly by the government, with insufficient connection with market demand. It has called for an enabling framework that would attract private investment in VET through Public-Private Partnership (PPP). Involving the private sector in VET has for decades been a successful part of the training systems of many countries. For example, the VET system in Germany is characterised by much higher proportion of youth participation, intensity of private participation and a basis in legislation (Mehrotra et al. 2014).

To foster public-private partnerships, the government of India has set up institutional capacity in the form of the NSDC and Sector Skill Councils (SSCs). These have spawned private vocational training providers (VTPs) or training service providers (TSPs) on a for-profit business model (Government of India 2013). NSDC, which came into existence only in 2010, has facilitated the setup of 2,856 skill development centres through its 203 training partners in the private sector, including 1148 mobile training units which are operating in 350 districts (covering 27 states and 4 union territories) or around half of India's 641 districts. These mobile units consist of fully equipped classrooms on wheels with laptops/tablets powered by solar panels to provide technology enhanced training in geographically diverse or remote areas. Around 14,00,844 people have been trained. The NSDC also operates a scholarship to encourage poor youth to take up vocational training.

The National Skill Development Agency (NSDA), now a part of the newly formed Ministry of Skill Development and Entrepreneurship, was created in June 2013 to coordinate and harmonise skill development efforts across various stakeholders. The Ministry works primarily through the NSDA, National Skill Development Corporation (NSDC), and the Directorate of Training (erstwhile Directorate General of Employment and Training of Ministry of Labour and Employment). The role of the new Ministry involves coordinating and evolving skill development activities, mapping of existing skills and certification, and developing industry-institute linkages, among others. The government is entering into partnerships with private players in these high growth sectors to promote innovative approaches in skill development.

The problem with the NSDC-funded VTPs is that they have mostly provided training for 3–4 months to each trainee (i.e. 300 hours or so), and then expect that they will find stable jobs in the organised sector of the economy. While the numbers trained under this scheme have been large, but because of lack of industry experience, the quality of training has been poor, and even more worrying, as it has not been driven necessarily by the demands of industry. This form of short-term training has neither improved the employability of youth trained nor met the needs of industry (see an expert group report on the website of Ministry of Skill Development and Entrepreneurship, www.skilldevelopment.gov.in/report-SSC.html).

The SDG 8 aims to promote economic growth, full and productive employment and decent work for all. But to ensure trainees usable employability skills in a supply-driven, government-financed TVET system (which is appropriate characterisation of India's TVET), greater autonomy would have to be given to VET Institutions to design their own programmes and use flexible delivery models, with the involvement of business and industry. The direct involvement of industry will have many benefits. There is a need to focus on structuring, organising, and sequencing information to facilitate optimal processing, active involvement of the learners in the learning process and meta-cognitive training in the skill development programmes so that the learners can get significant exposure of the workplace related skills. Training quality can be enhanced by making provisions for developing well-trained teachers and instructors with pedagogical skills and experience from the world of work. The integration of ICT and technology-mediated teaching and learning into training provision can also contribute to quality delivery of skills. Training for high-quality skills is also closely linked to the building of strong, professional management and leadership capacity as well as a suitable quality monitoring and evaluation mechanism to drive the entire system (Afeti and Adubra 2014).

In most developing countries formal VET systems coexist with education and training outside the formal system with diverse socio-economic contexts. In India too, about 90 per cent of the working population is employed in the informal or unorganised sector of the economy. People, especially those who are traditionally burdened with social and economic responsibilities within the household often prefer the informal training, which offers flexibility and participation in terms of entry and the period of training. The unorganised sector contributes more than 60 per cent share to the GDP and people working in the unorganised sector need a system for recognition of prior learning so that they get an opportunity to obtain relevant certification of their competencies acquired through informal learning and enter the formal education system, thus becoming lifelong learners. The non-formal VET system is fragmented and largely uncoordinated. Non-government organisations (NGOs) and specialised VET institutions are offering short duration vocational courses, without proper curriculum and adequate training of trainers. A very large number of workers in the informal/unorganised sector have acquired skills through experience or other non-formal learning channels. However, because of lack of formal certification, they are unable to properly market their services. Those who are traditionally burdened with social responsibilities within the household, often prefer non-formal training, which offers "flexibility in terms of entry and period of training" and also enable them to "earn while they learn" (Mehrotra and Sacheti 2009). However, the "technical" skills imparted to youth through the system of informal vocational training does not provide them the "life-long learning" opportunity which is necessary to bring about necessary behavioural or attitudinal changes and to make them aware of their social rights. They may wish to study part-time or at a flexible pace; their home and/or workplace may be away from the learning centre, so distance learning options may be attractive.

Addressing challenges of sustainable development through changes in work based skills

Work-based learning encompasses a diversity of arrangements, including apprenticeships, on-the-job training, internships and work placements that form part of formal vocational qualifications. Managed effectively, it delivers benefits for all participants and contributes to better labour market and economic outcomes (OECD 2014). Work experience is a critical component of preparing youth for transition to the world of work. The discourses of "learning in the workplace" (Marsick and Watkins 1990), "work based learning" (Boud and Solomon 2001) and "informal learning" (Garrick 1998) all promote learning that takes place at and through work and learning unmediated by educational institutions or practitioners (Chappell

2003). Potential benefits for youth who participate in work experiences include 1) gaining career readiness skills including the "employability skills" that employers look for in entry level workers, 2) increasing one's knowledge of specific occupational skills and workplace settings, 3) establishing a work history and connections with employers that can aid in future job searches, and 4) developing an understanding of different occupations in order to make informed career choices.

However, of all registered enterprises in India only 16 per cent were providing in-firm enterprise-based training in 2009 (according to a World Bank survey). By 2014 that share had risen to 36 per cent of firms. But that means that two-thirds of firms are not providing in-house or in-firm training to their staff. In countries that had successful industrial policies (e.g. in East and South east Asia, see Mehrotra 2016a), and in which manufacturing accounts for a much higher share of employment and output than in India, the share of firms that provide in-firm training is much higher.

Critical to ensure recognition of prior learning

Half the workforce of 490 million is either illiterate or has primary or less education. Adults with limited formal education can re-enter education by validating the competences they have acquired through work. This requires that India will have to put in place mechanisms for Recognition of Prior Learning (RPL), which are not in place today. This requires that 3–4 month long courses are offered to those who are already in the workforce, though had earlier dropped out without any formal certification. They may be lacking foundational cognitive skills, and RPL must ensure that this gap in their education is filled. Second, RPL courses should ensure that the soft skills or transferable (or soft) skills that they would never have had the opportunity to be trained in are imparted to them (e.g. computing skills, team work, communication skills) – depending upon their field of work. Finally, they should be given a chance to upgrade their vocational skills. This combination can constitute a course of 3–4 months that should entitle them to a RPL certificate.

This will have particular relevance to potential migrants with skills and qualifications formally and informally to enable them to migrate, within the country or even abroad. SDG Target 4.6 calls upon all youth and substantial proportion of adults to achieve literacy and numeracy. Non-formal education programmes, often provided through youth and community based organisations in India, facilitates the learning of knowledge and skills, especially for employment.

Market demands for sustainable products and services, adopting to new sustainable practices and developing the competence of employees in new and emerging areas for green economy will bring about necessary changes in VET provisions. Greening the curriculum, which refers to the infusion of environmental and sustainability perspectives into the curriculum at all stages could help students to understand environmental science and related social issues to make well-reasoned and ethically appropriate environmental decisions across different areas at workplace. The demands of green products and services, energy efficient building, meeting renewable energy targets, waste management, water management and emission control requirements will have an overall impact on business activities and skill development ecosystem. Green job profiles should form the basis on which new curricula and new teaching methods should be built. Old curricula should be reviewed and re-oriented to promote green economy. The government should develop a robust framework and guidelines for education, with a focus on learning outcomes, so as to achieve the objectives of equity with sustainable development.

Generic skills, which apply across a variety of jobs and life context, are important in all aspects of life. These are skills that employers expect workers to have from day one. These include communication skills, interpersonal skills, decision making skills, and lifelong learning skills. One promising approach is to integrate these soft skills with vocational training so that these skills are acquired in meaningful practical contexts (OECD 2014). The National Policy on Skill Development and Entrepreneurship 2015 provides directives to include basic modules of computer literacy, finance, language and generic skills like etiquette, appreciating gender diversity in workplace, building positive health attitudes and social and life skills in skill development programmes so as to enable youth to be employable and market ready. The curriculum should be so designed as to develop skills of the levels and quality acceptable to the employing agencies; the acid test of effectiveness of the curriculum will lie in the employability of the learner. Increasing the employability of people will help them to get entry-level jobs, innovate, and adopt new technologies. It will promote labour adaptability to changing skill needs, new tasks and job roles, improve productivity, and labour mobility in search of new avenues and opportunities. Increased attention to improving participation rates of young people, particularly marginalised youth, is needed to ensure that they acquire the knowledge, capacities, skills and ethical values needed to fulfil their role as agents of development, good governance, social inclusion, tolerance and peace. However, gender disparities in non-formal training do exist. According to the 68th round of NSSO, nearly 1.6 per cent of males in rural areas compared to 0.9 per cent of females and in urban areas, nearly 5 per cent of males compared to 3.3 per cent of females received formal vocational training. The situation is complicated by the fact that half the workforce of 490 million is either illiterate or has primary or less education. Another 16 per cent of the workforce has only 8 years of education, which means the number of adults that need vocational, cognitive and non-cognitive skills has to expand, if these youth are to become employable in the non-agricultural workforce. The Target 4.5 of SDG 2030 exhorts countries to eliminate gender disparities in education and ensure quality vocational training for youth. The only way forward for this to happen rapidly is through the recognition of prior learning (RPL) on a vast scale. Recognition of Prior Learning is a process of certifying pre-existing skills and knowledge, used in many Organisation for Economic Cooperation and Development (OECD) countries to make the skills of prospective and current students visible to both education and training institutions and employers (OECD 2014). It encourages an individual to return to education through the certification of relevant skills, and associated course exemptions. It is, therefore, important that training providers should offer RPL as part of the range of services offered to adults (OECD 2014). Some efforts in this direction have been made but quality of RPL efforts will need to improve. The NSDA has launched pilots on RPL in four sectors – agriculture, domestic work, health care and gems and jewellery. A separate pilot for the construction sector has also been initiated by the Ministry of Skill Development and Entrepreneurship. However, clarity in the role and functions of the various stakeholders is needed for greater acceptance and impact of RPL. Effective implementation of RPL will help to promote transition for further and supplementary education and training.

Conclusion

India is one of the fastest growing economies in the world, but its growth can only be sustainable if it has the skills to drive it forward. By 2030, substantial increase in the number of youth and adults who have relevant skills, including technical and vocational skills, will be required for employment, decent jobs and entrepreneurship. The long term relationship between industrial and sustainable development for meeting economic, social and environmental goals can be achieved through partnerships between various government and private agencies. It will require training of youth in different content and new skills through formal and non-formal VET programmes with curriculum designed to suit the requirements for developing skills for sustainability. The creation of the national skills qualifications framework with level descriptors and clearly defined national occupational standards and benchmarks will lead to quality assurance in both the formal and informal training sector. General awareness about sustainability issues and the generic skills that may be applied across all occupations needs to be improved for ensuring engagement of all the stakeholders. The implementation of an integrated system of formal, non-formal and informal VET sectors still remains a challenge in India, and incorporating the concept of lifelong learning and environmental sustainability would require a comprehensive conceptual framework to promote industry engagement in green skills and economic growth through effective implementation of VET programmes.

Notes

1 The official labour force participation rate for men, which measures the proportion of the total male population in the labour force, stood at 55.6 per cent in 2011–12, unchanged from its level in 2004–5. For women, already scarcely represented in India's labour market, the labour market participation in the same period dropped from 29.4 per cent to 22.5 per cent.
2 Sectoral skill gap based on a nationally or sectoral representative sample of a rigorous nature do not exist in India. That requires that the National Sample Survey Organization begin to conduct quenquennial surveys assessing skill gaps. Without such regular surveys, there is no possibility of a Labour Market Information System emerging in India.
3 The National Youth Policy 2014 has defined 'youth' as persons in the age-group of 15–29 years.
4 Employability skills are also sometimes referred to as generic skills, capabilities or key competencies. Employers consider that employability skills are as important as job-specific

or technical skills. There are two facets to employability skills: generic skills (skills that apply across a variety of jobs and life contexts) and personal attributes (loyalty, enthusiasm, motivation and sense of humour). Generic skills are also known by other names, such as key skills, core skills, essential skills, key competencies (widely used in Australia, Germany, United Kingdom, European Union and OECD countries) and transferable skills.

5 The NSQF consists of 10 levels, with level 1 representing the lowest and level 10 the highest level of complexity. It provides an opportunity for enhancing the quality assurance and recognition of skills gained through formal, non-formal and informal learning. As per the NSQF implementation schedule, after the third anniversary date of the notification of the NSQF (i.e. after 27th Dec 2016), government funding would not be available for any training/ educational programme/ course that is not NSQF compliant. All accredited training providers would need to comply with this requirement of the NSQF, failure to do which would lead to their de-listing by the NSDA or the concerned Ministry.

6 Learning outcomes are defined in the European Qualifications Framework (EQF) as 'statements of what a learner knows, understands and is able to do on completion of a learning process, which are defined as knowledge, skills and competences'.

References

Afeti, Goerge and Ayélé Léa Adubra. 2014. *Skilling Africa: The Paradigm Shift to Technical and Vocational Skills Development*. Available at: www.adeanet.org/en/system/files/adea_tvsd_paradigm_shift_paper.pdf [Accessed September 22, 2016].

ASER. 2014. *Annual Status of Education (Rural) Report 2014*. New Delhi: ASER Centre. Available at: http://img.asercentre.org/docs/Publications/ASER%20Reports/ASER%202014/fullaser2014mainreport_1 [Accessed September 22, 2016].

Boud, D. and Solomon N. (eds.). 2001. *Work-based Learning: A New Higher Education?* Buckingham: Society for Research into Higher Education/Open University Press.

Chappell, C. 2003. "Researching Vocational Education and Training: Where to from here?" *Journal of Vocational Education and Training*, 55(1): 21–32.

Ertmer, P.A. and Newby, T.J. 2013. Behaviorism, Cognitivism, "Constructivism: Comparing Critical Features from an Instructional Design Perspective." *Performance Improvement Quarterly*, 6(4): 50–72.

Garrick, J. 1998. *Informal Learning in the Workplace: Unmasking Human Resource Development*. London: Routledge. doi: 10.1177/103841119903700212.

Government of India. 2013. *Twelfth Five Year Plan 2012–2017*. New Delhi: Planning Commission.

Marsick, V.J. and Watkins, K.E. 1990. *Informal and Incidental Learning in the Workplace*. London: Routledge.

Mehrotra, Santosh. (ed.). 2014. *India's Skills Challenge: Reforming Vocational Education and Training to Harness the Demographic Dividend*. New Delhi: Oxford University Press.

———. 2016a. "Technical and Vocational Education in Asia: What can South Asia Learn from East/ South East Asia?" *The Indian Journal of Labour Economics*, 59(4): 529–552.

———. 2016b. "What has the SDG4 Brought to India's Education and Training Transformation?" *NORRAG News*, 54: 61–62. Available at: www.norrag.org/fileadmin/Full%20Versions/NN54.pdf.

Mehrotra, Santosh, Gandhi, A., Sahoo, B.K. 2013. "Estimating the Skill Gap on a Realistic Basis for 2022." *IAMR Occasional Paper 1/2013*. New Delhi: Institute of Applied Manpower Research (National Institute of Labour Economics Research).

Mehrotra, Santosh, Raman, R., Kumra, N., Kalaiyarasan, Röß D. 2014. "Vocational Education and Training Reform in India: Business Needs in India and Lessons to be learned from Germany." *Working Paper*. Bertelsmann Stiftung, p. 60.

Mehrotra, S. and Parida, J. 2017. "Why the Female Labour Force Participation is Falling in India?" *World Development,* 98(C): 360–380.

Mehrotra, S. and Sinha, S. 2017, "Explaining falling Female Labour Participation in a Period of High Growth." *Economic and Political Weekly,* 52(39).

Mehrotra, V.S. 2012. "Integrating Academic and Vocational Education: Making the Link through National Vocational Education Qualifications Framework." *COMOSA Journal of Open Schooling,* 3(1): 30–48.

Mehrotra, V.S. and Sacheti, A.K. 2009. "Integrating TVET with Open and Distance Learning: Taking Skills Training to the Doorstep." In Maclean, R. and Wilson, D. eds., *International Handbook of Education for the Changing World of Work: Bridging Academic and Vocational Learning.* Netherlands: Springer.

MoL&E. 2009. *National Skill Development Policy.* New Delhi: Ministry of Labour & Employment, Government of India. Available at: http://msde.gov.in/assets/images/NationalSkill Development PolicyMar09.pdf [Accessed September 22, 2016].

MSDE. 2015. *National Policy for Skill Development and Entrepreneurship 2015.* New Delhi: Ministry of Skill Development and Entrepreneurship, Government of India. Available at: www.skilldevelopment.gov.in/assets/images/Skill%20India/policy%20booklet%20 Finalpdf [Accessed September 22, 2016].

———. 2016. *Expert Group Report on the Rationalization of Sector Skills Councils.* New Delhi: Government of India. Available at: http://msde.gov.in/report-ssc.html [Accessed 15, 2016].

NSSO. 2015. *NSS Report No. 566: Status of Education and Vocational Training in India (July 2011- June 2012).* New Delhi: National Sample Survey Office, Ministry of Statistics and Programme Implementation.

OECD. 2013. *Skills Development and Training in SMEs: Local Economic and Employment Development (LEED).* Paris: OECD Publishing. http://dx.doi.org/10.1787/9789264169425-en.

———. 2014. *Skills beyond School: Synthesis Report. OECD Reviews of Vocational Education and Training.* Paris: Organisation for Economic Co-operation and Development Publishing.

Pilz, Matthias. 2016. "A View from the Outside: India's School-to-work Transition Challenge: Strengths and Weakness." In *India: Preparation for the World of Work: Education System and School to Work Transition.* Koln: Springer.

U-DISE. 2010. *State Report Cards 2009–10: Elementary Education in India – Where do we stand?* New Delhi: NUEPA.

UN Habitat. 2013. *State of the Urban Youth, India 2012: Employment, Livelihood, Skills.* Mumbai: IRIS Knowledge Foundation.

PART IV
Health, nutrition and food security

6
ACHIEVING SUSTAINABLE DEVELOPMENT GOAL 3 IN THE INDIAN CONTEXT

The policy-action incoherence

T. Sundararaman and Alok Ranjan

On the face of it the Sustainable Development Goals (SDGs) have only one goal dedicated to health – namely goal 3 and even this is articulated in a broad sweep: "Promoting healthy lives and wellbeing at all ages for all". However, all the other 16 goals also have a bearing on health and some of them are proximate and direct social determinants of health, as powerful in their influence as anything that the health sector contributes. These include goal 1 on poverty, goal 2 on food security and nutrition, goal 4 on education, goal 5 on gender equity and goal 6 on water and sanitation. All the other SDGs also have an effect on health, mostly indirectly, and some like goal 7 on cities have components or targets under them with more direct influence on health outcomes.

These Sustainable Development Goals have been criticised (The Economist 2015; Tom Paulson 2015) for being aspirational rather than guiding immediate action, and with too many targets without a clear focus. However others have argued that having been made with greater participation, they are much more representative of what nations want and they serve an important purpose – to articulate a political consensus around the values that inform the kind of growth and human development that the people of the world want and need (Jason Hickel 2015).

Whereas Millennium Development Goals (MDGs) would only call for a reduction of poverty as defined by a low set numerical threshold, the SDGs explicitly call for a reduction of poverty in all its forms plus access to social protection measures as affirmative actions that the poorest and most marginalised need. More interesting, it calls for wealth to be shared and income inequality to decrease. In almost all its goals SDGs reiterate the need to address inequity. Taken together the 17 goals and 169 targets of the SDGs creates a vision which demands an alternative growth and development strategy to the one we have, one which is more democratic and people-centred and sustainable.

It would be unrealistic to expect that the adoption of the SDGs implies that the case has been won for an alternative model of development and growth. Past experience teaches us that even the best laid of policies get filtered by the actions of global institutions and national governments, so that what is implemented in its name could be quite far removed from the original intention as articulated in policy statements.

The adoption of SDGs by India is no different. India's experience in social policy, especially in health policy is similar. Public health in India has been characterised over the years by a sharp and growing divergence between policy statements and actual implementation (Sen 2012). Not surprisingly, the recent pronouncements of the government of India to achieving universal health coverage (UHC) has also been viewed with considerable skepticism within the Indian public health community (Singh 2013).

Nevertheless, both the academic community and civil society that has been arguing for health as a right could benefit from taking the SDGs seriously and using it as an advocacy tool for influencing both direction and magnitude of change. The Indian government is a signatory to the implementation of the Sustainable Development Goals and has set up mechanisms to oversee its implementation. SDGs have an international and national legitimacy which provides scope for civil society, not only to monitor and insist on implementation, but also to push for the requisite changes in policy that would be essential for progress towards these goals.

In this chapter we limit ourselves to the SDG on health and trace the changing discourse around health care as reflected in global policy statements and how global health institutions as well as Indian policy and implementation has responded to these. This chapter sets out examples of a regular and repetitive divergence between policy pronouncements and actual direction of policy action which it characterises as a "structured policy incoherence". It then explores the factors that lead to this. It calls for reducing this incoherence and generating a better public understanding of how health policy is shaped, which in turn somewhere down the line could lead to the alternate policies that we need and which are the underlying spirit of the SDG.

The SDG on health

In contrast to the MDG health goals, that limited itself to maternal mortality, child mortality and disease specific mortality of three diseases, the SDG health goals call for "wellbeing for all at all ages". This is much more in the spirit of the Health for All Declaration of Alma Ata that called for the attainment of the highest possible level of health as the most important social goal.

But the health goals of the MDGs are not lost to the SDGs. They appear as the first three targets – clearly putting forth the continuity with the MDGs, and underlining their continued relevance. Though reduced in hierarchy from goal to target – they now call for achievement of a fixed numerical value, instead of a proportional reduction over baselines, which for Maternal Mortality ratio (MMR) is pegged at 70 per 0.1 million live births, for neonatal mortality is 12 per 1000 live births and under 5 mortality is 25 deaths per 1000 live births. In the more detailed list of indicators that goes with each target, even still-birth rates are included.

In target 3, the call is for ending the epidemic of the three diseases that MDGs had selectively flagged – Acquired Immunodeficiency Syndrome (AIDS), tuberculosis and malaria – but to this list neglected tropical diseases[1] are added. Further the target, in a clear effort to be comprehensive, adds on – "combat hepatitis, waterborne diseases and other communicable diseases". In India, the first three diseases that were flagged in the MDGs represents approximately 6 per cent of morbidities, but redefined thus to include all communicable diseases it is 28 per cent of all morbidities that come under the scope of action (John et al. 2011).

Targets 4 to 6 make the efforts to expand the scope of the health goal to include all diseases that contribute significantly to the global burden on diseases. Target 4 is a very comprehensive definition for non-communicable diseases (NCDs) which defines the targets as premature mortality and then calls for a one-thirds reduction – similar to the proportional reduction target as was used for maternal and child mortality in the MDGs. Target 5 brings in the challenge of addressing all forms of substance abuse. Target 6 gets more ambitious and demands halving of deaths because of injuries and road traffic accidents, and that too by 2020 which was then just five years away. This is as compared to 2030 for all other targets. By 2020 even a plateauing of deaths because of injuries would have been challenging. In target 9, no numerical target is indicated, since there are no reliable baseline measures and not even an agreed upon methodology of how it can be measured.

The third category are process targets, calling for what are essentially measures of health sector performance, as compared to the other indicators so far, which are all measures of health outcomes. Target 7, relates to reproductive health and emphasises its integration with national strategies, underlining the fact that under the MDGs it had been largely a vertical programme. Universal Health Coverage comes in as target 8, a modest place for what was during the run-up discussions considered as one of the options to articulate the overall health goal. The target description of UHC, specifies financial protection as well as access to medicines and health services as distinct objectives.

Finally, in the fourth and last category we have four means of implementation targets which spell out four measures, some of which would be clearly unpalatable to corporates and many global institutions. These include implementation of the Framework Convention on Tobacco Control, the implementation of the TRIPS flexibilities and Doha declaration, and the emphasis on expanding the health workforce.

The policy incoherence in financing

These SDG-3 targets described come as a surprise for two reasons. Firstly, many of them run counter to the ideological directions of health sector reforms advocated by global health institutions. Secondly even as goals become more ambitious, the commitment to increasing financing is muted, and in practice there is little or no increase in public financing. While most nations struggled to find investments to meet the MDG goals, the SDG requires a much higher investment and that too almost immediately. There was a UN summit held in Addis Ababa in June 2016 on financing which should have come up with the financing required, but the summit concluded without any clear commitments (Center of Concern 2016; McArthur 2016). No major international development agency or global health institution has held out any promise of making any significant increase in financing (Center of Concern 2016; McArthur 2016). On the other hand a lot of discussion also went into how health systems should be designed to withstand shocks because of reduced public financing, a discussion that happens often under the sobriquet of resilient health care systems (Thomson et al. 2014).

In India this incoherence with respect to policy pronouncements on financing is now well established. In 2009 to 2011, there was a lot of talk of the 12th Five-year Plan becoming the health plan and the prime minister made an announcement to that effect from the ramparts of the Red Fort as part of his Independence Day speech. Then there was a high-level expert group set up by the Planning Commission to recommend towards achievement of universal health coverage. There were solemn discussions whether 2.5 per cent of the GDP would be an adequate public spend or it should rise even higher. The draft of a new health policy that was put up on website for public discussion on 31 December 2014 stated:

> The National Health Policy (NHP) accepts and endorses the understanding that a full achievement of the goals and principles as defined would require an increased public health expenditure to 4 to 5% of the GDP. However, given that the NHP, 2002 target of 2% was not met, and taking into account the financial capacity of the country to provide this amount and the institutional capacity to utilise the increased funding in an effective manner, this policy proposes a potentially achievable target of raising public health expenditure to 2.5 per cent of the GDP. It also notes that 40% of this would need to come from Central expenditures. At current prices, a target of 2.5% of GDP translates to Rs. 3800 per capita, representing an almost four-fold increase in five years. Thus, a longer time frame may be appropriate to even reach this modest target.

The final health policy that was adopted in 2017 commits to the more limited 2.5 per cent of GDP target and that too by 2025 (Government of India 2017).

But throughout this period from the adoption of the 12th Plan, to the declaration of the National Health Policy there has been no increase in budgetary allocations in real terms and in one year it even fell (Sundararaman et al. 2016). This failure to increase budgetary allocations is justified in policy in one set of articulations – small base of tax payers, responsibility of the state government, poor absorption etc. (Niti Aayog 2015; Sethi 2015). Simultaneously in another set of policy articulations a case is made out to increase public expenditure on health (Government of India 2017). This is what we term a structured policy incoherence.

The policy incoherence in access

Achieving SDG 3 clearly requires expanding the basket of services that are publicly provided and financed. Every policy document of this period – the 12th Five Year Plan on health, the National Health Policy and the budget speech of the finance ministers all call for such an expansion. Universal health coverage by definition also calls for making a more comprehensive list of health care services available. However, in practice, there has been very limited movement beyond the traditional reproductive and child health (RCH) area, partly because of funds and partly because of the focus imposed by development partners and their funding. But it is also because selective health care as a concept is so embedded in the institutions of health governance and health provisioning that it is not easy to change. Instead a new range of terms now enter the discourse – targeted universal care or progressive universalism (Gwatkin and Ergo 2011) and defining essential health packages, based on computations of cost-effectiveness for different interventions. Whereas targeted universal care is an easy to spot oxymoron, progressive universalism posits that we start with a very selective essential health package that is universally accessed and as funds come in, the package is gradually extended. The line of argument is that since resources are limited, the equity imperative is best met by a few essential services that achieve universal coverage. However the essential health package is defined so narrowly, that for the majority of health care needs the majority of the population would have no access except the unregulated and unaffordable private provider. The rate of progressive expansion is also unstated. As a result, on the ground, public facilities are unable to cater to many health care needs and thereby lose their credibility.

An alternative interpretation to progressive universalism would have been to make all services completely free/subsidised to the poor and then slowly expand to include higher income groups. This approach is criticised on two grounds. Firstly that a health care approach that targets only the poor would be poor (quality) health care. This is not necessarily true, but due to both poor investment and poor governance, it is often the case. And secondly that means testing to identify the poor is never satisfactory. This is true and the solution would lie in making access to public services universal and without any restrictions, and by self-selection – many who can afford it would seek private care. As public investment grows, the capacity of public facilities can expand to provide care to larger sections of the population.

Policy incoherence in strategy to achieve UHC

The other incoherence is as regards the strategy to achieve universal health coverage, one of the main targets under SDG-3. Again, the official position of the World Bank, of the World Health Organization, of USAID and of different national committees is that they are not imposing any particular road map of how to reach universal health coverage, nor are they insisting on a shift from public provisioning based systems to purchasing care from private providers using insurance or public-private partnerships. How important is this clarification is evident from an open letter from World Bank and WHO to the UN Statistical Commission that finalises the indicators for measuring progress towards UHC disagreeing with the then definition of the indicator and asking for a change which is neutral between public provisioning and insurance based purchasing of care.

However, in this period, in India the World Bank team is closely associated and indeed along with the German Aid Agency, the sole technical support for the roll out of a nationwide insurance programme and the public funded health insurance programmes of many states. This World Bank intervention replaces an earlier generation of reforms in the nineties that were called "state health systems development programmes". These programmes were most active in the nineties and they led to the introduction of user fees, restriction of public health systems to a very selective and sub-critical package of care, and wide-spread efforts at public-private partnership (PPP) along with funding for infrastructure. The resulting growth of the private sector is now seen as the justification for shifting government to a role in purchasing care from private through insurance means – in preference to its own provisioning. The bank's private finance wing – the International Finance Corporation has India as the second largest destination for investments in health – and much of it is to building models of health care around the commercial private sector (Provost and Kennard 2016). Agencies like Gates Foundation and USAID are also engaged in efforts to shift government from provision of primary care to purchasing it (CHMI 2016). The bank's series of monographs reviewing progress towards Universal Health Coverage also largely equates the introduction of insurance based models as the introduction of universal coverage (Cotlear et al. 2015).

The government's National Health Policy 2017 also reflects this incoherence. In its paragraph 3.3 of the policy, it reserves all primary health care provision for the public provider and then states:

> The policy envisages strategic purchase of secondary and tertiary care services as a short-term measure.... The order of preference for strategic purchase would be public sector hospitals followed by not-for profit private sector and then commercial private sector in underserved areas, based on availability of services of acceptable and defined quality criteria. In the long run, the policy envisages to have fully equipped and functional public-sector hospitals in these areas to meet secondary and tertiary health care needs of population, especially the poorest and marginalised. Public facilities would remain the focal point in the healthcare delivery system and services in the public health facilities would be expanded from current levels.

However, a few pages later in para 13.6 the National Health Policy states that strategic purchasing is for directing areas for investment for the commercial health sector – and goes on to list opportunities for investments in insurance, fully functional primary health care facilities, operationalising such health and wellness centres to provide a larger package of comprehensive primary health care across the country, and specific gaps in public services that would include diagnostics services, ambulance services, safe blood services, rehabilitative services, palliative services, mental health care, telemedicine services, managing of rare and orphan diseases.

Since 2008, though funds for strengthening public services have grown modestly, government investments in insurance has increased. Most studies indicate that for a number of operational and design reasons, these public funded health insurance schemes and public-private partnerships fail to provide financial protection or increase access to health care.

Policy incoherence in the means of implementation

The SDG 3 also has four targets that relate to the means of implementation. Of these the second target 3.b or target 11 calls for research and development and providing access to medicines in line with the Doha Declaration on the Trade Related Aspects of Intellectual Property Rights (TRIPS) agreement, and then goes onto emphasising "the right of developing countries to use to the full the provisions in the Agreement on Trade-Related Aspects of Intellectual Property Rights regarding flexibilities to protect public health, and in particular, provide access to medicines for all". The US has consistently resisted such widespread use of these flexibilities which include compulsory licensing beyond a narrowly defined public health emergency. India is a signatory to the Doha declaration, and indeed, this is a provision that enables the Indian pharmaceutical industry to emerge as the pharmacy of the developing world. It is key, not only to affordable drugs for India – but for the entire developing world.

But the ink on the signature adopting the SDGs has not yet dried when the government announces a new policy on patents that fails to recognise this, and even worse is the instance of US business interests which gives an informal assurance that it will not use these flexibilities.

On the ground, the country which could once boast of making almost all the pharmaceuticals it needs, has become increasingly dependent on imports of active pharmaceutical ingredients (API) or bulk drug and there is a loss of national capacity in this area (Jha 2007). Compounding this is a takeover of Indian pharmaceutical companies by multinationals. The domestic sector of the Indian pharmaceutical industry so necessary for our drug security has weakened, as they cannot enter the new drugs segment because of the change in the patent regime nor are they able to export to developed nations since a number of non-tariff barriers come in the way. Such are the problems that in recent time, to quote DG Shah, Indian Pharmaceutical Alliance (IPA) director "over 25,000 crores (250,000 million) of Indian capital for pharma-manufacture has gone to the USA".

The incoherence on target 3.c, another means of implementation target is similar. The target commits us to an increase in health workforce, implicitly in this context a public health workforce. In practice increases in regular salaried workforce in the public health sector are resisted, and funding for more health workers has stagnated and in most states. There is also a contractualisation of the public health workforce (Kumar et al. 2014). Meanwhile a large number of tax concessions and facilitation provided to private health care, the introduction of publicly financed health insurance programmes and the promotion of medical tourism has all created a favourable climate for the growth of corporate health care industry which in turn leads to an internal brain drain of health professionals from public services and rural areas into the growing corporate segment. Target 3.c also calls for substantial increase in health financing and we noted earlier that public health expenditure stagnates or even as a proportion of GDP in real terms declines (Sundararaman et al. 2016).

As for target 13 (or 3.d) this calls for an adequate public health surveillance capacity. But as of today the integrated disease surveillance programme is limited to the information from the public sector and has a considerable gap in the necessary laboratory support it needs, does not integrate with mortality data and has a poor use of information (IDSP 2015).

The only target on which the government of India has made significant progress is target 10 which refers to the implementation of the Framework Convention on tobacco control.

Measurement as re-interpretation of SDGs

Recent presentations of SDG-3 have tended to draw a visual image of SDG3 where the 13 targets are aggregated into 3 groups or pillars of four targets each and UHC, which is one of the targets, is now amplified into an all-embracing ceiling. The UHC target is seen as an adequate umbrella to subsume all SDG-3 related targets within itself and provide at one level a comprehensive understanding of how to achieve all the SDG3 targets and therefore of how to measure progress towards SDG3. In parallel to re-interpreting SDG-3 as almost synonymous with UHC are the trends that were discussed earlier for re-interpretation of UHC as financial protection, preferably by insurance for a limited set of services.

This re-interpretation of SDGs could justify limiting measurement of progress to a few convenient indicators. It could be argued that only those indicators should be selected where there are ongoing public health interventions, and where data is already available. Since data sources are more developed only where there are vertical selective health care services in operation, this too would justify limiting measurement and intervention to such areas. Measurement of progress along select indicators would in turn justify and amplify action on these intervention, and attenuate the need for action on other areas.

Such a re-interpretation, if it happens, would not be for the first time in global public health. The international political consensus at Alma Ata was for a comprehensive primary health care. But this was successfully re-invented as selective primary health care in the mid-1980s and early 1990s, at the initiative of agencies like Rockefeller Foundation, UNICEF, World Bank and USAID, with WHO having to trundle along (Sengupta 2013). It is not very different now – though we now have more global health institutions and the Gates Foundation also – playing similar roles.

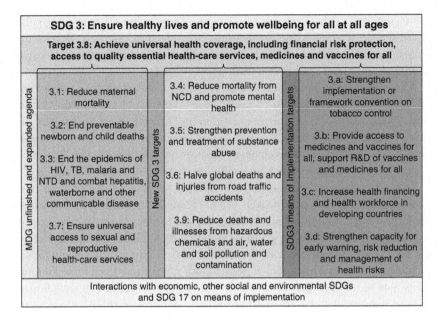

FIGURE 6.1 Sustainable development Goal 3 and its targets

Source: Presentation by Dr Ties Boerma, Head, Department of Measurement and Statistics, WHO, May 2016, in WHO-MOHFW–organised meeting on SDGs

The underlying logic of what appears confusing and chaotic in policy articulations and practice could become much more explicable when we trace out the contestations on directions of reform and the different stakeholder interests at work. We need to examine whether the various policy incoherences described represent the unstable and ad hoc balance between the democratically articulated need for people in developing nations to have better health outcomes and the economic policies and efforts at shaping of health markets to suit the requirements of monopoly capital, both national and international.

The incoherence between economic and health policies

One must therefore seek to understand the direction of reforms not on its technical soundness (which has never been established), but in the changing economic and political contexts.

The first wave of health sector reforms that took place in India in the early nineties was part of structural adjustment that the Washington Consensus had mandated (Williamson 1993). This had led to limitation of government health services to a few selective interventions, with the understanding that the market would take care of the others (McPake and Mills 2000), the introduction of user fees, and decreased government investment, sharp decreases in the workforce and initiation of a wave of public-private partnerships (LaFond 1995; Leighton 1996; Russell and Gilson 1997). These reforms have been held responsible for weakening public health systems which became unable to perform effectively even on select vertical programmes, and which in turn resulted in a shift to use of private providers and a resulting huge rise in costs of care (Nandraj et al. 2001).

These structural adjustment reforms and consequences were not confined only to India. They were a feature of almost every third world nation (McPake and Mills 2000). There were important exceptions in Thailand, Brazil, Sri Lanka, Cuba, Costa Rica etc. Within India, Tamil Nadu and Kerala stayed out of these externally funded state health systems development reforms and continued to invest in public health systems throughout the nineties though nowhere near the scale required.

In the last decade the rising costs of care led to renewed demands for more public expenditure. But policymakers had to reconcile the demand for investing in public health systems with the continuing demand for increasing private participation in health care. With the global recession of 2008, global and national capital accelerated its engagement with the health sector as an area for investment and sought a greater proportion of such public health expenditure to be routed through the private sector. The period since 2008 has also seen a lot of hot money flowing in from industrialised nations and foreign direct investment (FDI) inflows in the health sector are estimated at over a few billion dollars annually. Corporate health care now seeks an entry into government funded primary health care as well and there are policy statements in the 12th Plan and the National Health Policy that provide space for such intervention (Planning Commission 2011).

Public financing in health is low at 1 per cent of GDP – but in absolute terms it is still large, close to Rs.1,000,000,000,000 (about $16 billion US) per year. Corporate India smells an opportunity here. Increasing public financing to 2.5 per cent of the GDP makes perfect sense to corporate India, if this increase can also be routed through corporates, who stand by willing to harness the rewards, without any risk, if contracted for delivering all health care services. This 2.5 per cent would be a tremendous stimulus to health care industry, which is one of the most robust growth engines within the services sector and which makes its contribution to India's relatively high economic growth rates. It is therefore not an expansion of public services that this set of stakeholders requires but a transfer of existing public services into private delivery mechanisms. In secondary and tertiary care, corporate hospitals have already established their space. The push now is for a major corporate entry into primary health care provision. Agencies like IFC, USAID and Gates Foundation (CHMI 2016) actively promote this, though there is little evidence over 20 years of reform and repeated efforts at public-private partnerships that this works (Chakravarthi et al. 2017). If we understand such a transfer to corporate hands as the unwritten terms for increasing public financing we can perhaps make better sense of the incoherence between oft-repeated statements of increasing financing and the failure to do so.

In the emerging architecture of recent decades, the role of the state changes from a limited provider of health care, leaving the rest to the markets to an interventionist state that re-organises the nature of production and re-sets the terms of the market so that monopoly capital, especially global financial capital can find entry and profit. Free market choice amongst competing private providers, with public providers taking care of the residual poor and some services which are in the nature of public goods is the prevailing architecture. This is now to be replaced by institutional choice, where choice is exercised by the state or intermediary institutions on behalf of the consumer, with state acting as purchaser on their behalf and consumer choice limited to choosing between a very limited number of intermediaries and providers who are now bound together in cartels as health management organisations. The USA is one of the best examples of this, and this is the model that despite all protestations and warnings we seem to be following. But in the USA, health care costs have reached almost 19 per cent of USA's GDP and yet one in four Americans has no coverage whatsoever or are seriously under-insured. This would be a dangerous path for the rest of the world to follow.

Conclusion

If we understand the structured policy incoherence around SDG3 and the mismatch between policy pronouncements and practice as reflective of different stakeholder pressures, then it becomes important for that constituency whose goal is equitable health outcomes to stay engaged with the debate and not abandon the field to health care industry and global health institutions that are dependent on corporate or US funding. SDG 3 can be achieved only if government's economic and industrial policies, at least with reference to the health sector, are subordinate to achieving health policy goals, and this needs to be articulated by civil society and the public health community. Otherwise like what happened with reinterpreting primary health care as selective primary health care, the SDG-3 can be re-interpreted as one narrow understanding of UHC which could then be used to further privatisation and corporate profits.

Given the unevenness in resources and influence that health activist groups, independent academics, and representatives of developing nations command, one has to strategise how such reinterpretation is resisted and how the discourse on SDGs is shaped to push for an equitable and sustainable development path. Such a strategy for SDG 3 would include insisting that measurement of progress should be against every one of the 13 targets under SDGs, (including for example such process targets as implementing the Doha declaration) and creating a public understanding on what a road map to move towards each of these SDG targets would look like and what are the barriers and the ways forward.

The SDGs represent a hard-won global political consensus that provides an opportunity and a space for building a better public understanding of health policy. Windows of opportunity to strengthen public services and claim health and health care as a human right would arise in each nation as they did in India in the early eighties and again in 2004–05. But when the opportunity arises there must be the capacity for making use of it to advance towards a holistic understanding of health which the SDG 3, like the Alma Ata declaration before it, represent.

Note

1 The currently used global definition of neglected tropical diseases is insufficient to add in Indian concerns like leprosy.

References

Center of Concern. 2016. *"Inaction agenda" from Addis Ababa Conference, criticized by CSOs.* Available at: www.coc.org/coc/%E2%80%9Cinaction-agenda%E2%80%9D-addis-ababa-conference-criticized-csos [Accessed December 3, 2017].
Chakravarthi, I., Roy, B., Mukhopadhyay, I., and Barria, S. 2017. "Investing in Health: Healthcare Industry in India." *Economic and Political Weekly*, 52(45).
CHMI. 2016. *Contracting of Selected District Healthcare Facilities in Uttar Pradesh.* The Center for Health Market Innovations. Available at: http://healthmarketinnovations.org/program/contracting-selected-district-healthcare-facilities-uttar-pradesh [Accessed August 12, 2017].
Cotlear, D., Nagpal, S., Smith, O., Tandon, A., and Cortez, R. 2015. *Going Universal: How 24 Developing Countries are implementing Universal Health Coverage from the Bottom up.* World Bank Publications.
Government of India. 2017. *National Health Policy, 2017.* New Delhi: Ministry of Health and Family Welfare.
Gwatkin, D.R. and Ergo, A. 2011. "Universal Health Coverage: Friend or Foe of Health Equity?" *Lancet*, 377(9784): 2160–2161. doi: 10.1016/S0140-6736(10)62058-2.
The Economist. 2015. *The 169 Commandments: The Proposed Sustainable Development Goals would be worse than useless.* Available at: www.economist.com/news/leaders/21647286-proposed-sustainable-development-goals-would-be-worse-useless-169-commandments [Accessed October 29, 2017].
IDSP. 2015. *Joint Monitoring Mission Report Integrated Disease Surveillance Programme 2015.* Available at: http://idsp.nic.in/index1.php?lang=1&level=2&sublinkid=5967&lid=3913&font=Increase [Accessed December 3, 2017].
Jason, Hickel. 2015. *The Problem with Saving the World.* Available at: http://jacobinmag.com/2015/08/global-poverty-climate-change-sdgs/ [Accessed October 29, 2017].
Jha, R. 2007. "Options for Indian Pharmaceutical Industry in the Changing Environment." *Economic and Political Weekly*, 42(39): 3958–3967.
John, T.J., Dandona, L., Sharma, V.P., and Kakkar, M. 2011. "Continuing Challenge of Infectious Diseases in India." *The Lancet*, 377(9761): 252–269.
Kumar, P., Khan, A.M., Inder, D., and Anu. 2014. "Provider's Constraints and Difficulties in Primary Health Care System." *Journal of Family Medicine and Primary Care*, 3(2): 102. doi: 10.4103/2249–4863.137610.
LaFond, A. 1995. *Sustaining Primary Health Care.* London: Earthscan.
Leighton, C. 1996. "Strategies for Achieving Health Financing Reform in Africa." *World Development*, 24(9): 1511–1525. doi: 10.1016/0305-750X(96)00058-7.
McArthur, J. 2016. "What Happened at the Addis Financing for Development Conference?" *Brookings.* Available at: www.brookings.edu/blog/up-front/2015/07/21/what-happened-at-the-addis-financing-for-development-conference/ [Accessed December 3, 2017].
McPake, B. and Mills, A. 2000. "What can we learn from International Comparisons of Health Systems and Health System Reform?" *Bulletin of the World Health Organization*, 78(6): 811–820.

Nandraj, S., Muraleedharan, V.R., Baru, R.V., Qadeer, I., and Priya, R. 2001. *Private Health Sector in India*. Mumbai, Madras, Delhi, India: Centre for Enquiry into Health and Allied Themes/Indian Institute of Technology/Jawaharlal Nehru University.

Niti Aayog. 2015. *Increasing Financial Resources for Health*. Available at: www.mygov.in/sites/default/files/master_image/Working%20paper%202-forTheme9-Increasing%20financial%20resources_0.pdf.

Planning Commission. 2011. *High Level Expert Group Report on Universal Health Coverage for India*. Working Paper id: 4646. eSocialSciences. Available at: https://ideas.repec.org/p/ess/wpaper/id4646.html [Accessed September 10, 2016].

Provost, C. and Kennard, M. 2016. "The World Bank is Supposed to Help the Poor. So Why is it Bankrolling Oligarchs?" *Mother Jones*. Available at: www.motherjones.com/politics/2016/03/world-bank-ifc-fund-luxury-hotels/ [Accessed October 30, 2017].

Russell, S. and Gilson, L. 1997. "User Fee Policies to Promote Health Service Access for the Poor: A Wolf in Sheep's Clothing?" *International Journal of Health Services*, 27(2): 359–379. doi: 10.2190/YHL2-F0EA-JW1M-DHEJ.

Sen, G. 2012. "Universal Health Coverage in India." *Economic & Political Weekly*, 47(8): 45.

Sengupta, A. 2013. "Universal Health Coverage: Beyond Rhetoric." *Municipal Services Project, Occasional Paper No*. Available at: www.phmovement.org/en/node/9160 [Accessed September 6, 2016].

Sethi, N. 2015. "NITI Aayog against Free Health Care, Bats for More Private Sector Role." *Business Standard India*. Available at: www.business-standard.com/article/economy-policy/niti-aayog-against-free-health-care-bats-for-more-private-sector-role-115082500061_1.html [Accessed December 3, 2017].

Singh, Z. 2013. "Universal Health Coverage for India by 2022: A Utopia or Reality?" *Indian Journal of Community Medicine: Official Publication of Indian Association of Preventive & Social Medicine*, 38(2): 70–73. doi: 10.4103/0970–0218.112430.

Sundararaman, T., Mukhopadhyay, I., and Muraleedharan, V.R. 2016. "No Respite for Public Health." *Economic & Political Weekly*, 51(16): 39.

Thomson, S., Figueras, J., Evetovits, T., Jowett, M., Mladovsky, P., Maresso, A., Cylus, J., Karanikolos, and Kluge, H. 2014. *Economic Crisis, Health Systems and Health in Europe: Impact and Implications for Policy*. WHO Regional Office for Europe.

Tom Paulson. 2015. "Gates Foundation Rallies the Troops to Attack UN Development Goals." *Humanosphere*. Available at: www.humanosphere.org/world-politics/2015/05/gates-foundation-rallies-the-troops-to-attack-un-development-goals/ [Accessed October 29, 2017].

Williamson, J. 1993. "Democracy and the 'Washington Consensus'." *World Development*, 21(8): 1329–1336.

7

PUBLIC HEALTH POLICIES

Generating revenues or relief?

Imrana Qadeer

The crisis in public health in India is linked to two major realities: one, the persistence of unacceptable levels of absolute and relative poverty; and two, a drastic shift in official approach towards a business model of health care. Both are related to the nature of development in India and its welfare policies. In the 1930s and 1940s the National Congress through its National Planning Committee, the trade unions, Gandhi himself, and the industrialists carved out value-loaded plans for India. Despite their differences in strategies to address poverty, all these broad plans proposed free basic universal health care, recognising the linkage between poverty and ill-health (Qadeer 2008). These exercises were used by both the colonial government's Health Survey and Planning Committee (Government of India 1946), and independent India's Five Year Plans to develop the health sector. In 1978, the country became a signatory to the WHO's Alma Ata declaration on comprehensive primary health care as a part of the newly emerging democracies demanding their space in the global arena. The declaration underlined that health was a human right and the responsibility of the state, rooted in welfare and social and economic progress, where people participated in planning. Primary health care was defined as the following:

> Essential health care based on practical, scientifically sound and socially acceptable methods and technology, made universally accessible to individuals and families in the community through their full participation, and at a cost that the community and country can afford to maintain at every stage of their development in the spirit of self-reliance and self-determination. It forms an integral part both of the country's health system, of which it is the central function and main focus, and of the overall social and economic development of the community. It is the first level of contact of individuals, the family and community with the national health system, bringing health

care as close as possible to where people live and work, and constitutes the first element of a continuing health care process.

(WHO 1978)

Health and nutrition thus, were always at the core of welfare that anchored Indian democracy. Inclusive development and universality of welfare is nothing new; it is part of a Constitutional commitment to expand the domain of basic rights by gradually including the key directive principles into it. Now, however, the Twelfth Plan has redefined its task:

> Work towards the long term objective of establishing a system of Universal Health Coverage (UHC) in the country. This means that each individual would have assured access to a defined essential range of medicines and treatment at an affordable price, which should be entirely free for a large percentage of the population. Inevitably, the list of assured services will have to be limited by budgetary constraints.
>
> *(Government of India 2012)*

This objective – by imposing limits on assured services and the notion of affordability – indicates that the state's commitment is shrinking. This shift is an outcome of changes – big and small – over the past three decades. It is different from the experience of many other middle income countries like Brazil and South Africa that have undertaken health sector reforms (HSR), but have managed to protect or revive their basic health service sectors and also invested higher proportions of their GDP in it. The issue then is not of right or wrong policies but one of perspectives. Political commitments may change in intensity and spheres over time within a given framework, but when the value framework itself changes then fissures of discontinuity appear. India is under one such shift and the present redefining of the health policy objective is reflective of the country's attempt to get integrated into a fast expanding neo-liberal global market through structural reforms, where health like many other services is a driver of revenue and wealth. Today the idea of a mixed economy is not considered viable. The challenge is no more to identify past mistakes and flaws to improve planning, but to withdraw from the earlier commitment of protecting the vulnerable and including them in the development process through a transparent systemic transformation. The state has become a true *steward* of the medical market that is accepted as the ideal distributor of welfare.

Interestingly, despite drastic cuts in financial allocations in welfare, promotion of markets, and rejection of participatory planning at all levels – for political reasons – the language of *universality, inclusion* and *assurance* for the disadvantaged, especially the very poor, continues and promotes targeting in official programmes. Above all, universal health care is projected as a new and unique idea. Thus, the country seems to be escalating, at war footing, the dismantling of its infrastructure for basic public health services, through partnership with the private sector and disinvesting in public health and food security systems. This chapter examines the shift in policy perspective through a review of four aspects of the Indian experience of health planning: (a) the intensification of health sector reforms in India and its gradual consolidation in the 21st century, (b) medical industry's perspective regarding the health sector, (c) the National Health Accounts estimation of expenditures for better planning and its official use, and (d) contribution of the National Institute for Transformation of India (NITI Aayog) to the HSR. The directions emerging out of these are then analysed for their value for the less privileged and the wisdom of the present policy, and the implications are considered.

Some of the conceptual underpinnings of this chapter need to be underlined at the outset. First, we consider medical care to be a key component and a major tool of public health which, apart from its value for individual patients, helps control diseases and changes their histories when used strategically with adoption of preventive and promotive methods by the health system. Public health is a broader concept than just medical care; it is about providing comprehensive health services. It has been accepted as "a discipline aimed at developing a health system to deliver equitable, appropriate and holistic care to improve the health status of the individual and health indices of the country at an affordable cost" (Government of India 2012, p. 132). Second, in the Indian context, prevention is primarily a socioeconomic challenge of dealing with inequalities (structural injustice) and inequities (distributive injustice), rather than health education and immunisation alone, as is often professed. Thirdly, feeding programmes, that started as short-term initiatives but continued because of failures of long-term policies, must not overshadow the importance of a national food security system. For health, this non-medical input is very critical because of the interdependence of health and nutritional status. To that extent the scope of this chapter is limited as it primarily addresses the growing shift towards individualised medical care away from the comprehensive approach of public health.

Planned reforms of the twenty-first century

The agenda of reforms was formally acknowledged in the 1990s with opening up of tertiary care to private providers, penetration of public sector institutions by private investors, user fee, casualisation of work force, a series of concessions announced for the medical industry promoting its growth, and the popularisation of medical tourism over time. Soon however, several problems, such as rising expenditures, poor and varying quality of care, lack of regulatory mechanisms, costs, and scope of services threw up a host of problems. The user fee could not mobilise sufficient resources nor could private insurances grow given the limited number of buyers who could afford it (Onotai 2008). The much talked about social security net remained a myth as the state stepped in to oversee the smooth expansion of the private sector's growth. What came handy at this point was the concept of UHC that, by its very definition, zeroed in on "essential medical care", protection from catastrophic expenditures, universalisation of medical care at affordable cost, and financial mobilisation through multiple providers rather than holding the state alone responsible for services.[1] The non-medical inputs into health like food, drinking water, environmental sanitation etc. again got side lined.

The Tenth Five Year Plan (2002–2007) referred to the 2002 National Health Policy, which emphasised Primary Health Care for all, and prophesied to revive the public sector by addressing "the increasingly complex situation regarding access to good quality care at affordable costs" (Government of India 2002, p. 82). It proposed to provide

> essential primary health care, emergency lifesaving services, services under the National Disease Control Programmes and the National Family Welfare Programme, totally free of cost to all individuals, and essential health care service to people below poverty line based on their need and not on their ability to pay for the services.
> *(Government of India 2002, p. 83)*

This called for overcoming the funding constraints, strengthening referrals between the three tiers of services, health management and information systems (HMIS), surveillance, district level planning, provision of drugs, horizontal integration of programmes, and skill development and education. The Plan perceived both government and private health services as "paid" social responsibility and commented that

> "Growing commercialisation of health care and medical education over the last two decades has eroded this commitment, adversely affecting the quality of care, trust and the rapport between health care seekers and providers".

Yet the need to build links with private and voluntary sectors was accepted under pressure of the "rising expectations", and "costs of new technologies" (Government of India 2002, p. 82). The document accepts this compulsion without making any distinctions between expectations or needs of different social groups or the relative value of new technologies in the Indian context! It also said that the systems approach is more appropriate, even though "both health care providers and health care seekers still feel more comfortable with the one to one relationship with each other than with the health system approach" (Government of India 2002 p. 82). Thus, ignoring that individual patient-provider relationships and provider behaviour constitute critical elements of a health care system, this illogical reason was used for ignoring a system's approach and shift its responsibility on care seekers. The demand for hi-tech personalized care of some, un-mindful of prevention also became a rationale for shifts in planning of public services after acknowledging the problems with commercialisation and hi-tech.

Yet another contradiction is the assertion of importance of the role of health insurance while accepting the risk of cost escalation and market failures. The Plan acknowledged the problems with the private sector as lacking quality, trained personnel, rational standardised treatment, and ethical practices, but professed that collaboration with private providers through contractual and part time appointments of doctors, their participation in national disease control programmes through free supplies of drugs and vaccines for their patients, subsidies to super specialty hospitals etc., gave poor results only because of inadequate monitoring. So the onus to improve public-private-partnerships through greater rationalisation, monitoring, regulation, and better evolved Memorandum of Understanding (MoUs), was placed on the state.

The Tenth Plan also proposed developing a National Health Accounts (NHA) for tracking resource flow into all components of health sector to rationalise and stream line this critical aspect of planning. It pointed out the high levels of out-of-pocket expenditure (OOPE) for both in-patient and out-patient care, in spite of the former being primarily from public sector, which despite its much lower costs incurs OOPEs because of the poor availability of drugs in public hospitals. The Plan was critical of externally funded schemes for bringing their own structures and monitoring systems that could not become sustainable. But, convinced of the economic advantages of investing in health, it observed that, "it is essential to quantify the interactions between the health of the population and economy, gauge essential potential benefits of various interventions and ensure adequate investment in chosen priority sectors" (Government of India 2002, p. 140). Clearly then, the push towards privatisation, commercialisation and medicalisation came despite full knowledge of the limitations and pitfalls of these strategies for a stratified iniquitous society; the distinction between need and demand was ignored; and a camouflage of "high expectations of people" was used instead!

The Eleventh Five Year Plan conceded failures in almost all previous commitments to strengthening infrastructure but, in the name of inclusive development, proposed targeting the poor in the time-bound frame of the MDGs. A list of drawbacks was also offered, such as:

- Centralised instead of decentralised and locally relevant planning;
- Institutions based on population norms rather than habitation;
- Fragmented disease specific approach rather than comprehensive health care;
- Inflexible financing and limited scope for innovations;
- Inability to mobilise Ayurveda, Yoga and Naturopathy, Unani, Siddha and Homoeopathy (AYUSH) and Registered Medical Practitioners (RMPs) and other locally available human resources.

But what was not acknowledged was that most of these drawbacks were due to the failure to implement the previous Plans' key recommendations: like strengthening the infrastructure, integration of programmes, monitoring private sector participation, and setting up regulatory systems. The Eleventh Plan, apart from reiterating the previous promises, again emphasised the *decentralisation of services even beyond districts and using locally appropriate strategies.* Using NSSO (1986–2004) it argued that the utilisation of public outpatient and inpatient facilities had declined while there was an increase in utilisation of the private health care in both rural and urban areas, and interpreted the shift as reflecting, "The people's growing lack of trust in the public system" (Government of India 2007, p. 68). Thus, after failing to protect public sector health infrastructure, the planners condemned it without any self-evaluation.

Despite these distortions of the initial public health perspective till the Eleventh Plan, health care at the primary and secondary level was still seen as part of NRHM. Tertiary care and medical education were to be strengthened separately through 6 AIIMS-like institutes and strengthening of existing hospitals and essential drug supply systems. The Plan encouraged the states to raise their investments to 7–8 per cent of state expenditure and to increase competition among providers, creating consumer choices, and ensuring oversight through elected local bodies. Further, it claimed that no amount of pure bio-medical research will be able to find solutions to health issues unless *it addresses upfront the social determinants of health!* Yet it left it to the states to achieve this integration through more resources for welfare sectors (water, housing, nutrition, sanitation, education etc.), and better fiscal management and reprioritisation. The Plan carried forward existing insurance schemes such as employees state insurance, central government health and ex-servicemen contributory health schemes. In addition, it proposed: (a) community based health insurance, "not-for-profit insurance scheme that is aimed primarily at the informal sector and formed on the basis of a collective pooling of health risks and the members participating in its management", with ACCORD, (Action for Community Organisation Rehabilitation and Development), BAIF (Bhartiya Agro Industrial Foundation), Karuna Trust, Self Employed Women's Association (SEWA), and Development of Human Action (DHAN Foundation; (b) schemes to train traditional birth attendants (TBAs) into skilled birth attendants (SBAs); and (c) reserved 65 per cent of the resources allocated to health for NRHM, which was one of the flagship programmes of Government of India. Still, its focus was PPPs (public-private-partnerships) and state funded insurance systems, and setting up diagnostic and therapeutic centres by private players in hospital premises wherever required, with the proposal to give them infrastructure status. This was also the first Plan to project the National Health Account (NHA) data on expenditures on health for the year 2001–02 that showed households account for 72 per cent share of the assessed expenditures. Interestingly, the information was partial as it did not cover the departmental reimbursements to employees for their health expenditures (Government of India 2002), nor the private sector's resource investments despite a growing partnership with it – a matter that we discuss later. The Plan emphasised the necessity of focusing on health outcomes rather than health outlays, including a disaggregated examination by gender, class, caste, etc. to assess their impact on different groups (Government of India 2007, p. 106). This however, has never been done officially.

The Twelfth Five Year Plan was guided by two almost contrary efforts at policymaking: the High Level Expert Group (HLEG) (2011) and the Steering Committee of the Planning Commission (2012). Highly influenced by the latter, it fragmented the system into NHM, UHC (seen as universal medical coverage), tertiary and primary health care (conceived as only the essential primary level care and yet separate from NRHM), and public health! This purposively fragmented vision lost all the strengths of a systemic approach to public sector services and became amenable to private penetration. The state financed insurance systems that were run mostly by the private providers, targeted the very poor, and thus over 70 per cent of the population was left to access the market. Even these insurance services for the poor were limited by the budget constraints and a managed care model. Government funding – which had risen from 0.9 per cent of GDP to 1.3 by 2010 – actually fell down to 1.1 by 2015 despite additional "sin taxes" (taxation of harmful industries, i.e. tobacco and alcohol) and corporate social responsibility funds imposed by the state. At the same time the state revenues shrank as the rich were exempted from appropriate levels of taxation by lowering general direct taxations and raising the indirect taxation, thereby shifting the burden on to the poor.

Inter-sectoral convergence, regulatory mechanisms, quality control, developing data base and research were all religiously repeated without any specific timelines or guidelines. In short, the Twelfth Plan fully committed itself to serve the private and corporate sectors by splitting UHC from tertiary care and NRHM, against all public health rationale, and made funding, "an instrument of reforms and incentive" (Government of India 2012, p. 18). Consequently, the funding for states was made conditional to their higher investments while the CSR funds of the corporate sector were devoid of any concrete conditions about areas of investment. The budget allocation for health sector and the corporate revenue foregone for the year 2017–18 were 350,000,000,000 and 620,000,000,000 respectively reflecting state priorities. Non-medical social determinants were mentioned but no concrete plans offered to strengthen the same. Above all, most of these responsibilities were shifted to the states. The Rashtriya Swasthya Bima Yojana (RSBY) through PPP arrangements was to deliver UHC to protect against "catastrophic expenditure"; its expansion thus became a priority while the funds for basic public sector health infrastructure and its programmes either did not improve or shrank! The state remained responsible for disease control programmes, family welfare, PHC infrastructure, education and training of medical manpower, health information system, monitoring and regulation. But all of these inevitably got undermined thereby creating more space for the private sector.

This undermining of the public sector is reflected in the slow but definite handing over of medical education to the private sector, discontinuation of monitoring systems for nutritional status and Plague surveillance,[2] declining investments in the NRHM (Ghosh and Qadeer 2017), and constant emphasis on partnerships with private providers, even for national disease control programmes such as National Tuberculosis Control Programme (NTCP) (Unger et al. 2010).

This arrangement was perfect for the corporate sector, with rights to retain profits without many risks. It increased corporate access to those uncovered with insurance in an unregulated market, and assured payment from the state for treating the poor. The state thus became both a client and a steward that fragmented even the WHO's framework for UHC and, in its name, provided the impetus to the medical industry to capture the tertiary care market, expand to other levels of medical care and, focus on diagnostics, therapeutics, drugs, and medical instrumentation for its business.

The corporate vision of health sector

The independent researchers of the private sector and the literature emerging from the research organisations of the corporate medical sector reveal a perspective where the business model dominates medical care in the health sector. Even if the corporate organisations delve on what the country's needs are, their main attraction is tertiary care, the emerging medical markets, and adding to the GDP. The discussions are around the drivers of industry in India, how capital can be mobilised for this business, and the government's role in a) supporting the industry and b) taking care of the residual health problems. In contrast to the hesitations and contradictions of the Tenth and Eleventh Plans prior to the complete coming together of the state and corporate vision in the Twelfth Plan, this section explores the confidence of the corporate perspective and its convictions.

Hopes

Despite all the talk by the Twelfth Plan of aligning private sector objectives with national goals wherever partnerships are forged, the perspectives of private sector policies – with minor variations – shows a clear focus on growth and maximisation of profits in the medical industry. The financial institutions, both foreign and domestic, see profitable opportunities in India's health care. The International Finance Corporation (IFC), for example, has a separate portfolio for this industry now, with a commitment of $450 million US (30 per cent of the IFC global investment in medical industry) for India. According to the IFC, "India is a very important market for the IFC and the World Bank group" (Gireesh 2014; Itumalla and Acharyulu 2012). Since 2009 it has funded the Apollo Chain to extend its network to tier II cities and their smaller hospitals to provide "affordable health care" to low income group through cross-subsidisation between them and the high income population (Chakravarthi 2013). Similarly, the McKinsey report for Confederation of Indian Industry (CII) finds "inspiring possibilities" in the Indian health care sector for private sector contribution which was expected to come up with innovative business models, specially a profitable model to penetrate the market of the underserved rural populations (McKinsey 2012). The fourth annual Global Healthcare Private Equity Report of Bain & Company offers equity as an innovation and equates strategic investments of over $1 billion US to "dry powder" for generating profits. It recognises the importance of a strong financial market and the large number of competing health care investors, for the strategic investors "to put their dry powder to work" (Bain & Company 2015). According to this report, investors faced high valuations, inflation fears about the rupee, election uncertainty, and concerns about patent protections and manufacturing quality. Yet, strategic investors remained active, demonstrating continued enthusiasm for the health care delivery segment in India.

> In India, provider activity was tempered relative to 2013; however, the sector remained the most active for PE investment activity in the country. Several deals involved hospital operators: Olympus Capital Asia Investments and India Value Fund Advisors (IVFA), for example, invested $60 million in Aster DM Healthcare, an India-based company that runs hospitals across India and the Middle East. Investments in primary and specialty care continued, spanning primary care/GP clinics and dialysis to aesthetics. Healthcare delivery in India also captured strategic interest, with DaVita HealthCare Partners taking a stake in Express Clinics, a primary and urgent healthcare delivery chain operator based in India, and South African hospital operator Life Healthcare increasing its stake investment in hospital chain Max Healthcare.
>
> Interestingly, companies that have developed cost-effective models for delivering healthcare in India are starting to expand into other emerging markets. For example, India-based hospital operator Manipal Hospitals is building a new tertiary care hospital in Malaysia, which is slated to open in 2015. Narayana Health, an India-based hospital operator backed by J.P. Morgan, Pine Bridge Investments and CDC Group, is building a heart hospital in the Cayman Islands in partnership with the US hospital system Ascension Health.
>
> *(Bain & Company 2015, p. 14)*

The professional consultancies like Bain & Company and Flanders and other private equity associations observed the intense competition among international financing organisations for entering India's medical market and the Indian industrial organisations welcomed it along with the political leaders (KPMG & ASSOCHAM 2011). Thus, it is clear that the interest of the investors is aroused for financial reasons as they see a market not the poor state of health of the majority, as well as a government keen on welcoming them. Chakravarthi (2013), while exploring the medical industry, has shown that even corporates other than the health industry see health care as a big business opportunity. She quotes Bose, the president and CEO of GE:

> India is the first country to have a large number of multinational healthcare providers. There are seven to eight very active MNCs. It opens a whole host of opportunities for us. I see the healthcare sector as one of the biggest opportunities.
>
> *(Bose 2012)*

Drivers of growth and its nature

The strong attraction of capital to this country is seen as rooted in its high demand for medical care against inadequate supplies, rising disposable incomes from 14 per cent to 26 per cent over 2008–9 to 2014–15 of the expanding middle class

(KPMG & ASSOCHAM 2011), demographic shifts, rising life style diseases (non-communicable), and the double burden of disease itself is seen as a driver of growth of the private sector. Added to this is India's weak regulatory mechanisms and its pro-market and pro-industry policies that promote FDI in the health care sector, especially medical tourism. Reduction in direct taxation with rise of indirect taxes, income tax exemptions for 5 years in case of rural hospitals, custom duty exemptions, higher depreciation on equipment, promotion of private insurance agencies, exemptions on health insurance, social health insurance schemes, land allocations, and human resource training (that makes personnel available to all infrastructure), promise of infrastructure development, relatively lower cost of setting up establishments, and possibility of lower cost of service packages, offered corporations increasing affordability by making economy of scales possible (McKinsey & Company 2012).

Indian business firms seem to be very optimistic with the success of the medical model of services. The estimate of the medical market has risen from $45 billion US in 2008 to $158 billion US by 2017 and $280 billion US by 2020 (Vidhya and Savitha 2015). This is said to be due to the fact that 74 per cent of hospitals and 40 per cent of hospital beds are in the private sector that secured Rs.124135.7 million of FDI over 2000–14 (ibid.). According to India Brand Equity Foundation (IBEF) this increase over 2008–20 is expected to remain at a compound annual growth rate (CAGR) of 16 per cent. It is reflected in the constant rise of private sector hospitals over the government hospitals. While the latter declined in proportion from 34 to 19 per cent, the top tier hospital and the nursing homes in the private sector have increased in proportion from 26 to 40 and 26 to 30 per cent respectively; only the mid-tier hospitals declined in proportion from 14 to 11 per cent over the same period (IBEF 2015, p. 10). The compound annual growth rate (CAGR) of government hospitals and hospital beds in India was 27.2 and 4.8 per cent over 2009–12. This varied heavily over states and was also often unreported. In contrast, it is argued that the CAGR of the private sector has increased and will continue to do so over time because of public-private spending. The Flanders report points out that, according to ASSOCHAM, medical tourism will double over 2011–15 ($980 million to $1.8 billion US), the per cent of foreign investment increased from 2.2 per cent to 2.7 per cent over 2009–10 and will continue to do so (IBEF 2015; Flanders 2015).

Advice to the government

The 2002 initiative of McKinsey and Confederation of Indian Industries (CII), on guiding India in health planning, continues to inspire the private providers to enter clinical care at all levels of services and expand. Beginning from tertiary care the corporates visualise a descent into secondary and primary levels (CII & McKinsey 2002). In 2012 they suggested that the government dialogues with the private sector and acts as payer, not provider, of medical care. The private sector could then retain a CAGR of 7–10 per cent with economy of scale (not possible with high levels of OOPE) and, fill the infrastructure gap. Also, using the rationale of standard of care and concern for the poor, the focus on non-communicable diseases (NCDs) for clinical care at the secondary and primary levels remained the agenda in 2012 as well (McKinsey 2012). The promoters of the private sector feared the insecurities of the macro-economic situation, threat of regulatory mechanism, corruption and slow official procedures, and expected that the state should remove these constraints for investors (Flanders 2015). However, they consistently pushed for standards derived from the developed nations with very different macro-economic and social situations. Thus, they advised India to catch up in training more doctors, nurses and technicians, and create doctors and beds, rather than promote paramedics and peripheral health centres. The comparisons were with the US and Japan when India, had one bed for 1050 population and 0.7 doctors, and 1.5 nurses for a 1,000 population, lower than the WHO average prescription of 2.5 doctors and nurses for a population of one thousand (Deloitte 2015). Federation of Indian Chambers of Commerce and Industry and KPMG (a partnership of Indian firms and a part of KPMG International), exclusively focused on employment (private sector, if supported, could create 7.5 million direct job opportunities). They argued that the private sector can open opportunities and contribute where there is increasing demand for tertiary care. The sector requires not only more nurses, doctors, technicians for diagnostic labs (biochemical and radiology), but also other indirect providers such as general administrative staff, business office manager, managed care administrative staff, housekeeping and security, medical receptionists, medical secretaries, transcribers, medical record keepers etc. Other areas of contribution were exports, productivity and entrepreneurship. India was advised to grab the opportunity to raising its investment share in GDP to two per cent over the next ten years from one per cent at present (KPMG & FICCI 2015). Others see a potential of 4 million jobs and more within the country, fulfilling the need to expand capacity and improve standards, but the emphasis is on its rising contribution to the GDP which could go up to 6–7 per cent according to McKinsey (Alam and Khader 2015). The shortage of beds, inadequate use of information technology, poor patient tracking and monitoring, and poor hospital and health information management systems (HIMS), are emphasised by these advisers pushing for modernisation and high tech services to attain international standards in a country that has as yet not been able to provide basic services. Their advice is promoting PPPs like the SRL Diagnostics in Himachal, which runs 24 district diagnostic labs with the state government as well as the use of IT, telemedicine and bio-technology industry. The industry also welcomed the government's decision to raise the FDI limit in the medical insurance business to 49 per cent (Deloitte 2015).

This focus on modern hospitals and infrastructure shows the mismatch between their vision of modern care and the alternate modern system needed by the country! The real challenges of public health facing the country are unattractive for the medical industry and hence left to the state; the exception being vaccines and telemedicine that are in the interest of biotech and IT firms. In short the industry recommendations are for strengthening the medical care system on the lines of developed nation's technological framework, inevitably for an elite market. These suggestions do not help in thinking of alternatives to address inequity in health services but push for straight-jacketed, ill-suited models of care prevalent in the developed countries.

The capital

It is argued that

> India's health care sector is capital-intensive, with long gestation and payback periods for new projects. Land and infrastructure costs account for 60–70 per cent of the capital expenditure for hospitals. Further, the industry also requires capital for upgrade/maintenance/replacement of medical equipment and expansion. Availability of capital at a reasonable cost remains a hurdle.
>
> *(Flanders 2015)*

It is worthwhile exploring, even if very often the land for private institutions comes from the government at throw away prices, where does the rest of the money come from?

The FDI in hospital and diagnostic sector, though rising over 2000–2013 to 25 per cent of the total FDI in health care ($2,514.13 US), is only a small share and can best be regarded as complementary to, and not as a substitute for, the private domestic investment. Yet it is a critical source which has acquired power to influence directions by greater control in institutional management and policy directions as a participant in provisioning. The Indian government permitted hundred per cent FDI in the hospital sector since 2000. This made it possible to purchase assets beyond 50 per cent to acquire rights in management of the establishment. Sixty per cent of the approved FDI owners now hold more than 49 per cent of the stakes in hospitals. The free flow of this capital is managed by the Reserve Bank of India (RBI), Foreign Investment Promotion Board (FIPB) and through acquisition (that primarily indicates cross border merger or joint ventures). The proportion of FDI flows are of the order of 74 per cent through RBI, 6 per cent via FIPB and 20 per cent via acquisition (Hooda 2015). Hooda also points out that FDIs are routed through countries where double taxation avoidance agreements exist for India (Singapore, Mauritius, South Korea and UAE, which act as tax havens). These are mostly the corporate multi-specialty hospitals where the foreign investors have voting rights and hence opportunities for controlling the direction of development of institutions, often in contradiction to national needs.

Over 2013–14, the beneficiaries of FDI have been Maharashtra, Karnataka, Uttar Pradesh, Haryana, Delhi, Tamil Nadu, and Punjab, i.e. the richer urban regions. The corporate groups involved are Fortis Global, its subsidiary Escorts, Apollo, Kanishka Hospital, Hrudayalaya Private Ltd., Columbia Asia, Nova Medical Centre, Kokilaben Dhirubhai Ambani Hospital, Aditya Birla Foundation, Wockhardt group etc. This growing corporate sector has overtime marginalised and over-shadowed the traditional small private providers (individuals and nursing homes) or, absorbed them as their franchises (Hooda 2015). An important trend is that the enterprise surveys have shown a decline of small providers from the earlier 1.3 million while the establishment hospitals have risen over 2000–2007 to 40,000 (Mukhopadhyay 2019).

Along with the private equity as a part of the FDI, domestic private equity firms, commercial loans, and individual investors constitute an important source of funding. From 29 investments from business houses in 2011 it rose to 71 in 2013 of which Max India, Life Cell India, Hind Computer Ltd (HCL), Hind Latex Ltd (HLL) are some. More have joined since then and help expand capital investments primarily through exits, mergers and initial public offerings (IPO). Exits helped to expand capital three and four-folds the initial investment, as in the case of Apax and Avenue Capital firms that invested in Apollo hospitals and Medanta between 2006 and 2007 respectively to 2013. The critical sources of private equity funds are endowments, insurance companies, pension funds, and trusts needing long term investments (Girija Kalyani and Vijya Laxmi 2015; Hooda 2015). For 2015, $2.9 billion US home-grown equity funds are reported from off shore and domestic investors. This sum has varied over the years with 2007 reporting the highest at $9 billion and $4 billion (US) more is expected next year (Sarkar 2016).

Inevitably, assistance at lower rates of returns attracts the private sector to Viability Gap Funding (VGF) and annuity funds, both from the Indian government. The government offers annuity funds for long term investment with conditionalities for return that vary from project to project (Infrastructure Today. 2012). The Ministry of Finance, defines VGF as a onetime government lending by the state which could be as high as 40 per cent of the total cost of the project.[3] The state has developed especial institutions to support and ease the flow of these funds such as the India Infrastructure Finance Corporation Limited[4] (IIFCL) and the India infrastructure Project development Funds[5] (IIPDF). According to its annual report 2014–15, the former disbursed a total of Rs.31,110 million over 2014–15 as direct lending to all infrastructure projects, as against Rs.25,880 million during 2013–14 (IIFCL 2015). The disbursement by IIPDF could not be compared as the available review was only for 2011–2012 with Rs.25.6 million (Nanda 2015).

These figures no doubt are not very high or systematically collected but they surely indicate that the private sector is borrowing and advancing resources to create infrastructure. Government loans for this specific purpose are a part of this borrowing and not accounted as health expenditure by NHA! Lastly, the much talked of corporate social responsibility (CSR) funds are actually managed by the corporates themselves to run a wide variety of small projects ranging from educational, preventive, clinical, or community based services to disabled, adolescents, treatment camps etc. which barely adds up to anything substantive (Vidhya and Savitha 2015). As pointed out earlier, the state does not even demand that the funds be invested in services specified within its priorities, nor is CSR accounted for as private health expenditure.

This hard push for mobilising finances from within the country and abroad, capturing tertiary medical care, percolating to secondary levels, and not accounting for the capital that is mobilised for private health infrastructure (as FDI, government loans, and domestic equity funds), is well protected by the national strategy to promote PPPs. The notions of integration, universality, primary health care, national health programmes, and social determinants of health become verbal assurances for populist consumption while, at best, UHC helps narrow down the basic services to some ill-defined essential clinical care. By adopting the international format for NHA, the 10th Plan appears to be opting for rational planning while the exercise actually focuses upon state expenditures, uses definitions that lack clarity, and avoid looking at expenditures (financial investments) of medical entrepreneurs. This makes its projections amenable to misinterpretation, especially about private expenditure on health. It does not even touch the fast growing finances of the corporate infrastructure and its underlying sources; a critical concern that we explore in the following section.

Biased harnessing of information

To make health planning more rigorous, the government had added to its Census, data from the National Sample Surveys, Central Bureau of Health Intelligence, office of the Registrar General monitoring causes of death, additional agencies including Plague Surveillance Units and National Nutritional Monitoring Bureau, National Family Health Survey (NFHS), District Health Surveys (DHS), and NHA for informed and epidemiologically rational health planning. The district survey constructed a wealth index but never used it to assess differentials in health indicators across social and economic groups. Unlike NSS, its unit data is not available to researchers. Shrinking funds led to closures of plague monitoring from 1990s and Nutrition Monitoring Bureau after 2012. The NHA has produced a second report only after seven years, without much attention to the PPP strategy in vogue. Dismantling of monitoring systems and use of inadequate methodologies has not only led to gaps in information but also made these instruments amenable to misinterpretation in favour of the medical industry. We discuss here the NHA as described by the economic advisor in 2004–05 as:

> An effective tool to support health system governance and decision making by not only capturing financial flows but by also providing information relevant to designing better and more effective health policies. By providing a matrix on the sources and uses of funds for health, the NHA framework facilitates in tracing how resources are mobilised and managed, who pays and how much is paid for healthcare, who provides goods and services, how resources are distributed across services, intermediaries and activities the health system produces etc. . . . The selection of the year 2004–05 has been consciously made so as to have a comprehensive baseline of the quantum of public and private spending and the components of public spending

given the launch of the major public health intervention, the National Rural Health Mission in 2005.

(NHA Cell 2009)

On scrutiny though, the NHA data neither fully captures the "resources mobilised" (expenditure) by the state, nor by their "*private*" counterparts. The current emphasis in planning has been on professional and financial partnership for resource mobilisation since the turn of the century; yet NHA makes no effort to grapple with the private investments in health sector or the state's spending on private sector, both as loans and indirect investments as concessions. It puts together OOPE (expenditure by families), social insurance schemes, and health expenditures paid for by firms, and calls them private expenditure For 2004–05, OOPE was 71.1 per cent and the other two constituted 6.8 per cent of the total health expenditure (THE); the private expenditure thus became 77.9 per cent of THE. The public investment against this was only 19.67 per cent. The catch in NHA 2009 is that

a   Both social insurance schemes and payments for health by firms include public as well as private schemes in NHA accounting and hence, cannot only be private!
b   It did not distinguish between direct expenditure for immediate utility by families, and expenditure for future security (premiums of individuals and financial investments for infrastructure strengthening by the state or the private sector), thus erasing the difference between "consumption" and "investment" of finances.
c   It also did not assess systematically the sources of investments (premiums, public and private entrepreneurial investments) as the matrix in the international accounting system provides space only for state expenditure and OOPE, and ***not*** corporate/private investments in infrastructure.

As a result the real private investment is never revealed. What is presented as private is the consumer expenditure by individual families and firms combined with social insurance! As price of service (OOPE) includes the profits of the investors, and the investment recovered, it can only be a bloated indicator of the actual private expenditure. This methodology has been uncritically accepted by the officials of National Commission on Macroeconomics and Health (Rao 2005) and even the HLEG (Planning Commission 2011, p. 8), that treated OOPE as a part of the health financing mechanism and projected a relatively high percentage of private investment in the health sector as compared to public spending.

Even for OOPE, the accounting system did not identify its flow into public or private institutions – which could be indicative of the state of the two sectors. Nor did it estimate catastrophic OOPE along with total OOPE which is bound to be high given a highly privatised medical system and a growing middle class in India. It is the catastrophic OOPE that is the critical element pushing families into poverty and not total OOPE. High total OOPE then became the rationale behind the policy to promote private partnerships and state led insurance schemes; in this process the focus on differential expenditures for long term strengthening of infrastructure through investments by the families as premiums and, public, private entrepreneurs, and corporate sector got lost. Hence, firstly only a fraction of the part that goes to public sector can be treated as revenues for health if it is reinvested and secondly, OOPE in the private sector is no reflection of private financial investment in health as there is no way to assess its reinvestments and division of profit.

The actual financial flows, when tracked, show an immense business potential for corporate medical company credits (domestic private equity, direct institutional investments, FDI, venture capital and government loans) that flow in and out of the hospital and diagnostics sector, to help build services, pay back the loans and shares, as well as make entrepreneurial profits out of the investments that start to pay back in about 7–8 years of setting up a hospital (Itumalla and Acharyulu 2012; Alam and Khader 2015). It is this profit that makes the medical market attractive for investors and entrepreneurs; a big chunk of it goes into their pockets. This is the expected blast mentioned as benefit of the *dry powder of the strategic investors* by the 4th Global Equity Report (Bain & Company 2015). The real private capital expenditure of the entrepreneur can only be a part of this profit and no effort is made to capture its extent.

The NHA in 2009 stated that data on private sector is difficult to acquire, hence it excludes expenditures (investment) of corporate or private business in building health sector infrastructure but today things are different. In the previous section we have looked at the private industry in medical care and found that several government sources such as the Department of Industrial Policy and Promotion (DIPP) of the Commerce Ministry, Centre of Monitoring Indian Economy, Financial Investment Promotion Board (FIPB), Security Exchange Board of India, and the currently set up institutions such as India Infrastructure Finance Corporation (IIFC) and the India infrastructure Project Development Funds (IIPDF) have been active in monitoring and promoting private investments in the medical market. If the corporate self-assessment of an expanded medical market of $160 billion US by 2017 (IBEF 2015) and the references to strategic investors, increasing domestic private equity, emerging domestic health financing firms and corporate groups are true then, private investment/expenditure too should be accounted for. The NHA system could now gauge the capital investment (expenditure) of the private sector for a more realistic accounting with the help of these institutions. The private sector may be under no compulsion to be transparent about its investments but, the state must assess its partner's financial investments in a shared responsibility; it has an obligation to be transparent in its partnerships. Unfortunately this has not happened.

The NHA has after ten years brought out a second report with a changed methodology, more varied and barely comparable with the 2009 document (NHSRC 2016). The categories of "capital" and "current" expenditures are introduced to differentiate between consumption and investment expenditures but capital expenditure is yet not calculated for the private sector. Current health expenditure is analysed by source of financing, health care schemes, providers and functions, yet public and private insurances and large enterprises are clubbed together, thereby confusing sector-wise expenditures. Continuing to respond to the international priorities, NHA 2013–14 is an opportunity lost to assess private capital investments. The flow of state funds into private enterprises are sidelined and OOPE decline to 62.4 per cent of THE, is explained as an outcome of rising social security without mentioning the shrinking proportions of THE as per cent of GDP (1.1 per cent) and rising catastrophic expenditures over time (Selvaraj et al. 2015), or the rising percentage of expenditure on health in total household expenditure (Selvaraj and Karan 2012) along with rising costs of care. These trends together raise serious doubts about the positive impact of social insurance schemes as they are.

The mystery of private financial investment and capital flows through the private medical market thus remains to be unpacked and its true extent unknown!

Transforming health sector without systematic planning

The tension between the Ministry and the Planning Commission was visible in 2012 itself when the Ministry asked for a revision of the chapter on health to align it with the recommendations of the HLEG. It reportedly argued that, under the Twelfth Plan, the government's primary health care function would be limited to essential interventions such as immunisation, antenatal care, and disease-control programmes, leaving clinical services to the private providers through a managed-care model. The government's role would, in effect, diminish from providing health services to managing the net-work (Krishnan Vidya 2012). When the new government took over in 2014, the first thing it did was to debunk planning itself. For a country as large and as complex as India, this was nothing short of a disaster. Though much of the criticism could be valid about the working of the erstwhile Planning Commission, it still had some procedural guidelines, a level of transparency and was a space where the civil society could intervene and raise issues concerning the common people. Its closure closed these doors and, except for the annual policy documents and a scanty web site, there is little access to the thinking process within the government.

The Policy document of 2015 and the annual budget made it clear that the agenda of reforms – undermining of public services and promotion of private medical markets – will only be strengthened. Niti Aayog's first working Paper in 2015, chose to show improvements since the 1990s and pointed out the gaps in outcomes, relating them to state's inability to invest where it should, absence of essential package of services, non-coordination between public, private and non-profit providers, doctor absenteeism, and lack of regulation which leads to poor quality and the inequity that prevails (Niti Aayog 2015a). Its second paper in the series proposed measures to encourage higher state spending on health by providing matching grants and giving additional incentives when they do so (Niti Aayog 2015b). In addition it proposed "sin tax", corporate social responsibility (CSR), and PPPs as sources of investment.

When in the same year a draft National Policy was circulated, asking for a sober increase of financial commitment of 2.5 per cent of GDP, NITI Aayog opposed it fervently, claiming that, "We need to assess whether drastically increasing investments will run in to the law of diminishing marginal returns, besides posing a challenge to the absorptive capacities of the state health systems" (Kumar 2015). The draft policy of the new government had itself said that India's investments in the health sector at large, and in public health sector specifically, are much lower than most other developing countries with better health statistics. The HLEG too had cut down its recommendation of 4 per cent because of pragmatic reasons to allocation of 2.5 percent of the GDP. According to a letter written to the Ministry of Health, the NITI Aayog's health advisor had said, "Even though one might find it morally and ethically reprehensible – this system of two-tier care – one for those with means and a voice and the other for the voiceless and indigent" will continue to exist in the short or even medium term (Kumar 2015). This understanding has persisted and expressed itself in a shift away from welfare towards handing over responsibility to families and civil society through cash transfers and voucher systems and state-funded insurances with provisioning by private providers.

The Draft Health Policy 2015, in contrast, had noted that, "The public sector is value for money as it accounts for less than 30 per cent of total expenditure, but provides for about 20 per cent of outpatient care and 40 per cent of in-patient care. This same expenditure also pays for 60 per cent of end-of-life care (RGI estimates on hospital mortality), and almost 100 per cent of preventive and promotive care and a substantial part of medical and nursing education as well" (Government of India 2015). In the afore-mentioned letter of the advisor health, NITI Aayog, to the Ministry in response to this draft, it was pointed out that the Ministry recognised the private providers as a major provider but,

> it is also a 40 billion industry growing at a CAGR of 15 per cent and the policy does not indicate a frame work for engaging these except for its regulation in filling critical gaps of public sector
>
> *(Kumar 2015)*

This was considered a major weakness of the policy draft!

The observers of NITI Aayog point out its dislike for welfare subsidies and its faith in the ability of the private sector to deliver (Sethi 2015). They also wonder about its thinking as it depends on CSR and a truncated NHM and "demands an 8 per cent rise in state budgets, a Rs.3,800 per capita/year public spending when, without private partnership, a Rs.1,700 per capita expenditure would have sufficed for the same purpose according to the advisor Planning Commission" (Duggal Ravi 2016). The Aayog is also exploring privatising even of primary care, introducing competition at secondary level for public hospitals, and reducing financial investment to 1.6 from 2.5 per cent of the GDP through more selective partnerships with innovative corporates (Krishnan 2016). The 2015 draft policy has been reportedly reviewed by the cabinet for its wisdom in bringing in a health rights budget. To avoid legal hassles, there is a reversal to "assured care" and a push to increase health budget to 2.5 per cent of the GDP (*The Times of India* 2016). The pressure of the coming election, and the thrust of the corporates to expand further the health assurance scheme, seems to be at work. The semblance of an expanded UHC contributing to private profits can kill two birds with one stone. Either way, a comprehensive vision of Primary Health Care as conceptualised by the WHO is far from the Niti Aayog's imagination.

What then is the dominant trend?

The trends since 2014–15 are reflected by the analysis of annual budgets of the past four years (Qadeer and Ghosh 2016; Ghosh and Qadeer 2017) that highlight:

1 The near stagnation of total budget and its reduction as a proportion of GDP.
2 Preference for investment in medical care – especially the hospital sector – over integrated public health programmes.
3 Rising investments in insurance/National Assurance Programme (RSBY mainly depends on private providers: 30–80 per cent across states), which does not leave sufficient resources for restoring infrastructure or securing other forms of necessary welfare (food, drinking water, sanitation etc.).
4 A reduction in allocation to the NHM which was the flagship programme for basic services, disease control programmes and, even in the Family Welfare budget. Drastically reduced, it now focuses on sterilisations and contraceptives at the cost of the maternal and child health safety components which earlier made this programme broad based and welfare oriented.
5 Drastic cuts in the investments in key social sectors critical for health, such as the ICDS, school health, women's social security, and MGNREGA, further undermines the constantly occurring theme of social determinants of health which all three Plans underlined but did little about.
6 Even the budget for the much talked of Swachh Bharat programme for sanitation appears to be high only when seen with water supply, by itself sanitation suffers a cut of over Rs.24,240 million in 2016–17.

The purpose of these budgets then is not increasing but *reallocating* resources, with a shift from primary to tertiary care, transfer of subsidies to the private sector in the name of assurance, and bringing large sections of the population into the sphere of the medical market as only the targeted population gets some limited coverage. There is little evidence of moving towards universal coverage at affordable prices and with free medicines and diagnostics even for the poor who continue with OOPEs.

Implications

For a country like India where inequality, poverty, gender discrimination, and social and religious stratification and exclusion are entrenched realities, what does this direction of development mean? This can be grasped best if we recognise that a focus on medical care alone – and that too at the tertiary level – can be a strategy for the developed countries with basic amenities, services, and employment, but not for those living in poor environments and engaged in work with unhealthy working conditions and poor access to health facilities. This is so because living environment, working conditions, and work opportunities have a major impact on health other than services, as shown by the Commission of Social Development of the WHO (CSDH 2008). Therefore, accepting international standards and ignoring the prevailing social context and the realities within a country, opting for short term solutions and succumbing to the demands of business and politically powerful, inevitably leads to a loss of balance in public health policy and a subsequent loss of trust of the majority in Planning processes. A pointer to the problem is a WHO report that estimates one quarter of the morbidity load in developing countries as rooted in their poor environment. Diseases most linked to environment were diarrhoea, respiratory diseases, malaria, accidents, heart diseases, tuberculosis, diabetes, under-nutrition etc. (Prüss-Üstün and Corvalán 2006). The report also points out the high risk posed to children and women in poor environmental conditions. The relationship between under-nutrition and ill health has long been established and the importance of mechanisms like changed gut flora, loss of gut villi, poor absorption, immunological changes, and increased metabolism, have only become better understood with time (Katona and Katona-Apte 2008).

In India, the official estimates of poverty vary from 37.2 per cent (Planning Commission: 2009) to 50 per cent (Government of India 2009). The methodological debate revolves around using Consumer Price Index–based estimates, the changing composition of the consumption basket used by the poor and other than food, key non-food items in measurement of poverty (ADB 2011). The critics using alternate methods estimate poverty to be as high as 74 per cent (Patnaik 2015). The deputy chairman of NITI Aayog accepts the fact that 90 per cent of the work force is engaged in low paying unorganised or informal sector jobs (The Hindu 2016). In addition, apart from those who remain unemployed all through the year, 40 per cent of the working population does not get work at all through the year on any regular basis even in better off areas like Chandigarh (Labour Bureau 2015). In this context, the persistence of a mixed pattern of communicable and non-communicable diseases reported from Chhattisgarh, representative of the disease burden of tribal and non-tribal populations of central India (Jain et al. 2016), matches the pattern of diseases of poverty reported by WHO experts. The reports of high prevalence of hunger and under-nutrition and its intimate association with tuberculosis, malaria, anaemia etc. is also not surprising nor is the fact that people delay accessing health care for lack of resources and let complications grow till survival is threatened (Jain et al. 2016). Between 1993–94 and 2009–10, the proportion of calorie deficient population increased in all monthly per capita income expenditure quintiles. While in the poorest quintiles the initial proportion of people getting less than the recommended calories (2200 R, 2100U) itself was above 90 per cent, in the rest it steadily rose touching 36 per cent even in the fifth quintile (Qadeer et al. 2016). Other factors in this context are caste and class that impact living and working conditions, access to service, its utilisation as well as outreach and hence the level of mortality, morbidity, stunting and anaemia especially among women and children (John 2017, Mukherji et al. 2011, Balarajan et al. 2011). The business model of health services can therefore hardly resolve the public health crisis under these conditions.

The Indian people require medical care of a different kind that is based on a strong and accessible comprehensive basic service network to help them not to neglect early treatment and to avoid hospitalisation for tertiary care of complications (even if through health insurance). Under-nutrition and social and economic constraints then are two key factors that the health policy of India has to address. In short we must redefine "profits" itself. It cannot just be about expanding capital without enhancing wellbeing by letting technology make its makers obsolete. Ensuring livelihoods, making people healthier, and recognising the value of those who produce the wealth: is a value shift that is crucial. Without it, like the MDGs, the SDGs too will be interpreted according to the convenience of business. This shift is reflected in the understanding of those who work directly with the people. That is how public health was born in Britain, through the local government county doctors and not specialists of the 19th century. A far sighted doctor from Liverpool, Benjamin Moore, in 1912 coined the idea of tax based National Health Service (NHS), that the British Labour government implemented in 1948 and was later undermined by the 1980s Reforms. Hope for India also lies in the democratic struggles of practitioners who have the courage to question the irrational practices of their peers (Gadre and Shukla 2016) and those who choose to work directly with communities to create new opportunities for learning to look at health through lenses other than technology alone (Jain with JSS 2016) and evolving health care with a difference.

Notes

1 WHO 2005: Sustainable health Financing, Universal coverage and Social Health Insurance, available at: www.who.int/health_financing/documents/cov-wharesolution5833/en/ [accessed June 16, 2016].
2 Dwindling resources of public heal led to closure of Plague monitoring units in the endemic states which culminated in the 1994 epidemic (Qadeer, Nayar, and Baru 1994) and the National Nutrition Monitoring Bureau of the NIN (ICMR) has stopped its reporting since 2012.
3 Ministry of Finance, Government of India. www.pppinindia.com/newFAQs.php), accessed on 2.7.2016,
4 IIFCL, 2015, annual report- 2014–15, New Delhi, www.iifcl.co.in/ accessed 2.7.2016.
5 www.pppinindia.com/IIPDF_Home.php [accessed July 2, 2016].

References

ADB (Asian Development Bank). 2011. *Understanding Poverty in India, ADB Publication.* Available at: www.adb.org/sites/default/files/publication/28930/understanding-poverty-india.pdf [Accessed May 14, 2016].

Arun, Drs Gadre and Abhay, Shukla. 2016. *Dissenting Diagnosis*. Gurgaon: Random House India.
Bain & Company. 2015. *Global Healthcare Private Equity Report, Bain and company in collaboration with the Healthcare Private Equity Association*. Available at: www.bain.com/Images/REPORT_Healthcare_Private_Equity_Report_2015.pdf [Accessed May 14, 2016].
Bose. 2012 (as quoted in Chakravarthi, Indira 2013). "The Emerging 'Health Care Industry' in India: A Public Health Perspective." *Social Change*, 43(2): 149–164.
CII and KcKinsey & Company. 2002. Health Care in India, the road ahead, New Delhi: CII.
CSDH (Commission on Social Determinants of Health). 2008. Closing the gap in a generation: health equity through action on the social determinants of health, Final Report of the CSDH. Geneva: WHO.
Deloitte, 2015. *Healthcare Outlook, India*. Available at: https://www2.deloitte.com/content/dam/Deloitte/global/Documents/Life-Sciences-Health-Care/gx-lshc-2015-healthcare-outlook-india.pdf [Accessed June 1, 2016].
Infrastructure Today 2012. "Annuity can Fast-track Investment in Soft Infra." *Infrastructure Today*, July 2012, p. 1. Available at: http://www.infrastructuretoday.co.in/News.aspx?nid=zBuFGfzV8j5NsMnwF/WRMA== [Accessed June 5, 2016].
Flanders. 2015. *Healthcare Sector in India, Flanders Investment and Trade Market Survey*. Flanders, New Delhi. Available at: www.flandersinvestmentandtrade.com/export/sites/trade/files/market_studies/864150615075708/864150615075708_1.pdf [Accessed June 14, 2016].
Gireesh, Babu. 2014. "IFC Eyes Strong Opportunities in India's Health Care Sector." *Business India*, November 7, Chennai November 7, 2014.
Girija Kalyani, B. and Vijaya Laxmi, B. 2015. "Private Equity in India: A Special Reference to Healthcare Sector." *Global Journal for Research Analysis*, 4(12): 306–308.
Government of India. 1946. *Report of the Health Survey and Development Committee, Vol. 1*. Delhi: Manager of Publications.
———. 2002. *Tenth Five year Plan 2002–07, Vol. II*. New Delhi: Planning Commission.
———. 2007. *Eleventh Five Year Plan 2007–12, Vol. II, Chapter 3*, pp. 57–127. New Delhi: Health and Family welfare and Ayush, Planning Commission.
———. 2009. "Report of the Expert Group to advise the Ministry of Rural Development on the Methodology for conducting the Below Poverty Line (BPL) Census, for 11th Five Year Plan [Saxena Committee Report]." *Ministry of Rural Development*, pp. 9–10, New Delhi, August.
———. 2012: *Twelfths Five Year Plan 2012–17, Vol. III, Chapter Health*, pp. 1–47. New Delhi: Health, Planning Commission.
———. 2015. *Draft National Health Policy*. New Delhi: Ministry of Health and Family Welfare.
The Hindu, 9th August, 2016, pp. 15 column 6–8.
The Hindu. 2016. "Panagariya Blames Industry for Employment Crisis." *The Hindu*, 9th August, p. 15.
Hooda, Shailender K., 2015. *Foreign Investment in Hospital Sector in India: Trends, Pattern and Issues, Working Paper181*. New Delhi: Institute for Studies in Industrial Development.
IBEF (India Brand Equity Foundation). 2015. *Health Care*. Available at: www.ibef.org/industry/healthcare-india.aspx 9.7.2016
IIFCL. 2015. *Annual Report 2014–15*. New Delhi: India Infrastructure Funding Corporation Limited, p. 4.
Itumalla, Ramaiah and Acharyulu, G.V.R.K. 2012. "Indian Healthcare and Foreign Direct Investment: Challenges & Opportunities." *Asia Pacific Journal of Marketing & Management Review*, 1(2): 57–69.
Izhar, Alam Md. and Ahamad, Khader Jameel. 2015. "An Analysis of Foreign Direct Investment Inflows in Healthcare Sector in India." *Pezzottaite Journals*, 4(2): 1669–1674.

Jain, Yogesh. 2016. "Health Through the Hunger Lens." In *Chronicles from Central India: An Atlas of Rural Health*. Chhattisgarh: Jan Swasth Sahyog.

Jain, Yogesh, Raman, Kataria, Sushil, Pael, Suhas, Kadm, Anju, Kataria, Rachna, Jain, Ranivdra, Kurbude, and Sharayu, Shinde. 2016. "Burden and Pattern of Illness among the Tribal Communities in Central India: A Report from the Community Health Programme." In *Chronicles from Central India: An Atlas of Rural Health*. Chhattisgarh: Jan Swasth Sahyog.

John, J. 2017. "Caste and Inequalities in Health." *The Hindu*, 2 November 2017. Available at: www.thehindu.com/opinion/lead/Caste-and-inequalities-in-health/article16876113.ece

Katona, Peter and Katona-Apte, Judit. 2008. "The Interaction between Nutrition and Infection." *Clinical Infectious Diseases*, 46(10): 1582–1588. Available at: http://cid.oxfordjournals.org/content/46/10/1582.full [Accessed August 8, 2016].

KPMG & ASSOCHAM. 2011. *Emerging Trends in Healthcare a Journey from Bench to Bedside, KPMG*. Available at: http://indiainbusiness.nic.in/newdesign/upload/news/Emrging_trends_in_healthcare.pdf [Accessed June 12, 2011].

KPMG & FICCI. 2015. *Health Care the Neglected Drivers Need for paradigm shift, FICCI*. Available at: http://ficci.in/publication-page.asp?spid=20634 [Accessed May 5, 2016].

Krishnan, Vidya. 2012. "Ministry Opposes Plan to Overhaul Healthcare: Plan Panel to Rewrite its Chapter on Health in the 12th Five-Year Plan Document." *Live Mint*, August 7th, Tuesday. [Accessed December 7, 2015].

———. 2016. "Niti Aayog Meet Seeks Reforms in Public Healthcare System." *Live Mint*, 6th August. Available at: www.livemint.com/Politics/rOamP33pmhUT3kFZ4uIoSO/NITI-Aayog-meet-seeks-reforms-in-public-healthcare-system.html [Accessed August 6, 2016]

Kumar, Alok. 2015. "Letter to the Ministry, from advisor Health." *NitiAayog*. Available at: http://phmindia.org/wp-content/uploads/2015/09/NITI-Aayog-Comments-on-NHP-1.pdf [Accessed March 26, 2017].

Labour Bureau. 2015. *Report of the 4th Employment & Unemployment Survey 2013–14, A Press Note*. Available at: http://labourbureau.nic.in/Press_note_4th_EUS.pdf [Accessed June 8, 2016].

McKinsey & Company. 2012. *Indian Healthcare Inspiring Possibilities, Challenging Journey, Prepared for CII*. Available at: http://docplayer.net/1652212-India-healthcare-inspiring-possibilities-challenging-journey.html [Accessed August 3, 2016].

Mohan, Ghosh Sourindra and Qadeer, I. 2017. "An Inadequate and Misdirected Health Budget." *The Wire*, 9(14).

Mukherji, S., Haddad, S., and Narayana, D. 2011. "Social Class related Inequalities in Household Health Expenditure and Economic Burden: Evidence from Kerala, South India." *International Journal of Equity Health*, 10: 1.

Mukhopadhyay Indranil. 2019. "National Health Policy. 2015: Growth Fundamentalism Driving Health Coverage Agenda?" In Qadeer, I., Saxena, K.B., Arathi, P.M. (eds.). *Universalising Health Care in India: From Care to Coverage*. New Delhi: Aakar, pp. 98–116.

Nanda, Sudhansu Sekhar. 2015. "Infrastructure Development in India: The Role of Public-private Partnership." *International Journal of Core Engineering & Management (IJCEM)*, 2(6): 60–70.

NHA Cell (National Health Accounts Cell). 2009. *National Health Accounts India 2004–05*. New Delhi: Ministry of Health & Family Welfare, GoI.

NHSRC (National Health System Resource Centre). 2016. *National Health Accounts- Estimates for India 2013–14*. Ministry of Health & Family Welfare. GoI, New Delhi.

NITI Aayog. 2015a. "Health Systems in India: Bridging the Gap Between Current Performance and Potential, Increasing Financial Resources for Health," *Working Paper series 1, Paper No. 1/2015*, Health Division, New Delhi.

———. 2015b. "Increasing Financial Resources for Health," *Working Paper Series 1, Paper No. 2*, Health Division, New Delhi.

Onotai, Lucky O. 2008. "A Review of the Appropriateness of User Fees and Social Health Insurance to Fund the Health Care Systems in Low and Middle-Income Countries." *The Nigerian Health Journal*, 8(1–2): 1–5.

Patnaik, Utsa. 2015. "Aspects of Food Security: The Production and Absorption of Food Grains in India in Recent Years." In Qadeer, I. (ed.). *India Social Development Report 2014 Challenges of Public Health*. New Delhi: Oxford University Press.

Planning Commission. 2009. *Report of the Expert Group to Review the Methodology for Estimation of Poverty, [Tendulkar Committee Report]*. New Delhi.

———. 2011. *High Level Expert Group Report on Universal Health Coverage for India*. New Delhi: Planning Commission.

Prüss-Üstün, A. and Corvalán, C. 2006. *Preventing Disease Through Healthy Environments. Towards an Estimate of the Environmental Burden of Disease*, pp. 11–12. Geneva: WHO.

Qadeer, I. 2008. "Health Planning in India: Some Lessons from the Past." *Social Scientist*, May–June, 36(5–6): 51–75.

Qadeer, I. and Ghosh, M. Sourindra. 2016. "Public Health in the Infirmary." *The Hindu BusinessLine*, 17 April. Available at: https://www.thehindubusinessline.com/opinion/public-healths-in-the-infirmary/article8486437.ece#!

Qadeer, I., Ghosh, M. Sourindra., and Presanna, Madhavan Arathi. 2016. "India's Declining Calorie Intake: Development or Distress?" *Social Change*, 46(1): 1–26.

Qadeer, I., Nayar, K.R., and Baru R.V. 1994. "Contextualising Plague: A Reconstruction and an Analysis," *Economic and Political Weekly*, 29(27): 2981–2989.

Rao, Sujata. 2005. *National Commission of Macroeconomics and Health, Financing and Delivery of Health Care Services in India, Background Papers*, pp. 239–242. New Delhi: Ministry of Health & Family Welfare.

Ravi, Duggal. 2016. "Is Niti Aayog Even Thinking About Health?" *Economic & Political Weekly*, 51(20): 12–14.

Sarkar, Pooja, 2016. "Home Grown PE Funds Raised $ 2.9 bn in 2015." *Live Mint*, 2nd August, 2016.

Selvaraj, Sakthivel, and Karan, Anup K. 2012. "Why Publically-Financed Insurance Schemes are Ineffective in Providing Financial Risk Protection." *Economic & Political Weekly*, 47(11): 60–68.

Selvaraj, Sakthivel, Karan, Anup K., and Mukhopadhyay, Indranil. 2015. "Publically Financed Health Insurance Schemes in India: How Effective Are They in Providing Financial Risk Protection?" In Qadeer, I. (ed.). *India Social Development Report 2014, Challenges of Public Health*. New Delhi: Oxford University Press.

Sethi, Nitin. 2015. "NITI Ayog against Free Health Care Bats for more Private sector Role." *Business Standard*, 25th August. Available at: www.business-standard.com/article/economy-policy/niti-aayog-against-free-health-care-bats-for-more-private-sector-role-115082500061_1.html [Accessed August 6, 2016].

The Times of India. 2016. "National Health Policy: Cabinet Note Proposes Assured Services to All". *The Times of India*, 25 July. Available at: http://timesofindia.indiatimes.com/india/National-Health-Policy-Cabinet-note-proposes-assured-services-to-all/articleshow/53380886.cms

Unger, Jean Pierre, Paepr, Pierre De, Ghilbert, Patrecia, Zocchi, Walter, Van, Dessel, Qadeer, Imrana, and Sen, Kasturi. 2010. "Privatisation (PPM-DOTS) Strategy for Tuberculosis Control: How Evidence Based is it?" In Unger, Jean Pierre, Papepr, Pierre De, Sen, Kasturi and Soors, Werner eds., *International Health and Aid Policies. The Need for Alternatives.* New York: Cambridge University Press, pp. 57–66.

Vidhya, K. and Savitha, P. 2015. "Corporate Social Responsibility of Health Care Sector." *International Research Journal of Business Management*, VIII(2): 20–24.

WHO and UNICEF, 1978. *Report of the International Conference on Primary Health Care, Alma Ata USSR, 6th-17th Sept.* Geneva: WHO.

Yarlini Balarajan, Selvaraj, S., and Subramanian, S.V. 2011. "Health Care and Equity in India." *The Lancet,* 377(9764): 505–515.

8

MACRO-MASKING OF MICRO REALITIES

Access to food and nutrition among tribals

Nitin Tagade and R. S. Deshpande

Food security has been a major concern in India for the last century and it remained as the central pursuit of our agricultural policy. India's policy could be traced from the official documents beginning from Food Grains Policy Committee of 1943 (Gregory 1943), Maitra (1950), Mehta (1957), Venkatappaiah (1966) to the Report of the High Power Committee (Government of India 1990a, 1990 b) covering major sectors of agricultural economy. A policy study by ASSOCHAM (1998), the Long Term Grain Policy Committee (Government of India 2002) and Farmers' Commission headed by Dr Swaminathan (Government of India 2004) have also focused on food security concerns. These important documents flag some of the issues in making India food sufficient through their wide ranging recommendations. The recommendations need some scrutiny. The period after independence witnessed broadly five important policy phases namely – (i) food security, (ii) institutions for food administration, (iii) introduction and dissemination of technology to increase food production, (iv) reaching food to the under-developed regions, classes, farmers, and (v) enabling access to food both in physical and economic terms. In any case, India is far away from the SDG mandated targets of food security. The questions raised include: Have we failed in framing the policy? Have our policy documents remained only in the shelves of the food ministry? Is the problem so enormous that we cannot grapple with it? Are the diversities posing a formidable challenge to us? These call for a scrutiny.

India has significant regional diversity in its agriculture and that is also reflected in the availability and access to food. It is not surprising to hear the reports of tons of grains rotting in the Food Corporation of India (FCI) godowns and at the same time some section of population in the country, is denied food. Unfortunately, even our definition of food grains is dominated only by wheat and rice (the food grains identified with rich/middle income groups) and if these two are taken out of the total, we are extremely insufficient on the availability. The often evaded issue in the food security analyses is the regional diversity and ethnic differentials of tastes, access and availability of food. Surprisingly, the states or regions that depict good economic progress also have a hungry belly deep inside their forested regions. Any analysis across states bears this out. Here we looked into the cross-section of the states briefly and then analysed the state of food and nutrition security in Maharashtra, a well-developed state to understand the micro scenario comparing with the given macro picture. The choice was purposive as the "advanced state" image of Maharashtra has a lot under its mask.

Sample and the design

We are using here both primary and secondary information. The secondary sources include data from National Sample Survey Organisation (NSSO), National Family Health Survey (NFHS) and Census of India for macro understanding. Primary level information was collected from the selected households about their socio-economic conditions along with dietary specification and anthropometric measures from four tribal dominated districts of Maharashtra for the year 2007–08. The survey covered 239 households having at least a child below age six years in tribal dominated areas of Maharashtra. Four-stage stratified sampling method was adopted. In the first stage, districts with a high tribal density compared to the state average were grouped into four categories based on the level of poverty and child malnutrition (Table 8.1). These four categories include high poverty and low malnutrition (HPLM), low poverty and high malnutrition (LPHM), high poverty and high malnutrition (HPHM) and low poverty and low malnutrition (LPLM). In these four categories, one district each are selected for the survey, namely Nagpur, Gadchiroli, Nandurbar and Raigarh. At the second stage, a tehsil (i.e. sub-district) was selected from each district based on high proportion of tribal population and

TABLE 8.1 Poverty and malnutrition in districts with ST population above state average

Groups	High malnutrition	Low malnutrition
High poverty	Nandurbar (65.5, 49, 67.4), Dhule (26, 49, 52.4), Nashik (23.9, 35.44, 58.8), Wardha (12.5, 30.5, 52.5), Chandrapur (18.1, 33.02, 59.1), Yavatmal (19.3, 30.43, 60), Amravati (13.7, 31.11, 55.9), Jalgaon (11.8, 44.3, 51.4)	Nagpur (10.9, 35.27, 46.2)
Low poverty	Gadchiroli (38.3, 26.67, 61.9), Thane (14.7, 13.11, 48.5)	Raigarh (12.2, 8.44, 39.4)

Source: IIPS 2006; Government of India 2001; Government of Maharashtra 2002; and Chaudhuri and Gupta 2009.

Note: 1, figures in parentheses indicate the percentage of ST population (2001), poverty ratio during 1993–94 and the percentage of malnutrition among children below six years during 1999–2000 in the district, respectively; 2, the threshold taken in the above table for ST population (2001), poverty (1993–94) and proportion of malnourished children below six years (1999–00) are 8.9, 28.4 and 47.7 per cent respectively.

two villages were selected as the third stage based on two criteria: (i) where the tribal population should account for a large share, and (ii) that one of the village should be closer to the market place while the other far away. The proximity to the market place is proxy for the relative level of development in the village.[1] In the last stage, 30 households having at least one child below six years of age were selected randomly from a list provided by the primary school in each selected village. Anthropometric data were collected from the households for children below six years of age from both tribal and non-tribal communities using World Health Organisation (WHO) method (WHO 2009).

Food and nutrition: the macro scene

Poverty has been accepted in the literature as one of the direct correlates of malnutrition and food insecurity. Most studies on poverty focus on the mundane measurement debates, statistical systems, small vs. large sample debates and the performance over time (decline or otherwise of head count ratios) (Subramanian 1997; Deaton and Kozel 2005). The level of poverty is estimated based on the Tendulkar Method for 2011–12 (Figure 8.1). Poverty is 43 per cent among tribals and 20 per cent among non-tribal. Accepting the official figures, the states with dominant tribal population continue to show high density of poverty. The difference in the poverty level between the tribal and non-tribal groups is 23 per cent points. Theoretically, we do not find significant answers to the higher poverty among Scheduled Tribes. Possibly the reason may lie in our definition of poverty or even the composition of food basket.

One way of looking at poverty among tribal could be through the differences between these two groups (Figure 8.2). The state wise differences are particularly

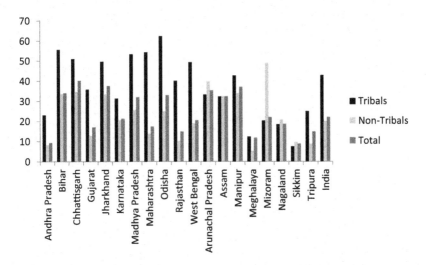

FIGURE 8.1 Poverty in India (%), 2011–12

Source: Based on unit level data of NSSO Consumption Expenditure, 2011–12

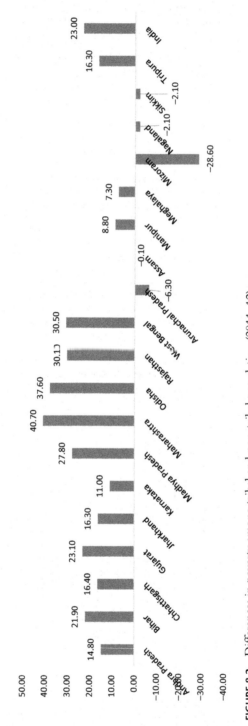

FIGURE 8.2 Differences in poverty among tribal and non-tribal population (2011–12)

Source: Based on unit level data of NSSO Consumption Expenditure, 2011-12

higher in the states in central tribal region ranging from 11 percentage points in Karnataka to 41 percentage points in Maharashtra. The differences in north-eastern regions like Mizoram, Nagaland, Sikkim, Arunachal Pradesh and Assam indicate otherwise. It is clear that the poverty among Tribal is higher in Maharashtra and this can also be due to the NSSO's approach in defining food. Tribal families largely consume fresh edible commodities available from forests of which nutrition calculation is neither possible nor undertaken under NSSO. Recent barrier created by the state forest policies restricting tribal people to use forest products snatches their regular food.

Micro realities – the primary survey

Aggregate scenario

Malnutrition has always been a major issue in India because it decides the cognitive development in the early age and future growth. Undernutrition is measured with the help of three indicators namely underweight, wasting and stunting. Underweight is a composite index of measuring acute and chronic undernutrition, shows the low weight for a given age, while wasting measures acute undernutrition that shows low weight for a given height and stunting measures chronic undernutrition that indicates low height for a given age (Mortorell and Ho 1984). In India, undernutrition or malnutrition is a universal problem.

In Table 8.2, the level of underweight among children below three years of age across states in India have been compared with the gross state domestic products (GSDP) for three time periods i.e. for 1991–92, 1998–99 and 2005–06 and classified the states. In this, Maharashtra comes consistently under the group of high GSDP, but the state could overcome the low level of undernutrition in next period and further slightly recovered. It is irony that a state with high economic performance has a pathetic performance in ensuring food security to the most vulnerable group.

In 2005–06, about 46 per cent of the children below five years, were malnourished with relatively high share in rural areas. These were largely from socially and economically weaker sections of Maharashtra. However, surprisingly the level of malnutrition is very high among Tribals (Figure 8.3).[2] About 57 per cent of the tribal children are underweight, 21 per cent wasting and 58 per cent are stunting; while this proportion among non-tribal is 34 per cent, 16 per cent and 44.6 per cent respectively. Undernutrition is visible and further becomes intense when we note that non-tribals also include the SC and OBCs.

The District Level Household Survey for 2011–12 presented in Figure 8.4 shows that Maharashtra has relatively higher proportion of underweight children (47.2 per cent) as compared to that of India (41.2 per cent). The differences between tribal and non-tribal communities are high again.

Our initial understanding of poverty and malnutrition in the study area clearly indicated that substantial non-food needs are not met. A significantly high share of

TABLE 8.2 Classification of states across the levels of GSDP and underweight

GSDP	1991–92		1998–99		2005–06	
	High under-nutrition	Low under-nutrition	High under-nutrition	Low under-nutrition	High under-nutrition	Low under-nutrition
High GSDP	Bihar and West Bengal	Andhra Pradesh, Bihar, Gujarat, Karnataka, Madhya Pradesh, **Maharashtra**, Punjab, Rajasthan, Tamil Nadu and Uttar Pradesh	Madhya Pradesh, Uttar Pradesh, Rajasthan, **Maharashtra** and West Bengal	Andhra Pradesh, Delhi, Gujarat, Karnataka, Kerala, Madhya Pradesh, Punjab, Rajasthan and Tamil Nadu	Gujarat, Madhya Pradesh, and Uttar Pradesh	Andhra Pradesh, Delhi, Haryana, Karnataka, Kerala, **Maharashtra**, Punjab, Rajasthan, Tamil Nadu, West Bengal
Low GSDP	Orissa	Tripura, Nagaland, Meghalaya, Manipur, Kerala, Himachal Pradesh, Haryana, Goa, Delhi, Assam, and Arunachal Pradesh	Orissa, Bihar	Arunachal Pradesh, Assam, Bihar, Goa, Haryana, Himachal Pradesh, Manipur, Meghalaya, Nagaland, Orissa, and Tripura	Bihar and Meghalaya	Arunachal Pradesh, Assam, Goa, Himachal Pradesh, Manipur, Nagaland, Orissa, and Tripura

Source: Compiled based on Nair 2007; IIPS 1994, 2007; IIPS and ORC Macro 2000; and CSO website

Notes: 1. Low and high levels of under-nutrition and Gross State Domestic Product (GSDP) is the lower and higher level of under-nourished children below three years.
2. Low and high levels of GSDP is the lower of higher GSDP than averages of all the states and UTs for the period of TE 1992–93, TE 1995–96, and TE 2005–06.
3. GSDP is at Constant Prices at 1993–94

Macro-masking of micro realities **173**

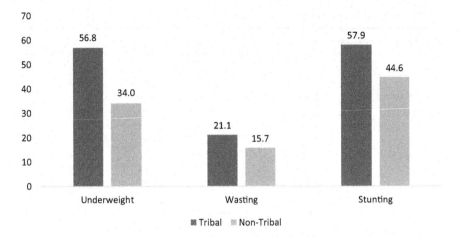

FIGURE 8.3 Proportion of undernourished children below 5 years in Maharashtra (%), 2005–06

Source: Author's estimates based on NFHS-3

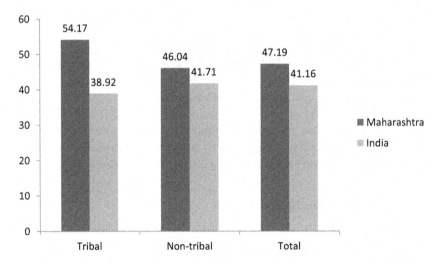

FIGURE 8.4 Proportion of underweight children below 5 years in Maharashtra (%), 2012–13

Source: Author's estimates based on DLHS-4

income spent on food is seldom associated with calorie intake not only because of low quantum of food but also because of low quality of food. As a result, the proportion of poor in the study area is remarkably high, at over 69 per cent, with mean calorie intake being far less than medically prescribed Indian Council of Medical Research (ICMR) norms (Table 8.3).[3] These together adversely influence the nutritional status among children below six years of age.

TABLE 8.3 Food insecurity in the study area

Indicator of food insecurity		Tribal	Non-tribal	All	N
Poverty (%)	BPL	88.27	70.13	69.30	197
	APL	11.73	29.87	30.70	42
Calorie Intake (kcal)	Mean	2,048	2,101	2,065	239
Stunting (%)	Severe	22.94	15.32	20.50	70
	Moderate	60.45	40.54	54.09	185
	Total	83.39	55.86	74.59	255
Wasting (%)	Severe	16.45	6.31	13.16	45
	Moderate	48.92	35.14	44.44	152
	Total	65.37	41.45	57.60	197
Underweight (%)	Severe	26.84	14.41	22.81	78
	Moderate	68.83	44.14	60.82	208
	Total	95.67	58.55	83.63	286

Source: Primary Survey

Note: 1, BPL and APL denotes below poverty line and above poverty line which has been estimated based on the Official Poverty Line provided by the Planning Commission of India; 2, the indicators of under nutrition are grouped as severe and moderate. It is to be noted that moderate under nutrition includes severe under nutrition.

It was found that five out of every six children are underweight in some way or the other, as 61 per cent children are moderately underweight and 21 per cent are severely underweight. The total chronically undernourished (stunting) children accounts about 75 per cent while acute undernourished (wasting) are 58 per cent. A relatively higher level of poverty and malnourished children and lower mean calorie intake are evident among tribal communities than the non-tribal. Among tribal communities, poverty is as high as 88 per cent, underweight about 97 per cent, wasting over 65 per cent and stunting over 83 per cent (Table 8.3).

Food insecurity at disaggregate level

The levels of undernutrition at disaggregated levels are presented in Table 8.4. Based on the extent of undernutrition, different regions can be grouped into three broader categories. These three categories include high, medium and low levels of child undernutrition.

The regions with the highest degree of severe and moderate undernutrition are included in the category of "higher extent of undernutrition". And the regions with a medium proportion of severe undernutrition but suffer from highest degree of moderate undernutrition are in "medium extent of undernutrition" whereas the third group, i.e. "low extent of undernutrition", includes regions with a low levels of both severe and moderate child undernutrition. The HPHM region falls under the first category while the LPHM region comes under the second category. The two regions, i.e. LPLM and HPLM, fall under the third category of lower extent of undernutrition.

TABLE 8.4 Prevalence of undernutrition across study regions (%)

Regions	Wasting			Stunting			Underweight		
	Tribal	Non-tribal	All	Tribal	Non-tribal	All	Tribal	Non-tribal	All
	Severely Undernourished								
HPLM	19.1	9.1	13.9	23.8	9.1	16.3	20.9	11.6	16.3
LPHM	17.2	0.0	14.3	17.4	20.0	17.9	25.7	35.7	27.4
HPHM	24.5	6.1	17.4	32.1	24.2	29.1	39.6	15.2	30.2
LPLM	7.7	4.8	7.0	21.5	9.5	18.6	21.5	4.8	17.4
	Moderately undernourished								
HPLM	45.2	54.6	50.0	59.5	29.6	44.2	67.4	48.8	58.1
LPHM	52.2	53.3	52.4	58.0	40.0	54.8	72.9	42.9	67.9
HPHM	56.6	15.2	40.7	67.9	72.7	69.8	64.1	48.5	58.1
LPLM	40.0	19.1	34.9	56.9	19.1	47.7	69.2	28.6	59.3

Source: Primary Survey.

Note: Abbreviations used are HPLM (high poverty and low malnutrition), LPHM (low poverty and high malnutrition), HPLM (high poverty and low malnutrition) and LPLM (low poverty and low malnutrition).

The HPHM region falls under the first category of high degree of undernutrition because, on the one hand, it shares the highest proportion of severely wasted, stunted and underweight children accounting for 17 per cent, 29 per cent and 30 per cent, respectively. In the LPHM region under the second group, poverty is highest with low per capita calorie intake in which the proportion of moderately wasted and underweight children is highest across regions, along with a relatively low levels of severely undernourished children compared to the HPHM region. The percentage of moderately wasted and underweight children in this region constitute about 52 and 68 per cent, respectively; while 55 per cent are moderately stunted. The third group includes the HPLM and LPLM regions. In the HPLM region, the proportion of severely stunted and underweight children is lowest, whereas, the proportion of severely wasted children is lowest in the LPLM region.

The share of moderately stunted children is lowest in the HPLM, while the proportion of moderately wasted children is lowest in the LPLM region. It is interesting to note that LPLM region has the lowest poverty ratio while the second highest poverty ratio is in the HPLM region. Thus, the extent of undernutrition is high in those regions which are selected based on high level of child undernutrition following the regions with high level of poverty. This is quite an intriguing result. Therefore, this issue was taken for further investigation in detail.

Prima facie the evidence on the basis of primary survey are corresponding with the broad expectations, as the extent of undernutrition is high in the HPHM region which declines in the LPHM, HPLM and LPLM regions. The macro level information for each of these regions is presented in Table 8.5 for further understanding how this information correlates with micro level understanding. The HPHM

TABLE 8.5 Basic socio-economic features

S. No.	Indicators	HPLM	LPHM	HPHM	LPLM
1	**Income and production indicators**				
1.1	Per Capita Net District Domestic Product (Rs.) (TE 2008)	46,662	24,006	30,561	50,593
1.2	Share of district Population to Total State Population (2001)	4.27	1.02	1.38	2.3
1.3	Share of Tribal Population to Total District Population (2001)	10.9	38.3	65.5	12.2
1.4	Share of Forest Area (2002–03)	21.21	69.87	20.27	32.35
1.5	Average Foodgrain Production in TE 2000–06 in 00' MT	1,942	1,679	1,717	3,379
1.6	Per Capita Foodgrain Production in 2001 (kg)	303.7	882.1	668.9	996.9
1.7	Productivity Foodgrain Production (TE 2000–06) in kg/hectare	851	938	810	2099
2	**Human development indicators**				
2.1	Total Literacy Rate (2001)	84.03	77.42	55.78	77.03
2.2	Male Literacy Rate (2001)	90.18	71.86	66.16	86.15
2.3	Female Literacy Rate (2001)	77.42	48.07	45.18	67.75
2.4	Human Development Indicator Rank (2002)	5	35	32	6
2.5	Poverty (1993–94)	35.27	26.67	49.00	8.44
2.6	Child Underweight (2002–04)	46.2	61.9	67.4	39.4

Source: Government of India, Census of India (various years); Government of Maharashtra, Directorate of Economics and Statistics, (various years); Government of India, Economic Survey of India (various years); and RCH 2 (2002–04), (IIPS 2006); (IIPS 2007); Government of India 2002b: EPWRF 2004.

Note: The information is compiled based on the districts.

region has highest share of ST population. Similar kinds of results are found in the case of LPHM region; however, forest coverage is highest. The LPHM and HPHM region differs mainly on two counts. The former region has advantage in terms of productivity of and per capita food grain availability, while it is in the disadvantaged position in terms of both male and female literacy rate as compared to the HPLM region (Table 8.5). Even though the inferences are tallying with the other observations, the gravity of the problem is much higher at the ground level.

Determinants of underweight

The discussion on food insecurity reveals high level of food insecurity in the study area, particularly among tribal communities. Further, the nutritional status of tribal children in a few regions is relatively better. The level of undernutrition among tribal communities is found relatively high when compared to non-tribal communities. The findings at the disaggregate level clearly indicate a contradictory scenario in the LPHM and HPHM regions. It is seen that a relatively low level of undernutrition among tribal children is observed when compared to non-tribal children. Therefore, an attempt is made to understand the factors affecting the nutritional status in the study area. This is an outcome indicator of deprivation. Such an understanding of factors affecting the nutritional status would naturally hold larger implications for policymakers. Here we have used Linear Regression Model for the reason that the dependent variable, {z-score of weight-for-age} is an anthropometry measure of underweight. The z-score is the standard normal variate, which indicates how far values of weight-for-age differ from the international threshold given by the WHO. The values range from the lowest (−) 6 to the highest (+) 6. The values indicate level of nutritional status. The explanatory variables include both linear and dummy variables (Table 8.6).[4] The linear variables are birth

TABLE 8.6 Linear regression results related to undernutrition {dependent variable: underweight (z-score of weight-for-age)}

Explanatory variables and variable information		Coeff.	Std. Err.	T
CONS	Intercept	−3.545	0.553	−6.41***
PRIMARY_EDU	Dummy for Primary Education of Mother (Primary Education = 1; Other = 0)	−0.340	0.183	−1.86*
MIDDLE_EDU	Dummy for Middle Education of Mother (Middle Education = 1; Other = 0)	0.339	0.134	2.53***
HIIGHER_EDU	Dummy for Higher Education of Mother (Higher Education = 1; Other = 0)	−0.251	0.261	−0.96
INTERIOR	Dummy for Interior Villages (Interior Village = 1; Close to Market Place = 0)	0.359	0.109	3.28***
TRIBE	Dummy for Tribal (Tribal = 1; Non-tribal = 0)	−0.727	0.212	−3.42***
HPLM	Dummy for HPLM Region (HPLM = 1; other = 0)	−0.219	0.151	−1.45
LPHM	Dummy for LPHM Region (LPHM = 1; other = 0)	−0.119	0.158	−0.75
HPHM	Dummy for HPHM Region (HPHM = 1; other = 0)	−0.375	0.159	−2.36**
B_ORD	Birth Order of the Child	−0.134	0.049	−2.74***
BMI_MO	Body Mass Index of Mother	0.092	0.023	3.92***
TRIBE_BO	Interaction between Tribal and Birth Order	0.202	0.073	2.75***
NTFP_MO	Dummy for mothers engaged in NTFPs (Yes = 1; No = 0)	0.359	0.136	2.64***
AGEGRP1	Dummy for age-group 3–4 (Age Group 3–4 = 1; other = 0)	−0.296	0.142	−2.09**
AGEGRP2	Dummy for age-group 5–6 (Age Group 5–6 = 1; other = 0)	−0.132	0.147	−0.89
N = 341, F (14, 326) = 6.08***, R-square = 0.19				

*Note:*1, ***, ** and * indicate p-value are significant at one per cent, five per cent and 10 per cent level, respectively; 2, HPLM, LPHM, HPLM and LPLM refer to high poverty and low malnutrition, low poverty and high malnutrition, high poverty and high malnutrition, and low poverty and low malnutrition regions respectively; 3, z-score varies from −5.99 to 0.46.

order of child, body mass index (BMI) of the mother and birth order of children belonging to tribal communities (interaction between tribal and birth order). On the other hand, the dummy variables are regions, i.e. HPLM, LPHM and HPHM regions, mothers engaged in collecting NTFPs, age group of children (age group 0–2, 3–4 and 5–6), literate mothers and proximity to market.

The results indicate that the nutritional status is the combined effect of non-economic factors that include social status, mother and child related factors and village and region-specific factors. The significance of non-economic factors in terms of determining the nutritional status, reaffirms our contention that deprivation has broader connotations than mere technical dimensions of poverty. In other words, factors such as mother being a literate, proximity to market place, BMI of mother, mother engaged in collecting non-timber forest produce (NTFPs) and birth order of children have a significantly positive impact on the nutritional status of children. On the other hand, being tribal, the HPHM region, birth order of children and age group of children (i.e. 3–4 years) have a significantly negative impact on the nutritional status of children.

The education-level of mother has a significant impact on the dependent variable, indicating that the nutritional status improves in relation to her educational level. Earlier studies have shown that the probability of mother with primary/secondary/higher levels of education having underweight children is very low (Radhakrishna and Ravi 2004). However, the results of the present analysis indicate a significantly negative impact for mothers with primary education and a positive impact for mothers with middle school education on the nutritional status of their children. This significant negative impact could be because a larger proportion of the sample mothers surveyed had only primary education.

BMI of mother and engagement or non-engagement of mother in the collection of NTFPs – have a positive impact on the nutritional status of children. The nutritional status of mother dictates that of the child. Additionally, a mother's engagement in the collection of NTFPs from the forest areas also has a positive impact on the nutritional status of children. This could be due to two factors: first, mothers engaged in the collection of NTFPs also collect edible material and second, it may be giving additional purchasing power to mothers in terms of ensuring nutritious food for their children.

It is observed that region-specific characteristics and proximity to the market place have a significant impact on the nutritional status of children. The HPHM region has a significantly higher proportion of underweight children compared to those of the LPLM region. However, far-flung villages share a better nutritional status among children compared to villages closer to the market place. The reason could be the dependence on agriculture-based economy and access to natural forest resources in the villages far from the market place.

The child-specific factors such as birth order and age of children have a negative impact on the nutritional status of children – with increasing birth order, the nutritional status of the children declines. It means that more the number of children in the households, higher will be the level of deprivation and underweight among children. However, it is to be noted that the interaction between tribal and birth order of children brings out a different dimension in terms of improvement in the nutritional status with increasing birth order among the tribal communities. This is because the livelihood of tribal community is dependent on the year-round livelihood pursuits unlike non-tribal communities. In addition, children under 3–4 years experience a low nutritional status compared to those 0–2 years. This also confirms the negative impact of birth order. This could be due to the fact that younger children benefit from breastfeeding, while sufficient and nutritious food may not be available to higher age group of children because of household poverty.

4. Conclusions

Food security has been a major concern in India since last century. Policies were made and strategies formulated to overcome food and nutrition deficiency. Even after seven decades of Independence, we cannot say that India is comfortable on food security front. The strategies thus far implemented focused largely on food distribution, employment generation and higher food production. In the recent past we witnessed some positive impact of the strategies implemented focusing on improvement in the food delivery system, increase in the food buffer stock and MGNREGS to create affordability to the poorest of the poor. Our analysis based on a field study was intended to understand the issues of food insecurity/access in the tribal dominated areas of Maharashtra. Analysts have missed the real picture because of the masking of facts taking place in the analysis of macro level data. A comparison of food insecurity between the two groups reveals a higher incidence of food insecurity among the tribes as compared to that of non-tribes. The nutritional status of tribal children is lower than that of their non-tribe counterparts. This finding, however, is difficult to be generalised and the situations elsewhere may be different or even worse. The vulnerability to food insecurity of tribal communities' would be further aggravated, if they were denied access to their forest based traditional livelihood systems. Their dependence for nutrition on the forest products to which the access is denied through the state control, need to be understood as an deliberate policy to keep them away from food of their liking. State should build the capabilities of the tribal communities to overcome food insecurity, particularly in distress situations with the help of their own initiatives. The target of SDG in the case of these ethnic groups is truly a distant dream of many a policymakers.

Notes

1 We define market place as a place with a relatively developed market on which people of adjoining villages depend for various purposes such as procuring consumption and non-consumption products, health care facilities and secondary education.
2 The Factsheet of NFHS 4 for 2015–16 shows that 36 per cent of children below five years are underweight in Maharashtra. These figures are 40 per cent in rural and 36 per cent in urban Maharashtra. However, proportion of malnourished children across social groups is not yet published.

3 Indian Council of Medical Research (1996) recommends 2400 kcal per day in rural areas for a healthy and active person.
4 The specification used in this paper for linear regression model is , where Y is dependent variable i.e. weight-for-age (z-scores) for measuring underweight among children below age six years, a is intercept, b is coefficient of X explanatory variables and e is error term. The explanatory variables include both dummy as well as linear variables.

References

ASSOCHAM. 1998. *Strategic Plan for Indian Agricultural Sector.* New Delhi: ASSOCHAM.
Chaudhuri, S. and Gupta, N. 2009. "Levels of Living and Poverty Patterns: A District-Wise Analysis for India." *Economic and Political Weekly,* XLIV(9): 94–110.
Deaton, Angus and Kozel, Valerie. 2005. *The Great Poverty Debate.* New Delhi: Macmillan India.
EPWRF. 2004. *District-wise Agricultural Data Base for Maharashtra: 1960–61 to 1997–98.* Mumbai: EPW Research Foundation.
Government of India. 1990a. *National Agricultural Policy Resolution: Comment by Standing Advisory Committee (Chairman, Sharad Joshi).* New Delhi: Ministry of Agriculture.
———. 1990b. *Agricultural Policies and Programmes: Report of the High Powered Committee (Chairman: Shri Bhanu Pratap Singh).* New Delhi: Government of India.
———. 2001. *Census of India: Social-Cultural Tables, Maharashtra, Census of India.* New Delhi: Government of India.
———. 2002a. *Report of the High Level Committee on Long-Term Grain Policy, (Chairman: Abhijit Sen).* New Delhi: Department of Food and Public Distribution, Ministry of Consumer Affairs, Food and Public Distribution.
———. 2002b. *National Human Development Report-2001.* New Delhi: Planning Commission, Government of India.
———. 2004. *Serving Farmers and Saving Farming: National Commission on Farmers (First Report).* New Delhi: Ministry of Agriculture, Government of India.
———. *Various Years. Census of India.* New Delhi: Government of India.
———. *Various Years. Economic Survey of India.* New Delhi: Government of India.
Government of Maharashtra. *Various Years. Economic Survey of Maharashtra.* Mumbai: Government of Maharashtra: Directorate of Economics and Statistic.
———. 2002. *Maharashtra Human Development Report, 2002.* Mumbai: Government of Maharashtra.
Gregory, Sir Theodore. 1943. *Report of the Foodgrains Policy Committee.* New Delhi: Government of India.
ICMR. 1996. *Some Common Indian Recipes and Other Nutritive Value.* Hyderabad: National Institute of Nutrition.
International Institute of Population Sciences (IIPS). 1994. *National Family Health Survey: India 1992–93.* Bombay: IIPS.
International Institute for Population Sciences (IIPS) and ORC Macro. 2000. *National Family Health Survey (NFHS-2), 1998–99: India.* Mumbai: IIPS.
International Institute for Population Sciences (IIPS). 2006. *Reproductive and Child Health: District Level Household Survey (RCH-DLHS):2002–04.* Mumbai: International Institute for Population Sciences.
International Institute for Population Sciences (IIPS). 2007. *National Family Health Survey 3: India, 2005–06.* Mumbai: International Institute for Population Sciences.
Maitra, Laxmi Kanta. 1950. *Report of the Foodgrains Investigation Committee.* New Delhi: Government of India.

Mehta, Asok. 1957. *Report of the Foodgrains Enquiry Committee*. New Delhi: Ministry of Food and Agriculture, Government of India.
Mortorell, R. and Ho, T.J. 1984. "Malnutrition, Morbidity and Mortality." *Population Development Report*, 10: 49–68.
Nair, K.R.G. 2007. "Malnourishment among Children in India: A Regional Analysis." *Economic and Political Weekly*, XLII (37): 3797–3803.
Radhakrishna, R. and Ravi, C. 2004. "Malnutrition in India: Trends and Determinants." In Irudaya Rajan, S. and James, K.S.(eds.). *Demographic Change Health Inequality and Human Development in India*. Hyderabad: Centre for Economic and Social Studies, Hyderabad.
Subramaniam, S. (ed.). 1997. *Measurement of Inequality and Poverty (Readers in Economics Series)*. Delhi: Oxford University Press.
Venkatappaiah, B. 1966. *Report of the Foodgrains Policy Committee*. New Delhi: Depart of Food, Ministry of Food and Agriculture, Government of India.
WHO. 2009. *Software for Assessing Growth and Development of the World Children*. Available at: www.who.int/growthref/tools

9
FOOD SECURITY AND SUSTAINABLE AGRICULTURE IN INDIA

Mondira Bhattacharya and Ankita Goyal

Food security is ensured when all people, at all times, have physical, social and economic access to sufficient, safe and nutritious food that meets their dietary needs and food preferences for an active and healthy life (FAO). The concept of food security has been undergoing changes over the last several years. In the 1950s, it was assumed that adequate agricultural production will assure adequate availability of food. In the 1970s, it became clear that along with production, affordability and accessibility to balanced diets is equally important. Affordability is related to jobs or livelihood opportunities. More recently, it is becoming evident that food security is also dependent on the biological absorption of food in the body through the consumption of clean drinking water, environmental hygiene, primary health care and primary education. Finally, ecological factors also determine the long term sustainability of food security systems (Swaminathan 2001). A recent empirical study on prioritising government spending shows that additional spending on agricultural research, education, health and rural infrastructure is the right strategy to ensure agricultural growth and poverty alleviation (Bathla et al. 2017). Taking cognizance of the various aspects of food security, the United Nations adopted SDGs on September 2015. SDGs are universally agreed intergovernmental set of 17 aspiration goals with 169 targets whose main agenda is transforming the world by 2030 through sustainable development practices. One of the SDG seeks to end hunger, achieve food security and improve nutrition and promote sustainable agriculture (United Nations, n.d.).

In the context of India, it is a well-known fact that agriculture is the mainstay of India's economy. The sector accounts for 17 per cent of GDP and 50 per cent of the workforce (2017–18). The economic contribution of agriculture in the GDP is steadily declining, yet it is demographically the broadest economic sector and the country remains an important global agricultural player. India is home to one-fourth of the world's undernourished people and around 21 per cent of the population lives on less than US$1.9 a day. Further levels of inequality and social exclusion are very high (World Food Program n.d.). The share of arable land in the country has declined from 61 per cent in 1990 to 59 per cent in 2014, and India has the world's largest area under cultivation of wheat, rice, pulses and cotton (FAOSTAT 2016). However, agricultural productivity is impeded by water shortages and recurrent droughts, while environmental degradation and vulnerability to weather-related disasters pose challenges to the country as a whole (Food Security Portal, IFPRI n.d.). Food security in India is challenged by three types of problems: (i) problems of availability of food, (ii) problems of accessibility to food, and (iii) problems of sustainable agricultural practices. This chapter attempts to demonstrate with empirical data the situation with respect to the three main challenges affecting food security and sustainable agriculture in India and also discusses the on-going interventions to address it.

The challenge of availability of food

This challenge relates to stagnating crop yields that are primarily due to imbalanced fertiliser usage, lack of crop diversification and dominance of rice-wheat crop rotation especially in the Indo-Gangetic plains that is resulting in soil degradation, water logging and over exploitation of natural resources.

The agricultural sector growth rates in India have been fluctuating over the years. It was 1.5 per cent in 2012–13, 5.6 per cent in 2013–14, −0.2 per cent in 2014–15, 0.7 per cent in 2015–16 and 4.9 per cent in 2016–17. This is explained by high dependence of Indian agriculture on rainfall which aggravates production risks. The average food grain production too has been stagnating at around 250 million tonnes for the last few years. The average yields of principal crops show an increase from period I (2005–06 to 2009–10) to period II (2010–11 to 2016–17). However the trend growth rates during the same period have shown a decline (Table 9.1).

TABLE 9.1 Crop yields and growth rates

Crops	Period I 2005–06 to 2010–11		Period II 2011–12 to 2016–17	
	Yield (Kg/Ha)	Growth Rate (%)	Yield (Kg/Ha)	Growth Rate (%)
Rice	2162.84	0.85	2425.93	0.34
Wheat	2810.60	2.42	3070.46	−0.51
Coarse cereals	1331.23	4.18	1659.43	1.15
Pulses	635.82	2.49	736.66	−0.05
Food grains	1828.01	1.98	2087.44	−0.14
Oilseeds	1031.99	2.59	1117.67	−1.08
Cotton	425.89	3.87	479.25	−1.06
Sugarcane	68246.97	0.60	70279.58	−0.20

Source: Directorate of Economics and Statistics, Ministry of Agriculture and Farmers Welfare, GoI

TABLE 9.2 Crop yield comparisons (2016–17) Kg/Ha

Crops	India	World	USA	China
Paddy	3790	4577	8112	6856
Wheat	3034	3401	3541	5396
Coarse cereals	1676	4036	10217	5712
Cotton	550	790	970	1680
Groundnut	1287	1607	4073	3675
Sunflower seed	628	1804	1940	2683
Rapeseed	1180	2094	2045	1982
Soybean	1144	2754	3494	1803
Pulses	589	958	2034	1732
Sugarcane	70394	70134	80033	73523

Source: FAOSTAT and OECD-FAO Agricultural Outlook

Comparison of crop yields with world averages, particularly with USA and China show that Indian crop yields are relatively lesser (Table 9.2). Crop yield gaps are high in India, leaving a lot of scope for improvement and adoption of practices that would lead to improved productivity.

The challenge of accessibility to food

This challenge relates to affordability, procurement and distribution of food. These include levels of poverty and malnutrition in the country along with government schemes that are meant to reduce them in rural areas, such as the Public Distribution System (PDS), Integrated Chid Development Services (ICDS) and Mid-Day Meal (MDM) schemes. It also includes within its ambit access to health care, safe drinking water and sanitation because these are needed for improving the food absorption capacity of people.

Levels of poverty

Over the years there have been different methodologies followed by the various expert groups to estimate poverty levels in the country, namely the Lakdawala committee, the Tendulkar committee and more recently the Rangarajan committee. Table 9.3 illustrates the estimates according to the Tendulkar methodology. It is seen that the poverty ratios have consistently declined since 1993–94 to 2011–12, both in rural as well as urban areas. The absolute numbers of poor have also registered a decline, while the average per capita expenditure has shown an increase.

Despite this development, the fractions of population living in households with per capita calorie consumption below stipulated norms have been increasing over the years (Table 9.4). Therefore, though the proportion of people living below the official poverty line has declined, there is an increase in the proportion of people consuming fewer calories than the stipulated norm. This is a paradoxical situation

TABLE 9.3 Official poverty estimates in India: percentage and number of poor (Tendulkar methodology)

Years	Poverty ratio			Number of Poor (million)			Average monthly per capita expenditure (Rs.)		
	Rural	Urban	Total	Rural	Urban	Total	Rural	Urban	Total
1993–94	50.1	31.8	45.3	328.6	74.5	403.7	–	–	–
2004–05	41.8	25.7	37.2	326.3	80.8	407.1	447	579	1026
2009–10	33.8	20.9	29.8	278.2	76.5	354.7	673	860	1533
2011–12	25.7	13.7	21.9	216.7	53.1	269.8	816	1000	1816

Source: Government of India 2014b

TABLE 9.4 Fractions of population living in households with per capita calorie consumption below stipulated norms

NSS rounds	Rural	Urban	Total
1983 (38th round)	66.1	60.5	64.8
1987–88 (43rd round)	65.9	57.1	63.9
1993–94 (50th round)	71.1	58.1	67.8
1999–2000 (55th round)	74.2	58.2	70.1
2004–05 (61st round)	79.8	63.9	75.8

Source: Deaton and Drèze (2009)

and raises doubts on the official poverty estimates. In fact it is argued that the decline claimed in the official poverty ratios is spurious (Patnaik 2013).

Extent of malnutrition

According to the FAO, India was home to 194.6 million undernourished people in 2015, which amounts to nearly 15.2 per cent of its population. The "Global Hunger Index" (GHI) developed to measure and track hunger globally and by country and region has been placing India at 46.2 out of 100 in 1992, 38.2 in 2000, 35.6 in 2008 and 31.4 in 2017. Thereby according to the GHI, India falls under the category of "serious hunger level" (Grebmer et al. 2017).

The per capita net availability of food grains per day increased marginally from 476 gms in 1990 to 487 gms in 2016 while the growth rate showed a negative trend of −0.13 per cent. However, the trend growth rate of pulses increased at 0.64 per cent. The per capita net availability of cereals per day is much greater than pulses (Figure 9.1).

The stipulated calorie intake as prescribed by the erstwhile Planning Commission was 2400 Kcals/day in rural areas and 2100 Kcals/day in urban areas. However, calorie intake has been lesser than the prescribed norms in both rural and urban

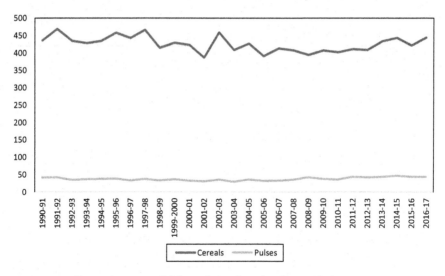

FIGURE 9.1 Per capita net availability of cereals and pulses (g/day)

Source: Government of India, Economic Survey (2017–18)

TABLE 9.5 Nutritional status

Nutrition intake	Areas	1993–94	2011–12
Calorie intake (Kcals/ capita/day)	Rural	2221	2099
	Urban	2089	2058
Protein intake (gms/ capita/day)	Rural	60.2	56.5
	Urban	57.2	55.7
Fat intake (gms/ capita/day)	Rural	31.4	41.6
	Urban	42	52.5

Source: Nutritional Intake in India – NSSO 68th Round (July 2011–June 2012), Government of India 2014a.

areas and the intake is also declining over the years. Further, protein intake is declining and fat intake is rising in rural areas (Table 9.5).

The on-going government schemes to tackle the problem of hunger and malnutrition are discussed in the following section.

Government schemes

Public Distribution System (PDS)

The Public Distribution System (PDS) in India strives to ensure food security through timely and affordable distribution of food grains to "below poverty line" population who cannot afford food grains at market prices. It is seen that the share of public distribution of food grains has been fluctuating over the years, though it is

Food security and sustainable agriculture 187

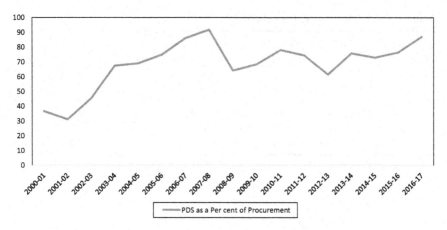

FIGURE 9.2 Public distribution of food grains as a percentage of procurement

Source: Department of Food & Public Distribution, Ministry of Consumer Affairs, Food and Public Distribution, Government of India, various years (a)

TABLE 9.6 Growth of food grains, procurement and public distribution (%)

Time periods	Years	Procurement	Public distribution
I	2000–01 to 2008–09	1.98	14.37
II	2009–10 to 2016–17	0.29	2.37
Overall	2000–01 to 2016–17	4.30	8.39

Source: Department of Food & Public Distribution, Ministry of Consumer Affairs, Food and Public Distribution, GOI

showing a rising trend since 2014–15 (Figure 9.2). However, the trend growth rate of both procurement and public distribution of food grains has declined in recent years (period II) (Table 9.6).

Various studies have estimated PDS leakages to be very large. They are as high as 54 per cent for wheat and 15 per cent for Rice. The leakages are falling though still unacceptably high (Sen et al. 2015).

Integrated Child Development Services (ICDS)

This scheme was launched by the Ministry of Women and Child Development for early childhood (below 6 years) development in 1975. It aims to reduce the incidence of mortality, morbidity, malnutrition and school dropout; to enhance the capability of the mother to look after the health and nutritional needs of the child through proper nutrition and health education.

From Table 9.7 it is seen that growth rates of operational anganwadi centres (AWCs), supplementary nutritional beneficiaries and preschool educational beneficiaries have declined in recent years (period II).

TABLE 9.7 Growth rate of ICDS in India (%)

Time periods	Years	Operational AWCs	Supplementary nutrition beneficiaries – children (6 mths – 6 yrs) and pregnant & lactating women	Preschool education beneficiaries
I	2002–08	10.05	15.07	12.32
II	2008–14	5.40	3.34	1.26
Overall	2002–14	8.59	9.93	7.18

Source: www.indiastat.com

According to the NFHS-3 report (2005–06), 72 per cent of the enumerated areas were covered by AWCs and 62 per cent enumerated area had AWCs that had existed for the last 5 years. Yet malnourishment was 40.4 per cent for children below 3 years and 48 per cent for those below 5 years. The incidence of anaemia in children between 6–35 months was 74 per cent according to NFHS-2 (1998–99) which increased to 79 per cent during NFHS-3 (IIPS 1998–99 and 2005–06). Only 39 per cent children between 12–23 months were fully immunised in rural areas. A high proportion of pregnant women (78 per cent) and lactating mothers (83 per cent) were not using ICDS facilities. The AWCs were typically located in the richer part of the villages which may have been out of reach for vulnerable children. The programme was also found to target children mostly after the age of 3 when malnutrition had already set in (Saxena 2010).

Mid-day Meal Scheme (MDM)

This scheme was launched by the Ministry of Human Resource Development in 1995. This is a school meal programme designed to improve the nutritional status of school-age children nationwide. This is done with a view to enhancing enrolment and attendance and simultaneously improving nutritional levels among children.

The midday meal statistics show that various services and infrastructure needed for smooth delivery of the scheme have been improving over the years (Table 9.8). However, evaluation studies showed that nutritional delivery through the meals was low in comparison to the daily requirements in general. The meals were much lower in nutrients such as protein, fat, iron, and iodine (Deodhar et al. 2010). Other problems reported were unavailability of proper kitchen sheds, unavailability of tumblers & plates, students washing utensils, reduction in teaching time by teachers involved in MDM and adulteration and leakages of food grains (Government of India, 2010).

Health and Sanitation

Access to health care

The National Health Mission (NHM) was started by the Ministry of Health and Family Welfare, as a welfare initiative to strengthen the health care infrastructure

TABLE 9.8 Midday meal statistics

Years	Government aided schools providing midday meals (%)	Schools providing midday meals having kitchen shed (%)	Schools providing midday meals but do not prepare in school premises (%)
2009–10	87.50	42.81	–
2010–11	88.24	41.19	–
2011–12	92.06	40.95	–
2012–13	94.83	60.43	12.53
2013–14	97.89	74.92	9.45
2014–15	96.94	77.37	9.80
2015–16	97.61	80.02	9.23

Source: DISE Flash Statistics, NUEPA, Government of India, various years (b) (Various Issues)

in the country. The mission has two components, the National Rural Health Mission (NRHM) that was launched in 2005 and the National Urban Health Mission (NUHM) that was launched in 2013.

Between 1995 and 2014 India's public expenditure on health care rose only from 1.1 per cent of GDP to 1.4 per cent. More than 70 per cent of health financing in India is through out of pocket (OOP) payments (Government of India, 2011). The Rashtriya Suraksha Bima Yojna (RSBY) has been the main insurance mechanism available to the poor, but its coverage is low and in many states it has a poor claims ratio. With rising life expectancy, health care costs are expected to rise as the population vulnerable to chronic non-communicable diseases (NCD) would increase. According to the 12th Plan document there were only 45 doctors per lakh (0.1 million) population in the beginning of the Plan (2012–17) while the desirable number was 85. Similarly there were only 75 nurses and Auxiliary Nurses & Midwives (ANM) per lakh (0.1 million) population while the desirable number was 225 (Government of India 2013b). Rural areas are typically poorly served. Between 2007 and 2011 rural sub-centres grew by 2 per cent, primary health centres by 6 per cent, community health centres by 16 per cent and district hospitals by 45 per cent. Yet shortfalls remain. In 2011 the gap between staff positioned and required was 52 per cent for ANMs, 72 per cent for doctors, 88 per cent for specialists and 58 per cent for pharmacists. Between 2007 and 2011, mobile medical units (MMU) was deployed in 449 districts, yet the outreach remained inadequate. The Janani Surksha Yojna (JSY) in rural areas saw a rise in institutional deliveries from 40 per cent to 68 per cent between 2005 and 2009, yet share of women coming in for antenatal care was a low 23 per cent (Government of India 2013a).

Access to safe drinking water

There has been marked improvement in access to better drinking water sources among households in both rural and urban India (Table 9.9).

A closer look at disaggregated data (Table 9.10) shows that the principal source of drinking water in rural areas is tubewell/borehole (52.4 per cent). While in

TABLE 9.9 Access to safe drinking water (%)

Years	Rural	Urban	Total
1991	55.5	81.4	62.3
2001	73.2	90	77.9
2011	82.7	91.4	85.5

Source: Economic Survey (2016–17)

TABLE 9.10 Number per 1,000 households in India by some "improved" and "unimproved" principal source of drinking water (1993–2012)

All-India	Rural				Urban			
Principle source of drinking water	49th Round (1993)	58th Round (2002)	65th Round (2008)	69th Round (2012)	49th Round (1993)	58th Round (2002)	65th Round (2008)	69th Round (2012)
Improved sources								
Bottled water			5	16			27	52
Piped Water (Dwelling, yard, Public tap)	189	275	301	312	704	736	743	691
Tubewell/borehole	445	513	547	524	185	196	175	199
Unimproved sources								
Surface water: tank/pond	8	4	3	5	4	0	1	1
Other surface water: River/Dam/Stream/Canal/Lake etc.	17	11	7	6	1	1	0	0

Source: NSSO 69th Round (July 2012 to December 2012)

urban areas it is piped water into dwelling (35.1 per cent) (69th Round, NSSO). "Tubewells" as a source of drinking water have been increasing in rural areas, but they are gradually increasing in urban areas as well. Use of "bottled water" had increased more than twice in rural India and almost doubled in urban India during the period 2008 and 2012. Use of "publictap/standpipe" had increased over time in rural India and decreased marginally in urban India between 2008 & 2012.

Further, households having sufficient drinking water throughout the year from principal sources declined marginally to 85.8 per cent in rural areas and 89.6 per cent in urban areas (Table 9.11). Households having principal source of drinking water outside their premises but within 0.2–0.5 km also increased in both rural and urban areas. Other parameters also showed improvement.

Access to sanitation facilities

Sanitation facilities are seen to be improving gradually in both rural and urban areas (Table 9.12). However, 62.3 per cent households in rural areas and 16.7 per cent

TABLE 9.11 Number per 1,000 households in India by some important characteristics of principal source of drinking water (1993–2012)

All India Characteristics	Rural 49th round (1993)	58th round (2002)	65th round (2008)	69th round (2012)	Urban 49th round (1993)	58th round (2002)	65th round (2008)	69th round (2012)
Households having sufficient drinking water throughout the year from principal source		887	862	858		892	911	896
Households having principal source of drinking water within premises	343	372	405	461	662	703	745	768
Households having principal source of drinking water outside premises but within 0.2–0.5km	81	90	92	93	25	29	20	29
Households having exclusive use of principal source of drinking water	206	254	311	337	402	438	470	468
Households having community use of principal source of drinking water	728	656	568	467	380	308	229	190

Source: NSSO 69th Round (July 2012 to December 2012)

TABLE 9.12 Number per 1,000 households in India by some important characteristics of bathroom and sanitation facilities (1993–2012)

Characteristics	Rural 49th round (1993)	58th round (2002)	65th round (2008)	69th round (2012)	Urban 49th round (1993)	58th round (2002)	65th round (2008)	69th round (2012)
Households without bathroom facility	870	760	644	623	465	315	215	167
Households having attached bathroom	54	98	125	155	275	411	480	554
Households without latrine facility	858	763	652	594	306	179	113	88
Households having exclusive use of latrine	102	173	279	319	404	535	581	639

Source: NSSO 69th Round (July 2012 to December 2012)

households in urban areas reported no bathroom facilities (69th Round NSSO). In fact households without bathroom facilities have shown a decline over the years. Only 15.5 per cent households in rural areas and 55.4 per cent households in urban areas reported attached bathroom in dwellings. 59.4 per cent households in rural areas and 8.8 per cent households in urban areas reported no latrine facilities. Lastly, exclusive use of latrine facilities was reported by only 31.9 per cent rural households and 63.9 per cent urban households.

Indicators of human development

Over the years India has shown improvement on most indicators of human development (Table 9.13). However, we have not been able to achieve targets set by the various Five Year Plans (FYP) for most indicators. In fact child sex ratio has shown deterioration.

The challenge of sustainable agriculture

This challenge is based on rising concerns over sustainability because of depletion of natural resources, environmental pollution and climate change, that are in turn resulting in stagnating crop yields in recent years. Therefore there is a need for sustainable agricultural practices such as complementarity between usage of

TABLE 9.13 Selected indicators of human development

Indicators	Baseline level	Recent status
Life Expectancy at Birth (Years)	64.3 (2001–05)	67.5 (2009–13)
Infant mortality rates (per 1000 live births)	57 (SRS, 2006)	44 (SRS, 2011)
Maternal mortality rate (per 100000 live births)	254 (SRS, 2004–06)	212 (SRS, 2007–09)
Birth rate (per 1000)	23.8 (2005)	21.4 (2013)
Death rate (per 1000)	7.6 (2005)	7 (2013)
Total fertility rate	2.8 (SRS, 2006)	2.5 (SRS, 2010)
Malnutrition among children 0–3 years	40.4 (NFHS, 2005–06)	No recent data available
Anaemia among women and girls	55.3 (NFHS, 2005–06)	No recent data available
Sex ratio (females per 1000 males)	933	943 (2013)
Child sex ratio (0–6 years)	927 (2001)	918 (2011)
HDI ranking	0.387 (1999–2000)	0.563 (2007–08)

Source: Twelfth Five Year Plan – Social Sectors, Vol. III & Economic Survey (2015–16)

non-chemical (organic) and chemical fertilisers, use of water efficient technologies and crop diversification towards water saving and leguminous crops to improve soil health and crop productivity.

Organic farming

Organic farming is a system which avoids or largely excludes the use of synthetic or chemical inputs. Latest data shows that the proportion of agricultural area treated with chemical inputs is much larger than that treated with Farm Yard Manure (FYM) and their shares are seen to be increasing over the years, while those of FYM are declining. Further, the use of chemical fertilisers is much higher in irrigated than in un-irrigated areas (Table 9.14).

Since the establishment of the National Centre of Organic Farming (NCOF) a decade ago, only 0.5 per cent arable land is under organic cultivation in India. This includes cultivated area which is under an organic certification process as well as wild areas that includes forest lands and shrubs and grasslands. Figure 9.3 shows that cultivated area undergoing the process of organic certification is less than 1 MHa and is increasing slowly in recent years. On the other hand, wild areas show much larger acreage, though their acreage is seen to be declining in recent years. The total acreage under organic farming is high because of the share of wild areas in it. Organic products are expensive as they are produced without the aid of relatively cheaper inorganic compounds. They are branded and marketed in a manner whereby they command a significant premium compared to products derived from crops that are grown using chemical inputs. The high price acts as a deterrent to demand which results in low acreages under organic cultivation.

It is important to understand that the organic farming cannot substitute chemical fertilisers but can only complement it. The combined and balanced use of organic as well as chemical fertilisers is important instead of complete organic farming. This is because the supply of organic manure is limited and thus more expensive as compared to chemical inputs, which would not be cost effective for the poor farmer.

TABLE 9.14 Farm area treated with chemicals and FYM

Areas	Area treated with fertilisers (%)		Area treated with FYM (%)		Area treated with pesticides (%)	
	2006–07	2011–12	2006–07	2011–12	2006–07	2011–12
Irrigated	91.77	89.75	21.94	18.24	52.20	48.70
Unirrigated	55.12	63.88	31.13	22.67	29.68	39.33
Total	72.62	75.88	26.74	20.62	40.44	43.67

Source: Government of India, Agricultural Census, Input Survey 2006–07 and 2011–12

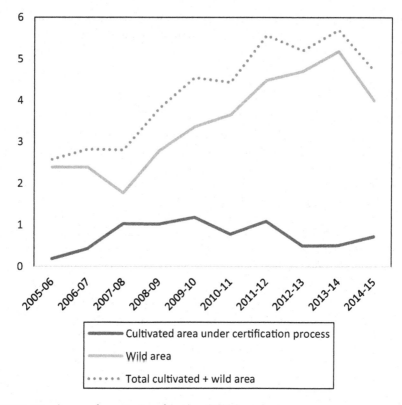

FIGURE 9.3 Area under organic cultivation (MHa)

Source: National Centre of Organic Farming, GoI & FIBL Research Institute of Organic Agriculture and IFOAM Organics International

System of rice intensification

System of Rice Intensification (SRI) is a climate-smart method for increasing the productivity of rice and more recently other crops by changing the management of plants, soil, water and nutrients. SRI spaces rice plants more widely and does not depend on continuous flooding of rice fields. It also uses lesser seed and chemical inputs. In India SRI cultivation in rice started in 2003 and its share in total rice area was just 1 per cent in 2008 (SRI India 2008). Since SRI uses less seed and chemical inputs, it offers a shrunk market for certain agro-based industries and thus does not attract their patronage. It also requires more commitment and involvement from farmers and extension personnel and is thereby more labour-intensive than conventional cultivation which is a factor for slow or non-adoption. Overall benefits of SRI to practicing farmers come in the form of higher profits, because of savings in seed and irrigation.

Water efficient agriculture

Irrigation is very critical to agriculture in India. However, irrigation problems range from high expenditure on large canal based surface irrigation projects and proliferation of schemes, rising gaps between irrigation potential created and utilised and dependence and over-exploitation of ground water. The growth rate of irrigated area has declined in recent years from 2.31 per cent between 2000–01 and 2006–07 to 1.54 per cent between 2007–08 and 2014–15. Area under tube-well irrigation stood at 46 per cent of the total irrigated area while the total irrigated area itself was 48.64 per cent in 2014–15. Hence in India there is high dependency on groundwater for irrigation as a result of which groundwater tables are on the decline. According to an estimate, ground water tables in India are declining at the rate of 1 Foot/Year (National Aeronautics and Space Administration). The declining ground water tables necessitate the need for Micro-Irrigation. This is a resource conservation technology and involves the use of Drip and Sprinkler System of irrigation. The technology involves irrigating crops at the root zone as per the crop requirement. This technology greatly enhances both water and fertiliser use efficiency. Till 2016 the cumulative area under micro-irrigation was 8.63 Mha. It covered only 9 per cent of the gross irrigated area and 12.42 per cent of the total micro-irrigation potential. The area under micro-irrigation has grown rapidly from 0.02 MHa in 2005 to 8.63 MHa in 2016. However, the rate of adoption of this technology across states is varied. The top adopting states till 2016 were Rajasthan (20.32 per cent), Andhra Pradesh and Maharashtra (approximately 15 per cent) and Gujarat 12.39 per cent. According to a study by Palanisami et al. in 2011 the poor adoption was attributed to factors such as high cost, complexity of the technology and socio-economic issues such as a lack of access to credit facilities, fragmented landholdings and localised cropping pattern. Farmers opined that the technology was suitable only for large farmers.

Water efficient and nutrient rich crop – coarse cereals

Coarse cereals that include crops such as Jowar, Bajra, Ragi and Millets are very rich in nutrients and also water efficient in nature. Coarse cereals occupy about 12.66 per cent of the cropped area but its area is on the decline (Figure 9.4). Trend growth rates in its production and yields have also declined over the years (Table 9.15).

Leguminous crops – pulses

Pulses are leguminous crops. These have nodules that fix nitrogen into the soil and enhance soil fertility and crop productivity. Pulses occupy around 12.13 per cent of the cropped area and it shows a fluctuating but increasing trend since 2014–15 (Figure 9.5). Though trend growth rates in its area have increased, the growth in its production and yields have registered a decline (Table 9.16).

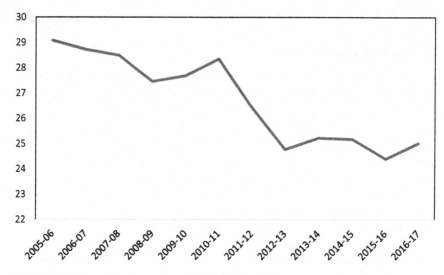

FIGURE 9.4 Area under coarse cereals (000 Ha)

Source: Directorate of Economics and Statistics, Ministry of Agriculture and Farmers Welfare, GoI

TABLE 9.15 Coarse cereal statistics

Years	Averages		Growth rates (%)	
	2005–10	2011–16	2005–10	2011–16
Area ('000 Ha)	28.29	25.16	−0.78	−0.92
Production ('000 tonnes)	37.62	41.75	3.37	0.23
Yield (Kg/Ha)	1330.01	1659.43	4.18	1.15

Source: Directorate of Economics and Statistics, Ministry of Agriculture and Farmers Welfare, GoI

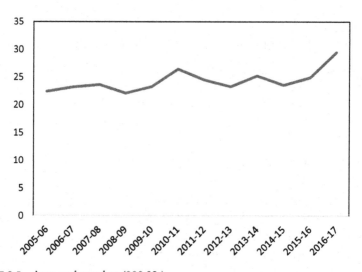

FIGURE 9.5 Area under pulses (000 Ha)

Source: Directorate of Economics and Statistics, Ministry of Agriculture and Farmers Welfare, GoI

TABLE 9.16 Pulses statistics

Years	Averages		Growth rates (%)	
	2005–10	2011–16	2005–10	2011–16
Area ('000 Ha)	23.50	25.14	2.22	3.09
Production (000 tonnes)	14.97	18.55	4.77	3.04
Yield (Kg/Ha)	637.94	736.66	2.50	-0.05

Source: Directorate of Economics and Statistics, Ministry of Agriculture and Farmers Welfare, GoI

TABLE 9.17 Area under crops as percentage of gross cropped area (triennium ending 2014)

Crops	Average of 2012–14
Rice	22.07
Wheat	15.49
Oilseeds	13.50
Coarse cereals	12.66
Pulses	12.13
Cotton	6.19
Sugarcane	2.54

Source: Directorate of Economics and Statistics, Ministry of Agriculture and Farmers Welfare, GoI

Area under coarse cereals and pulses occupy a smaller share in the cropping pattern of India compared to crops like rice (22.07 per cent), wheat (15.49 per cent) and oilseeds (13.50 per cent). The shares of cotton and sugarcane are 6.19 per cent and 2.54 per cent respectively. The shares of rice and wheat are high because they are staple crops. Oilseeds, sugarcane and cotton are commercial crops and hence are promoted more compared to coarse cereals (also referred to as "poor man's food") and pulses (Table 9.17).

Budgetary allocations

Table 9.18 shows budgetary allocations in agriculture, rural development and social sectors. It is seen that outlays in agriculture, irrigation, education, health, rural development and drinking water showed a decline in 2015–16 from their 2014–15 levels. However

TABLE 9.18 Budgetary allocations (percentage of GDP)

Items	2014–15	2015–16	2016–17
Agriculture & irrigation	0.25	0.19	0.32
Social sectors including education & health	1.09	1.03	1.01
Rural development & drinking water	0.66	0.66	0.68
Food subsidy	0.94	1.03	0.9
Fertiliser subsidy	0.57	0.53	0.46

Source: Bose (2016)

they increased marginally in 2016–17. Subsidies on food and fertiliser have been decreasing too. It is imperative to increase allocations in these sectors. India has a very low tax to GDP ratio. It is around 18 per cent compared to 28 per cent for USA and around 45–50 per cent for Scandanavian countries. Hence budgetary allocations towards various sectors can be increased by improving the tax to GDP ratio (Right to Food Campaign).

Conclusions and way forward

The paper has demonstrated with empirical data that the situation with respect to food security in India is quite fragile and the on-going interventions are inadequate. Also, sustainable agricultural practices adopted in the country are too meagre to impact the situation positively. The small and declining share of agricultural GDP is unable to support half the workforce of India as it currently does. It increases the vulnerability of the poor. High poverty levels and malnutrition have been a consistent problem in India and in order to tackle it, schemes such as the ICDS, MDM, PDS etc. have been introduced. However, their performance reveals a mixed picture and the set of food insecure people remain large. Access to safe drinking water, sanitation and health care facilities are increasing but rural areas are lagging behind their urban counterparts. Over the years, India has shown improvement on most indicators of human development, but in spite of this several FYP targets remain unaccomplished. Hence, if India has not been able to meet its FYP targets on time, achieving SDGs by 2030 seems a very difficult if not an impossible proposition. A lot of concerted efforts and political will is needed for achieving SDGs. Some of these, as discussed in the paper, could be to promote crop diversification towards water-efficient crops (coarse cereals) as well as leguminous crops (pulses). Crop productivity could be raised by using cost-effective, ecologically sound and sustainable technologies (SRI and micro irrigation). There has been significant decline in calorie intake eventhough official poverty estimates are also declining. This makes the official estimates of poverty seem ambiguous and misleading and thereby need to be amended. Budgetary allocations to agriculture, rural development and other social sectors could be increased by generating more resources for public welfare programmes by improving the tax to GDP ratio through progressive direct taxation.

References

Bathla, S., Thorat, S.K., Joshi, P.K., and Yu, B. 2017. "Where to Invest to Accelerate Agricultural Growth and Poverty Reduction." *Economic & Political Weekly*, 52(39).

Bose, Prosenjit. 2016. "A Budget that Reveals the Truth about India's Growth Story." *The Wire*. Available at: http://thewire.in/23392/what-the-budget-tells-us-about-indias-growth-story/, [Accessed June 10, 2016].

Deaton, A., and Drèze, J. 2009. "Food and Nutrition in India: Facts and Interpretations." *Economic & Political Weekly*, 44(7).

Deodhar, S.Y., Mahandiratta, S., Ramani, K.V., Mavalankar, D., Ghosh, S., and Braganza, V. 2010. "An Evaluation of Mid-Day Meal Scheme." *Journal of Indian School of Political Economy*, 22(1–4).

FAOSTAT 2016. Available at: www.fao.org/faostat/en/#compare [Accessed February 26, 2016].
FiBL Research Institute of Organic Agriculture. Available at: www.fibl.org, [Accessed June 30, 2016].
Government of India. 2006–07 and 2011–12. *Agricultural Census, Input Survey*. New Delhi: Department of Agriculture, Cooperation & Farmers Welfare, June 5, 2016. Available at: http://inputsurvey.dacnet.nic.in/ [Accessed June 30, 2016].
———. 2017–18. *Economic Survey 2017–18*. New Delhi: Ministry of Finance. Available at: http://mofapp.nic.in:8080/economicsurvey/ [Accessed February 26, 2019].
———. 2010. *Performance Evaluation of Cooked Mid-Day Meal*. New Delhi: *Planning Commission*, Programme Evaluation Organization.
———. 2011. *Report of the Working Group on National Rural Health Mission (NRHM) for the Twelfth Five Year Plan (2012–17)*. New Delhi: Planning Commission.
———. 2013a. "Key Indicators of Drinking Water, Sanitation, Hygiene and Housing Condition in India." *National Sample Survey Office (NSSO), Ministry of Statistics and Programme Implementation, 69th Round (July 2012 to December 2012), December*. Available at: http://mospi.nic.in/sites/default/files/publication_reports/nss_rep_556_14aug14.pdf, [Accessed July 5, 2016].
———. 2013b. *Twelfth Five Year Plan – Social Sectors*, Vol. III. New Delhi: Planning Commission.
———. 2014a. "Nutritional Intake in India." *Ministry of Statistics and Programme Implementation, National Sample Survey Office (NSSO) 68th Round (July 2011–June 2012), October*. Available at: www.indiaenvironmentportal.org.in/files/file/nutritional%20intake%20in%20India%202011-12.pdf [Accessed July 6, 2016].
———. 2014b. *Report of the Expert Group to Review the Methodology for Measurement of Poverty*. New Delhi: Planning Commission.
———. *National Centre of Organic Farming*, Department of Agriculture, Cooperation and Farmers Welfare, Ministry of Agriculture and Farmers Welfare. Available at: http://ncof.dacnet.nic.in/ [Accessed June 30, 2016].
———. *Various Years, Department of Food & Public Distribution*, Ministry of Consumer Affairs, Food and Public Distribution. Available at: www.dfpd.nic.in [Accessed February 17, 2019].
———. *Various Years.a. Directorate of Economics and Statistics*, Department of Agriculture, Cooperation and Farmers Welfare, Ministry of Agriculture and Farmers Welfare, Government of India. Available at: http://eands.dacnet.nic.in/ [Accessed February 17, 2019].
———. *Various Years.b. District Information System for Education (DISE) Flash Statistics*, National University of Education. Planning and Administration (NUEPA), Ministry of Human Resource Development.
Grebmer, K., Bernstein, J., Hossain, N., Brown, T., Prasai, N., Yohannes, Y., Patterson, F., Sonntag, A., Zimmermann, S.M., Towey, O., and Foley, C. 2017. *2017 Global Hunger Index: The Inequalities of Hunger*. Washington, DC: International Food Policy Research Institute; Bonn: Welthungerhilfe; and Dublin: Concern Worldwide. Available at: www.globalhungerindex.org/pdf/en/2017/appendix-d.pdf [Accessed October 12, 2017].
IFOAM Organics International. Available at: www.ifoam.bio/en. [Accessed June 30, 2016].
IFPRI. n.d. – Food Security Portal. Available at: www.foodsecurityportal.org [Accessed October 20, 2017].
Indiastat.com. Available at: www.indiastat.com [Accessed July 10, 2016].
IIPS. 1998–99 and 2005–06. *National Family Health Survey (NFHS) 2 & 3* – Mumbai: International Institute for Population Sciences. Available at: http://rchiips.org/NFHS/nfhs2.shtml & http://rchiips.org/NFHS/nfhs3.shtml [Accessed June 25, 2016].
National Aeronautics and Space Administration (NASA). 2009. Available at: www.nasa.gov/topics/earth/features/india_water.htm [Accessed July 12, 2016].

OECD-FAO Agricultural Outlook. Available at: https://stats.oecd.org/Index.aspx?dataset code=HIGH_AGLINK_2018 [Accessed February 27, 2019].

Palanisami, K., Kadiri, M., Kakumanu, K.R., and Raman, S. 2011. "Spread and Economics of Micro-irrigation in India: Evidence from Nine States." *Economic & Political Weekly*, 46(26/27).

Patnaik, Utsa. 2013. "Poverty Trends in India 2004–05 to 2009–10: Updating Poverty Estimates and Comparing Official Figures." *Economic & Political Weekly*, 48(40).

Right to Food Campaign. *Food Security: What the Government Says and What We Want*. Available at: www.indiaenvironmentportal.org.in/files/food_security_what_the_government_says_and_what_we_want.pdf [Accessed August 20, 2017].

Saxena, N.C. 2010. "Hunger, Under-nutrition and Food Security in India." *Chronic Poverty Research Centre (CPRC) & Indian Institute of Public Administration (IIPA), Working Paper 44*. Available at: www.files.ethz.ch/isn/128320/CPRC-IIPA per cent2044.pdf [Accessed July 7, 2016].

Sen, A., Himanshu, Drèze J., and Khera, R. 2015. "Clarification on PDS Leakages." *Economic & Political Weekly*, 50(39).

SRI Fact Sheet India 2008, ICRISAT-WWF Project. Available at: www.sri-india.net [Accessed June 15, 2016].

Swaminathan, M.S. 2001. "Food Security and Sustainable Development." *Current Science*, 81(8).

Food and Agriculture Organisation. 2015. *The State of Food Insecurity in the World – Meeting the 2015 International Hunger Targets: Taking Stock of Uneven Progress*. Rome: FAO, IFAD and WFP. Available at: www.fao.org/3/a-i4646e.pdf [Accessed June 18, 2016].

United Nations, n.d, *Sustainable Development Goals Knowledge Platform*. Available at: https://sustainabledevelopment.un.org/topics/foodagriculture [Accessed October 20, 2017].

World Food Programme. n.d. Available at: http://www1.wfp.org/countries/india [Accessed October 20, 2017].

PART V
Gender equality

10

GENDER AND SUSTAINABLE DEVELOPMENT GOALS

Suneeta Dhar

2015 was an exceptional year for women's rights globally. New data reported the gains made and challenges faced in advancing women's rights through the 20-year review of the implementation of the UN Beijing Platform for Action (1995) and the completion of the 15-year UN Millennium Development Goals (September 2000). These agreements paved the way for a new set of global agreements to emerge – the UN Sustainable Development Goals (September 2015). The Sustainable Development Goals (SDGs) underscore the areas where states have failed to meet with their gender-equality obligations. The SDGs represent the evolution of a new compact on women's human rights and gender equality that has been universally endorsed by governments, donors, women's movements, civil society and other international and national stakeholders.

This chapter traces the key commitments made to women's rights through the three major conferences in the last two decades, previously mentioned. It engages the context and framing of the women's rights agendas by global and regional women's advocacy groups, their organising efforts and their impact on UN agendas. Women's groups imprinted upon the worlds' consciousness the need to develop enabling policy frameworks (that are pro-women), and fast-track their implementation to ensure significant changes in the lives of women and marginalised populations. They also raised critical questions of how equality, inclusion and participation would be embedded in a world that was structured around grave inequalities and exclusions.

Whereas the framework of the paper is global, the final section of the paper suggests what it would require for countries to meet SDG goals. Using India as a case study, it examines two critical areas among the SDGs – the Economic Empowerment of Women and Ending Violence Against Women in India – with pointers regarding how India could better meet its commitment vis-à-vis these two goals. India's policy initiatives and budgetary commitment to advance women's rights in the context of the SDGs is also reviewed in the light of the SDG commitments urging the need for instituting effective mechanisms and additional fund flows to meet the gender equality goals intrinsic to the SDGs. While some civil society and Indian women's movement groups have been engaged with global policy in the context of advancing women's rights in the SDG framework, it is hoped that they will continue to play a strong role nationally and regionally.

The paper concludes with a broad-brush snapshot of how other countries are developing mechanisms to advance their SDG commitments. Key areas of focus being identified by various countries are described, noting how the North and developing countries are engaged in the process. The lack of data and measurement on gender equality is a key concern in the SDG process, and the efforts underway to improve data collection for monitoring processes are underlined and national plans to create the infrastructure for this described.

Clearly, the SDGs mark a new phase in the struggle for gender equality. This can only be realised with women's voices, a rights-based framework and lived realities informing this process, together with broad-based partnerships with civil society and government.

Women's rights: the journey from the Beijing platform for action to sustainable development goals

189 countries adopted the Beijing Declaration and Platform for Action (BPfA) in September 1995[1] during the Fourth World Conference on Women. Beijing followed the three major international conferences for women that were held in Mexico City (1975), Copenhagen (1980) and Nairobi (1985) as part of the UN Decade for Women. The participants at these meetings raised critical concerns pertaining to the promotion of equal rights and opportunities for women around the world.[2] The Beijing Conference is considered to be one of the major achievements of global and local women's movements in the early 1990s as the women's movements were extremely effective in their organising and took their agenda to governments and other state actors, generating broad-based public support for women's equality. Women from the global South also played a critical role in framing and advancing their concerns in global agendas.

The 12 areas of concern in the BPfA were women and poverty; the education and training of women; health; violence against women; armed conflict; the economy; women in power and decision-making; mechanisms for the advancement of women; human rights; the media; women and the environment; and the girl child. Most importantly, the BPfA called for strong commitments on the part of governments, national governments, international institutions and other partners to fully support and realise the advancement of women's human rights and gender equality. Several grassroots women's groups, community organisers, feminist academicians and others from India had participated in the lead-up preparations to the Beijing conference and sought commitments from both local and national stakeholders.

As the implementation of the Beijing agenda proceeded, regional and global reviews and appraisals occurred on a five-year basis to track progress.[3] Through this period women's groups and networks prepared alternative reports to highlight the gaps and achievements been made at the national, regional and global levels. In this way they sought to push their governments and relevant bodies to meet their commitments. For example, in India, the National Alliance of Women[4] (NAWO) held regular reviews and the United Nations Development Fund for Women (UNIFEM) South Asia[5] convened bi-annual regional review meetings with government and civil society to support the implementation of BPfA with governments in South Asia.

For the 20-year Beijing review, the United Nations Entity for Gender Equality and the Empowerment of Women (UN Women) in 2015[6] continued its dialogue and assessment process with the government and civil society in India, and convened a National Consultation in partnership with the Bejing+20 Civil Society Working Group and a wide set of stakeholders. Key issues discussed were that of disability and sexuality, the need for using an intersectional lens across gender issues, the impact of information technology and social media on gender and rights, and newer forms of violence faced by women and girls. The need to work with men in ending violence against women, and with the LGBTIQ (lesbian, gay, bisexual, transgender, intersex and queer) and young people as allies was also raised. The findings were thereafter presented at regional and global review meetings.

At the 20-year review of the BPfA, held by the United Nations Commission on the Status of Women[7] in New York in September 2015, a political declaration was adopted by member states (UN Women 2015). The Declaration recognised that no country had fully achieved equality and empowerment for women and girls. It further noted that progress across the 12 critical areas has been uneven and that there were persistent obstacles and structural barriers to achieving gender equality.

Currently available gender statistics at the UN underscore severe gender gaps in some critical sectors. Worldwide, 58 million children of primary-school age are out of school (more than half of them being girls), with nearly three-quarters living in sub-Saharan Africa and South Asia. Nearly two-thirds of the world's illiterate adults are women, and this number has remained the same over the last 20 years. Worldwide, 35 per cent of women have experienced either physical and/or sexual intimate partner violence or non-partner sexual violence. So far, it has been noted, not one country has reached or surpassed gender parity. At the legislative level, while a record 143 countries had guaranteed equality between women and men in their constitutions by 2014, there were still 52 that had not (UN Women 2015).[8]

In response to these persistent inequalities, governments pledged to take further concrete actions to achieve gender equality, including strengthening the implementation of laws, policies, strategies and institutional mechanisms, as well as work towards transforming discriminatory gender norms and practices. Governments committed to significantly mobilising additional financial resources and strengthening accountability mechanisms. Most importantly, governments seemed to have welcomed the contributions of civil society, including women's and community-based organisations, to support implementation at all levels.

Whether these commitments translate into action is needed to be seen over time. In some countries, it has been noted that governments have not to date sufficiently embarked on translating women's rights using the normative framework of equality and non-discrimination at the national level, nor have they partnered with women's groups for implementation of this important agenda. India prepared its National Plan of Action for Women post the Beijing Conference and instituted several steps to meet with its obligations. The brief findings from the India review reports and its evolving plans for the SDGs are highlighted in the section under India in more detail.

Changing contexts from MDGs to SDGs

Before the turn of the last century, and in preparation for the 2000 Millennium Summit, the UN Secretary-General launched his report, *We the peoples: The role of the United Nations in the 21st century* (Annan 2000). A Millennium Forum was convened that brought together several representatives of non-governmental and civil society organisations from over a hundred countries to discuss issues such as poverty eradication, environmental protection, human rights and protection of the vulnerable. In September 2000, leaders of 189 countries signed the historic Millennium Declaration[9] and adopted the Millennium Development Goals (MDGs), committing themselves to achieving a concrete set of eight measurable goals by 2015. The goals addressed extreme poverty in its many dimensions – income poverty, hunger, disease, lack of adequate shelter, and exclusion – while promoting gender equality, education and environmental sustainability. They also included basic human rights – the rights of each person on the planet to health, education, shelter and security.

Among the eight goals was Gender Equality and Women's Empowerment (MDG3). According to the World Health Organization (WHO), the indicators of MDG3 were formulated to track key elements of women's social, economic and political participation, and to guide countries towards building gender-equitable societies.[10] It is worth noting here that the goals and targets for the MDGs were framed around key development concerns – primary education, nutrition and health – that are largely relevant to developing countries and were thus not considered universally applicable.

Despite the intentions, the MDGs were met with much dismay by women's groups across the world. There were concerns about their being located within a development framework rather than a rights-based one. The MDGs neither mentioned nor identified a target for ending violence against women (VAW), the care work of women, women's autonomy or agency. Feminists continued to underline the missing agendas and advocated for their inclusion. They also critiqued and challenged the inadequacy of the framing of targets and indicators, and outlined the difficulties of capturing the goal of women's empowerment (Kabeer 2005).

Women's advocates argued that the MDGs represented a contraction of commitments in relation to the previous UN agendas empowering women. Sen and Mukherjee (2014) observed that only about one-quarter of the targets in the BPfA were (directly or indirectly) covered by an MDG target and indicators. These targets were primarily related to education, health, women's employment, political representation and access to water and sanitation. Furthermore, education and health rights were given a higher priority than women's economic and political rights. Maternal health and HIV/AIDS were considered more relevant than sexual and reproductive health, again underlining the fact that the MDGs were development oriented but not rights based. Women's groups insisted that a rights-based approach drive the development agenda. The insistence by women's groups did lead to an additional MDG target, the "universal access to reproductive health" (Sen and Mukherjee 2014). Women's groups were simultaneously working at the national level, advocating with their respective governments to build in additional targets on VAW into national plans. At this level they met with limited success.

To bridge deficits on gender issues within the MDGs, women's groups also strongly advocated for deploying "lessons learnt" from the various outcome documents of the Beijing reviews, country CEDAW (Convention on the Elimination of all Forms of Discrimination against Women) reports,[11] and other global reviews (Security Council Resolution 1325), so as to inform the MDG implementation plans. UNIFEM too raised these concerns and strongly advocated for the need to address women's rights as had been enshrined within international obligations embodied in the BPfA, CEDAW and other international documents (Waldorf 2003). Fears about dilution in human rights standards for women and unmet state obligations continued to remain at the heart of the struggles of women's groups through this entire process.

On the completion of 15 years of MDGs, while some significant gains were seen to have been made regarding several MDG targets worldwide, uneven progress across regions and countries was also noted in the global report (United Nations 2015). There were concerns raised in the report about millions of people being left behind (especially from among the poorest and disadvantaged sections of society) because of their sex, age, disability, ethnicity or geographic and other social locations. These findings further corroborated the concerns raised by women's groups regarding the persistence of gender gaps that require more systemic attention.

As global efforts progressed within the UN, it was at the Rio+20 Conference on Sustainable Development (2012) that a global development framework was being envisioned, which was to go far beyond the time frame of 2015 and carry forward the momentum generated by the MDGs. It led to the formulation of the UN General Assembly Open Working Group (2014) that drafted a document with 17 goals for the General Assembly's approval, spanning the years 2015 to 2030.[12] On 25 September 2015, 193 member states of the United Nations adopted the SDG global framework[13] to end poverty, protect the planet and ensure prosperity for all. The United Nations Development Programme (UNDP) noted that the SDGs were based on an inclusive agenda that could help tackle some of the immense development challenges facing the world, such as poverty, climate change and conflict.[14]

It is instructive to note at this point that the MDGs were formulated in the post-cold war geo-political context, when the neo-liberal globalisation agenda was dominant. They were thus driven by the aid agenda from the North and formulated for developing countries only (Fukuda-Parr 2016). The SDGs, on the other hand, set out a universal set of goals with targets for all countries. The SDGs were thus based on key principles, such as being inclusive in nature and "leaving no one behind" – universally applicable and based on human rights.

Voices from the women's movements

Because of the sustained efforts of women's groups, UN Women, and other gender equality champions, a stand-alone Goal 5 on Women's Empowerment and Gender Equality was adopted within the SDGs with gender targets included across other goals as well. This was marked as a great step forward. The SDG Goal 5 encompasses a multi-dimensional approach to gender equality with a wide range of targets that include ending discrimination and violence against women, including trafficking and sexual (and other types of) exploitation; ending child, early and forced marriage, and female genital mutilation; recognising unpaid care and domestic work; promoting women's participation and opportunities for leadership; ensuring universal access to sexual health and reproductive rights; enabling ownership of land and other property, including natural resources; and providing access to intermediate technology (Stuart and Woodroffe 2016). The 17 goals are interconnected; that means that gains in any one area would catalyse achievements in others, with the potential to create greater synergies and impact.

Given the limited success that women's movements, networks and groups had in integrating gender and rights issues within the MDGs, they engaged far more extensively in the lead-up processes to the adoption of the SDGs. Among the prominent women's groups and networks engaging with the process were Post-2015 Women's Coalition, Women's Major Group (WMG), Development Alternatives with Women for a New Era (DAWN),[15] Association of Women in Development (AWID) and Asia Pacific Women's Law and Development, as well as other regional networks. Each of them, independently and collectively, raised concerns throughout the negotiation processes with member states and UN bodies regarding the structural nature of poverty and the neo-liberal macroeconomic framework and their impacts on women and marginalised people. Others, too, highlighted the deepening of gender inequalities and the differential impacts of the neo-liberal economic framework and globalisation upon women's care work and on environmental sustainability (Ponte and Enríquez 2016).

The Post-2015 Women's Coalition (March 2015) demanded dramatic changes in macroeconomic policies. They called for the development of an alternative economic framework that would end the feminisation of poverty and address the multiple burdens of unpaid care and non-care work, disproportionately borne by women and girls around the globe. Among the key outcomes of the organising and critiques by women's groups was the establishment of the High Level Panel on Women's Economic Empowerment by the Secretary-General in January 2016,[16] post the adoption of Agenda 2030.

Women's groups have also been critical about governments' disregard of women's human rights and have unequivocally demanded that states fulfil their obligations under CEDAW and its optional protocols. They have consistently advocated for the inclusion of diverse women's voices and the need to move away from the reductive nature of targets and indicators under the SDGs. AWID, a global women's coalition (Abelenda 2015), welcomed the inclusion of decent work, social protection and the institution of a new multi-stakeholder technology facilitation mechanism in the SDGs. However, they expressed some alarm at the binary notion of gender equality that was being adopted by some states. This had resulted in the exclusion of LGBTIQ rights and non-protection against discrimination for persons with different sexual orientation and gender identities. The Women's Major Group (WMG) (July 2014) amplified these concerns during the negotiations. They called for a truly universal agenda grounded in human rights, asserting that woman's bodies and lives cannot and should not be subjected to national agendas. In a strongly worded statement to governments, the WMG stated

> To those who are still denying our rights we reaffirm, again, that we will always refuse to have our lives used as bargaining chips. No agenda should be traded off. The entire world is at stake because of the narrow ways in which policies and actions are implemented. The significant global challenges we face require a comprehensive ambitious agenda.

Khan and Lappin (APWLD) flagged concerns regarding how the SDGs had undermined agreements reached at Beijing. Essentially, they argued, the SDGs did not reflect an understanding of the deeper structural nature of inequalities experienced by women as was in the Beijing documents. They stressed the lack of firm commitments to reducing military expenditures by governments and to reducing arms manufacturing and trade. They also noted that the right of female workers to organise and collectively bargain for eliminating their wage inequality was unattended to within the SDGs, and, there was need for more state commitments to analyse and adjust macroeconomic policies (including taxation and external debt policy) utilising a gender perspective:

> The objectives of Beijing were consistent with recognition of the deeply structural nature of the inequalities experienced by women. By openly challenging austerity programmes and the impact of macroeconomic policies on women, the platform acknowledged that the neoliberal, "trade not aid" model of development was – and is – failing the majority of the world's women. Despite the intervening impact of two global financial crises,

rocketing wealth inequality, growing fundamentalisms, and a steadily worsening climate crisis, the SDGs fail even to match the Beijing agreement's level of ambition, let alone build on it to meet our current challenges.

(Khan and Lappin 2015)

Clearly it pointed to the fact that the SDGs lacked a coherent socio-economic and political framework that was pro-poor and pro-women.

The Asia-Pacific Women's Alliance for Peace and Security (APWAPS 2015)[17] underlined issues of peace and security, particularly highlighting concerns of women in conflict situations, within the ambit of the SDGs. They stressed the concerns of the Beijing+20 reviews and of the Global Study of the Implementation of UN Security Council Resolution 1325 (UN Women 2015) that focused on six key areas: (1) addressing issues of lack of accountability and continued impunity; (2) the impacts of militarisation, small arms and the continuum of violence in everyday life; (3) the nature of structural inequalities and climate injustice and their links to current development policies and practices; (4) the phenomenon of rising cultural and religious fundamentalisms; (5) unaddressed issues of victim/survivor recovery and reparation; and (6) ensuring women's full and meaningful participation in building peace and security. They called for periodic reviews that would fully integrate commitments to the women, peace and security agenda.

While conversations continue on the development of strategies to respond to the framing, application and limitations of the SDGs, there are apprehensions about the nature of effective public financing by the state to meet these commitments. Women's groups have learnt from the Beijing process that lack of budgetary support to their programmes results in ineffective and partial implementation of planned commitments. They are organising to secure increased investments and intentional support for gender budgeting through innovative financing mechanisms. While there is some disquiet about the increasing corporate control over development agendas (the corporate sector is a key stakeholder in the SDGs), there have been suggestions to institute adequate mechanisms to advancing human rights and gender justice within the corporate sector. These have been followed with discussions to enforce accountability standards within the SDGs, and not leave them to "voluntary" reporting processes (DESA 2015).

Mary Shanthi Dairiam (IWRAW-AP 2016), a leading human rights activist and former CEDAW Committee Member (2005–08) asserts: "There is a need for a consistency of approach that integrates equality and non-discrimination as normative standards across not only all the goals, but importantly across institutions using legal, policy, and programmatic measures".

SDGs in the context of India

In the context of India, it is important to understand how SDGs are framed and what the mechanisms being developed are to deliver them. India has a long history of work and a vibrant women's movement on the ground, which has consistently raised concerns and engaged in advancing the status of women in the country. The movement is diverse and works with an intersectional lens at policy and field levels.

Several initiatives have been underway in India on women's equality. *Towards equality* (Government of India 1974), the historic and path-breaking first report of the Committee on the Status of Women in India, was led by the late feminist academics Vina Mazumdar and Lotika Sarkar. The report drew the country's attention to discriminatory socio-cultural practices and how economic and political processes disempowered women. It issued an alert to the problem of the declining sex ratio that in turn led to the development of gender-sensitive policy-making and an increased focus on the education of girls.

Forty years later, the second report was prepared by a High Level Committee on the Status of Women (2015). This report highlighted key gender gaps, applying an intersectional lens, and covered the diversity and complexity of women's lives in the country. Along with several other reports – Shram Shakti (1989), Justice Verma Committee Report (Verma et al. 2013), United Nations (2014) – there has been an extensive and informed analysis of the pathways that can be traversed to enhance women's status. Despite all such commitments, a greater political will is needed to transform gender relations and inequalities. There is need for deeper commitment in enacting sustained institutional reforms and in changing patriarchal, feudal and misogynist mindsets.

India has been a signatory to the Beijing, CEDAW, MDGs and SDGs agendas. The Beijing report of the Indian government, as reported in the news, stated that deep-rooted gender inequalities remain and undermine the country's potential to translate economic growth into inclusive development, and that gender inequalities persist in education, income and employment and women's health (Menon 2014). In its MDG report, India claimed that it had halved its incidence of extreme poverty from 49.4 per cent in 1994 to 24.7 per cent in 2011, despite the large numbers of underweight and malnourished children and women in the country (Raghavan 2015). The report highlighted deficits on several health parameters, such as maternal mortality, infant mortality and basic sanitation. Referencing the MDG 3 targets (on gender equality), India claimed to being close to target, achieving higher enrolment and female youth literacy than earlier, with women in wage employment increasing to 22.28 per cent by the year 2015. It also noted that there was a higher representation of women in parliament (12.24 per cent), a figure still far below the 33 per cent being advocated by women's groups (Dubbudu 2015).

In its Concluding Comments to India's fourth and fifth reports, the CEDAW Committee made some observations regarding steps that could be taken towards progress on women's rights (United Nations 2014). It noted the absence of a comprehensive anti-discrimination law in the country to effectively address all aspects of discrimination and all forms of intersectional discrimination against women. The Committee also observed that the two declarations made by India to the CEDAW Convention were incompatible with its constitutional guarantees of equality and non-discrimination. It noted the persistence of patriarchal attitudes and deep-rooted stereotypes that were entrenched in the social, cultural, economic and political institutions and structures of Indian society and in the media, and stated that sustained action was needed to eliminate harmful discriminatory practices.

In a follow-up consultation, post the adoption of the SDGs, UN Women convened the Global Leaders' Meeting on Gender Equality and Women's Empowerment: A Commitment to Action. More than 90 leaders made national commitments that would close the gender equality gap – from laws and policies to national action plans and adequate investment.[18] India was not among the countries listed on the previously mentioned commitments.

The key challenge for India is to understand more deeply why, despite constitutional guarantees on women's equality and rights and the adoption of several policies and programmatic directions over the years, patriarchal mindsets and misogyny continue to persist and limit women's freedom, voices and dignity.

A more in-depth analysis is provided in the next section on some of the barriers to realising women's rights in two key areas, economic rights and the pandemic of violence against women, and is supplemented by a brief analysis of the data from select policy measures and budgetary investments for women.

Barriers to economic rights of women

Despite the economic growth in the country in the past decade or so, the declining workforce participation rates for women have been cause for concern. It is well known that women face a host of barriers to realising their economic rights. They are largely employed in the informal sector that is marked by insecure and precarious work conditions with little or no access to social protection. Rigid gender norms impact their employment opportunities and mobility patterns. Labour markets also provide fewer and low-paid work options for women. Women bear the brunt of time-poverty because of unpaid and care work. Gender gaps persist in infrastructure and public services and place enormous pressure on their daily lives, including the poor availability of drinking water, sanitation facilities, fuel, fodder and transport.

The UN Global Report on Economic Empowerment and SDGs (United Nations 2016a), has found that only one in two women (aged 15 and over) is in paid employment as compared with three in four men. That amounts to about 700 million fewer women in paid employment than men (that is, 1.27 billion women as against 2 billion men). The report also found that women take on about three times more unpaid work than men do and hundreds of millions of women work informally without social and labour protection in law or in practice.

In India, there are about 120 million women who work informally. According to the report of the Labour Bureau, there are 149.8 million women workers, of which 121.8 million and 28 million are in rural and urban areas respectively. Of these 35.9 million work as cultivators, 61.5 as agricultural labourers, 8.5 in the household industry, and 43.7 are classified as "other workers" (Government of India 2014; Ravichandran n.d.). Even though India's economy grew at an average of 7 per cent between 2004 and 2011, its female workforce participation fell by seven percentage points, to 24 per cent from 31 per cent (Pande and Troyer 2015). This then amounts to more than 25 million women missing from the labour force.

NSS data show that while participation rates for women workers is highest in the 34–44 age group, the decline is highest in the 25–34 age group (ISST 2015). Rohini Pande et al. (2016) noted that if efforts were made to close the gender gap in labour-force participation in India, there would be a 27 per cent net increase in the GDP. According to the ILO, 865 million women in the world have the potential to contribute more fully to their national economies and 94 per cent (812 million) of them live in emerging and developing economies (ILO 2016).

Well-known Indian feminist economist Jayati Ghosh (2016) offers an explanation for the missing women in the economy. She points out the limitations of the NSSO definition of employment that has excluded some important activities that need to be counted as work. This is specific to two NSSO codes, 92 and 93, that exclude certain activities that are largely in the domain of domestic duties and care work.[19] The data suggest that shifts have taken place from recognised work to unpaid work. Ghosh further adds that as per the ILO definition (Castillo 2014), if such activities were counted as work, the data would certainly read otherwise. Additionally, and as is well known, women's work is affected by their limited agency in bargaining, both within the family and outside.

Studies have indicated that female workforce participation is affected because of child care, particularly for women from urban areas with children less than five years old (Sudarshan 2016). Neetha N. (cited in ISST 2015) points out that it is difficult to separate unpaid economic work and social reproduction work while computing women's actual contributions to the economy.

There is a need to develop methodologies to accurately capture women's care and unpaid work in the country, as well as an urgency to free women workers from disadvantaged backgrounds from exploitative work conditions. A recent study (Centre for Equity Studies 2016) flags the abysmal living and work conditions of women from specific social groups. They suffer sexual violence, harassment and have little or no control over and access to land, assets, housing and other community resources. Domestic workers, women manual scavengers and women sex workers are particularly subject to severe discrimination, violence and social stigma.

To advance women workers' rights within the SDGs, secure livelihoods and enabling conditions must be created. The UN Global Report on Economic Empowerment and SDGs underscores some of the systemic constraints that need the attention of policymakers and planners. These include (1) addressing adverse social norms, (2) reforming discriminatory laws and building legal protection, (3) ensuring sufficient access to financial, digital and property assets and (4) recognising and redistributing unpaid household and care work. It adds that women's access and ownership of property and greater access to resources along with collective mobilisation to negotiate and bargain is the only way towards reversing their lower status and reclaiming their rights.

India needs to step up to this challenge urgently. It needs to address Goals 1 and 5 of the SDGs in a continuum and plug the gender gaps highlighted earlier. It needs to make unequivocal and sufficient investments for maternity and child care and for social security. It needs to ensure access to not only meaningful livelihoods (in farm- and non-farm sectors) but also quality gender-based skill training, and to institute enabling policies that result in greater access and control over resources for all women. It can no longer pursue economic policies that benefit large corporations that displace women from their traditional lands, forests and livelihoods, forcing them into an insecure pool of migrant labour and distressed human beings. The impacts of such economic policies only further erode women's rights and deepen the feminisation and inter-generational transfer of poverty, and need to be reversed.

Pandemic of violence against women

The second thematic area being highlighted is that of the pandemic of violence against women, a missing target of the MDGs, as mentioned earlier, but the SDGs have undone that injustice, stating a commitment to ending all forms of violence against women under Goal 5.

The UN Special Rapporteur on Violence against Women noted in her India mission report that Violence against Women (VAW) in India is systemic in nature, and occurs both in public and private spaces. She observed the persistence of patriarchal social norms, structural and institutional forms of inequalities and other gender hierarchies that underpin violence against women (Manjoo 2014). The special rapporteur further noted that there are high levels of tolerance in society with regard to violence. This is a disturbing observation that requires both government and society at large to work at transforming social norms.

Data from reliable national sources, the National Family Health Survey 3, state that one out of every three ever-married women has experienced spousal violence (Kishore and Gupta. 2009). Other national data indicate an increase of 9.2 per cent in the reporting of crimes against women (CAW) for the year 2014. The data further reveal an over 50 per cent increase since 2010 in such reporting.[20] This is a good trend as it is hoped that increased reporting will result in firmer actions against the perpetrators of violence and more action regarding preventive measures. The difficulty is that, according to the data, in more than 90 per cent of the cases the perpetrator is known to the victim, and is often a member of the family in incidents of incest and sexual assault (NCRB 2015).

Even though reporting on VAW has increased, there are barriers faced by women survivors of violence. These include delays in the timeliness of the response system and the process of re-victimisation faced by them at police stations, courts and hospitals. This is also accompanied by a very long period of the trial system and an overall lack of support. Many survivors also fear lack of support from family members and the breaking of family honour codes, especially if the perpetrator is a relative.

The national capital of Delhi accounts for approximately 21 per cent of all crimes against women, despite being home to less than 1.4 per cent of India's population (*Indian Express* 2016). There was a 27 per cent increase in 2014 (Mukherjee

2016) over the previous year on reporting on rapes and sexual assaults. A multi-site study by Women in Cities International (2009–10) and Jagori reported that 75 per cent of women respondents identified gender as the main contributory factor to their lack of safety in urban spaces (Jagori 2010). In another study, Jagori reported that two out of three women reported facing incidents of sexual harassment more than once during the year. In particular, young women below the age of 25, women from low-income communities (particularly the homeless), single women and women from marginalised communities were the most vulnerable (Jagori & UN Women 2011).

Following the brutal gang rape on 16 December 2012 in Delhi that led to massive street protests by citizens and women's groups nationwide, far-reaching changes in laws (that could impact upon women's right to equality and right to dignity) were recommended by the committee headed by the late Justice Verma (Report of the Committee 2013b).

The recommendations led to the adoption of the new Criminal Law (Amendment) Act 2013 and the Sexual Harassment of Women at Workplace (Prevention, Prohibition and Redressal) Act (2013). Women's groups continue to demand actions on the recommendations, and the inclusion of issues that were left out, such as sexual violence during situations of communal violence; structural violence faced by women from Dalit, Adivasi and minority communities; violence on women with disabilities, single women and LGBTIQ women; and women who are internally displaced and living in militarised zones and fragile regions. Women's groups continue to raise concerns also about women facing communal- and caste-based violence that deprives them of fair and just access to redress, reparation and justice, and have continually raised issues of impunity of both state and non-state actors.

A network of women activists has also been working on peace, security and development for women living in conflict areas, advocating the repeal of the Armed Forces (Special Powers) Act (AFSPA). Irom Sharmila led this charge for 16 years through a peaceful hunger strike. This courageous woman ended her fast on 9 August 2016 with, regrettably, little change in the situation.[21] The Supreme Court on 8 July 2016 did, however, note that the indefinite deployment of armed forces in the name of restoring normalcy under AFSPA "would mock at our democratic process", apart from symbolising a failure of the civil administration and the armed forces (Anand 2016).

In undertaking their campaigns to support women victims of violence, women's groups and activists have faced repression, intimidation and severe threats to their lives. Attacks on women human-rights defenders have been on the rise and their voices are being stifled through a slew of counter-legal and other threats.[22] Women's groups are also facing an enormous backlash as they continue to demand due diligence and effective implementation of the various laws and procedures to end VAW as well as hold institutions and alleged perpetrators to account. In a stunning reversal, in a case of sexual harassment in Delhi, an injunction against one of the woman complainants and her lawyer was filed by the defendant's lawyer in a civil suit that demanded 10 million rupees in damages from the complainant (Venkat 2016).

Unheard of in legal procedure so far, it will discourage women survivors from speaking up in future. The Special Rapporteur on VAW in her report also noted threats faced by women rights defenders in India.

While India has ratified several human rights instruments and despite progressive laws and policies,[23] effective implementation and preventive measures fall far short of requirements. The issues of impunity and immunity enjoyed by perpetrators under the guise of tradition, culture, and other factors, and the low rates of prosecution and conviction undermine the drive to reduce VAW. Unless the state steps in and takes urgent measures to respect the rights of women as constitutionally mandated and supports the elimination of structural barriers that impede women's human rights, all efforts towards reducing VAW will be stymied. To tackle these deep-seated problems requires a transformative vision and an approach that sees women as autonomous and equal citizens, with rights to bodily integrity and the right to assert their sexualities, freedoms and voice.

Policy initiatives and budgetary investments for gender equality

The Indian government in recent years has expressed its commitment to the SDGs and has catalysed several programmatic initiatives, which include Make in India, Digital India, Smart Cities and Skills India, aimed at boosting economic and skill development as well as manufacturing to help lift millions out of poverty (*Indian Express* 2016). Other prominent schemes such as Beti Bachao Beti Padhao and Swachh Bharat were rolled out earlier in an effort to advance girls' and women's rights and dignity. Women's groups have suggested that such initiatives need to be developed with a rights framework that would ensure elimination of structural barriers for girls and women.

NITI Aayog, the new planning body set up in 2014, has mapped the core central schemes of the government in line with SDG areas. In June 2016, NITI Aayog put online a comprehensive list of targets and interventions by the respective ministries with regard to SDGs in India.[24] It is believed that state governments are in the process of formulating their plans based on the SDGs, and these will culminate in a 15-year plan to be adopted by NITI Aayog (Mishra 2016). NITI Aayog recently presented India's first Voluntary National Review on the implementation of SDGs to the 2017 High-level Political Forum (HLPF) in New York on 19 July 2017.[25]

In the meanwhile, the Ministry of Women and Child Development (MWCD) placed two draft policies, the Draft National Policy on Women (MWCD 2016a) and the Draft Trafficking in Persons Bill (MWCD 2016b), in the public domain for feedback. While some rounds of consultations with women's groups have been held by the National Commission for Women (NCW), and recommendations received online, the final documents are not yet in the public domain. The MWCD has been given a nodal role for Goal 5 of the SDGs (women's empowerment and gender equality), and has been assigned a role in addressing other goals too. However,

MWCD seems to have no role to play on SDG Goal 11, which is to make cities inclusive, safe, resilient and sustainable.

Smart cities and urbanisation processes need to be seen through a gender and rights lens. There is no information available to date about the setting up of any dedicated task force for the SDGs, nor one specifically for contributing to and monitoring the gender targets under Goal 5. Women's groups have suggested establishing consultative mechanisms for the implementation and monitoring of the policies and plans. In the meanwhile, some informal groups and coalitions of civil society have set up platforms to share and monitor developments in the context of the SDGs, such as a National Coalition – Wada Na Todo Abhiyan (WNTA), which also released a Civil society report on SDGs: Agenda 2030[26] in July 2017.

As far as budgetary investments are concerned for women's development, a recent study reveals that the total magnitude of funds (budget estimates, or BE) in the Gender Budget Statement (2016–17) was Rs.906,250 million. Allocations for the MWCD amounted to 19 per cent of this total amount. While major allocations were made for the Integrated Child Development Scheme (ICDS), about Rs.20,000 million was allocated for cooking gas connections (for 15 million families below the poverty line, in women's names) and another Rs.5,000 million for the Stand Up India scheme (to promote entrepreneurship among women from the scheduled castes and scheduled tribes). This confirms lower budgetary investments for women's development and empowerment. Because of fiscal devolution, the fund-sharing pattern between the centre and states has changed over two years, from a 75:25 ratio to 60:40. Intensive efforts would be needed to advocate with state governments for adequate investments to fulfil their obligations to women's rights (CBGA 2016).

The CBGA report also noted that two schemes continue in pilot mode, a maternity benefit scheme or the Indira Gandhi Matritva Sahyog Yojana (IGMSY), and Sabla, a centrally sponsored scheme for adolescent girls. The IGMSY continues as a pilot scheme and cannot adequately cover all pregnant and lactating women, as mandated by the National Food Security Act (2013). In the budget announced on 1 February 2017, while there has been a notable increase in the allocation to the Maternity Benefit Programme (formerly known as IGMSY) from Rs.4000 million in 2016–17 (BE) to Rs.27,000 million in 2017–18 (BE), it still does not meet the estimates of the Standing Committee on Food, Consumer Affairs and Public Distribution (2012–13) that had projected the total expenditure for approximately 22.5 million pregnant and lactating women to be around Rs.145,120 million per annum (to be borne by both the centre and states). The current allocation continues to fall short and will not enable universalisation of the scheme (CBGA 2017).

Though allocations for the umbrella scheme for the Protection and Empowerment of Women (covering eight schemes) increased in 2016–17 (BE), the total amount remains rather inadequate and certainly affects the quality and coverage of services for women survivors of violence. Besides, there are concerns about ineffective utilisation of funds meant for women. Of the two central schemes for women in distress, CBGA found that a mere Rs.130 million was utilised of 1,110 million allocated for the one stop crisis centres, and Rs.175 million of the 560 million allocated for the Helpline. Another scheme for women in difficult circumstances (Swadhar Greh) has limited outreach, covering 311 homes (2014) with a capacity of only 17,370 inmates.[27] This only points to the ineffectiveness of programmes in not meeting the huge needs of women survivors for shelter and safe spaces.

A new initiative, the Central Victim Compensation Fund Scheme, has been set up with an initial corpus of Rs.2000 million to support victims of sexual assault, acid attacks and human trafficking and for women killed or injured in cross-border firing. The Nirbhaya Fund set up in 2013 has Rs.30,000 million (as of 2016–17). However, this too has remained largely unspent in the initial period, as observed by a Parliamentary Standing Committee (Madhukalya 2016). An analysis of recent proposals to the Fund was for Rs. 22,000 million (Kaul and Shrivastava 2017).

The Justice Verma Committee Report was resolute about the need for police reforms. This would need a host of steps that includes not just enhanced budgetary allocations and more women in the force at all levels (currently 9 per cent), but more importantly changes in how policing is undertaken and the law implemented. The need to fill the additional 4,700 posts and develop an action plan for women's safety, particularly in Delhi's outer areas where the transition from rural to urban is in progress, has been brought to the attention of the police by the High Court of Delhi (Mathur 2016). It is interesting to note that the CBGA study (via spatial data mapping) found a greater concentration of police stations in the centre of the city rather than on the periphery. The parliamentary panel noted the need for sensitisation programmes on behaviour towards women, among other measures ((PTI) 2015). Lalita Panicker noted in her op-ed piece that

> while technology can aid in addressing women's safety, the certainty and severity of the law needs to be in place. Without follow-up actions by the law – of filing and accepting FIRs in time and taking prompt actions against stalkers and harassers – there will be little progress.
>
> *(Hindustan Times 2017)*

Needed also is an outcome evaluation of funds made available for women's safety, the key question being whether investments in technology-based surveillance (CCTV cameras, GPS devices and other equipment) have led to any significant changes, and an estimate of the costs incurred because of ineffective funding for victim support, rehabilitation and restorative justice. It is imperative that many more investments be made to bridge the gaps in the continuum of services for victims/survivors of violence, for prevention and the changing of mindsets and, more importantly, for ensuring zero tolerance to violence and access to justice for women human-rights defenders. The key recommendations emerging from CEDAW's Concluding

Comments, Report of the UN Special Rapporteur on VAW and the High Level Committee on Women should be built into the SDG national plans.

Initial global efforts to advance Goal 5 of the SDGs

Some countries have a head start in developing mechanisms for SDGs. As part of the first year of the SDGs, 22 countries volunteered to present their national reviews to the High-level Political Forum at a meeting convened by the United Nations. These reviews assessed gaps between their national contexts and policies in the context of the SDGs. From the presentations, UN Women found that 17 countries had made specific references to gender equality issues. For example, Estonia raised the issue of tackling the gender pay gap as a priority. Germany was working towards good governance by cross-cutting it with gender equality. Other countries reported specific challenges in addressing Goal 5 relating to violence against women and children (Egypt and Finland), gender inequality (Egypt, Finland, France, Germany and Norway), gaps in wellbeing and health between genders and across regions (Finland), youth and long-term unemployment (Finland, Egypt, Republic of Korea, Sierra Leone), and addressing the needs of an ageing population (Republic of Korea). Mexico specifically noted challenges in bringing in, among others, women, indigenous peoples and communities, youth, LGBTIQ groups, migrants, and persons with disabilities and of African descent into the implementation efforts (United Nations 2016b).

At the 68th Session of the Nordic Council, the prime ministers of Denmark, Finland, Norway and Sweden discussed how they could be leading examples in achieving the SDGs. The European Union has developed a Gender Action Plan (2016–20), which is aligned with SDG 5 (Wahlen 2016). The government of Malaysia, in partnership with UNDP, has agreed to introduce the Gender Equality Seal Certification, in collaboration with the private sector, which is aimed at equal opportunities and inclusive work environments for women (UNDP 2016).

The International Centre for Research on Women, with leading feminist thinkers and others, presented six overarching recommendations on gender equality and women's rights to the new Secretary-General of the United Nations on his taking office, calling for the highest level of support for the effective implementation and accountability of SDGs, in particular SDG 5, and the mainstreaming of gender through all the goals (Thompson 2017).

In the last few years, attention has focused on gender responsive data collection and its use for monitoring purposes. Of the 14 indicators to monitor SDG 5, there are no comparable data for six indicators in most countries, including women's rights to land, and an agreed standard for measurement is missing. In this regard, UN Women has stepped up its efforts towards building accurate and comparable gender data that could monitor the progress of SDGs and provide the data to citizens to hold leaders accountable. They plan to build the capacities of National Statistics Officers and national administrations, civil-society organisations and academics from select countries. In a period of five years they expect the availability of reliable and comparable gender data on the extent of legal discrimination, women's asset ownership and, specifically, a comprehensive data base on ending violence against women and women's unpaid care work (UN Women September 2016).

As data measurement processes get institutionalised, there may be a need to develop adequate ethical measures to ensure women's privacy and confidentiality. In India, far greater effort is needed to not only upgrade the framework and collection of gender-disaggregated data, but also to analyse data with a gender lens to understand the differential impacts of policies and programmes on diverse sections of women in the country.

Conclusion

Meaningful and transformative changes cannot take place unless governments step up their efforts at all levels to address the deep gender inequalities, as well as partner women's organisations, collectives and civil society in policy and implementation efforts. Empirical data from 70 countries over the last four decades reveal that the presence of autonomous feminist organisations is among the single most important factor in advancing actions to tackle violence against women. The writer points to the fact that this seems more significant than the wealth of a country or the number of women in government (Moosa 2015).

Women's movements have been pushing the boundaries to build strategic partnerships with the government and have been advised to use SDG Target 5.5 and demand resources for their work as well (Esquivel and Sweetman 2016). In India there is urgent need for multi-sector approaches and partnerships to advance work on women's rights within the SDG plans. Alliances across civil society, trade unions, academic institutions and international bodies need to be forged more strongly to build effective accountability measures for the implementation of SDGs.

Notes

* The author acknowledges the review and feedback provided by Dr Mary John, Senior Fellow at the Centre for Women's Development Studies (CWDS), New Delhi and thankful to Dr Jael Silliman, women's studies scholar and writer, for editing this chapter. An expanded version of the paper was published in *Indian Journal of Gender Studies*, vol. 25, no. 1 (2018). Used with permission.
1 United Nations: Beijing Declaration and Platform for Action, 15 September 1995. See www.un.org/womenwatch/daw/beijing/beijingdeclaration.html
2 The United Nations has organised four world conferences on women. These took place in Mexico City in 1975, Copenhagen in 1980, Nairobi in 1985 and Beijing in 1995. See more at www.unwomen.org/en/how-we-work/intergovernmental-support/world-conferences-on-women
3 Five-yearly reviews and appraisals have been undertaken by the UN on the Beijing Platform for Action. All reports are available at www.un.org/womenwatch/daw/beijing/index.html
4 National Alliance of Women (NAWO) is an umbrella organisation of women's groups formed in 1995 post the Beijing Conference; it is now located in Bangalore. See more: https://karnataka.ngosindia.com/national-alliance-of-women-bangalore/

5 The United Nations Development Fund for Women (UNIFEM) has supported women's empowerment and gender equality through its programme offices since 1976. In January 2011, UNIFEM was merged into UN Women, a composite entity of the UN, with the International Research and Training Institute for the Advancement of Women (INSTRAW), the Office of the Special Adviser on Gender Issues (OSAGI), and the Division for the Advancement of Women (DAW). See more: www.wikigender.org/wiki/united-nations-development-fund-for-women-unifem/

6 A wide-ranging consultation was held covering several issues in this review process, which subsequently led to inclusion in the regional and global processes. A report of the consultation is available with UN Women. See http://beijing20.unwomen.org/en/news-and-events/stories/2014/8/diversity-of-voices-at-beijing-20-consultations-in-india

7 The Commission on the Status of Women (CSW) is the principal global intergovernmental body exclusively dedicated to the promotion of gender equality and the empowerment of women. See more at www.unwomen.org/en/csw

8 UN Women works to empower women and girls in all of its programmes. Its two central goals are the advancement of women's political participation and leadership and their economic empowerment. To this end, it maintains a global data base and supports research and data-gathering on women. See more at www.unwomen.org/en/news/in-focus/women-and-the-sdgs/sdg-5-gender-equality#notes

9 The General Assembly, by its resolution 53/202 of 17 December 1998, decided to designate the 55th session of the General Assembly as 'The Millennium Assembly of the United Nations' and to convene, as an integral part of the Millennium Assembly, a Millennium Summit of the United Nations.

The Millennium Summit was held over 6–8 September 2000 at the United Nations Headquarters in New York with 149 heads of state and government and high-ranking officials from over 40 other countries. The main document, unanimously adopted, was the Millennium Declaration, which contained a statement of values, principles and objectives as the international agenda for the 21st century. It also set deadlines for many collective actions. See the United Nations Millennium Development Goals website www.un.org/en/events/pastevents/millennium_summit.shtml

10 WHO works to advance the empowerment of women, especially in its intersection with health issues, and supports the prevention of and response to gender-based violence, also promoting women's leadership in the health sector. See www.who.int/topics/millennium_development_goals/gender/en/

11 The Convention on the Elimination of all Forms of Discrimination Against Women (CEDAW) is an international treaty adopted in 1979 by the United Nations General Assembly. See more at www.un.org/womenwatch/daw/cedaw/

12 The Rio+20 outcome document, *The future we want*, set out, inter alia, a mandate to establish an Open Working Group to develop sustainable development goals for consideration and appropriate action at the 68th session of the UN General Assembly. It also provided the basis for the SGDs' conceptualisation, and the mandate that they should be coherent with and integrated into the UN development agenda beyond 2015. See the proposal drafted by the Open Working Group for Sustainable Development Goals at https://sustainabledevelopment.un.org/focussdgs.html

13 The outcome document of the United Nations Summit for the post-2015 development agenda was adopted by the General Assembly on 25 September 2015 at its 70th session: Transforming Our World, the 2030 Agenda for Sustainable Development. For more see www.un.org/en/ga/search/view_doc.asp?symbol=A/RES/70/1&Lang=E

14 The UNDP, as a lead UN agency for human development, has had its development and funding policies working in 70 countries and territories guided by the SDGs. See more at www.undp.org/content/undp/en/home/sustainable-development-goals.html

15 The Post-2015 Women's Coalition is an international network of feminist, women's rights, women's development, grassroots, peace and social justice organisations focused on the realisation of women's rights and gender equality (www.post2015women.com/mission/).

The Women's Major Group is self-organised, comprising more than 500 organisations and recognised by the UN, including in the UN processes on Sustainable Development, and facilitates women's civil society inputs into the policy space (https://sustainabledevelopment.un.org/majorgroups/women).

Development Alternatives with Women for a New Era (DAWN) is an international feminist network of advocates and researchers (http://dawnnet.org/).

16 The UN Secretary-General announced the first-ever High Level Panel on Women's Economic Empowerment to provide thought leadership and mobilise concrete actions aimed at closing economic gender gaps that persist around the world. The Panel provided recommendations for the implementation of the 2030 Agenda for Sustainable Development to improve economic outcomes for women and promote women's leadership in driving sustainable and inclusive, environmentally sensitive economic growth. It has recently published its findings. See more at www.unwomen.org/en/news/stories/2016/1/wee-high-level-panel-launch

17 The Asia-Pacific Women's Alliance for Peace and Security creates spaces for women to discuss peace and security that matters to women. It brings together feminist organisations, women human-rights defenders, women peace builders and others from across Asia and the Pacific.

18 A campaign was launched by UN Women for Planet 50–50 by 2030: Step It Up to make governments commit nationally to closing gender-equality gaps, formulating laws and policies and action plans and making adequate investments. See more at www.unwomen.org/en/get-involved/step-it-up

19 Census Code 92, relating to those who 'attended to domestic duties only' thus includes all activities that constitute the care economy – looking after the young, the sick and the elderly as well as other healthy household members; cooking, cleaning and provisioning for the family; and so on.

Code 93 relates to those who 'attended to domestic duties and were also engaged in free collection of goods (vegetables, roots, firewood, cattle feed), sewing, tailoring, weaving, etc for household use'.

Jayati Ghosh has suggested the need for a re-read of the data as 'Women's workforce participation rate in 1999–2000 would increase to 89 per cent in rural areas, and only decline to 85 per cent in 2011–12. In urban areas, the participation rate would show an increase to 81 per cent in 1999–2000 and remain around 80 per cent in 2011–12.' See more at www.theguardian.com/global-development-professionals-network/2016/jul/16/womens-workforce-participation-declining-india

20 NCRB data (2015): A total of 3,37,922 cases of crimes against women were reported in 2014 as compared to 3,09,546 in 2013. There were 2,13,585 reported cases in 2010, which increased to 2,28,649 cases in 2011, and further increased to 2,44,270 cases in 2012.

21 See more at standwithiromsharmila.in

22 The groups include the Jagdalpur Legal Aid Group (Chhattisgarh), Lawyers Collective among others, in addition to individual activists in different parts of the country.

23 These include the International Covenant on Civil and Political Rights; the International Covenant on Economic, Social and Cultural Rights; the Convention on the Elimination of All Forms of Discrimination against Women; the International Convention on the Elimination of All Forms of Racial Discrimination; the Convention on the Rights of the Child; and the Convention on the Rights of Persons with Disabilities.

24 Niti Aayog: Sustainable Development Goals (SDGs), Targets, CSS, Interventions, Nodal and other Ministries (as on 08.06.2016), can be accessed at http://niti.gov.in/writereaddata/files/SDGsV20-Mapping080616-DG_0.pdf

25 Niti Aayog presented India's first Voluntary National Review on implementation of SDGs on 19 July 2017. It can be accessed at http://niti.gov.in/content/voluntary-national-review-report

26 *Civil society report on SDGs: Agenda 2030* is a civil society initiative anchored by Wada Na Todo Abhiyan. The report was released in Delhi on 6 July 2017 at a large gathering

of 225 participants comprising academicians, members of the media, networks working on SDGs, organisations/individuals engaged with marginalised groups, and members from civil-society organisations from across 18 states of India. It can be accessed at http://wadanatodo.net/highlight/civil-society-report-on-sdgs-agenda-2030/
27 This was revealed through a Lok Sabha Unstarred Question (No. 4519) for answer dated 19.12.2014. (See CBGA study, 2016.)

References

Abelenda, Ana. 2015. *2020 Development Agenda Gets Adopted – Strong on Gender but Structural Obstacles Remain.* Press release, AWID. Available at: www.awid.org/news-and-analysis/2030-development-agenda-gets-adopted-strong-gender-structural-obstacles-remain

Anand, Utkarsh. (July) 2016. "Manipur Probe: Indefinite AFSPA is Failure of Army, Govt, says SC." *Indian Express*. Available at: http://indianexpress.com/article/india/india-news-india/excessive-force-cant-be-used-by-army-or-police-even-in-afspa-areas-rules-supreme-court-2900857/

Annan, Kofi A., Secretary-General of the United Nations. 2000. *We the Peoples – the Role of the United Nations in the 21st century*. United Nations Department of Public Information New York, NY 10017. Available at: www.un.org/en/events/pastevents/pdfs/We_The_Peoples.pdf

APWAPS. 2015. *Grounding 2015 Global Commitments for a Transformative Agenda on Peace and Security in Asia and the Pacific*. Available at: https://apwaps.files.wordpress.com/2016/01/grounding_lr.pdf

Castillo, Monica D. 2014. *The Decent Work Measurement Framework and the 19th ICLS Resolution Concerning Statistics of Work, Employment and Labour Underutilization*. Available at: http://www.ilo.org/wcmsp5/groups/public/---dgreports/---stat/documents/presentation/wcms_323478.pdf

Centre for Budget and Governance Analysis. 2016 March. *Connecting the Dots: An Analysis of Union Budget 2016–17*. Available at: www.cbgaindia.org/wp-content/uploads/2016/03/Connecting-the-Dots-An-Analysis-of-Union-Budget-2016-17.pdf

———. 2017 February. *What do the Numbers Tell: An Analysis of the Union Budget 2017–18*. Available at: www.cbgaindia.org/wp-content/uploads/2017/02/Analysis-of-Union-Budget-2017-18-2.pdf

Centre for Equity Studies. 2016. *India Exclusion Report 2015*. New Delhi: Yoda Press. Available at: www.im4change.org/docs/91763text-final_India-Exclusion-Report-round2Final.pdf

Centre for Women's Development Study. 2015. *Towards Equality: Report of the Committee on the Status of Women in India* (reprint). Mazumdar, Dr. Vina (general ed.), Sharma, Kumud, and Sujaya, C.P. (eds.). Pearson.

Dairiam, Mary Shanthi. 2016. "IWRAW Asia Pacific." Presented at *CSW 60*, March 2016.

Department of Economic & Social Affairs. 2015 June. *CDP Background paper no. 25 ST/ESA/2015/CDP/25*. Available at: www.un.org/en/development/desa/policy/cdp/cdp_background_papers/bp2015_25.pdf

Dubbudu, Rakesh. 2015. "Has India Achieved the Millennium Development Goals (MDG)?" *Factly*. Available at: https://factly.in/millennium-development-goals-achieved-by-india/

Esquivel, Valeria and Sweetman, Caroline. 2016. "Gender and the Sustainable Development Goals." *Gender & Development*, 24(1): 1–8. doi: 10.1080/13552074.2016.1153318.

Fukuda-Parr, Sakiko. 2016. "From the Millennium Development Goals to the Sustainable Development Goals: Shifts in Purpose, Concept, and Politics of Global Goal Setting for Development." *Gender & Development*, 24(1):43–52. doi:10.1080/13552074.2016.1145895.

Ghosh, Jayati. 2016 July. "Women are the Engines of the Indian Economy but We are Ignored." *The Guardian*. Available at: www.theguardian.com/global-development-professionals-network/2016/jul/16/womens-workforce-participation-declining-india

Government of India. 1974. *Towards Equality: Report of the Committee on the Status of Women in India*. New Delhi: Department of Social Welfare.

———. 2014. *Statistical Profile on Women Labour 2012–13*. Chandigarh: Labour Bureau. Available at: http://labourbureaunew.gov.in/UserContent/Statistical_Profile_2012_13.pdf

High Level Committee on the Status on Women. 2015. *Report on the Status of women in India*. Four volumes and summary report. Available at the website of MWCD, India Govt. http://wcd.nic.in/documents/hlc-status-women

Indian Express. 2016 January. "United Nations Ushers in Ambitious 2030 Sustainable Development Goals." PTI & *Indian Express*. Available at: http://indianexpress.com/article/world/world-news/united-nations-ushers-in-ambitious-2030-sustainable-development-goals/

ISST. 2015. *Gender and Economic Policy Discussion Forum: Placing Women's Unpaid Work in Development Policy*. Briefing note 17. New Delhi: Institute of Social Studies Trust. Available at: https://in.boell.org/sites/default/files/uploads/2013/10/briefing_paper_17.pdf

International Labour Organisation. 2016. *World Employment and Social Outlook – Trends 2016*. Summary document. Available at: www.ilo.org/global/about-the-ilo/newsroom/news/WCMS_443500/lang--en/index.htm

Jagori. 2010. *Understanding Women's Safety: Towards a Gender Inclusive City*. Research findings, Delhi 2009–10. Jagori, WICI & UN Trust Fund. Available at: www.safedelhi.in/understanding-womens-safety-towards-gender-inclusive-city.html

Jagori & UN Women. 2011. *Safe Cities Free of Violence Against Women and Girls Initiative – Report of the Baseline Survey in Delhi* (2010). Jagori & UNIFEM. Available at: http://safedelhi.in/baseline-survey-womens-safety-nine-districts-delhi2010.html.

Kabeer, Naila. 2005. *The Beijing Platform for Action and the Millennium Development Goals: Different Processes, Different Outcomes*. Paper for the United Nations Division for the Advancement of Women (DAW) Expert Group Meeting. EGM/BPFA-MD-MDG/2005/EP.11 4 February 2005. Available at: www.un.org/womenwatch/daw/egm/bpfamd2005/experts-papers/EGM-BPFA-MD-MDG-2005-EP.11.pdf

Kaul, Kanika, and Shrivastava, Saumya. 2017. *Safety of Women in Public Spaces in Delhi: Governance and Budgetary Challenges*. New Delhi: Centre for Budget and Governance Analysis.

Khan, Tessa, and Lappin, Kate. 2015 September. "Global Goals on Women's Rights are a Pale Imitation of Promises Made in Beijing. Asia Pacific Forum on Women, Law and Development (APWLD)." Originally published in *The Guardian* and available at: http://apwld.org/global-goals-on-womens-rights-are-a-pale-imitation-of-promises-made-in-beijing/

Kishore, Sunita and Gupta, Kamal. 2009 August. "Gender Equality and Women's Empowerment in India." *National Family Health Survey (NFHS – 3)*. Mumbai: International Institute of Population Studies (IIPS). Available at: http://rchiips.org/nfhs/a_subject_report_gender_for_website.pdf

Madhukalya, Amrita. 2016 April. "Nirbhaya Funds Lying Idle While Crimes Against Women Rise: Parliament Committee." *Daily News and Analysis* (DNA). Available at: www.dnaindia.com/india/report-nirbhaya-funds-lying-idle-while-crimes-against-women-rise-parliament-committee-2206928

Manjoo, Rashida. 2014 April. *Report of the Special Rapporteur on Violence Against Women, its Causes and Consequences. Mission to India*. United Nations. A/HRC/26/38/Add.1, 1 April 2014.

Mathur, Aneesha. 2016. "Delhi High Court Pulls up Govt, Police over Women's Safety." *Indian Express*. Available at: http://indianexpress.com/article/cities/delhi/delhi-high-court-pulls-up-govt-police-over-womens-safety/

Menon, Meena. 2014. "India Admits to Gender Inequalities in Beijing Plus 20 Review." *The Hindu* (15 November 2014). Available at: www.thehindu.com/news/india-admits-to-gender-inequalities-in-beijing-plus-20-review/article6603307.ece

Ministry of Women and Child Development (MWCD). 2016a. *National Policy for Women 2016* (draft). *Articulating a Vision for Women's Empowerment.* Government of India. Available at: http://wcd.nic.in/sites/default/files/draft%20national%20policy%20for%20women%202016.pdf

———. 2016b. *Trafficking of Persons (Prevention, Protection and Rehabilitation) Bill, 2016* (draft). Government of India. Available at: http://wcd.nic.in/acts/trafficking-persons-bill-2016-draft

Mishra, Mona. 2016 September. "One Year Since the SDGs, How Committed is the Indian Parliament?" Blog. *Huffington Post.* Available at: www.huffingtonpost.in/mona-mishra/one-year-since-the-sdgs-how-committed-is-the-indian-parliament/

Moosa, Zohra. 2015. "Movements, Money and Social Change: How to Advance Women's Rights." *Open Democracy.* Available at: www.opendemocracy.net/5050/zohra-moosa/movements-money-and-social-change-how-to-advance-women%E2%80%99s-rights.

Mukherjee, Sharmistha. 2016 March. "Time to Make Delhi Safe for Women." *The New Indian Express.* Available at: www.jagori.org/sites/default/files/publication/SAFE_CITIES_FOR_WOMEN_AND_GIRLS_0.pdf

National Crime Record Bureau of India. 2015. *Crime Against Women.* Chapter 5. Available at: http://ncrb.nic.in/StatPublications/CII/CII2014/chapters/Chapter%205.pdf

Neetha, N. 2015. *Gender and Economic Policy Forum.* Institute of Social Studies Trust. 2015 August. Cited in Briefing Note 17. Available at: www.isstindia.org/research-details/gender-and-economic-policy-discussion-forum/3/1/

Pande, Rohini, and Moore, Charity Troyer. 2015. "Why aren't India's Women Working?" *New York Times.* Available at: www.nytimes.com/2015/08/24/opinion/why-arent-indias-women-working.html?_r=0

Pande, Rohini, with Moore, Charity, and Johnson, Jennifer (8 March) 2016. "Five Key Lessons about Women and Work in India." *Harvard.Edu.* Available at: http://scholar.harvard.edu/rpande/news/five-key-lessons-about-women-and-work-india

Panicker, Lalita. 2017 January. Our Cities Cannot be Called Smart Until Women Feel Safe." *Hindustan Times.* Available at: www.hindustantimes.com/columns/our-cities-cannot-be-called-smart-until-women-feel-safe/story-HYBjewRfPQwMJTDcMwxzWN.html

Ponte, Nicole Bidegain and Enríquez, Corina Rodríguez. 2016. "Agenda 2030: A Bold Enough Framework Towards Sustainable, Gender-just Development?" *Gender & Development*, 24(1): 83–98. doi: 10.1080/13552074.2016.1142227.

Post-2015 Women's Coalition. 2015 March. *Press Release for CSW 59.* Available at: www.post2015women.com/press-release-for-csw59/

Press Trust of India (PTI). 2015 February. "Women Constitute Only a Little Over 9 Per cent of the Delhi Police Force: Panel." *News Nation.* Available at: www.newsnation.in/article/106141-women-constitute-a-9-delhi-police-force-panel.html

Raghavan, T.C.A. Sharad (8 July) 2015. "India on Track in Reducing Poverty." *The Hindu.* Available at: www.thehindu.com/news/national/millennium-development-goals-report-2015-india-on-track-in-reducing-poverty/article7396544.ece

Ravichandran, V. n.d. "Female Workforce Participation in India." *Academia.Edu.* Available at: www.academia.edu/14623355/FEMALE_WORKFORCE_PARTICIPATION_IN_INDIA

Sen, Gita and Mukherjee, Avanti. 2014. "No Empowerment Without Rights, No Rights Without Politics: Gender-equality, MDGs and the Post-2015 Development Agenda." *Journal of Human Development and Capabilities*, 15(2–3): 188–202. doi:

10.1080/19452829.2014.884057. Available at: http://dx.doi.org/10.1080/19452829.2014.884057

Stuart, Elizabeth and Woodroffe, Jessica. 2016. "Leaving No-one Behind: Can the Sustainable Development Goals Succeed Where the Millennium Development Goals lacked?" *Gender & Development*, 24:1, 69–81. doi: 10.1080/13552074.2016.1142206.

Sudarshan, Ratna. 2016 March. *Financial Chronicle*. My digitalfc.com. Available at: www.mydigitalfc.com/leisure-writing/womens-work-counts-558

Thompson, Lyric. 2014. July 18. *Concluding Observations on the Combined Fourth and Fifth Periodic Reports of India*. Adopted by the Committee at its 58th session (30 June – 18 July 2014). Committee on the Elimination of Discrimination against Women. Available at: www.google.co.in/webhp?sourceid=chrome-instant&ion=1&espv=2&ie=UTF-8#q=CEDAW%2BConcluding%2BComments%2BIndia+2014.

———. 2015. *The Millennium Development Goals Report – Summary*. New York: United Nations. Available at: www.un.org/millenniumgoals/2015_MDG_Report/pdf/MDG%202015%20Summary%20web_english.pdf

———. 2016a. *Leave No One Behind. A Call to Action for Gender Equality and Women's Economic Empowerment: Report of the UN SG's High-level Panel on Women's Economic Empowerment*. United Nations. Available at: www.womenseconomicempowerment.org/assets/reports/UNWomen%20Full%20Report.pdf

———. 2016b. *Synthesis of National Voluntary Reviews*. Division for Sustainable Development, Dept. of Economic and Social Affairs, United Nations. Available at: https://sustainabledevelopment.un.org/content/documents/126002016_VNR_Synthesis_Report.pdf

———. 2017 January. "Towards a Feminist United Nations: A Six-point Agenda for the New SG." *50,50, Inclusive Democracy*. Open Democracy. Available at: www.opendemocracy.net/5050/lyric-thompson/towards-feminist-united-nations-six-point United Nations (September 1995). Beijing Declaration and Platform for Action, *Fourth World Conference on Women*, Beijing 1995. Available at: www.un.org/womenwatch/daw/beijing/platform/declar.htm

United Nations. 2014. *Concluding Observations on the Combined Fourth and Fifth Periodic Reports of India: Committee on the Elimination of Discrimination against Women*. New York: United Nations. Available at: https://digitallibrary.un.org/record/778815/files/CEDAW_C_IND_CO_4-5-EN.pdf

———. 2015. *The Millennium Development Goals Report 2015*. New York: United Nations. Available at: http://mdgs.un.org/unsd/mdg/Resources/Static/Products/Progress2015/English2015.pdf

———. 2016a. *Leave no one Behind: A Call to Action for Gender Equality and Women's Economic Empowerment*. Report of the UN Secretary General's High-Level Panel on Women's Economic Empowerment. New York: United Nations. Available at: https://d3jkvgmi357tqm.cloudfront.net/1504462664/unwomen-leave-no-one-behind.pdf

———. 2016b. *Synthesis of National Voluntary Reviews*. New York: Division for Sustainable Development, Department of Economic and Social Affairs, United Nations. Available at: https://sustainabledevelopment.un.org/content/documents/127761701030E_2016_VNR_Synthesis_Report_ver3.pdf

UNDP. 2016 November. "Michelle Yeoh urges Asia-Pacific governments to adopt UNDP Gender Equality Seal." *UNDP Pacific Office in Fiji* (website). Available at: www.pacific.undp.org/content/pacific/en/home/presscenter/pressreleases/2016/11/24/michelle-yeoh-urges-asia-pacific-governments-to-adopt-undp-gender-equality-seal.html

UN Women. 2015a. *Political Declaration on the Occasion of the Twentieth Anniversary of the Fourth World Conference on Women*. Adopted at the CSW 59. 9–20 March 2015. New York:

UN Women. Available at: http://www2.unwomen.org/~/media/headquarters/attachments/sections/csw/59/declaration-en.pdf?v=1&d=20151208T214833

———. 2015b. *Transforming Justice, Securing the Peace: A Global Study on the Implementation of the United Nations Security Council Resolution 1325*. New York: UN Women. Available at: http://wps.unwomen.org/themes/

———. 2016 September. *Take Five with Papa Seck: Getting Better at Gender Data – Why Does it Matter?* UN Women press release. Available at: www.unwomen.org/en/news/stories/2016/9/feature-story-take-five-with-papa-seck-on-gender-data#sthash.jNfJbDct.dpuf

Venkat, Vidya. 2016 April. "Women Activists Object to Pachauri's Civil Suit Against Vrinda Grover." *The Hindu*. Available at: www.thehindu.com/news/national/women-activists-object-to-pachauris-civil-suit-against-vrinda-grover/article8465697.ece

Verma, Justice, J.S. (Retd.), Seth, Justice Leila (Retd.), and Subramanium, Gopal. 2013. *Report of the Committee on Amendments to criminal law*. Available at: http://www.prsindia.org/uploads/media/Justice%20verma%20committee/js%20verma%20committe%20report.pdf

Wahlen, Catherine Benson. 2016. *Nordic Countries Advance Cooperation on SDGs*. IISD. SDG Knowledge Hub. Available at: http://sdg.iisd.org/news/nordic-countries-advance-cooperation-on-sdgs/

Waldorf, Lee. 2003. *Pathway to Gender Equality: CEDAW, Beijing and MDGs*. UNIFEM in cooperation with GTZ sector project 'Strengthening Women's Rights', with support of BMZ. New York: UNIFEM. Available at: http://iknowpolitics.org/sites/default/files/pathway20to20gender20equality20part201.pdf

Women's Major Group. 2014. *Statements on final SDGs*. Press release, July 2014. Available at: DAWN website. www.dawnnet.org/feminist-resources/content/womens-major-group-release-statements-final-sdgs.

11
WOMEN'S WORK PARTICIPATION AND MATERNITY PROTECTION CONUNDRUM IN INDIA

Call for high-priority interventions

Lakshmi Lingam

The SDG framework adopted by the UN as post-2015 development agenda has Goal 5 as a stand-alone gender equality goal. In consonance with reduction of poverty and inequalities, and focusing on sustainability – Goal 5 provides an opportunity to bring the intersectional nature of gender to the fore. Several targets within each SDG overlap with targets in other Goals creating the need for synergetic policy and programmatic response to address complex problems of the world.

In this chapter an attempt is made to closely examine gender equality (Goal 5) with reference to No poverty (Goal 1), Reduce Inequalities (Goal 10) and Good Health and Wellbeing (Goal 3) particularly with reference to women's roles co-terminously as mothers and paid and unpaid workers.

Women as bearers and caregivers of children provide the foundation for generating future labourers for any economy. Reproduction involves not only procreation but also nurturing and caring for a growing child. Additionally, women contribute to social reproduction by means of care work for the family and household, transmitting culture and maintaining social bonds and community. Women's commitment to their households and care work often create labour market entry barriers as well as the basis for discrimination. Further, lack of access to, ownership of and control over resources compromises women's agency, autonomy and decision-making within families and across various institutions. Women have been witnessing various forms of violence and violations of their rights. Development indicators on a variety of gender indicators as well as indicators related to education, employment, health, political participation, incomes, wealth and overall wellbeing, are worse for women and girls. Poverty and social inequalities impact women and girls much more severely and gender inequality is exasperated at the intersections of multiple stratifiers (Kabeer and Cook 2010).

Among several enabling equity policies that contribute to strengthening women's participation in the labour force, maternity benefits and support to care work have a proven track record. The most productive years of a woman's life are also the reproductive years. In the absence of maternity protection[1] particularly for the unorganised sector, a woman has to forego her employment with adverse consequences not only for herself but also her family, through reduced income and enhanced medical expenses. It has been observed that women in paid or unpaid work carry on with most arduous work almost till their delivery and return to work at the earliest (Sinha et al. 2016). This has deleterious effect on childbirth and the health of the child. It affects the infant's health, for according to health specialists babies need six months of full breast-feeding and supplemented by solid food for the next two years. Breast-feeding is energy intensive for mothers, who require extra nutrition as well as extra calories. However, despite several positive global pronouncements it has been observed that maternity protection, support to care work and recognition of unpaid work continues to be overwhelmed by poor policy commitment, preoccupation with population control goals and budgetary underfunding.

Maternity protection could be an important means of increasing participation of women in the labour market. Although social mores and attitudes, lack of education and skill formation as well as lack of suitable opportunities have a role in keeping female work participation in India at abysmally low levels, there is a strong possibility that the provision of maternity protection and child care facilities will increase the participation of younger women (20 to 30 years) in the labour force by reducing the costs to the woman and her family of entering the labour market. This will in turn increase their participation in education and skill formation, thus opening up avenues for empowerment.

Among several gender issues that impinge on gender equality, in this chapter an attempt is made to centre stage maternity protection within the Sustainable Development Goals framework, particularly with reference to maternity benefits as a mechanism to fulfil women's rights as workers and citizens.

This chapter is structured into three sections. This introduction lays the ground for the chapter, which attempts to address the peculiar conundrum of women's work participation at the intersections of social reproduction and household poverty. **Section One** lays out the ground realities of the globalising economy and its impact on poverty and maternity, while **Section Two** attempts a comprehensive outline of the macro picture pertaining to women's work and children's nutrition. This spans an interrogation of their labour force participation, links between fertility, education and employment, and the utilisation of maternal health services. These arguments are tied together through an exploration of the pathways between women's work and child nutrition, to make a strong case for the universal coverage of maternity benefit schemes. **Section Three** lays out the policy context connecting maternity protection, women's rights and gender equality. This section reviews select maternity benefit schemes in India in terms of their design and implementation.

Gender, poverty and globalising economy: ground realities

Women work long hours though they are not recorded as workers. Unpaid care and housework represents 35 per cent of all work time in India, and women are responsible for 91 per cent of it. Women also do 29 per cent of all market work. The pattern of women spending more time in non-market work also exists for girls compared to boys. Valuing time spent on unpaid care and house work at market value amounts to 43 per cent of GDP (Ladusingh 2016). Women earn less income despite the fact that they are responsible for meeting 40 to 100 per cent of a family's basic needs. Because of low levels of literacy, skill training and bargaining capacity, women are more often compelled to resort to jobs that are low paid, monotonous, seasonal, labour-intensive, and carry considerable occupational risk. As a result, poverty among women is more perverse than among men. Coupled with the household poverty that women have to deal with, they also face enormous disadvantage that is embedded in gender relations, for example, domestic violence, poor access to intra-household resources, the responsibility of social reproduction under adverse conditions and lack of access to decision-making and power.

It has been observed that women bear the major brunt of macro-economic changes (Elson 2014). Concepts like "feminisation of poverty" and "feminisation of the labour force" are used to describe increasing poverty among women especially among households headed by them and increased participation of women in the labour force, especially at the lower rungs of manufacturing and services sectors. Deepening poverty among women, a product both of their low status and general economic decline, is contributing to a rise in prostitution, sexual violence, unsafe sex and vulnerability to trafficking. Prostitution, labour migration and illegal trafficking of women and children for the sex industry constitute the "shadow economy" of globalisation, an indicator of "feminisation of survival" (UNRISD 2010). Rural agrarian distress coupled with high indebtedness is leading to migration to the cities and cross-border transfer of women resulting in increasing vulnerability to risky sexual life and contraction of HIV/AIDS (for a detailed review see Lingam 2006).

In the era of globalisation, there are severe constraints in the growth of secure employment. While public sector employment has declined, the additional employment generated was entirely in the category of unprotected regular, casual or contract wage-work, which constitutes informal employment. The workforce in the informal sector grew from 361.7 million in 1999–2000 to 422.6 million in 2004–05. The emerging evidence shows that job losses have far outpaced job creation in the formal sector, forcing those thrown out of employment to eke out a living in the informal sector (Parasuraman 2009). Since the mid-1990s, the unbundling of manufacturing processes and the outsourcing of sub-processes and services as well as an expansion in contract services in the manufacturing and service sectors has led to a greater degree of flexibilisation of employment. These changes have led to the growth not only in unorganised sector employment but also to the growth of informal employment within the organised sector (NCEUS 2007).

Decline in social-sector funding by the Government particularly in public goods like health and education, governed by neo-liberal policies has brought in fresh shocks to the Indian society. Major shifts in Government policies and expenditure patterns in the social sector, particularly the health sector, are leading to a steady increase in poverty and indebtedness. Lower expenditures in public health systems, introduction of user fees, higher push for privatisation coupled with poor state regulation has led to higher out of pocket expenses for catastrophic illnesses, thus adding to India's poverty head count (Chandrashekhar and Ghosh 2011). In an essay that attempts to look at what produces and perpetuates persistent poverty, Barbara Harriss-White (2014) points to debt-related pauperisation and development induced displacement as major factors that contribute to persistent poverty in India. The reach and utilisation of public funded insurance is still in its infancy in the country. Women's attempt to manage reproductive labour, care work, unpaid and paid work, has to be understood within this context.

Women's work and child nutrition

Declining labour force participation of women

The positive contribution of greater gender equality in education and employment to economic growth is now fairly well established. Greater participation of women in employment leads in turn to positive effects on the "next generation of workers, parents and citizens" (Kabeer 2012). However, with reference to participation of women in employment, the World Employment and Social Outlook Report (2017) notes that

> Southern Asia exhibits one of the lowest rates of female labour force participation, at 28.5 per cent, while close to 82 per cent of working women in the region are in vulnerable employment. In fact, the female vulnerable employment rate in Southern Asia is the highest globally, slightly ahead of the second highest rate, in sub-Saharan Africa. The gender gaps in the labour market also extend to the differences in remuneration between men and women across all levels of occupation and sectors.
>
> *(ILO 2017, p. 8)*[2]

The last two decades of rapid GDP growth in India, have not only failed to create significant employment opportunities for women but also led to the withdrawal of women from the labour force according to Indian labour surveys (NSSO 66th round – 2009/10). About 21 million female workers were out of the workforce between 2004/05 and 2009/10. Contrary to a quantum leap of 13 million in the rural male workforce, the rural female workforce recorded a decline of 19 million during the same period, of which scheduled tribe, scheduled caste and other backward classes combined to add up to a significant proportion. Interestingly, there is an increase in the number of females attending educational institutions, however, women receding into carrying out domestic duties accounted for a large-scale decline in the female workforce (Muniyoor 2014). Although there was some reduction in participation for women in higher income classes as well, traceable to the income effect, this was small.

There is a strong possibility that women are withdrawing from the labour market because of, on the one hand, lack of opportunities (Choudhury 2011) and on the other, to the high costs of undertaking productive work in addition to reproductive work in comparison to the (low) expected returns from work. More primary research is called for to capture class and caste-wise variations in women's work participation linked to maternal causes. A strong case exists for encouraging the participation of women in the economy by positively addressing the key barriers to participation.

Fertility, education and employment

Work participation in India is characterised by women with low levels of literacy and women who have completed child bearing and initial years of child rearing. Further, work participation rates are closely linked with low levels of literacy and higher fertility. Steady increases in education among women in India, is not automatically leading to an increase in employment rates and this is a peculiar conundrum.

Illiteracy and low levels of education attainments impose severe disadvantages in terms of bargaining power in the labour market or with the government. The Scheduled Tribe (ST) and Scheduled Caste (SC) women remain the most severely disadvantaged. Even membership in organisations such as labour unions or welfare boards requires literacy and the awareness that it engenders. Educational deprivation renders women workers acutely open to exploitation – circumvention by employers of maternity benefit laws – in addition to being given low wages, experiencing job insecurity and even minimal conditions of decent work (Lingam and Kanchi 2013).

According to National Sample Survey Organisation (NSSO) data, 2009–10, the majority of women in the reproductive age bracket, particularly in the prime childbearing age, not only remains out of the labour market but also enters the workforce after completing child bearing. Besides social norms, low levels of education and skills, lack of maternity benefits and child care and elderly care facilities on the supply side and a general lack of opportunities and discrimination against younger women, particularly newly wedded or potential mothers, on the demand side, could be some of the important reasons for the low participation of younger women in the labour market.

Further, women receive fewer years of schooling than men in all segments of the workforce and the educational attainments of female workers continue to be at low levels. In 2009–10, amongst women workers of the reproductive cohort, 34.4 per cent (rural and urban) were illiterate. Despite considerable improvement since 2004–05, a little less than half the female ST (48.2 per cent) and SC (45.6 per cent) workers remained illiterate in 2009–10, the highest rates for any group.

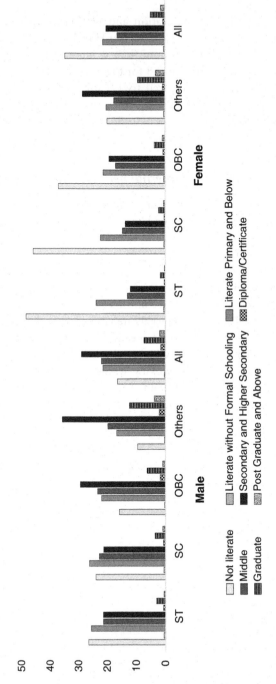

FIGURE 11.1 Percentage distribution of male and female workers 15–49 years by education level and social group (2009–10)

Source: Calculated from NSSO 66th round, 2009–10

Women's fertility linked to education and household income level

Women's fertility rate differs by education and wealth or income quintiles. According to National Family Health Survey (NFHS)-4, women in the poorest households have about 1.6 children more than women in the richest households. The total fertility rate (TFR) is 2.5 for the STs, 2.3 for the SCs, and 2.2 for the other backward classes compared to 1.9 for "others" and the overall average is 2.2 (IIPS 2017). Figure 11.2 provides an understanding of fertility rate by various key background variables like education, caste status and income groups.

Employment and utilisation of maternal health services

Poverty and vulnerability prompt women to seek some form of work at the expense of their health, child care, rest and leisure. It has been observed that working-women have lower levels of maternal health care utilisation and higher levels of anemia and poor health.

NFHS-4 (2015–16) data shows that employment does not necessarily ensure higher utilisation of maternal health care services. Among women aged 15–49, who had a birth in the 12 months preceding the survey, a lesser percentage of employed women received at least 3 antenatal care visits compared with non-working women (43 per cent and 58 per cent, respectively). The percentage of women who had institutional delivery and delivery by a health professional is also higher amongst non-working than amongst working women. There are significant disparities in health and also utilisation of health care services including maternal care by caste, economic status and education.

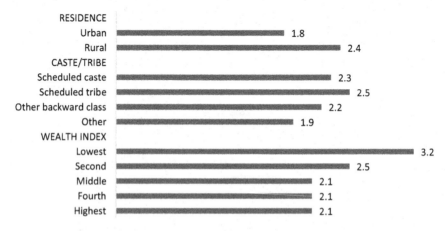

FIGURE 11.2 Total fertility rate by background characteristics (NFHS-4)

Source: National Family Health Survey 4 (2015–16), IIPS, Mumbai

Several reasons like opportunity costs of utilising maternal care in terms of loss of work day and income and lack of time must be inhibiting the use of medical services amongst the employed women among the lower income groups.

Presence of children & labour force participation

A UN Women Discussion Paper articulates,

> the participation rates of women and men belonging to households with small children up to the age of three moves in opposite directions with increasing number of children. While the Labour Force Participation rates of men in households with small children are relatively high, the participation rates of women in such households are fairly low. Women from households not having small children are more likely to be in the labour force than those from households with small children.
>
> *(Raveendran 2016)*

In the absence of child care arrangements that go beyond the nominal four hours that are available at the Integrated Child Development Scheme (ICDS) run anganwadi centres, women in the childbearing years, whether pregnant or lactating or with small children are forced to choose to stay at home despite economic deprivations. Women who leave their small children behind with other care givers like older women or small children risk the health of the small children. The care of the child and the need to work for a wage or carry out a range of social provisioning tasks (collecting firewood, fodder and water) continue to make demands on women's energy and time.

In India, apart from ongoing efforts to strengthen state initiatives to address child survival and nutrition, several child development researchers and civil society organisations have been highlighting the issue of "care" and a "caring environment" as critical components required by infants and young children in the early years of

TABLE 11.1 Labour force participation rates of women and men by number of children in the household

No. Children up to the Age of 3	1999–2000 Men	1999–2000 Women	2004–05 Men	2004–05 Women	2011–12 Men	2011–12 Women
0	80.3	38.9	80.9	43	76.7	31.5
1	89.5	37.3	89.7	39.5	88.6	28
2	89.9	36.2	91.6	39.4	90.7	28.3
3	88.8	34.1	90	37.1	88.7	27.6
4+	90.3	29.5	89.2	36	88.7	31.4
Total	83.4	38.1	83.8	41.8	79.7	30.7

Source: (Raveendran 2016).

rapid development. Responsive care, provided by a care-giver, is considered to be an essential component contributing to cognitive development, emotional wellbeing and health, not to mention the safety and protection of young children.

Profile of maternity and vulnerability

The SDGs for maternal mortality (Target 3.1) require governments to reduce maternal mortality to less than 70 per 100,000 live births by 2030. Several high-income countries have already achieved maternal mortality at 16 and less per 100,000 live births. So the figure of 70 is still an unacceptable figure given that the state of Kerala in India has achieved 61 and Maharashtra has 68.[3] The overall Indian maternal mortality figure of 167 (2011–13) tells us the story of neglect of women during their most vulnerable period of pregnancy and childbirth. Women belonging to SC, ST and lower-income groups record high levels of infant and child mortality. Poverty, poor access to services and low utilisation of maternal care services contribute to this scenario. Institutional deliveries are steadily growing with a huge push through schemes like *Janani Suraksha Yojana*, to the neglect of and strengthening health systems and providing comprehensive health care services to pregnant women. Maternal death reviews point to high levels of undetected anaemia among pregnant women leading to obstetric emergencies, poor response and unnecessary referrals and lack of transportation services as major contributing factors leading to maternal deaths. It is not surprising that maternal deaths and belonging to marginalised communities go together (Subha Sri and Khanna 2014).

Pathways between women's work and child nutrition: the need for social support programmes

There have been considerable research efforts aimed at identifying and exploring pathways linking women's work and autonomy with child nutrition. One of the most common hypotheses to have been examined is that a higher level of autonomy of women is strongly correlated to a lower level of malnutrition in children. Haddad (1999) reaffirms across 7 countries (including India) that as women's status becomes more equal relative to men, there is a positive impact on child growth and negative impact on gender-based inter-generational discrimination. Shroff et al. (2009) examined NFHS-2 data for Andhra Pradesh to examine the relationship between maternal autonomy and child stunting, and found that women with more autonomy were significantly less likely to have a stunted child, and that two different measures of women's autonomy had an independent effect on child growth.

Recent review papers highlight that women's engagement in agriculture and allied activities contribute to child undernutrition in number of ways, like less time to participate in the care work of the household, improper child and infant feeding practices, lack of time for provisioning of clean water and accessing health care (Kadiyala et al. 2014). A recent paper in six districts of six states (empowered action group states another name for states performing poorly on several human development indicators) observed high levels of malnutrition among mothers who are constrained by working long hours, multi-tasking within a context of dwindling family support, declining food security and poor access to child care services (Chaturvedi et al. 2016).

It is not women's employment that compromises the health of their children but it is the lack of social security and availability of state run services that compound matters for women who make the Hobson's choice between paid work and hunger.

This issue is compounded in the case of poor women and single mothers, who are forced to work to make ends meet and earn for the family. In such a situation, the burden of care work falls on eldest female children, for whom the cost of carrying out this work comes in the form of reduced or removed educational opportunities. This in turn compounds and perpetuates inter-generational gender inequalities and gender division of labour as well as the cycle of poverty.

Malnutrition and early child development

According to a Lancet paper published in 2007,

> Development consists of linked domains of sensori-motor, cognitive-language and social emotional function. Poverty and the socio-cultural context increase young children's exposure to biological and psychosocial risks that affect development through changes in brain structure and function, and behavioural changes. Children are frequently exposed to multiple and cumulative risks. As risks accumulate, development is increasingly compromised.
>
> *(Walker et al. 2007, p. 145)*

According to these researchers,

> Socio-cultural risk factors include gender inequity, low maternal education, and reduced access to services. Biological risks include prenatal and postnatal growth, nutrient deficiencies, infectious diseases, and environmental toxins. Psychosocial risks include, parenting factors, maternal depression and exposure to violence.
>
> *(Walter et al. 2007, p. 146)*

Children with poor access to a range of household and public resources are likely to remain in poverty as adults and contribute to transmit inter-generationally the same disadvantages to their offspring and reproduce poverty. Hence, addressing the issue of early child malnutrition and development by simultaneously connecting the issue to its associated factors is a key to national development.

Multi-dimensional household poverty and maternal health significantly affect child growth and development. Hence, apart from child survival it is important to also prioritise a variety of vulnerabilities and development risks that children face closely linked to issues of maternal health and household

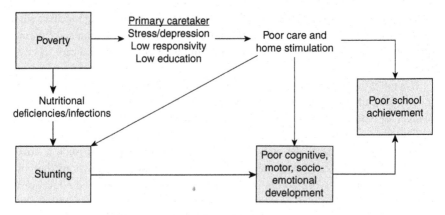

FIGURE 11.3 Hypothesised relations between poverty, stunting, child development and school achievement

Source: Grantham-Mcgregor et al. 2007.

poverty (Abraham and Kumar 2008). The answer to several of these serious concerns linked to poverty, changing economic context, rapid rural-urban migration, poor access to health care, nutrition, child care and schooling is embedded in public policies, programmes and government budgets.

Maternity protection, women's rights and gender equality: policy context

Maternity protection is recognised as an essential prerequisite for women's rights and gender equality, with the right to maternity protection enshrined in International Human Rights Instruments (for example: International Covenant on Economic, Social and Cultural Rights 1966), International Labour Conventions (no. 3, no. 102, no. 103 and no. 183) and in national legislations in several countries. In 1975, International Labour Organisation (ILO) adopted Declaration on Equality of Opportunity for Women Workers expressing the belief that equality of opportunity and equal treatment of women require the elimination of maternity as a source of discrimination and the protection of employment during pregnancy and maternity. In 2004, at the 92nd International Labour Conference, ILO member states adopted a resolution calling on all Governments and social partners to, among other objectives, provide all employed women with access to maternity protection, to develop gender sensitive social security schemes, and to promote measures to better reconcile work and family life.

In 1979, the Convention on Elimination of All Forms of Discrimination Against Women (CEDAW) took forward the work of the 1966 International Covenant on Economic, Social and Cultural Rights. Of interest is its expansion of the economic rights of women, which include the right to work, right to equal employment opportunities, right to equal remuneration, and right to equal treatment at the workplace. The Convention specified women's rights to social security and paid leave in case of situations creating incapacity to work, and demanded paid maternity leave – if not paid then compensated with the requisite social benefits. Crucially, it supported parents who were obligated to combine work and child care responsibilities by promoting the establishment of child care facilities, family benefits, and various forms of financial credit, with special policy recommendations for women in rural areas.

The focus on "maternity" had been part of public policy to protect maternal and infant health in India even prior to India's independence. One of the earliest was the Punjab Maternity Benefit Act (1943), which provided cash benefits to women workers for specified periods before and after confinements. The protection of women workers' maternity related rights were governed by the Factories Act 1948, which in turn was influenced by various conventions of the International Labour Organisation. The report[4] by the Bhore Committee (1946) pointed out to the inadequate availability of crèche facilities in several industries and poor implementation of Maternity Benefit provisions by various Union Provinces of pre-independent India (Government of India 1946).

When policy indeed recognised the link between maternity and women's work in much more explicit ways and addressed it in the Indian Factories Act 1948, it by design got limited to the organised sector where the presence of women is low (compared to the unorganised sector). The perspective that factory is the setting for "work" and "man" as an industrial worker governed the dominant thinking of this Act.

This male-stream thinking meant that the *protective* aspects of providing for leave during pregnancy and after child birth, providing for non-arduous work; and the *promotive* aspects of providing for transport, crèche facilities at the work place were unevenly implemented linked to the presence of women workers at the work place and the level of technology and mechanisation of the industry.

The Constitution of India stipulates in its Directive Principles that states should make provisions for securing just and humane conditions of work and for maternity protection. Accordingly, the government of India promulgated the Maternity Benefits Act in 1961 and the Employees State Insurance (ESI) Act in 1948. The MB Act, 1961, protects the employment of a woman during the time of her maternity and entitles her to full paid absence from work of 12 weeks. A comprehensive review of the maternity benefits in India concluded that the ESI and MB Acts are designed to cover workers in the organised sector (Lingam and Kanchi 2013). The Acts are biased in favour of permanent, full-time workers, workers with identifiable employers and/or a designated place of work. Although "contract workers" are included, they need to be shown on the books of the employer to be eligible. Finally, ESI and MB schemes suffer from an urban bias since they focus on non-agricultural sector and regular salaried workers. Thus maternity benefit cover is restricted largely to the tiny segment of formal workers in the organised sector who form a miniscule percentage of the total female workforce. Coverage of even organised sector workers is segmented and incomplete.

The MB Act has been amended in 2016 such that women working in the organised sector will now be entitled to paid maternity leave of 26 weeks, up from 12 weeks. This amendment will benefit about 1.8 million women. The new law will apply to all establishments employing 10 or more people, and the entitlement will only be applicable for the first two children. For the third child, the entitlement will be for only 12 weeks. Women in public sector organisations are also entitled to 730 days of child care leave during their entire career before their children cross the age of 18 years and this is permitted for two children.

Women organised sector workers and maternity

Maternity benefits, which encompasses several provisions including leave, wage compensation, nursing breaks as well as strictures against discrimination of women on account of reproduction, is an important tool that levels the playing field for women in the labour market.

The overwhelming majority of workers (more than 95 per cent), being informal workers, are out of the ambit of the MB and ESI Acts. Workers in agriculture, unorganised manufacturing and services and informal workers in the organised sector are thus without maternity cover.

The Committee on the Status of Women in India (1974) pointed out a large proportion of women workers are in the agriculture sector and in traditional home based industries with very poor public policy support through maternity benefits, avenues to improve their incomes and livelihoods. The Report of the Commission for Self-Employed Women "Shram Shakti" (1988) had documented the weak legal framework that governs the informal sector women workers and the lack of implementation, monitoring and supervision of whatever that exists (Government of India 1988).

The report pointed out the need to expand the understanding of "work" and "worker" and strongly recommended the need to create a policy framework for ensuring social protection on the one hand and women's rights as workers on the other. However, the neglect of the informal sector in India, despite its large numbers and contributions has been a cause for concern.

Based on the National Commission for Enterprises in the Unorganised Sector (NCEUS) 2006 report's recommendations, a draft bill was passed as the Unorganised Workers Social Security Act, 2008. Notwithstanding several limitations and gaps to the legislation it is significant to state that the Act mentions maternity entitlements to be provided for women working in the unorganised sector. This was expected to cover a larger section of women than covered by the other labour/sectoral laws and or Maternity Benefits Act.

Another significant legislation that has been passed is the National Food Security Act, which came through national campaigns to counter hunger and impoverishment. The Act provides for the following as maternity rights: Entitlement of one free meal to address women's nutritional needs during pregnancy and during lactation period for the first six months and further Entitlement of not less than

Rs.6000 to all pregnant and lactating women (except those working in Government employment or covered by benefits under similar laws). The *Indira Gandhi Matrutva Sahyog Yojana* in 2010 and the *Pradhan Mantri Matru Vandana Yojana in 2017* (to be discussed in a later section) have emerged from the commitments made in this legislation.

However, several of these commitments are problematically conceptualised and poorly implemented. The significance of maternity benefits linked to women's health as mothers and women's rights as workers and citizens are often diluted with population control agenda and thereby turn anti-poor and anti-women.

Maternity benefits: exclusion galore

Maternity Benefit schemes in India have been in existence for over five decades, yet the vast majority of Indian women do not get any maternity entitlements as the legislation does not apply to the unorganised sector. There are at least 19 maternity benefit schemes across all states, run by the Department of Health and Family Welfare and Department of Labour. Except Dr Muthulakshmi Scheme of Tamil Nadu, other schemes have recorded poor performance in terms of targeting the number of pregnant women (Balasubramanian and Ravindran 2012). Two recent schemes are discussed in the following sections.

Janani Suraksha Yojana

JSY is a conditional cash transfer (CCT) mechanism and is a safe motherhood intervention aimed at promoting institutional deliveries as noted earlier. JSY is not exactly a maternity benefit but a cash compensation to cover travel costs and to cover out of pocket expenses to a certain extent. The women have to be from below poverty line households. The allocations, expenditures and number of claimants vary across and within the states. The per-capita expenditure on women also varies across the states. Of the most important limitations, is the exclusion of the poorest because of lack of awareness and high transaction costs (Lim et al. 2010).

Indira Gandhi Matritva Sahyog Yojana (IGMSY): old scheme with limited coverage

The Ministry of Women and Child Development, had framed a scheme titled Indira Gandhi Matritva Sahyog Yojana (IGMSY) for pregnant and lactating (P&L) women which was piloted in 53 districts in 2010. This is a centrally sponsored scheme in which conditional cash transfers (CCTs) are to be made directly to the beneficiaries. The basic objective of the scheme is to support women with nutrition and enhance early infant nutrition and survival through protection and promotion of early breastfeeding within one hour and exclusive breastfeeding for the first six months in order to improve child health and development. Beneficiaries who fulfil the scheme conditionalities will be paid Rs.4,000 in three instalments between the second trimester till the child attains the age of 6 months on fulfilling specific conditions related to maternal and child health. The scheme eligibility criteria restricts it to mothers older than 18 years age and for only two childbirths. Studying the scheme design, Lingam and Yelamanchili (2011) demonstrated that, 48 per cent of deserving pregnant women who often are SCs, STs, illiterate and minority women are likely to be excluded from the benefits of the IGMSY. The Ministry of Women and Child Development's administrative data had observed that the scheme reached only 22.9 per cent of the targeted coverage (Government of India 2015). Two field studies in select states (Chhattisgarh, Uttarakhand and Uttar Pradesh; and West Bengal, Odisha, Jharkhand and Uttar Pradesh) pointed to several implementation related issues and the shortcomings in the conditionalities as well as the conditional cash transfers (Sahayog 2012; Sinha et al. 2016).

Pradhan Mantri Matru Vandana Yojana (PMMVY): new scheme with further limited coverage

In the place of IGMSY, the Government of India had approved the implementation of Pradhan Mantri Matru Vandana Yojana (PMMVY) in all districts of the country w.e.f. 01.01.2017 under which the eligible beneficiaries get Rs.5,000/- and the remaining cash incentive as per approved norms towards Maternity Benefit under Janani Suraksha Yojana (JSY) after institutional delivery so that on an average, a woman gets Rs.6000/-. The scheme is applicable only for one pregnancy event and to women who have not availed any other maternity scheme.

The objectives of the scheme are: (i) providing partial compensation for the wage loss in terms of cash incentives so that the woman can take adequate rest before and after delivery of the first living child; and (ii) the cash incentives provided would lead to improved health seeking behaviour amongst the Pregnant Women and Lactating Mothers.

Most crucially, where the IGMSY was open to women for the first two live births, the Maternity Benefit Programme (MBP) 2017 is restricted to only the first live birth, halving the number of beneficiaries. Moreover, the amount set aside for this programme is only around one fifth of the recommended amount by the Standing Committee on Food, Consumer Affairs and Public Distribution in 2013; and the amounts promised in the three-tier cash transfer process decreased between the January 2017 to the May 2017 press release of the MBP from Rs.6000 to Rs.5000.[5]

This reflects a doublespeak between the expressed objectives of the programme and its implementation. There seems to be a clash between the objectives of recognising women's unpaid work and right to wage compensation during maternity; and of addressing population control and ensuring behavioural change among women. As the current scheme stands, one has to carefully assess if the scheme is advancing women's wage compensation requirement and whether the stipulation of *Aadhar*[6] card and independent bank account is enabling access or impeding it.

Conclusion

Women bear the weight of reproduction and child care and support social reproduction through care work. Through these roles they generate future workers for the economy. Intersectional inequalities compound the risks and impacts of poverty for women and girls. However in the matter of allowing women to enter the workforce and supporting their agency, one of the social policies with maximum impact is maternity benefits, ideally supplemented by schemes to support women's care work.

This chapter centrally locates social protection within the SDGs, focusing on maternity benefits as a mechanism to fulfil women's rights as workers and citizens. The social policy context for maternity benefit schemes in India is linked to vulnerability and exclusion, set against the background of a globalising economy and ground realities of poverty and social exclusion. In this context, it outlines the macro picture pertaining to women's work and children's nutrition. Here, the chapter draws a strong link between women's declining labour force participation, the role of children and utilisation of maternal health services. This exposes the relationship between fertility, education and employment as well as the effects of women's work on child nutrition and wellbeing.

The chapter makes a strong case for the universal coverage of maternity benefit schemes as follows. First, they would facilitate women's entry into the labour market, with multiplier effects for economic growth as well as opening up avenues for women's empowerment. Second, they would enhance women's autonomy, financial independence and decision-making power, which in turn would have positive effects on their children's nutrition and health. Third, by shifting the burden of care work outside the family, they would help to cut short inter-generational cycles of poverty and gender-based discrimination.

Notes

1 The term maternity protection refers to legislations made in order to promote equality of all women in the workforce and the health and safety of the mother and child. The term maternity benefits refer to actual provisions made in the Acts and schemes in terms of number of weeks and months of maternity leave, wage compensations and other employer related commitments to be made to ensure equality, non-discrimination, health and safety of the mother and child.
2 World Employment and Social Outlook Report, ILO, Geneva, 2017
3 NITI Ayog website http://niti.gov.in/content/maternal-mortality-ratio-mmr-100000-live-births
4 Report of the Health Survey and Development Committee (1946): Vol. I – Survey, New Delhi: Government of India Press.
5 http://pib.nic.in/newsite/PrintRelease.aspx?relid=156094
6 Aadhaar is a 12-digit unique identification number issued by the Indian government to every individual resident of India upon application based on biometric and demographic data.

References

Abraham, A.R. and Kavi Kumar, K.S. 2008. "Multidimensional Poverty and Vulnerability." *Economic and Political Weekly*, 43(20): 77–87.

Balasubramanian, P. and Sundari Ravindran, T.K. 2012. "Pro-poor Maternity Benefit Schemes and Rural Women, Findings from Tamil Nadu." *Economic and Political Weekly*, 47(25).

Barbara-Harriss-White. 2014. "The Dynamic Political Economy of Persistent Poverty." In Gooptu, Nandini and Parry, Jonathan (eds.). *Persistence of Poverty in India*, pp. 370–395. New Delhi: Social Science Press.

Chandrasekhar, C.P. and Ghosh, J. 2011. "Latest Employment Trends from the NSSO", *Business Line*, 12.

Chaturvedi, S., Ramji, S., Arora, N.K., Rewal, S., Dasgupta, R., and Deshmukh, V. 2016. "Time-constrained Mother and Expanding Market: Emerging Model of Under-Nutrition in India." *BMC Public Health*, 16(1): 632.

Choudhury, S. 2011. "Employment in India: What does the Latest Data Show?" *Economic and Political Weekly*, 46(32): 23–26.

Elson, D. 2014. "Economic Crises from the 1980s to the 2010s: A Gender Analysis." In Rai, S.M. and Waylen, G. (eds.). *New Frontiers in Feminist Political Economy*, pp. 189–212. Abingdon, UK: Routledge.

Grantham-McGregor, S., Cheung, Yin Bun, Cueto, Santiago, Glewwe, Paul, Richter, Linda, Strupp, Barbara and the International Child Development Steering Group. 2007. "Developmental Potential in the First 5 years for Children in Developing Countries." *Lancet*, 369: 60–70.

Government of India. 1946. *Report of the Health Survey and Development Committee: Volume I – Survey*. New Delhi: Government of India.

Government of India. 1988. *Shram Shakti: National Report of National Commission on Self-Employed Women and Women in the Informal Sector*. New Delhi: Government of India.

———. 2015. *Parliamentary Standing Committee Report 268: Demand for Grants 2015–16*. New Delhi: Ministry of Women and Child Development, Rajya Sabha, Government of India.

Haddad, Lawrence. 1999. "Women's Status: Levels, Determinants, Consequences for Malnutrition, Interventions, and Policy." *Asian Development Review*, 17(1&2): 96–131.

ILO. 2017. *World Employment and Social Outlook Report*. Geneva: ILO.

International Covenant on Economic, Social and Cultural Rights. 1966. Available at: https://www.ohchr.org/Documents/ProfessionalInterest/cescr.pdf

International Institute for Population Sciences (IIPS) and Macro International. 2017. *National Family Health Survey (NFHS-4), 2015–16: India*: Mumbai: IIPS.

Kabeer, N. 2012. "Women's Economic Empowerment Offers a Win-Win Scenario." *The Guardian*. Available at: www.theguardian.com/global-development/poverty-matters/2012/nov/06/women-economic-empowerment-win-scenario [Accessed June 13, 2017].

Kabeer, N. and Cook, S. 2010. "Introduction: Overcoming Barriers to the Extension of Social Protection: Lessons from the Asia Region." *IDS Bulletin*, 41(4): 1–11.

Kadiyala, S., Harris, J., Headey, D., Yosef, S., and Gillespie, S. 2014. "Agriculture and Nutrition in India: Mapping Evidence to Pathways." *Annals of the New York Academy of Sciences*, 1331(1): 43–56.

Ladusingh, L. 2016. *Counting Women's Work in India: The Market and the Household in India*. Available at: www.cww-dpru.uct.ac.za/sites/default/files/image_tool/images/74/Country%20Report%2002%20-%20India.pdf [Accessed April 11, 2018].

Lim, S.S., Dandona, L., Hoisington, J.A. James, S.L.K., Hogan, M.C., and Gakidou, E. 2010. "India's Janani Suraksha Yojana, Conditional Cash Transfer Programme to Increase Births in Health Facilities: An Impact Evaluation." *Lancet*, 375: 2009–23.

Lingam, L. 2006. "Gender, Households and Poverty: Tracking Mediations of Macro Adjustment Programmes." *Economic and Political Weekly*, 41(20): 1989–1998.

Lingam, L. and Kanchi, A. 2013. *Women's Work, Maternity and Public Policy*. New Delhi: Ministry of Labour & Employment and ILO.

Lingam, L. and Yelamanchili, V. 2011. "Reproductive Rights and Exclusionary Wrongs: Maternity Benefits." *Economic & Political Weekly*, 46(43): 94–103.

Muniyoor, K. 2014. "Employment in India: Emerging Dynamics." *World Economics*, 15(4): 19–44.

NCEUS. 2007. *National Commission for Enterprises in the Unorganised Sector, Report on Conditions of Work and Promotion of Livelihoods in the Unorganised Sector*. New Delhi: NCEUS.

Parasuraman, S. 2009. "Economic Liberalisation, Informalisation of Labour and Social Protection in India", George Simmons Memorial Lecture delivered at the 31st Annual Conference of the IASP on "Population and Disease." *Tirupathi*, 4 November 2009.

Raveendran, R. 2016. "The Indian Labour Market: A Gender Perspective." *UN Women*, Discussion Paper No. 8.

Sahayog. 2012. *The Crisis of Maternity: Healthcare and Maternity Benefits for Women Wage Workers in the Informal Sector in India – A Compilation of Two National Studies*. Lucknow: SAHAYOG. Available at: https://aditigondal.files.wordpress.com/2012/08/the-crisis-of-maternity.pdf [Accessed June 13, 2017].

Shroff, M., Griffiths, P., Adair, L., Suchindran, C., and Bentley, M. 2009. "Maternal Autonomy is inversely related to Child Stunting in Andhra Pradesh, India." *Maternal & Child Nutrition*, 5(1): 64–74.

Sinha, D., Nehra, S., Matharu, S., Khanuja, J., and Falcao, V.L. 2016. "Realising Universal Maternity Entitlements." *Economic & Political Weekly*, 51(34): 49.

Subha Sri, B. and Khanna, R. 2014. "Dead Women Talking: A Civil Society Report on Maternal Deaths in India." *Common Health and Jan Swasthya Abhiyan*. Available at: https://cdn2.sph.harvard.edu/wp-content/uploads/sites/32/2015/12/Subha-Sri-B.pdf [Accessed June 17, 2017].

United Nations Research Institute for Social Development (UNRISD) (eds.). 2010. *Combating Poverty and Inequality. Structural Change, Social Policy and Politics* (Geneva).

Walker, Susan P., Wachs, Theodore D., Gardner, Julie Meeks, Lozoff, Betsy, Wasserman, Gail A., Pollitt, Ernesto, Carter, Julie A., and the International Child Development Steering Group. 2007. "Child Development: Risk Factors for Adverse Outcomes in Developing Countries." *The Lancet*, 369: 145–157.

PART VI

Poverty, employment and inequality

12

ARE WE REALLY CONCERNED ABOUT EMPLOYMENT?

Some reflections on India's current macroeconomic policy regime

Praveen Jha

It hardly needs any emphasis that sustained and inclusive economic growth, and not simply high rates of growth *per se*, is critical for eradicating poverty and promoting decent work in general. This of course requires necessary intervention on several fronts, in particular adequate macroeconomic space for national governments while being open to equitable multilateral trading systems. Investments in physical and social infrastructure with due emphasis on rural areas, necessary structural reforms, appropriate fiscal and monetary policies and a climate favourable to micro, small and medium enterprises are among the more important elements in a coordinated macroeconomic policy framework that can take the country in the direction of sustainable and inclusive growth, which also addresses the issues relating to decent employment. In fact it is important to emphasise that without addressing the concerns relating to employment, sustainability of any growth process may not be feasible and, in any case, it is not desirable.

It is well-acknowledged that the period since the early 1990s has witnessed a fundamental repositioning of the state versus the Market in the Indian economy. Essentially, the transition has been characterised by a strong push towards a neo-liberal policy regime, resulting in a very substantial degree of internal and external economic liberalisation. Although the process had begun in the second half of the 1980s, it was in July 1991 that a rapid and sharp shift in the economic policy towards neo-liberalism was officially enunciated, which justifies the view of the Indian case that of a transition from a "mixed economy" policy framework to a "market-driven" paradigm. Such a paradigm has been seriously deficient in terms of a whole range of macro-economic interventions required for a growth process which can be inclusive and promote decent work. Sure enough, as per the official figures, the period since the early 1990s clearly shows an acceleration in the trend growth rate compared to the 1980s, but it has been seriously flawed in terms of labour market outcomes. Furthermore, it may not be advisable to see the spurt in growth rates in some years, since the early 1990s, as a decisive transition to a significantly higher growth path.

This chapter is structured as follows: Section 2 provides a brief overview of the development strategy and economic performance of the Indian economy and also highlights important dimensions and policies relating to manufacturing sector. Section 3 seeks to examine the challenges of industrial policy in India to underscore the argument that there is hardly any strategy to realise the promise of adequate and decent employment. Section 4 concludes the paper.

Economic "reforms" and employment prospects

The performance of the Indian economy in the neo-liberal era continues to be a subject of intense debate, especially with respect to adequate and sustainable livelihood options for a large section of the population. In my assessment the essential picture that emerges is one of overall worsening in employment and conditions of work even though there has been a significant acceleration in output growth in the non-agricultural sector.[1] As regards the agricultural sector, its performance has tended to worsen considerably not only with respect to employment but also output growth. Fundamentally, there has been a change in the pattern of growth where the non-agricultural sector (essentially the services) has shown substantial acceleration in output per worker compared to the agricultural sector, and thus the gap between the two has tended to increase very substantially. Furthermore, employment content of growth process has gone down significantly during the reform era. In particular, rural India which houses more than two-thirds of the working population of our country has been among the worst hit during the period of reforms.

In terms of the five year plan chronology since the beginning of the new macroeconomic policy regime India has completed five FYPs, i.e. 8th (1992–97), 9th

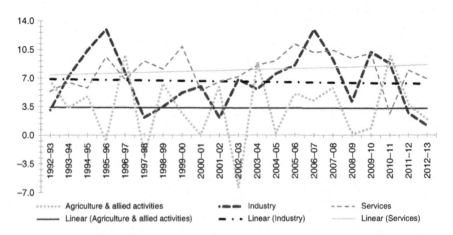

FIGURE 12.1 Sectoral growth rates (at 2004–05 prices) since the early 1990s

(1997–2002), 10th (2002–07), 11th (2007–12); and the 12th FYP (2012–17). The experience of the last two and half decades has been quite mixed; for instance, as already mentioned at the outset, a sustained high GDP growth rate for much of this period is well acknowledged but in terms of the structure of growth as well as its distribution, employment outcomes etc., there have been serious concerns. In fact, it is such concerns which give us an insight into the basic professed philosophy of the last two plans (11th and 12th), namely "inclusive growth" and "faster, more inclusive and sustainable growth". These two plans aimed to spread the benefit of growth process "to the mass of the population". Further, the twelfth FYP aimed to shift substantial population from agricultural to higher productivity non-agricultural occupations, and to accelerate the growth rate of the manufacturing sector. It also claimed to sharpen the thrust in terms of redefining the role and responsibility of state for delivering social services, like health and education and essential services and advocated further reduction in the role of state where private sector is able to deliver these services.

The sectoral composition of the employment and value added has witnessed a major change in last three decades. Since the employment intensity in the non-agricultural sectors is lower than that of agriculture, employment diversification of the economy has not kept pace with the diversification of the economy in terms of value added. Consequently, although the share of agriculture in GDP went down significantly from 38 per cent to 16 per cent over the period 1981–2012, the structure of the workforce was still dominated by agriculture (68 per cent in 1983 to almost 50 per cent in 2011–12). However, the current federal Indian government has changed the methodology of calculating GDP, with the 2011–12 prices as the base, and has adopted "System of National Accounts" (SNA), 2008 methodology (UNSTATS 2009) with a new classification system. Even if we choose to ignore the contention issues regarding the changed methodology, the point worth highlighting is that there is a significant deceleration during the last couple of years, even with the new series (of sector wise gross value added (GVA)). In fact the industry and services sectors have logged slowing down of their growth rates since 2014–15 (Figure 12.2).

Although there have been frequent loud claims regarding pro-growth measures such as "Make in India", "Digital India", "Smart City mission" etc. by the current government led by Mr Modi, most of these are on the same track as the policies of previous United Progressive Alliance (UPA) Government between 2004–14; at best the current government can claim, further acceleration with respect to some of these initiatives. The big ticket new interventions by the current government appeared to be a mixed bag, for instance, the 2016 insolvency and bankruptcy code which seeks to address the problem of bad loans and non-performing assets (NPAs) may be promising; however, its implementation is likely to be a long drawn and complex process. On the other hand we have highly controversial measures such as demonetisation and the rolling out of the Goods and Services Tax (GST). By now there is a substantial literature on demonetisation experiment – the goals, intended objectives and actual outcomes – from different quarters and there is near

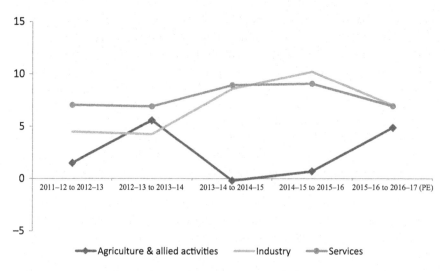

FIGURE 12.2 Sectoral growth rates (at 2011–12 prices) since 2011–12

consensus, explicit or implicit, that this has been an unmitigated disaster (Ghosh et al. 2017). It is quite clear that there has been a steady decline of the rate of growth of GDP in the quarters of 2016–17: from 9.2 per cent at the end of the quarter ending March 2016, to 7.9 per cent, 7.5 per cent, 7.0 per cent, 6.1 per cent and then 5.7 per cent at the end of the June quarter in the fiscal year 2017. Recent growth performance of the Indian economy has received flak from whole spectrum of economists and policy think tanks including many staunch advocates of neo-liberal reforms, as also prominent leaders and economist within the ruling party.[2]

Apart from the poor performance in terms of the GDP growth rate, there are serious concerns relating to almost every macro indicator, as is evident even from most official reports in the last few months. It is estimated that on an average 10–12 million new job seekers enter the labour market every year which obviously requires a massive upscaling of job generation; the trends regarding employment generation since the early 1990s have been seriously inadequate, to say the least, to meet the requisite demand for jobs. As regards generation of decent job the story is even more dismal. The latest estimates, available from the Labour Bureau, paint an extremely depressing picture with respect to the pace of job creation in the formal sector. Apart from being nowhere near what would be required to facilitate near full employment, there has been a staggering decline by about 90 per cent as new jobs has come down from about 1.1 million in 2010 to 150 thousand in 2016.[3] For reasons of space, it is not possible to examine many of these challenges in a satisfactory manner here.

The GDP share of the manufacturing sector has been almost stagnant at around 15 to 16 per cent since the early 1990s to 2012–13, and the same is true of its share of employment, which increased marginally from 11.24 per cent in 1983 to 12.20 per cent in 2004–05 and 12.6 per cent in 2011–12. In other words, the shift away from agriculture has not led to a significant increase in the share of employment in the manufacturing sector. On the other hand, the GDP share of trade, hotels and transport, storage, and communication increased by almost ten percentage points between 1981 and 2013. The new methodology of GDP accounting also shows a similar decline in the trend for manufacturing sector till 2016–17.

Further, dividing the overall manufacturing sector into registered and unregistered manufacturing industries, the former which is, in general, characterised by relatively high earnings and better working environment, appears to have played a very insignificant role in overall occupational transformation of the labour force in India for over last three or more decades. As per the Annual survey of Industries (ASI) and Directorate General of Employment and Training (DGET), as reported in the Handbook of Statistics on Indian Economy by the Reserve Bank of India (RBI), which provide figures on registered manufacturing sector employment, we get slightly different trends. The figures given by ASI show that registered manufacturing employment rose between the mid-1980s and mid-1990s and declined subsequently for a few years touching a low in 2002–03, before picking up again. As should be clear from figure 12.3, there is some increase between early 80s and the present, but figures available for the recent couple of years show a flattening again.

Figure 12.4 plots the change relating to the organised manufacturing sector using the DGET data reported in the RBI Handbook of Statistics on Indian Economy. As is clear, since the early 1990s, there has been a small decline in the number employed in the public sector along with a small increase of the private sector: on the whole there is little to cheer about.

As per the National Sample Survey (NSS), for rural male, the proportion of regular employed was about 10.3 per cent in 1987, which declined to 8.5 per cent in 2009–10, and again improved to 10 per cent in 2011–12. Also, in urban areas, the share of regular employed in male category, declined from 43.7 per cent in 1987–88 to 40.6 in 2004–05 and again improved and reached 43.4 per cent in 2011–12. The increase in regular employment during the period from 1983 to 2011–12, for both rural and urban females, was too small to raise the share of regular employed in total employment. We may also note that the annual increment in regular employment was about 2 million during 1993 to 2005, which declined to approximately 1 million during 2005 to 2010. Although, the data for the 61st and 68th NSS rounds show that the rate of regular employment generation in the private organised sector has picked up recently, it is also clear that this was more than offset by decline in the share of regular employment in rest of the economy. In fact, it is quite striking that over 80 per cent of all new jobs created in the recent years have been of casual nature, with construction alone accounting for a substantial share (Jha 2016; Chandrasekhar and Ghosh 2007, 2015).

In other words, in spite of the high growth rate in the Indian economy the process of informalisation and casualisation in the world of work has been on the rise during the last three decades. A substantial segment of workers who are unable to find even casual employment often remain "self-employed", which, to a large extent, is same as being underemployed or disguisedly unemployed. Further it is

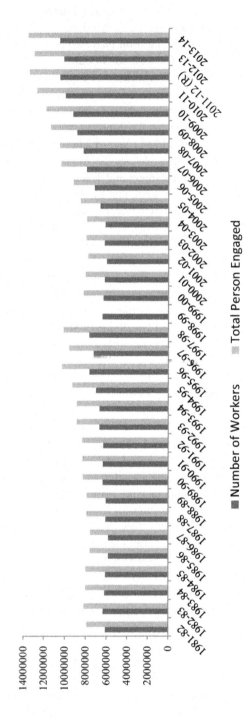

FIGURE 12.3 ASI estimates of registered manufacturing employment

Source: Annual Survey of Industries, Central Statistical Organization, 2013–14

Concerns about employment? 255

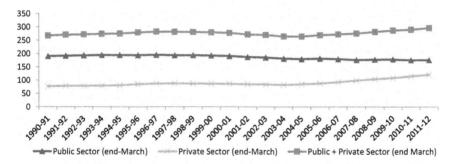

FIGURE 12.4 Employment in organised sector manufacturing (100,000 persons)
Source: Handbook of Statistics on Indian Economy, 2014–15

quite clear that the process of casualisation and contractual employment has gained momentum in the organised sectors. As regards sectoral distribution, the proportion of informal workers to total workers has been highest in trade, followed by manufacturing, transport and real estate, and business services. In terms of composition of employment, manufacturing and trade constitute around 70–75 per cent of total informal sector employment (NSS 67th round). In urban areas, the share of trade exceeds the share of manufacturing. Hence, the dominance of the tertiary activities in the informal sector, which was observed almost three decades ago, does not appear to have undergone any major change.

As per the latest (6th) Economic Census (EC), conducted from January 2013 to April 2014, there are 58.5 million establishments in the country. It may be noted that the said EC enumerated all establishments engaged in various activities excluding crop production, plantation, public administration, defence and compulsory social security. Thus it is a good source to draw the sketch of non-agricultural sector, both for output and employment. As per this source, of the total enumerated establishments, 35.02 million (59.9 per cent) were in rural and the remaining 23.45 million (40.1 per cent) were in urban areas. Furthermore 20.5 per cent of the establishments operate from outside household without fixed structure and these obviously constitute extremely vulnerable entities. Almost 74 per cent are employed in private proprietary establishments and it is worth noting that almost 45 per cent of all private proprietary establishments do not hire even one worker.

The comparable information on non-agricultural establishments, taking both organised and unorganised sectors together, can also be collated from the ASI and the NSSO. As is well known, for Indian economy, the ASI is the most important source of industrial statistics for the registered/organised manufacturing sector, whereas the NSSO plays a similar role for the unorganised sector as it provides requisite information on unincorporated non-agricultural enterprises and various indicators of economic and operational characteristics of enterprises in manufacturing, trade and other service sector (excluding construction) at national and state level. As per the recent relevant data from the ASI and NSSO, the total number of non-agricultural establishments in India was 57,832,182 of which the organised component accounted for 158,877 only or barely 0.275 per cent. If we take into account only the manufacturing sector, the share of the organised component was just about 0.85 per cent. These are indeed startling numbers as regards the structure of Indian industry/broader economy. It is true that in terms of the contribution to the GDP, the organised sector punches hugely above its weight with respect to its numerical share, as indeed in guiding the economic policy destiny of the country, especially at the current juncture. The contribution of the organised and unorganised non-agriculture GVA in Indian economy is almost evenly matched, although the distribution of specific sub-sectors varies dramatically.

It is evident from ASI data that there have been some notable changes across a few sub sectors (both within "traditional" as well as modern activities) in terms of their contributions. What may well be a matter of serious concern is the slippage with respect to presumably the cutting edge manufacturing segments such as "computer, electronic and optical products" and "pharmaceuticals, medicinal, chemical and botanical products", whose shares in number of factories, output as well as employment have plummeted dramatically. We may also recall here that generation of employment in organised sector has been a major challenge, particularly in the recent years; employment elasticity of output for the economy as a whole and in particular for the organised sector, in fact, has come under considerable pressure during the period of economic reforms.[4]

As regards the Unincorporated Non-Agricultural Enterprises (excluding Construction), taking both rural and urban India, almost 60 per cent of these operate with only 1 worker and another 26 per cent with 2 workers. Obviously this sums up not only the overwhelming smallness of the Indian non-agricultural sector but also its vulnerability. As is evident from NSS 67th round, manufacturing is just about 30 per cent of the total number of enterprises as well as the total number of workers in these activities. Furthermore, the distribution of unincorporated enterprises, in the aggregate, across rural and urban India is almost even, although the rural areas account for a much larger share of the Own Account Enterprises (OAEs). For the country as a whole, over 98 per cent of the enterprises and close to 90 per cent of the workers constitutes the informal component. Furthermore, if we look at the distribution of the formal, as well as informal in the unincorporated enterprises, manufacturing accounts for just about one-third of both the estimated number of enterprises as well the workers. We may also note here that in the recent years there has been a significant acceleration in the growth of informal employment even in the formal sector. In 1999–2000 the share of informal workers in the formal sectors was already 37.8 per cent which jumped to 54.4 per cent in 2011–12 (NSS 68th round). Thus, as per the latest count of workers in the country, which stood at 484.7 million in 2011–12, 447.2 million were informal workers.

There are a number of indicators which seem to indicate that the overall industrial structure and dynamics have come under severe stress during the reform era. In a careful study (Chaudhuri 2015), it is argued that there is a veritable manufacturing crisis since the early 1990s; in fact, the author argues that India is experiencing "premature deindustrialisation" and the argument is backed by a careful consideration of the evidence of "manufacturing crises". Almost all the correlates of manufacturing dynamics seem to indicate that the period since the early 1990s has been a difficult one and hence it is hardly surprising that the share of manufacturing in the GDP has stagnated during this period. Trends relating to manufacturing growth rate, trade balance, import dependency, or any other critical indicator for that matter, clearly suggest considerable stress for the period since the early 1990s. Going by the Index of Industrial Production (IIP), either by major sectors or in overall terms, it is clear that there is no significant improvement in the relevant rates during the post-reform period. If anything, the last decade shows a discernible worsening in the major segments, as also in the general IIP. In fact, during the last few years (since 2010–11), there has been virtual stagnation and of course the ongoing global recession has not helped matters. It is true that one can point to a few bright spots in India's industrial landscape since the early 1990s, but the point is that the expectations of a dramatic improvement as promised by the advocates of new economic policy in growth and overall performance of the manufacturing sector has certainly been belied.

We have noted earlier that the share of manufacturing in GDP has stagnated around 15–16 per cent, and its share in total employment has been stuck between 11 and 13 per cent, since 1991. In fact the growth of employment in manufacturing, in particular in its organised segment, has been more of a challenge compared to the growth of manufacturing value added. As per Economy Survey 2014–15, the share of employment of registered manufacturing in total employment marginally declined between 1984 and 2010 (from 0.027 to 0.026) and the annual growth rate of this segment over the same period was a negative 0.2 per cent. Further, as Chaudhuri (2015) notes, the organised manufacturing employment had witnessed a steady growth between early 1970s to mid-1990s (4.8 million in 70–71 to 7.1 million in 1996–97), before going down in absolute terms during the next decade (5.8 million in 2006–07), followed by a mild recovery (6.6 million in 2009–10). In any case, point worth highlighting is that given the size of India's workforce and the challenges of decent employment, these numbers and the changes therein are too small to make any song and dance about them. Apart from the overall manufacturing sector not doing too well, the situation of the unincorporated enterprises may be of greater concern, given their role in employment and livelihood generation. As may be seen from the recent rounds of the NSS data, employment elasticity of output even in unorganised manufacturing sector has tended to decline significantly; we already know that the story in the organised sector is much worse.

Some pointers for an appropriate industrial policy

It should be obvious from the foregoing discussion of India's industrial structure that policy obsession almost entirely with "big players" needs to be revisited. As is amply clear, the context and prospects of India's industrial landscape, particularly from the point of employment, are organically connected with the unorganised segments/micro, small and medium enterprises (MSMEs) etc. The country needs, first and foremost, a robust industrial policy (hence forth IP) for them, embedded in an overall macro-economic policy regime. Substantive measures are required which include boosting support for domestic manufacturers through a variety of channels, in particular through development of appropriate infrastructure for broad based manufacturing (with a clear focus on "small players"), encouragement of adequate technology policies etc. It is also worth noting that the need for a synergy between manufacturing and other sectors needs lot more attention, a problem which has been compounded during the era of reforms. Although some of the issues may be addressed in a piece-meal manner in the currently dominant neo-liberal policy framework, it is our contention that a serious rethink of the framework itself is required. Unfortunately there is little evidence of any such move at the current juncture. In fact, the so called "Make in India" programme[5] of the current National Democratic Alliance (NDA) government at the Centre is, to a large extent, reminiscent of the National Manufacturing Policy (NMP) of the erstwhile UPA regime. As in the case of the NMP, the thrust of the "Make in India" initiative is on the corporate sector, the Foreign Direct Investment (FDI) and the so-called "ease of doing business". It identifies 25 sectors in particular which currently account for approximately 20 per cent of the country's workforce (NSS 68th round).

For generation of adequate and decent employment, several key policies need to be in place. One of these is what gets highlighted as IP in the relevant literature. Meaning and scope of IP has generated substantial literature, emphasising different elements and aspects, and for many it may well seem akin to the proverbial elephant in the room. IP ought to be viewed as a number of strategic objectives and tools embedded in the larger development strategy and overall macroeconomic framework. As a recent United Nations Conference on Trade and Development (UNCTAD) report (2014), based on the deliberations of a panel of experts drawing on the collaborative research of the UNCTAD and the International Labour Organization (ILO) notes, the canvas of IP includes not only the manufacturing sector but also agriculture and services. The policy challenge is to put in place conducive structures and processes to facilitate economic diversification which hinges on higher value additions and returns; high road to transformation and broad based development would be the end objectives for any worthwhile set of industrial policies.

Clearly, strait-jackets and "one-size-fits-all" will not do and historically there has been space for a variety of industrial policies although, generally speaking, these are invariably about structural transformation with emphasis on industrialisation. It was such an understanding that informed the development discourses soon after the World War II, in the heyday of "Development Economics" during the 1950s and the 1960s, particularly in the Global South. The core concern was to "catch-up" with the industrially advanced countries through a set of strategies to facilitate broad based structural economic transformation and decent employment, with the manufacturing sector on the front burner. Creation of domestic manufacturing capabilities, sustained technological up-gradation, economic diversification, rising incomes etc. were supposed to be the important indicators of the process of catching up. It was argued that such a prospect could not and would not materialise without visible hand of the state and well-designed industrial policies. Unfortunately, as is well-known, the rise of neo-liberal order with accent on market fundamentalism, since the 1970s tended to negate, at least in official pronouncements in most countries in the world, the role and significance of industrial policies.

Thus, there is no one magic bullet in the name of IP and it is bound to be different across time and space. Initial conditions and the larger context obviously matter. However, the history of economic transformation across the World teaches us a number of important lessons which is worth paying attention to in any developing country. For instance, the role of pro-peasant land reforms in conjunction with appropriate macro-economic policies, which requires significant economic space for the state, disciplining of corporate powers and rentier classes, a long term vision for economic transformation and industrialisation etc. are among the critical elements that the policymakers must grapple with. It hardly needs emphasis that any coherent development strategy has to be steered through the state; but of course it also begets the question, whose state, what kind of state and is there a socio-political mobilisation to have a state conducive to progressive economic transformation?

In view of the sketch provided in section II, what can be said of India's IP at the current juncture? In sum, our contention is that, in spite of all the official discourses and claims regarding some kind of IP being in place in the country, even a preliminary assessment for the last three decades or so would seems to indicate that such claims are highly exaggerated. At best what we have had during this period are knee-jerk reactions and piece-meal interventions and grand slogans (such as "Make in India"), which do not cohere well; in fact, a more realistic conclusion may well be that we simply do not have an IP in place. As hinted earlier, the focus of the policymakers has been to integrate the country's economy in the global production systems, to have a slice of the pie either through an increase in exports in particular sectors or to get a share of the global capital in expanding domestic manufacturing. Sure enough, in both these respects, there have been some "gains" in specific sectors but, in an aggregate sense, these have been modest and possibly with significant costs to segments of manufacturing (particularly MSMEs) and sections of workers. As discussed earlier, the objective of getting integrated in the global manufacturing value chains required significant deregulation and liberalisation in cross-border movements with respect to almost all the factor and product markets and were often accompanied by various questionable concessions to corporate investors, both domestic and foreign. Furthermore, obsession with "sound finance", which is at the core of neo-liberal macroeconomic strategy, in conjunction with liberalisation, has resulted in fiscal stringency and massive erosion in the capacity of the state to intervene in the economy.

During the *dirigiste* era, India's economic federalism gave lot of space for the state governments to have their own policy interventions. As noted earlier, there is considerable differentiation, in terms of industrial performance, across major states of India and some of it is on account of historical legacies and policies prior to Independence. However, there have been important differences, with respect to

IP, across states after Independence as well. Thus there may be a good deal to learn from experiences of each other; emergence of industrial hubs in particular sectors in some of the southern states in the recent years may well be worth careful examination to draw some lessons regarding creation of appropriate economic environments. However, as a word of caution we must note here that any IP which is exclusively concerned with output expansion without caring for employment generation ought to be viewed, at best, as a limited success, (if not a failure), particularly so at the current juncture in case of most developing countries where creation of decent employment outside agriculture has been among the biggest challenge.

As should be evident from the structure of India's non-agricultural sector, for healthy and sustained growth in manufacturing the focus on the MSMEs will have to be critical and the relevant policy interventions must be tailored to their needs and conditions. In particular Government policies for MSMEs should help them improve their technological capabilities by focusing on: (i) Providing access to risk capital, (ii) Setting up of standards for the industry, (iii) Improving Industry/research institute/academia, interaction, mostly in clusters, (iv) Stimulating demand/providing scale through preferential treatment in government purchases, Modular industrial estates/laboratories near premier technical institutions with the required plug and play facilities. As per recent estimates, MSMEs contributes approximately 8 per cent of the country's GDP, 45 per cent of the manufacturing output and 40 per cent of the country's exports, and the sector is the second largest provider of employment in the country, after agriculture. Thus it is quite evident that a conducive policy towards MSMEs will play a critical role in India's broad based industrialisation and employment engendering drive.

As noted earlier, an obvious critical obstacle in the country's growth towards a significant "manufacturing hub" happens to be a serious inadequacy of infrastructure (such as ports, roads, power, etc.), for instance, in comparison to a country like China. It is well-known, during the last few years different governments have tended to rely on so-called "public-private partnerships", or on private investments, for the funding of quality infrastructure; most of these have been limited to a few pockets (by and large in urban areas) and the track records of such initiatives have hardly inspired confidence. Given the fiscal orthodoxy, which is the lynchpin of economic reforms, the Union as well as the state governments are generally loathe to expand overall public expenditure which, of course, has impacted on public provisioning for a whole range of critical pre-requisites, including infrastructure, for expansion of manufacturing. On the "supply side" apart from the infrastructural constraints, there are other gaps in terms of institutional constraints at different levels which impinge on the prospects of broad-based industrialisation. We may also note that there are significant problems on the "demand side" as well which require careful consideration. Given very high levels of mass poverty, massive disguised unemployment and serious deprivations afflicting large sections of the masses, there is an obvious problem of domestic demand. In the era of economic reforms, the pressure to squeeze labour cost has of course added to the problem further. Moreover, in the neo-liberal global economy in general, there have been similar pressures, thus contributing to the "race to the bottom" in terms of overall wellbeing of the workers, with adverse impacts on the level of demand everywhere. In fact, the neo-liberal pressures to outcompete each other amongst countries (in particular in the developing world) leading to "beggar thy neighbour" to a large extent operates through "beggar thy workers".

Apart from the issue of the squeeze in domestic demand, we also need to reckon the dynamics of overall demand in the global economy. As already hinted in the preceding paragraph, neo-liberalism invariably results in strong tendencies of compression of demand, through wage squeeze and worsening labour standards, almost everywhere. On top of this, there are other factors which may create serious demand pressures, as has been the case with the world economy because of a recession which started in developed countries in the aftermath of the well-known financial crisis beginning 2007–08. Given such a context, it is highly unlikely that India, or for that matter, most developing countries can hope to gain from the strategy of "export-led" manufacturing growth, which had been significant in the case of a handful of East-Asian countries. To the extent that one relies on such a strategy, it may certainly help a small set of big corporate players, both domestic and foreign, but the gains are unlikely to go beyond the confines of such players. In fact, majority of the workers and the masses in general, may well get a short shrift precisely because of the favourable conditions created for the small set of big players mentioned earlier. In other words, one of the big challenges confronting any strategy of broad-based industrialisation is to engage with the issue of broad-based domestic demand. This has been a major lacuna in all official policy discourses on industrialisation in India since the early 1990s. To the extent some important constraints and challenges have been flagged, they are almost invariably with respect to the "supply side" and the good deal of it has remained mere lip-service!

Concluding remarks

India's chequered record of industrial development since the early 1990s raises several important concerns with respect to overall economic policies and, in particular its IP. One of the major casualties of the neoliberal globalisation has been the shrinking of the national economic policy space. Post the Uruguay Round Agreements (URAs), creation of the World Trade Organisation (WTO) in 1995, subsequent proliferation of the regional trade agreements (RTAs) with their WTO-plus and WTO-extra provision etc., the conduct of the industrial and trade policies have been subjected to significant to severe restrictions. These have impacted adversely on many developing countries. In conjunction with their respective domestic contexts and capabilities, it is hardly surprising that the economic performance of different countries throw up a somewhat mixed picture, with handful appearing to be relative gainers whereas the overwhelming majority seems to be losers.

Sure enough, as mentioned earlier in terms of the GDP growth rates, the performance of the economy in the era of economic reforms has been a notch higher, compared to the preceding decade. The fact of high and sustained GDP growth rates, along with low to moderate inflation for much of the period since the early 1990s, significant achievements in Information and Communication Technology (ICT) segment and few other sectors are the obvious positives. Furthermore, India's attractiveness for foreign investors has certainly increased and shows up in the rising levels of foreign exchange reserves which stood at $402 billion US (as on 22 September 2017). Putting all these positives together, India does look like a "success story" (although not quite in the same league as China even in terms of the noted select indicators); however, as soon as one starts probing into further details relating to the structure and process of growth, in particular the performance of the manufacturing sector, and whether high GDP growth has generated positive outcomes for the majority of the population, the "success story" becomes seriously contentious.

The well-known major challenge, possibly the most daunting, that India's growth strategy confronts at the current juncture, is that of generating adequate employment and decent jobs. For the period since early 1990s, overall employment growth has been relatively sluggish compared to the preceding couple of decades, with very few opportunities for quality employment. In fact, as highlighted earlier manufacturing in India contributes only approximately 11–12 per cent of total employment. This compares unfavourably to several so called emerging economies where the share of employment in manufacturing ranges from 15 to 30 per cent. It was hoped by the advocates of the economic liberalisation that greater integration with the global economy would provide significant boost to expansion of the manufacturing sector and overall employment generation, while also improving the prospects for other variables impacting on the wellbeing of labour. However, by now it is well-acknowledged that most of the important labour market outcomes have shown little improvement during the reform period. Furthermore, deterioration with respect to employment is also reflected in different dimensions of quality such as growing informalisation, high incidence of vulnerable self-employment etc. Clearly, a rethink on overall policy regime is required and such a rethink must include Labour as a partner instead of viewing it as a hindrance to economic and social progress. Social dialogue in a genuine tripartite spirit, involving employers, unions and governments can go a significant distance in overcoming the employment crisis that the country is confronted with. One of the key elements in the dialogue will have to be the issue of reclaiming the national economic policy space, the overall macroeconomic policy regime and, of course, the IP.

Notes

1 It is symptomatic of the employment crisis in the country that even for a relatively lower ranked government job vacancy applications pour in thousands; according to a recent report in The Hindu, "Over 2.3 million candidates, including 222,000 engineers and 255 Ph.D. holders have applied for 368 posts of peon in the State Secretariat, Uttar Pradesh", 17, September, 2015.
2 The former Finance Minister (during the first NDA government), Mr Yashwant Sinha has expressed his disappointment in a scathing piece, and argues that the current government lacks any coherent economic strategy. For some recent commentaries, readers

may look at pieces by economist such as Ghosh and Chandrasekhar in Frontline and Business Line, Ranade (2017), Dubey (2017).
3 Recent report suggests significant job losses across sectors. As per a recent report in Indian express, 67 textile units closed down recently impacting over 17,600 workers; Larsen &Turbo has laid off about 14000 employees during the first two quarters of the fiscal ended March 31, 2017. Among the ICT majors Tata Consultancy Services, Infosys and Tech Mahindra have downsised their workforce by 1414, 1811 and 1713 respectively. As the news report puts it: "Textile to capital goods, banking to I-T, start-ups to energy, the economy's downward spiral is leaving a trail of job losses across both old and new economy sectors. In the near absence of consolidated employment numbers, disaggregated data collated from across these sectors by The Indian Express points to spreading employment distress in a market where fresh hiring opportunities are increasingly limited", Indian Express, Delhi Edition, 3rd October, 2017.
4 This comes out clearly from NSS 1983 and 2011–12. The same is also confirmed by assessments done by other well-known institutions. For instance, as per the RBI's report on Estimating Employment Elasticity (2014), UNDP Population Estimates and the HDFC Bank estimates, during the period 1977–78 to 99–00 employment elasticity was 0.39, which declined to 0.23 between 99–00 to 11–12 and further to a measly 0.15 between 2012–13 to 2015–16. It is important to highlight that this is happening at a juncture when addition to working age population is around 12 million per annum.
5 As per the press note issued by the Ministry of Commerce and Industry, Government of India: "The 'Make in India' programme aims at promoting India as an important investment destination and the global hub for manufacturing, design and innovation. The 'make in India' initiative does not target manufacturing sector alone, but also aims at promoting entrepreneurship in the country. The initiative is further aimed at creating a conducive environment for investment, modern and efficient infrastructure, opening up new sectors for foreign investment and forging a partnership between government and industry through positive mindset".

References

Chandrasekhar, C.P. and Ghosh, Jayati. 2007. *Growth and Employment in Organized Industry*. Available at: www.macroscan.com, January 30.
———. 2015. "Understanding 'Secular Stagnation'." *The Business Line*, October 12, 2015. Available at: https://www.thehindubusinessline.com/opinion/columns/c-p-chandrasekhar/the-common-mans-guide-to-secular-stagnation/article7753993.ece
Chaudhuri, Sudip. 2015. "Premature Deindustralization in India and Re thinking the Role of Government." FMSH-WP-2015–91. 2015. halshs-01143795
Dubey, Amitabh. 2017. "Fact Check: Have Modi Government's Reforms Really Transformed India?" *The WIRE*, 5th July, 2017.
Ghosh, Jayati, Chandrasekhar, C.P., and Patnaik, Prabhat. 2017. *Demonetisation Decoded: A Critique of India's Currency Experiment*. New Delhi: Routledge.
Jha, Praveen. 2016. *Labour in Contemporary India: Oxford India Short Introductions*. New Delhi: Oxford University Press.
Ranade, Ajit. 2017. "Economy Outlook Still Cloudy." *The Hindu*, September 4, 2017. Available at: https://www.thehindu.com/opinion/lead/economy-outlook-still-cloudy/article19615988.ece
UNSTATS. 2009. *System of National Accounts 2008*. New York: European Communities, International Monetary Fund, Organisation for Economic Co-operation and Development, United Nations and World Bank. Available at: https://unstats.un.org/unsd/nationalaccount/docs/SNA2008.pdf

13
EXPLORING THE RELATIONSHIP BETWEEN ECONOMIC GROWTH, EMPLOYMENT AND EDUCATION IN INDIAN STATES

Mona Khare

The circular relationship between economic growth, employment and education is widely discussed theoretically as well as empirically in existing literature. While the traditional approach as propounded by Nurkse (1953) in his model of vicious circle of poverty speaks of a circular nature of low income leading to low productivity because of low savings, low capital formation, leading back to low income, Meier and Baldwin (1957) ascribe it to market imperfections and quality of human resource. According to them, existence of market imperfections prevents optimum allocation and utilisation of natural resources, resulting in underdevelopment and economic backwardness. Giving importance to the character of human resources, they further explain that because of lack of skills and low levels of knowledge, natural resources remain unutilised, underutilised and misutilised, so that people continue to remain backward: "underdeveloped resources becoming, both a consequence and cause of backwardness" initiating a mutually aggravating cycle. The proposition is further supported by the Human capital theory of later years that provides ample evidence of increasing investment in education to develop human capital and its contribution to economic development and growth (Shultz, Becker, Hanushek and Kimko 2000; Krueger and Lindahl 2000; Hanushek and Woessmann 2007; Kingdon and Soderbom 2007a, 2007b; Chadha 2004, Mathur 1990). The new wave of linking "education to work" resultant from emerging labour market needs, evidences of higher salaries and better quality jobs with rising "skills hierarchy" from the primary to the tertiary levels are further empirical evidences of the proposition stated earlier. Such that obtaining quality education as the foundation to improving people's lives and sustainable development has become a widely accepted model of equitable growth. In this light Meier and Baldwin's explanation of vicious circle and market imperfections seem to fit the contemporary concept of sustainable development to a greater extent.

The market of today, is beset with imperfections of all kinds, and the newly emerging human capital market and a highly complex as well as dynamic labour market are no exceptions. The imperfections in human capital market are twofold – supply side educational inequalities and demand side employment inequalities. The interplay of these two inequalities, in turn, propagates economic inequality, that may become a vicious circle of unequal growth. The two way relationship between economic growth (EG) and human development (HD) can also become reinforcing as evidenced by literature such that nations may enter into an upward spiral of development i.e. the virtuous cycle of High Growth and large gains in HD or get trapped into a poverty trap i.e. the vicious cycle of low growth and low rates of HD (Ranis 2004; Ranis et al. 2000; Mayer-Foulkes 2003). The third case may be that of lop-sided economic growth i.e. relatively good growth and relatively poor HD or vice versa. Studies have shown that most nations with lopsided EG are not able to sustain their growth momentum and later move to the vicious cycle of low EG/low HD (Ranis et al. 2000). Such experiences prove that HD is a necessary pre-requisite of long term sustainable growth. However, equally important is the distributive angle of growth, increased investment, higher productivity and improved employment so as to leverage successes in HD into sustainable economic growth – the sustained upward spiral of virtuous economic growth.

What is the relative status of Indian states in experiencing this EG/HD relationship in terms of a virtuous, vicious or lopsided circle of EG is the major concern of this chapter. Which Indian states are poised to embark on the path of a virtuous circle of inclusive development and which are the ones that face the challenge of getting trapped in the lopsided growth-poverty model? Two main questions that this chapter attempts to explore are: whether the states that experienced a high rate of growth over a long period of time can be deemed to be better off in terms of lesser inequalities, better quality of employment and better status of education and two, if targeting a higher rate of growth in itself is a sufficient condition to achieve better quality of living – defined here as better quality of employment and higher education status.

The paper, thus traces Indian experience within the framework of a virtuous circle of sustained EG/HD relationship (Figure 13.1). High growth leads to high per capita incomes and low unemployment, in turn leading to better quality employment and better education status leading to lesser inequalities and sustained equitable growth in a circular fashion reinforcing each other. The paper is divided into four sections. Section I tries to study the growth profile of major Indian states in post-liberalisation period exploring the relationship between growth and income inequality. Section II focuses on the inter-state scenario in terms of employment and its relationship with inequalities in education and income. Section III attempts to identify the states trapped in the vicious circle of unsustainable growth. Unsustainable growth, here, may be defined as lopsided economic growth (EG) leading to a downward spiral of low educational status (ES) and poor quality of employment (EQ), reinforcing inequalities. Section IV dwells on major observations from the analysis.

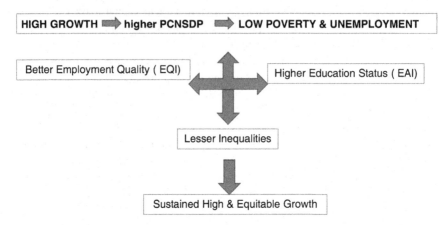

FIGURE 13.1 Framework for virtuous circle of EG/HD growth

Growth profile of major Indian states

India has been considered to be experiencing a reasonably high rate of economic growth during the past few decades but, whether this is a reason enough to rejoice is something that requires a deeper look into the growth patterns across its largely diverse state economies. Studies reveal that India's objective of "growth with equity" continues to elude it and remains a matter of grave concern for policymakers (Ravallion and Datt 2002; Kundu and Varghese 2010). In order to diagnose this situation across Indian states, LTGR (long term rates of growth) of NSDP (net state domestic product) were calculated for the post-reform period starting 1993–94 to 2011–12. The whole period was then divided into two – period I (1993–94 to 2000–01) and period II (2001–02 to 2011–12); period II was further subdivided into two sub-periods – period II.1 (2001–02 to 2005–06) and period II.2 in order to assess the states performance in sustained growth (Table 13.1).

The state-wise LTGRs (Col.2 Table 13.1) reveal that as in the earlier years, the States of Bihar, Madhya Pradesh, Uttar Pradesh, Odisha and West Bengal experienced low GRs while the States of Gujarat, Tamil Nadu, Haryana and Himachal Pradesh witnessed relatively high GRs. Based on LTGRs (1993–94 to 2011–12), States can be ranked as shown in Figure 13.2.

However, analysis of the growth profiles of the states during different sub periods unfolds harsher realities, the one positive feature being reduction in interstate disparities in growth in period II (coefficient of variation (CV) going down from 30 per cent to 18 per cent) as higher GRs were manifested by most of the low growing states, namely Odisha, Madhya Pradesh, Uttar Pradesh, Bihar and Rajasthan. In fact, the increase in their GRs were among the top five during the 1st and the 2nd sub-periods of the decade beginning 2001–02. Similar observations of

TABLE 13.1 Net state domestic product growth (base year: 2004–05)

States	1993–94 to 2011–12	1993–94 to 2000–01	2001–02 to 2011–12	2001–02 to 2005–06	2006–07 to 2011–12
Andhra Pradesh	6.61	5.08	7.30	5.74	6.79
Assam	3.73	1.73	4.96	3.71	5.25
Bihar	6.00	4.89	7.39	2.97	8.30
Gujarat	7.74	4.57	9.32	9.01	8.12
Haryana	7.24	5.24	7.98	6.66	7.16
Himachal Pradesh	6.69	6.52	6.32	5.88	5.36
Karnataka	6.12	5.54	6.37	5.47	5.38
Kerala	6.30	4.38	7.24	6.63	6.40
Madhya Pradesh	5.19	3.44	5.81	2.72	6.89
Maharashtra	6.57	4.02	8.13	7.46	6.37
Odisha	5.05	2.79	6.16	6.08	4.16
Punjab	4.86	3.81	5.51	3.54	5.37
Rajasthan	6.63	5.67	6.29	3.84	6.37
Tamil Nadu	6.93	5.43	8.22	6.45	7.09
Uttar Pradesh	4.36	2.59	5.50	3.85	5.54
West Bengal	5.95	5.82	5.38	4.43	4.85
Mean	6.00	4.47	6.74	5.28	6.21
SD	1.09	1.32	1.24	1.77	1.16
CV	18.15	29.60	18.40	33.63	18.64

Source: computed CAGRs for NSDP at factor cost, RBI Database from NAS, CSO

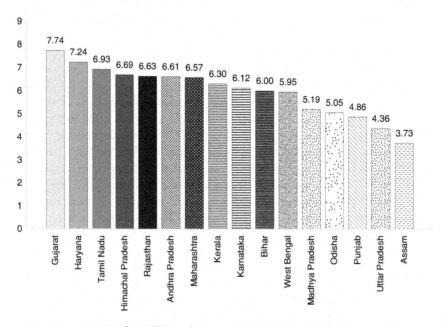

FIGURE 13.2 LTGRs for NSDP at factor cost (1993–94 to 2011–12)

Source: computed GRs for NSDP at factor cost, RBI Database from NAS, Central Statistics Office (CSO), Ministry of Statistics and Programme Implementation, Government of India.

low growth states of the earlier decades (60s, 70s, 80s, 90s) achieving a breakthrough by realising higher growth in the decade after early 1990s is evidenced in literature (Ahmad and Narain 2008; Kundu and Varghese 2010; Ahluwalia 2000; Bhattacharya and Sakthivel 2004). But, unfortunately, many could not sustain this high growth as revealed by sub-period wise analysis of the growth results. Those that showed a high GR during the period of 1990s but could not sustain it in the following decade are Himachal Pradesh falling from rank 1 in the period I to rank 9 in the period II, West Bengal from 2nd to 15th and Rajasthan from 3rd to 10th, Bihar from 8th in period I to 15th in period II.1, and Karnataka from 4th in period I to 11th in sub-period II.2. Similarly, Odisha that had improved its position to number 6 in sub-period II.1 slid down to 16th position in sub-period II.2

If consistency of high growth be the yardstick of sustainability, then the states can be divided into four categories.

> *Category I: Sustained High GR* – these include by far the developed states of Gujarat, Haryana, Tamil Nadu, Maharashtra, those that seem to have been maintaining high GRs during all the periods and sub-periods from 1993–94 to 2011–12.
> *Category II: Sustained Moderate GR* – Those consistent with a moderate growth during the periods and sub-periods are Andhra Pradesh, Karnataka and Kerala
> *Category III: Sustained Low GR* – Those consistent with a low growth during the periods and sub-periods are Uttar Pradesh, Assam and Punjab.
> *Category IV: Unsustained High/Low GR* – This category includes those that realised a very high growth in few earlier periods/sub-periods but slid down in the later periods i.e. West Bengal (high to low) Odisha (high to low), Rajasthan (high to low), Himachal Pradesh (high to low) and those that have taken to the high growth path recently i.e. Madhya Pradesh (low to high) and Bihar (low to high).

It can clearly be seen that the states that could sustain a high or moderate rates of growth are the relatively developed ones and the ones that could not, include largely the group of least developed states (based on Multi dimensional Index) One can, although note with some satisfaction that few from the latter category could break through the low growth trap in recent years (2006–07 to 2011–12 as in Table 13.1). These include Bihar, Madhya Pradesh and Rajasthan. But, there is every possibility that these may observe similar fate as that of other low growing states that rose to higher levels of growth in the earlier periods but could not keep up their relative ranks in later periods by sustaining high GR.

Therefore, this paradigm shift in the growth pattern of the country, gives little reason to rejoice because of following observations:

1   Despite registering higher GRs in recent decades the lesser developed states (LDS) have not been able to touch the per capita income mark of the developed states (DS). With sustainability of high GR by less developed states seen as a challenge, the concerns about their catching up with DS continues to remain a difficult proposition.

2   Their high growth does not seem to have made any dent on the rising regional disparities/imbalances as depicted by their per capita NSDP figures. Although the CV in the growth rates have gone down from 29.6 to 18.40 per cent in the decade starting 2001–02 the disparities in per capita NSDP have grown from a high of 57.2 per cent in 2000–01 to 62.64 per cent in 2011–12, as measured by the CV in per capita NSDP.
3   The LDS – Madhya Pradesh, Uttar Pradesh, Bihar, West Bengal and Odisha – thus continue to remain at the lower rungs of the ladder of per capita income. These states barring West Bengal are among the least developed states based on MDI scores of the Rajan Panel (Government of India 2013).

This analysis indicates that the states falling in both, categories III and IV are susceptible to remain trapped in the vicious circle of low growth and not be able to enjoy the virtuous circle despite realising high growths for short intermittent durations. The problem will become all the more challenging if such states also suffer from higher inter-personal inequalities of various forms – income, employment, education etc.

In the light of this analysis it would be interesting to explore the EG/HD relationship for the Indian states under study with employment.

Economic growth-employment – education inequalities

Relationship between Education, high growth, and increased productivity because of better human capital has found evidence in a large body of literature (Barro 1991, 1997; Mankiw et al. 1992; Temple 2001; Krueger and Lindahl 2000; Sianesi and Van Reenen 2003; Sala-iMartin et al. 2004). Literature on the subject has explained this positive association in three ways:

- Education brings increase in labour productivity, thereby "engendering transitional growth towards a higher equilibrium level of output" (Mankiw et al. 1992).
- Education adds to the innovative capacity and technology assisted growth (Lucas 1988; Romer 1990; Aghion and Howitt 1998; Nelson and Phelps 1966; Benhabib and Spiegel 1994), and last but not the least
- Education brings change in the nature of job skills demanded, that determines the labour market growth trajectory (Brynjolffson and McAfee 2014).

The human capital theorists attributed variations in skills to levels of education and years of schooling (Schultz 1963; Becker 1993; Mincer 1974; Ferrer and Riddel 2002). Since, the labour market is disproportionately in favour of workers who are more educated and better skilled, the HC market remains differentiated. Such imperfections on the supply side of the HC market may have the tendency to perpetuate inequalities of income (Schultz 1993). The challenges are complex as both the labour market and the education system have become more segmented in recent years (Khare 2016).

Implications of labour market segmentation and differentiated human capital on the relationship between economic growth and poverty reduction have been discussed in four contexts:

1. Segmented conditions inhibit the free and efficient flow of labour between jobs so that the overall rate of economic growth is likely to be lower;
2. In a segmented market, growth in one sector may not have positive impact on others because the factor returns are not likely to equalise across sectors or to which they at least have access by way of HC earned;
3. If growth results in increased employment opportunities in "less productive" job sectors, where those with low HD are predominantly employed it may not be able to make any reasonable dent on the vicious circle of EG/HD. As these sectors are characterised by low wages, poor work conditions, exploitative tendencies of underemployment and casualisation they tend to perpetuate inequalities;
4. Even if growth results in an increase in the number and productivity of jobs, it may be required to be supported by policies to reduce barriers of various kinds including that of HC formation for upward mobility of the poor. Only then can growth become pro-poor. The participation of the poor in growth will depend in part on concerted efforts to identify and remove these obstacles (Hull 2009; Leonardi 1998).

It is such imperfections as inherent in rising heterogeneity that are posing a challenge to equitable growth. When the heterogeneity of the employment quality and education intertwine in a highly segmented labour market of a knowledge intensive economy the challenge is to reap the virtuous circle of growth and break the vicious circle of low EG/HD/EQ. The fear that imperfections in the HC as well as the labour market can reinforce to act as a potential threat to reap the virtuous circle of high growth may not sound ungrounded.

This section traces the experiences of the Indian states in the context previously mentioned. High ROG is deemed to be associated with high per capita incomes, low poverty and unemployment. It is also associated with good employment and education. We define Employment Quality here by way of an Employment Quality Index (EQI) based on two indicators: percentage of main workers to total workers and proportion of Regular wage/salaried employee. The status of education is defined by way of Education Attainment Index (EAI) based on two indicators i.e. Average years of schooling (AYS) and Proportion of 15+ population with secondary education and above. The choice of these two indicators is guided by the fact that AYS is generally used to determine the education status of a population and secondary education is the minimum degree for a skilled workforce (ILO 2013; UNESCO 2012; GMR 2012) as stated by the ILO.

> Secondary school is an important channel through which young people acquire skills that improve opportunities for good jobs. High quality secondary education that caters for the widest possible range of abilities, interests

and backgrounds is vital to set young people on the path to the world of work as well as to give countries the educated workforce they need to compete in today's technology driven world.

(ILO 2010, 2013)

In OECD countries too, an upper secondary qualification has become the norm for young people. Today it is considered the minimum qualification for successful participation in the labour market and for integration in society (OECD 2012). With GER at the primary stage in India reaching almost 100 and now aiming at universalisation of secondary education the indicator seemed apt to be included in the Index.

Growth, employment quality and education status

The disconnect between India's recent GDP growth and decent employment has been evidenced by many scholars (Ghosh and Chandrasekhar 2007; Jha & Mario Negre n.d.; Chandrasekhar and Ghosh 2015). As highlighted in earlier section growth in the Indian states have had a very feeble but positive relationship with unemployment (0.15) which proves that high growth states do not necessarily have low unemployment. Out of the first eight high growth states only two, namely Himachal Pradesh and Maharashtra, are in the lowest unemployment quadrant. This, certainly is an issue of grave concern. But, what is even more worrisome is the fact that Employment Quality(EQ) is poor in low growing states despite the fact that many of them have been able to break the low growth trap to achieve higher rates of growth in recent years. The states of Bihar, Madhya Pradesh, Uttar Pradesh, Odisha and West Bengal along with the low growing Assam are in the poor EQI quadrant. The first quadrant of high EG and EQI has only two states of Gujarat and Tamil Nadu (Table 13.2). These two are also the states that have maintained high LTGR and despite higher inequality show better EQ.

A look at growth and education attainment index shows clearer division of high EG states in the higher EAI quadrants and the lower EG states in the lower EAI quadrants (Table 13.3).

The relationship of growth with both indicators of educational attainment is positive but not very significant. It may also be noted that the relationship is stronger with secondary plus population. Same is the case with indicators of employment quality. A positive but not a very significant relationship. Interestingly, growth is negatively related with Edu gini thereby indicating that high growth reduces educational inequalities (because higher the GR lower is the edu gini). But, the relationship is so feeble that one can conclude that high growth has not been able to make much impact on reducing educational inequalities in the states.

Employment, education and inequalities

A look at the last row of Table 13.4 has large scale implications. It can be seen that consumption gini is positively correlated with all positive and desirable

TABLE 13.2 Growth rate and employment quality, 2011–12

Eq \ H	NSDP at Factor Cost (At Constant Prices) (1993–94 to 2011–12)	Eq_1 (above Q_3 = above 6.03)	Eq_2 ($Q_2 - Q_3$ = 5.36 – 6.03)	Eq_3 ($Q_1 - Q_2$ = 3.90 – 5.36)	Eq_4 (less Q_1 = less 3.91)
H_1 (above Q_3 = above 6.64)	1 Gujarat (7.740) 2 Haryana (7.238) 3 Tamil Nadu (6.925) 4 Himachal Pradesh (6.680)	Gujarat (6.09) Tamil Nadu (6.29)	Haryana (5.85)	Himachal Pradesh (4.35)	—
H_2 ($Q_2 - Q_3$ = 6.21 – 6.64)	5 Rajasthan (6.631) 6 Andhra Pradesh (6.610) 7 Maharashtra (6.571) 8 Kerala (6.301)	Maharashtra (6.55)	Kerala (5.83) Andhra Pradesh (5.67)	Rajasthan (4.61)	—
H_3 ($Q_1 - Q_2$ = 5.15 – 6.21)	9 Karnataka (6.121) 10 Bihar (6.001) 11 West Bengal (5.954) 12 Madhya Pradesh (5.188)	—	Karnataka (6.01)	West Bengal (5.07) Madhya Pradesh (4.56)	Bihar (3.61)
H_4 (below Q_1 = 5.15)	13 Odisha (5.053) 14 Punjab (4.863) 15 Uttar Pradesh (4.362) 16 Assam (3.729)	Punjab (6.46)	—	Assam (4.81) Uttar Pradesh (4.30) Odisha (3.94)	—

Note: H1 – very high growth rate, H2 – high growth rate, H3 – moderate growth rate, H4 – low growth rate state. Eq1 – very high employment quality, Eq2 – high employment quality, Eq3 – moderate employment quality, Eq4 – low employment quality.

TABLE 13.3 Growth and education attainment index, 2011–12

H \ Edq	NSDP at factor cost (at constant prices)	Edq₁ (above Q₃ = above 5.497)	Edq₂ (Q₂ – Q₃ = 4.51 – 5.49)	Edq₃ (Q₁ – Q₂ = 4.20 – 4.51)	Edq₄ (below Q₁ = 4.20)
H₁ (above Q₃ = above 6.64)	1 Gujarat (7.740) 2 Haryana (7.238) 3 Tamil Nadu (6.925) 4 Himachal Pradesh (6.680)	Himachal Pradesh (5.94) Haryana (5.79)	Tamil Nadu (5.15) Gujarat (4.66)	—	—
H₂ (Q₂ – Q₃ = 6.21 – 6.64)	5 Rajasthan (6.631) 6 Andhra Pradesh (6.610) 7 Maharashtra (6.571) 8 Kerala (6.301)	Kerala (6.34) Maharashtra (5.83)	—	Andhra Pradesh (4.27)	Rajasthan (3.57)
H₃ (Q₁ – Q₂ = 5.15 – 6.21)	9 Karnataka (6.121) 10 Bihar (6.001) 11 West Bengal (5.954) 12 Madhya Pradesh (5.188)	—	West Bengal (5.07) Karnataka (5.29)	—	Madhya Pradesh (3.90) Bihar (3.61)
H₄ (below Q₁ = 5.15)	13 Odisha (5.053) 14 Punjab (4.863) 15 Uttar Pradesh (4.362) 16 Assam (3.729)	—	Punjab (5.39)	Assam (4.34)	Uttar Pradesh (3.91) Odisha (3.46)

Note: H₁ – very high growth rate, H₂ – high growth rate, H₃ – moderate growth rate, H₄ – low growth rate state, Edq₁ – very high EI, Edq₂ – high EI, Edq₃ – moderate EI, Edq₄ – low EI.

TABLE 13.4 Relationships: growth, education, employment, inequality

States	NSDP CAGR	Secondary and Above (15+ Age Group)	AYS	Edu Gini	Regular Wage / Salaried Employee	Per cent Age of Main Workers to Total Workers	Consumption Gini Index
	1993–94 to 2011–12	68th Round 2011–12			2011–12	2011	2010
Andhra Pradesh	6.61	31.43	5.24	0.56	179	83.8	32.33
Assam	3.73	25.65	6.09	0.39	142	72.6	28
Bihar	6.00	24.10	4.53	0.58	58	61.5	27.45
Gujarat	7.74	31.89	6.02	0.46	247	82.2	28.69
Haryana	7.24	43.68	6.97	0.43	239	78.7	32.72
Himachal Pradesh	6.69	45.44	7.08	0.39	182	57.9	33.04
Karnataka	6.12	39.06	6.47	0.45	225	83.9	27.76
Kerala	6.30	42.66	8.27	0.26	225	80.3	45.48
Madhya Pradesh	5.19	25.19	5.21	0.53	113	71.9	32.28
Maharashtra	6.57	42.17	7.24	0.39	265	88.5	32.93
Orissa	5.05	19.82	4.93	0.52	106	61	31.5
Punjab	4.86	39.81	6.60	0.43	275	85.4	32.87
Rajasthan	6.63	23.59	4.71	0.58	130	70.5	29.64
Tamil Nadu	6.93	36.37	6.51	0.43	255	85	29.47
Uttar Pradesh	4.36	26.36	5.09	0.56	106	67.8	30.65
West Bengal	5.95	23.80	5.43	0.49	168	73.9	29.94
All India	6.00	31.42	5.85	0.48	179	75.20	
SD	**1.09**	**8.67**	**1.06**	**0.09**	**67.45**	**9.66**	**4.21**
Average	**6.00**	**32.56**	**6.02**	**0.47**	**182.19**	**75.31**	**31.55**
CV	**18.15**	**26.61**	**17.67**	**18.72**	**37.02**	**12.82**	**13.34**
Correlation Coefficients							
with AYS	0.28	0.89	1.00	−0.95	0.77	0.47	0.64
with sec + population	0.45	1.00	0.89	−0.73	0.79	0.47	0.47
with Edu gini	−0.10	−0.73	−0.95	1.00	−0.65	−0.35	−0.62
with growth	1.00	0.45	0.28	−0.10	0.47	0.31	0.10
with consumption gini	0.10	0.47	0.64	−0.62	0.28	0.16	1.00

Sources: net state domestic product CAGR (self-computed) from Handbook of Statistics on Indian Economy (various years), RBI; per cent age of main workers to total workers – Census of India (2001 and 2011), Office of the Registrar & Census Commission, India; GINI Index – Ghosal, R. (); average year of schooling – NSSO 68th Round (2011–12); education Gini (self-computed); secondary and above (15+ age group); unemployment rate (UR) by different age groups (in Per 1000) 15 to 59 age and per cent of main worker and regular/salaried workers – NSSO Report No. 554 (68th Round) "Employment and Unemployment Situation in India", Ministry of Statistics & Programme Implementation, Government of India.

TABLE 13.5 Relationship between growth rate and education Gini (2011–12)

E \ H	NSDP at Factor Cost at Constant Prices (1993–94 to 2011–12)	E_1 (below Q_3 = below 0.41)	E_2 ($Q_2 - Q_3$ = 0.45 – 0.41)	E_3 ($Q_1 - Q_2$ = 0.53 – 0.45)	E_4 (above Q_1 = above 0.53)
H_1 (above Q_3 = above 6.64)	1 Gujarat (7.740) 2 Haryana (7.238) 3 Tamil Nadu (6.925) 4 Himachal Pradesh (6.680)	Himachal Pradesh (0.39)	Haryana (0.43) Tamil Nadu (0.43)	Gujarat (0.46)	–
H_2 ($Q_2 - Q_3$ = 6.21 – 6.64)	5 Rajasthan (6.631) 6 Andhra Pradesh (6.610) 7 Maharashtra (6.571) 8 Kerala (6.301)	Kerala (0.26) Maharashtra (0.39)	–	–	Andhra Pradesh (0.56) Rajasthan (0.58)
H_3 ($Q_1 - Q_2$ = 5.15 – 6.21)	9 Karnataka (6.121) 10 Bihar (6.001) 11 West Bengal (5.954) 12 Madhya Pradesh (5.188)	–	Karnataka (0.45)	West Bengal (0.49) Madhya Pradesh (0.53)	Bihar (0.58)
H_4 (below Q_1 = below 5.15)	13 Odisha (5.053) 14 Punjab (4.863) 15 Uttar Pradesh (4.362) 16 Assam (3.729)	Assam (0.39)	Punjab (0.46)	Odisha (0.52)	Uttar Pradesh (0.56)

Note: 1 H – State wise growth rate of NSDP at Factor Cost (1993–94 to 2011–12) at constant Prices. 2 E – Education Gini (2011–12). 3 H_1 – Very High growth rate, H_2 – High growth rate, H_3 – Moderate growth rate, H_4 – Low growth rate State. 4 E_1 – Low Education Gini, E_2 – Moderate Education Gini, E_3 – High Education, E_4 – Very High Edugini.

indicators – long-term growth, average years of schooling (AYS), secondary education population (SEP), regular salaried workers (RSW), main workers (MWR) but negatively related to Edu gini. Thus, higher growth, better education attainment and better employment are not necessarily reducing consumption inequalities.

With better education, unemployment is lesser (negative significant correlations) and employment quality is better (significant positive correlation), but if education inequalities are ignored there may be problems of greater consumption inequalities despite high growth as the case currently is. It can be seen that higher the Edu gini more the unemployment rate, (approx 0.5) higher the Edu gini lesser the RSW (-0.65) as also main workers. Thus, any attempt at improving the general education level has to be matched with reducing educational inequalities for better EQ.

This further is substantiated by the relationships between the Employment Quality Index (EQI) and Education Status Index (ESI). While quality of employment has a strong and positive relationship with education status index, it has a negative relationship with education inequalities (negative correlation between employment quality and Edu gini). This shows that if the education inequalities are lesser the employment quality is better. But inequalities of income (expenditure gini) have a positive but feeble correlation with EQ. Better the EQ higher the income inequalities. It may, thus, be inferred that just by creating more regular and stable jobs may not help reduce inequalities until it is simultaneously matched with reducing educational inequalities such that more and more people can gain the capabilities to engage themselves in more productive employment aiding in reduction of income inequalities. This is proven by a very high negative correlation between AYS and Edu Gini (−0.95). As the general level of education improves, inequalities of education get reduced, and is also likely to increase demand and capabilities for better employment. If high growth is not just made to create jobs but to create jobs of better quality and sustainable nature, the virtuous cycle of high growth can be initiated. While AYS and SEP both have a significantly high and positive correlation with consumption gini, both have a very high negative relationship with Edu gini (Table 13.4). It may thus be inferred that a high education may not necessarily mean low inequalities of income but certainly lower inequalities of education. Also, since AYS, SEP both have a significantly high positive correlation with RSW and a significantly negative correlation with Edu gini, it can be inferred that better education and lesser education inequalities are related to better EQ by way of both, more RSW and MWR which in turn may end up reducing the consumption inequalities and help sustain high growth.

But, one thing is for sure, that, generally those states that have better employment quality are the ones that have a better education status, too. A moderately high degree of correlation can be observed between employment quality and education attainment Index (0.68).

Those that are trapped in the double vicious circle of low growth, poor employment quality and poor education status are Uttar Pradesh, Rajasthan, Odisha, Madhya Pradesh and Bihar. Same is the relationship between Per Capita Net State Domestic

Product (PCNSDP) and the two indicators previously mentioned, richer states being in a better position on both fronts. Such a relationship is but expected and obvious.

A classification of the states under consideration divides them into the following categories.

- High growth high EA and low edu inequalities – Himachal Pradesh;
- High growth high/moderate EA and moderate edu inequalities – Kerala, Haryana, Tamil Nadu and Maharashtra;
- High growth moderate EA and high edu inequalities – Gujarat;
- Moderate growth moderate EA moderate edu inequalities – Karnataka;
- Low growth moderate EA and low edu inequalities – Assam, Punjab;
- Low growth low EA and low edu inequalities – Madhya Pradesh, Uttar Pradesh, Bihar, Odisha and West Bengal.

A similar kind of a categorisation can be seen in terms of indicators of quality employment. Most high growing states flock together with larger percentage of main workers as well as regular salaried workers and the low growing states are at the lower quadrants of employment quality.

It can thus be inferred that only 5 out of the 16 major states are on a virtuous Growth cycle and the rest are on a lopsided growth cycle with tendencies to either remain trapped in the vicious circle of low growth – low employment – low HD or slump back into this vicious trap. In the latter category are Gujarat and Karnataka, which are also the two exceptions.

States trapped in the vicious circle of unsustainable growth

Based on the above analysis, the states in India can be divided into the following categories:

Category I: virtuous cycle of high growth and large gains in HD – Himachal Pradesh, Haryana, Kerala and Maharashtra
Category II: vicious cycle of low growth and low rates of HD – Madhya Pradesh, Uttar Pradesh, Bihar, Odisha and Assam
Category III: lop-sided economic growth – (relatively good growth and relatively poor HD or vice versa)
III.a – EG lop-sided (relatively good growth and relatively poor HD) Andhra Pradesh and Rajasthan, Tamil Nadu & Gujarat, West Bengal & Karnataka
III.b – HD lop-sided (relatively low growth and relatively high HD) – Punjab

All four Sates in the virtuous circle category have high ESI and also low education inequalities as revealed by their low Edu gini. All four are in the 1st quadrant of education status i.e. high EAI and also the 1st quadrant of Edu gini i.e. lowest educational inequalities. All category II states have lower education status but very high education inequalities so that they all lie in poor quadrants of EQ. Category three states present a moderate picture on all fronts. Thus, as a policy matter category II states should be on the radar first followed by category III and then category I states as there is ample scope of improvement in the absolute status of all states.

Major observations and policy implications

Given the highly intertwined nature of education and employment, targeting a high rate of economic growth should undoubtedly be supported by policies to address issues of enhanced capabilities and as well as generating quality employment. Such capability building requires not only increase in education status but more importantly reducing education inequalities.

It is equally important to look into employment quality – education relationship keeping in view the sectoral profile and potential of Indian states that vary significantly. Depending on the state context, a substantive but differential employment and education development policy is desirable.

With the projections on sectoral employment elasticities for the 12th Five Year Plan being different for different sectors, the states having a higher share in employment as well as output in the two sectors of manufacturing and community, social and personal services are likely to have a potential to sustain a higher rate of growth and the resultant virtuous circle of high growth, better employment quality and higher education status. For such states the focus may be more on education so that a larger population is able to reap the benefits of the high growing high skilled sectors. For others, the strategy may start at structural transformation from low employment generating agricultural to non-agricultural sectors but if such a shift is not matched with improving the skills of the masses (higher levels of education and lower educational inequalities) in order to enhance their capabilities for upward labour market mobility, the result would only be increasing income gaps reinforcing education and skill gaps and increased susceptibility to remain trapped in lopsided growth. Thus, as a second stage of intervention, attempt should be made to transform "low productive sectors" into "more efficient high productive sectors". Here again the role of human resource development by way of more educated, skilled persons capable of innovation, creativity so as to bring out the low productivity sectors out of stagnation, becomes important. Experiences of many countries have evidenced that education, in its various guises, is often a crucial precondition for – labour market adjustment to more profitable economic activities. These may be by way of creating of a considerable mass of secondary educated workers for enabling participation in more technologically advanced sectors as evidenced in Ecuador; strong links between training institutes and private sector sources of demand, as a means of increasing market relevance of the labour force (Egypt, Kenya) shifting comparative advantage towards products and services based on skilled labour in Moldova (Hull 2006). The positive impact of education is not just restricted to the new technology driven sectors but also seen in even small size farm sector of rural economies. Educational improvements have helped even small scale farmers reap increased benefits as they are more adept to absorb new production techniques and innovate (Radwan 1995; Maddison 2007). The next important point that needs to be kept in mind is that whatever increases in jobs are happening in whichever sectors, quality of jobs should find priority over the quantitative numbers for any growth to become sustainable as well as equitable. The last but most important observation emerging from the analysis in the earlier sections is that until and unless inequalities of employment quality and education status are reduced and made more inclusive, it would be difficult to sustain economic growth and the risk of lop-sided growth shall keep looming large for most Indian states.

During the past two decades while the Indian economy has grown at an unprecedented high rate with several poorer states experiencing higher growth in recent years. However, inter-state disparities of per capita income continue to remain very high and there is hardly any change in the relative position of the poorer states in terms of growth. The aim should not just be high growth but sustained long term economic growth. Inequality seems to be a greater menace than low economic growth in itself in order to move into a virtuous growth cycle.

The problem of low growth in several of these states is coupled with problems related to employment and education. With growth having little dent on unemployment and quality of employment (jobless growth, growth in less productive jobs, casualisation etc.) the tendency of a vicious circle of poor employment leading to poor education is likely to continue in future if region specific policy initiatives are not taken. The concerns are becoming deeper given the persistence of the problem of poor quality of employment – less stable, non-regular and low remunerative employment. If education inequalities are ignored there may be problems of greater consumption inequalities despite high growth as the case currently is. Creating more regular and stable jobs may not help reduce inequalities until it is simultaneously matched with reducing educational inequalities. As a policy measure the country should aim at minimum threshold level of compulsory education (secondary level) to develop skilled and quality human resource capable of ensuring – regular inflow of income.

While there is a case of accelerating the economic growth, there is need for a comprehensive policy for quality employment by improving productivity through restructuring the state economies towards high growth sectors with higher employment elasticities to reduce demand side labour market imperfections. But, there is also a need for matching and equally comprehensive education policy aiming to reap the gains of good education – higher education attainments matching with low educational inequalities to address the supply side inequalities.

By and large, the richer states have the best of all worlds and there seems to be little likelihood of any major change in near future. These have greater regular/salaried workers, higher education status, a larger share of secondary school graduates, lower educational inequalities, less poverty and casual labour. But, most important of all, in general, they have maintained a long term high rate of economic growth. Therefore, if the first condition for creating a roadmap to better employment and education is a sustained high growth, the second is to make it equitable. Thus, for any attempt at making a dent on the vicious circle of low growth, poor quality employment and education, there is a need for structural transformation of the state economies. Transition from low productivity to high productivity of dominant sectors has to be coupled with policies that reduce inequalities in education attainment and improving quality of employment across the board keeping regional dimensions in focus.

Only then can India start its journey towards sustainable growth – growth for all. As an end note, a high rate of economic growth may be a necessary condition but is certainly not a sufficient one. It may only kick start a virtuous circle of high growth but it is only a differentiated regional policy of strengthening quality of employment and improved education status that can sustain this virtuous circle.

References

Aghion, Philippe and Howitt, Peter. 1998. *Endogenous Growth Theory*. Cambridge, MA: MIT Press.
Ahluwalia, M.S. 2000. "Economic Performance of States in Post Reform Era." *Economic and Political Weekly*, 35(19): 1638–1648.
Ahmad, Ahsan and Narain, Ashish. 2008. "Towards Understanding Development in Lagging Regions of India", paper presented at the Conference on Growth and Development in the Lagging Regions of India, Hyderabad: Administrative Staff College of India.
Barro, R. J. 1991. "Economic Growth in a Cross Section of Countries." *Quarterly Journal of Economics*, 56: 407–443.
———. 1997. *Determinants of Economic Growth: A Cross-country Empirical Study*. Cambridge, MA: MIT Press.
Becker, Gray S. 1993. *Human Capital: A Theoretical and Empirical Analysis with Special Reference to Education*. 3rd ed. Chicago: University of Chicago Press.
Benhabib, J. and Spiegel, M.M. 1994. "The Role of Human Capital in Economic Development: Evidence from Aggregate Cross-country Data." *Journal of Monetary Economics*, 34(2): 143–173.
Bhattacharya, B.B. and Sakthivel, S. 2004. "Regional Growth and Disparity in India: Comparison of Pre- and Post-Reform Decades." *Economic and Political Weekly*, 39(10): 1071–1077.
Brynjolffson, E. and McAfee, A. 2014. *The Second Machine Age: Work, Progress and Prosperity in a Time of Brilliant Technologies*. New York: W.W. Norton & Company Inc.
Chadha, G.K. 2004. "Human Capital Base of the Indian Labour Market: Identifying Worry Spots." *The Indian Journal of Labour Economics*, 47(1): 3–38.
Chandrasekhar, C.P. and Ghosh, Jayati. 2015. "Growth, Employment Patterns and Inequality in Asia: A Case Study of India." *ILO Asia-Pacific Working Paper Series*, January 2015.
Datt, G. and M. Ravallion. 2002. "Is India's Economic Growth Leaving the Poor Behind?" *Policy Research Working Paper 2846*. Washington DC: The World Bank.
EFA GMR. 2012. "Ecuador – Investment Climate Assessment" 2005 Egypt – Country Assistance Strategy." Idem, Kenya.
Ferrer, A.M. and Riddell, W.C. 2002. "The Role of Credentials in the Canadian Labour Market." *Canadian Journal of Economics*, 35(4): 879–905.
Ghosal, Ratan. 2012. "Growth, Poverty and Inequality Paradox in India: A Panel Data Approach." Available at: www.iariw.org.
Ghosh, Jayati and Chandrasekhar, C.P. 2007. "Economic Growth and Employment Generation in India: Old Problems and New Paradoxes." *Paper presented at the IDEAs International*

Conference on Sustainable Employment Generation in Developing Countries: Current Constraints and Alternative Strategies, January 25–27, 2007, University of Nairobi.

Government of India. 2011. *Statistics of Higher & Technical Education 2009–10 (Provisional)*. New Delhi: Ministry of Human Resource Development, Government of India.

———. 2013. *Report of the Committee for Evolving a Composite Development Index of States*. New Delhi: Ministry of Finance, Government of India. Available at: https://finmin.nic.in/sites/default/files/Report_CompDevState.pdf

Hanushek, Eric A. and Dennis, D. Kimko. 2000. "Schooling, Labor Force Quality, and the Growth of Nations." *American Economic Review*, 90(5): 1184–1208.

Hanushek, Eric A. and Woessmann, Ludger. 2007. "The Role of Education Quality for Economic Growth." *Policy Research Working Paper No. 4122*. Washington, DC: The World Bank.

Hull, K. 2006. "An Overview of World Bank Analytical and Advisory Activities Addressing the Labour Market and Employment, 2004-Present." Mimeo, Washington, DC: World Bank.

———. 2009. "Understanding the Relationship between Economic Growth, Employment and Poverty Reduction – Promoting Pro-Poor Growth: Employment." OECD.

ILO. 2010. *A Skilled Workforce for Strong, Sustainable and Balanced Growth: A G20 Training Strategy*. Geneva: ILO.

———. 2013. "Enhancing Youth Employability: What? Why? and How?" *Guide to Core Work Skills International Labour Office, Skills and Employability Department*. Geneva: ILO.

Jha, Praveen and Mario Negre. n.d. *Indian Economy in the Era of Contemporary Globalisation: Some Core Elements of the Balance*. Available at: https://myweb.rollins.edu/tlairson/asiabus/indiaeconomy.pdf

Khare, Mona. 2016. "Taking the Skills March Forward in India: Transitioning to the World of Work." In Pilz, Matthias (ed.). *India: Preparation for the World of Work – Education System and School to Work Transition*. Wiesbaden: Springer, pp. 103–140.

Kingdon, Geeta and Soderbom, Mans. 2007a. *Education, Skills and Labor Market Outcomes: Evidence from Ghana*. Background paper prepared for the World Bank study, *Linking Education Policy to Labor Market Outcomes*. Washington, DC: World Bank.

———. 2007b. *Education, Skills and Labor Market Outcomes: Evidence from Ghana*. Background paper prepared for the World Bank study, *Linking Education Policy to Labor Market Outcomes*. Washington, DC: World Bank.

Krueger, Alan and Lindhal, Mikael. 2000. *Education for Growth: Why and for Whom?* Working paper 808. Princeton University, Department of Economics.

Kundu, Amitabh and Varghese, K. 2010. *Regional Inequality and 'Inclusive Growth' in India under Globalization: Identification of Lagging States for Strategic Intervention*. India: Oxfam.

Leonardi, M. 1998. "Segmented Labour Markets: Theory and Evidence." *Journal of Economic Surveys*, 12(1): 103–109.

Lucas, Robert E. 1988. "Mechanics of Economic Development" *Journal of Monetary Economics*, 22: 3–42.

Maddison, D. 2007. "The Perception of, and Adaptation to, Climate Change in Africa." *World Bank Policy Research Working Paper No. 4308*. Washington, D.C.: World Bank.

Mankiw, N.G., Romer, D. and Weil, D. 1992. "Contribution to the Empirics of Economic Growth." *The Quarterly Journal of Economics*, 107(2): 407–437.

Mathur, Ashok. 1990. "Human Capital, Spatial Disparities and Economic Development." *Manpower Journal*, 26(3).

Mayer-Foulkes, David. 2003. "Human Development Traps and Economic Growth." In Lopez-Casasnovas, Guillem, Rivera, Berta and Currais, Luis (eds.). *Health and Economic Growth: Findings and Policy Implications*. Cambridge, MA: MIT Press, pp. 115–142.

Meier, Gerald M. and Baldwin, Robert E. 1957. *Economic Development: Theory, History and Policy*. New York: John Wiley & Sons.

Mincer, J. 1974. *Schooling, Experience and Earnings*. New York: Columbia University Press.

Nelson, R. and Phelps, E. 1966. "Investment in Humans, Technological Diffusion, and Economic Growth." *American Economic Review*, 56: 69–75.

Nurkse, Ragnar. 1953. *Problems of Capital Formation in Underdeveloped Countries*. New York: Oxford University Press.

OECD. 2012. Education Indicators in Focus, September. Available at: www.oecd.org/education/skillsbeyondhool/Education%20Indicators%20in%20Focus%207.pdf

Radwan, S. 1995. "Challenges and Scope for an Employment-Intensive Growth Strategy." In Von Braun, Joachim (ed.). *Employment for Poverty Reduction and Food Security*. Washington, D.C.: International Food Policy Research Institute (IFPRI).

Ranis, G. 2004. "Human Development and Economic Growth." *Centre Discussion Paper No. 887*, Economic Growth Centre, Yale University, USA.

Ranis, G., Stewart, F. and Ramirez, A. 2000. "Economic Growth and Human Development." *World Development*, 28(2): 197–219.

Ravallion, Martin and Gaurav Datt. 2002. "Why Has Economic Growth Been More Pro-Poor in Some States of India Than Others?" *Journal of Development Economics*, 68(2): 381–400.

Romer, P.M. 1990. "Human Capital and Growth: Theory and Evidence." *Carnegie – Rochester Conference Series on Public Policy*, 32(1): 251–286.

Sala-I-Martin, X., Doppelhofer, G. and Miller, R.I. 2004. "Determinants of Long-term Growth: A Bayesian Averaging of Classical Estimates (BACE) Approach" *American Economic Review*, 94(4): 813–835.

Schultz, T.W. 1963. *The Economic Value of Education*. New York: Columbia University Press.

Schultz, T.W. 1993. *Origins of Increasing Returns*. Oxford: Blackwell.

Sianesi, B. and Van, Reenen, J. 2003. "The Returns to Education: Macroeconomics", *Journal of Economic Surveys* 17(2): 157–200.

Temple, T. 2001. "Growth Effects of Education and Social Capital in the OECD Countries" *OECD Economic Studies*, 2001(2): 57–101.

UNESCO. 2012. *EFA Global Monitoring Report 2012 – Youth and Skills: Putting Education to Work*. Paris: UNESCO.

14
ELITE DOMINANCE AND RISING INEQUALITY IN INDIA

Zoya Hasan

In *The Great Escape*, Angus Deaton (2013) argued

> If democracy becomes plutocracy, those who are not rich are effectively disenfranchised. The political equality that is required by democracy is always under threat from economic inequality, and the more extreme the economic inequality, the greater the threat to democracy. If democracy is compromised, there is a direct loss of wellbeing because people have good reason to value their ability to participate in political life, and the loss of that ability is instrumental in threatening other harm.

Nowhere is this truer than in India. To quote Deaton again: "To worry about these consequences of extreme inequality has nothing to do with being envious of the rich and everything to do with the fear that rapidly growing top incomes are a threat to the wellbeing of everyone else (Ibid.)".

Growing inequality is one of the central issues of our time that requires close examination. India is one of the most unequal countries in the world, whether one measures inequality on the basis of income or wealth. To understand rising inequality, apart from an economic analysis, it calls for an analysis of political and policy processes that allow certain politically and economically powerful groups to control and manipulate not just economic activities but also democratic processes. The upshot of inequality is elite dominance which in turn has consequences for the operation of democracy and eventually for people's wellbeing. This chapter does not provide a comprehensive account of inequalities in India or the political economy of the Indian state. It examines in brief the politics and policies affecting inequalities in the context of the interaction between economic and political processes in the past two decades chiefly the impact of elite dominance on inequalities. It explores how political processes especially elite capture intensifies inequalities with regard to income and wealth, often referred to as vertical inequalities.[1] Inequalities among groups (horizontal inequalities) or those based on factors that determine identity, such as ethnicity and gender, are not dealt with here. While we need to be aware of inequality in its entirety taking into consideration the social and economic dimensions of inequality, the major concern of this chapter is an exposition of the political factors driving inequality and the changing thrust of social welfare in India.

Rising inequality

India is one of the most robust democracies in the world; people enjoy far greater political freedoms than in many other countries. But greater equality in the political sphere has not translated into more equal social outcomes for its people than for example in China which has invested heavily in health and education under Communism before it turned to market led growth model.

Economic growth averaged 8 per cent in the first decade of this century. However, this has not resulted in inclusive development and significant improvements in wellbeing. Instead of accelerated growth positively impacting human development indicators, it seems faster GDP/per capita growth begets slower growth in human development. This is clearly the result of an impoverished understanding of development as merely growth, rather than ensuring basic human capacities and dignity (Mannathukkaren 2015).

Despite rapid growth India is one of the poorest countries in the world that is often lost sight of (Dreze and Sen 2014). The country is home to the largest number of poor in the world (World Bank 2013). Though the rate of absolute poverty has declined India now has a greater share of the world's poor than it did thirty years ago. Then it was home to one fifth of the world's poorest people, but today it accounts for one-third, i.e. 400 million (Ibid.). While a majority of Indians live on less than a dollar a day (at nominal exchange rates); the country boasts a significant number of billionaires on Forbes' 2015 list. The 2014 *Human Development Report*, found that "inequality in the distribution of human development is distinctly pronounced in India" compared to other countries (Chandrasekhar and Ghosh 2014).

In India, income and wealth inequalities have been on the rise since the beginning of economic liberalisation. From the 1990s a series of market-oriented, business – friendly economic reforms have contributed significantly to rising inequality. Inequality of income in India is among the worst in the world. If one were to bring in social inequalities (based on caste and gender), the picture becomes even worse. An Oxfam report released in 2017 underscores the dramatic increase in wealth inequality in India which has been on the rise over the last few years (Oxfam 2018). According to Credit Suisse Global Wealth data, 73 per cent of the increase in wealth in India went to the top one per cent (Shorrocks et al. 2016). A year ago, the top one per cent owned 58 per cent of the stock of wealth (Cited in Patnaik 2018). In short, India is shining for its top one per cent and for another top 10 per cent and this "one per cent are not sharing anything with anyone" (Agarwal 2018). Much of this wealth was derived from land, real estate, construction, mines etc. It was created through crony capitalism and inheritance while people at the bottom saw their shares being reduced further (Oxfam 2018).

The huge growth of economic inequality in India is confirmed by French economists Lucas Chancel and Thomas Piketty using other data sources. Using a range of sources including tax returns, they have argued that income inequality in India today is higher than any time since 1922 when income tax was first introduced (Chancel and Piketty 2017). According to them, India has emerged as the country that has recorded the highest increase in the share of the top 1 per cent in national income over the past three decades, from 6.2 per cent in 1982–83 to 21.7 per cent in 2013–14. This rising inequality contrasts to the 30 years following Independence, when income inequality was widely reduced and the incomes of the bottom 50 per cent grew at a faster rate than the national average (Ibid.).

India's rising inequality is multi-dimensional and multi-structural and there are inequalities in wealth, income and consumption, as well as structural inequalities of opportunity, region and social groups. India is becoming more unequal, not just between rural and urban areas but also within rural and urban areas. Though the planning process tried to bridge the gap between different states inequality across states has grown over time (Oxfam 2018).

What is driving inequality?

The unmistakable increase in inequality is linked to neo-liberal economic policies and the economic and social institutions that underpin it. It is a consequence of deliberate policy choices based on the neoliberal growth model. Socio-economic policies that dominate India's development agenda since economic liberalisation are the most influential force driving wealth inequalities. This is responsible for widening gap between the rich and the poor. It results in a severely skewed distribution of assets, including land and capital, access to education, coupled with growth imbalances, slow job creation and worsening income distribution which favours the rich.

The details of the economic policies that came to be adopted in India since 1991, are well known, and need not be repeated here. What is clear is these policies aggravate inequalities in several ways. Specific policy choices which favoured capital rather than labour, and favoured skilled rather than unskilled labour, are part of the structure of the growth trajectory in India. The policy regime further entails a withdrawal of state support from peasant agriculture and neglect of millions of small farmers, landless agricultural workers, rural non-agricultural workers, and urban informal workers. It typically involves giving tax concessions and tax rebates to big corporations for ushering in "faster growth". Such tax concessions to corporations aggravate wealth inequality (Patnaik 2018). The biggest drawback of this model is the shortage of jobs. The Report "Reducing Inequalities" shows that

> while India witnessed rapid output growth especially from 2003–04 onwards, it was not manifested in rapidly growing employment in productive sectors

or in the expansion of decent work. Income generating opportunities have been getting severely limited for both rural and urban households, whether headed by males or females. More than half of all India's workers remain self-employed and there has been significant rise in casualisation of the workforce in both rural and urban sectors. All casual and self-employed, and a significant proportion of regular workers, are unsupported by any form of social security.

(Save the Children 2013)

In other words, public policy which would deliver basic benefits to the entire population has not been made a priority by any government. These policies in the Indian context would include: agrarian reform, food procurement, education, public health, employment creation, changes in governance through decentralisation and devolution of resources.

Elite capture and economic concentration

The second powerful force driving the 'rapid rise' in inequalities in India is the elite capture of policy space which has worsened economic inequality, and undermined the rules and regulations that give the poorest and the most marginalised citizens a fair chance. Concentration of economic and political power goes hand in hand as the state, prone to capture by special interests, has pulled its weight behind the corporate-capitalist elite which further intensifies disparities. Over time, the state has taken on a strongly pro-business orientation with a conspicuous dominance of the corporate elite (Kohli 2007). Businessmen have become increasingly cynical in manipulating the state to corner scarce resources and earn rent and super-profits.

A pro-business policy framework rather than a pro-market one is arguably a striking feature of the Indian policy regime. The last twenty years have seen a massive growth of corporate power which has gained a position of unparalleled significance displacing the legitimacy previously enjoyed by the developmental state (Chatterjee 2012). Elites use their political influence to curry government favours – including tax exemptions, sweetheart contracts, land concessions and subsidies – while blocking policies that strengthen the rights of the poor (Oxfam 2014). The strong mutually beneficial relationship between business and politics eventually leads to distorted economic priorities and developmental outcomes. The massive lobbying power of corporations to bend the rules in their favour has increased the concentration of power and money in the hands of the few. This challenge lies at the heart of the massive controversies in India today with regard to acquisition of land for industry and plunder of natural resources by the corporate class with the help of bureaucrats and politicians.

The former Reserve Bank of India Governor Raghuram Rajan had warned against crony capitalism which creates oligarchies and slows down growth (Rajan 2014). He underlined the role of special interests and clarified how lobbying produces policy changes to benefit these interests in collusion with politicians (Ibid.). According to him many business houses enjoyed 'riskless capitalism': in good times they enjoy profits and in bad times they are bailed out by the banks. Some of these indebted corporate groups were listed by reputed independent research institutions as defaulting on loans (Venu 2016). Credit Suisse India was regularly putting out the names of the top ten business groups that owed about Rs.7500 billion to the banks and nearly 50 per cent of this was close to default status (Pandey 2016). Some of these corporate houses had already got their loans restructured – a euphemism for postponement of interest and principal repayment during the United Progressive Alliance (UPA) regimes, especially after the global economic slowdown deepened post-2012. The close relationship between crony capitalism and corruption was a major concern for the public and "if the debate during the elections is any pointer, this is a very real concern of the public in India today' (BS Reporter 2014)". This concern was partly responsible for the crushing defeat of the Congress party in the 2014 elections (Sen 2014).

Crony capitalism was palpable in the sweetheart deals between political and economic elites in mining, land acquisition and telecommunications during UPA-2 (Mohanty 2012). However, this model did not change after the 2014 election. Economic liberalisation has encouraged a large section of land hungry sharks disguised as corporate sector to demand prime agricultural and forest land at throw away prices. This section had bankrolled the Bharatiya Janata Party (BJP)'s election campaign in the hope that it would dilute if not undo the Land Acquisition Act enacted by the UPA government. Not surprisingly, the BJP government did so with alacrity. Singled out by the corporate sector as the main obstacle in the path of development the Modi government issued three ordinances to amend the Land Acquisition Act passed in 2013. It tried hard to sell the amendments as a pro-reforms measure and making it easier for the state to acquire land for infrastructure and industry. However, it failed to persuade the farmers and the Opposition parties to pass it in Parliament. Eventually it had to revert to the situation prevailing before 2014 thus admitting that the Land Acquisition Ordinance was a mistake.

Manipulation of political processes

The third closely related issue is that of political processes that allow certain politically and economically powerful groups to control and manipulate not just economic activities but also democratic processes. Today, we are witnessing an unprecedented increase in the instances of politicians or their next of kin establishing businesses themselves either overtly or very often in a covert fashion. This has to be read with changing economic profile of elected Member of Parliament (MPs). With 82 per cent of the new MPs having assets worth over Rs.10 million each, 16th Lok Sabha is the richest when compared to the 15th (58 per cent) and 14th Lok Sabha (30 per cent) (Rukmini 2014). In the 2014 Lok Sabha there is a striking increase in the number of MPs who have declared business as their primary occupation. At 20 per cent this is higher than the 15 per cent for the previous Lok Sabha. By contrast in the very first Lok Sabha the percentage of MPs who had listed business as their occupation was 12 per cent (PRS legislative Research 2015). The failure to institute a transparent mechanism to fund politics leaves Indian democracy to be funded by corruption and making politics the shortest route to personal riches.

Inequality is also perpetuated by unequal access to health and education between the poor (whose ability to pay for better quality private services is very limited) and the rich. The actual public expenditure on education, health, agriculture and social security remains abysmal. The global average on social spending is 8.8 per cent of GDP. Among BRICS nations, India spends the lowest proportion of public expenditure on social protection at 2.5 per cent, while the highest is Brazil with 21.2 per cent, as of 2010. China, more populous than India, spends 6.5 per cent of total expenditure on social-protection schemes (*The Times of India* 2011).

India needs to increase its social sector spending substantially. With inequality rising, the government needs to spend more on social protection programmes, but this is not happening. Social under-spending has been a feature of India's development story. India's public expenditure on social protection is among the lowest in Asia, far lower than China, Sri Lanka, Thailand, and even Nepal.

The tax system is the most important tool at the disposal of the government to address these inequalities because public spending and redistribution are crucial for reducing poverty along with a corresponding investment by government to reduce inequality (Oxfam 2014). At 15.5 per cent, India has one of the lowest tax-to-gross domestic product (GDP) ratios, says a recent study by the Centre for Budget and Governance Accountability (Business Standard 2013). Only 3.01 per cent of Indians pay income tax. The data further reveal that there are just over 1.33 million income-tax assesses in India declaring income of more than Rs.1 million per year (Saha 2016). The government earned Rs.7420 billion as direct taxes in 2015–16, a 66 per cent increase from Rs.4450 billion in 2010–11. According to economists, Thomas Piketty and Nancy Qian, the tax base in China in the meantime increased from under 1 per cent to nearly 20 per cent (Piketty and Qian 2009).

Social welfare

India's growth story of the last two decades has had one recurring theme: that the pattern of economic growth is accentuating inequalities and insecurities previously mentioned. Indian democracy has struggled to provide even the basic minimum welfare to its more vulnerable citizens. There is almost no safety net (in practical terms, apart from the public distribution system) for the poor. Yet, there continues to be a deep divide over whether the gains from growth ought to be ploughed back to achieve social security for everyone or should we continue to rely on the trickle down effects of growth. The most vehement opposition to welfare has come from the middle classes who claim that they are not opposed to welfare measures per se but to the corruption and how it is implemented, when, in fact, opposition is often to the idea of welfare in its totality perceived as a handout to the poor.

Post-independence, there have been several social policies and programmes for the provision of public goods to the poor, indeed, a wide range of social welfare initiatives were introduced but these were conceived and implemented through policies rather than the acquisition of rights on the part of the people. India's overall success in promoting social opportunities on the basis of these policies was quite limited as these were initiated without altering structural inequities and were not embedded in a redistributive ethos. In short, we have a long way to go before we can ensure decent living conditions for all our citizens.

Between 2004 and 2014, India began to introduce a series of path breaking social legislations to expand the economic security and social opportunities for its citizens. Three distinct processes have catalysed this agenda in recent years: socio-legal activism, the expanding ambit of social movements, and the substitution of political patronage with legal rights (Ruparelia 2013). The last of the three is particularly important as it established belatedly a welfare policy framework on the basis of new laws that broke the traditional division of civil, political and socio-economic rights and provide incentives for collaboration across state and society (Idiculla 2013). In consequence, work, education, food, and health etc. are looked upon as rights which are legally enforceable whereas earlier these were completely dependent on the largesse of the state. The idea was not merely to introduce pro-poor schemes but to enshrine them in legal guarantees. This approach stems from a belief that growth alone is not enough to address the plight of the poor (Sampath 2015). The flagship initiatives were the right to information, employment, education and food. These legislations enshrined a number of new entitlements through legally enforceable rights (Hasan 2018).

While the intentions of the UPA government were extremely progressive, the practice was unimpressive and the welfare measures were unevenly implemented. The frequent declarations of intent were not matched by actual spending, and the amounts disbursed have been pathetically low and even declining in real terms under UPA-2 (2009–14). Furthermore, despite an ideology of universalism, social programmes were often targeted, this is true of both the right to employment and right to food. By creating a targeted group of beneficiaries, it also created the scope for a contradiction between those included within its welfare programmes and those excluded.

Public pressure played a crucial role in the process of policy-making in this period (Hasan 2018). In response, the government created institutionalised mechanisms of consultation with civil society to shape its social policies. New spaces of engagements evolved at various levels. The formation of the National Advisory Council (NAC) in 2005 was a product of this shift. It was established to provide advice on social policies and to monitor their implementation. It drafted much of the signature welfare legislation of the UPA. Prior to the NAC, several advisory committees had been set up but either their life span was short lived or did not gain much significance. These multiple processes began to shape welfare and the politics of development in India. Also a discernible shift in strategy on the part of social movements from opposing the state to engaging and partnering it facilitated this. It effectively forged links between social movements/campaigns and party processes which included building wider social alliances with other social movements, the intelligentsia, and the media, and these networks contributed to its success.

What about welfare policies of the Modi government? While the neo-liberal economic policies pursued by the previous government are being pursued by the present one, so, in this respect there is no difference between the UPA and NDA. But neo-liberalism under UPA was offset by a kind of ideological pluralism embodied in the varied policy positions taken by Prime Minister Manmohan Singh and Congress President Sonia Gandhi. The existence of different voices in the UPA and their accommodation facilitated the adoption of a welfare framework by the UPA government from 2005–09. This diversity of ideas and policies is completely absent in the NDA government which is highly centralised with a concentration of political authority in the Prime Minister's Office (PMO). The space for independent voices and discussion of varied approaches and policies at the level of the executive is very limited. NDA's neo-liberalism is consequently more hardnosed which is evident from their approach to social welfare.

Social sector schemes introduced by the previous UPA government haven't disappeared, in fact many of the UPA schemes have been relaunched under new names. There is no frontal attack on rights-based welfare schemes, but the government has undercut many rights-based welfare acts. Modi government has been largely dismissive of the welfare regime put in place by the previous government: nowhere is this more evident than in the government's treatment of Mahatma Gandhi National Rural Employment Guarantee Act (MGNREGA), which entitled rural households to demand from the state a hundred days of paid employment at stipulated minimum wages. Modi repeatedly mocked it as a monument to 60 years of failure of the previous government to develop the countryside. Despite its vehement denials, there are indications that the government is not keen on the rural jobs scheme and is sometimes quite unmindful of its legal obligations under it. It had attempted several dilutions as soon as it took office – restricting it to the poorest districts, reducing the wage component, introducing greater rigidity in the type of works that could be taken up. There is growing evidence that MGNREGA is being whittled down significantly and this is happening in a context where inequality has actually been rising in the country.

In the 2017 budget, the government claimed that the allocation under the MGNREGA has been increased but this is misleading (*Wire*, February 1). The outlay of Rs.480 billion for 2017–18 is just about the same as the revised outlay for 2016–17, which is Rs.475 billion. It is misleading also because the MGNREGA is a demand-driven programme, and the government is statutorily bound to provide work as long as there is demand for work (Ghosh 2017).

The major social welfare initiatives launched by the Modi government, include Pradhan Mantri Jan Dhan Yojana, the Pradhan Mantri Jeevan Jyoti Bima Yojana, the Pradhan Mantri Suraksha Bima Yojana and the Atal Pension Yojana. It is evident from these schemes that the government has reverted back to the scheme mode for welfare spending. Subscribers to all the three new insurance schemes had to acquire a bank account through the Pradhan Mantri Jan Dhan Yojana. This is the most important scheme in the social security framework of this government and yet the share of people with inactive accounts is very high, suggesting that not all beneficiaries of the scheme have been able to reap the full benefits (Kundu 2018). It is the basis for the life insurance, accident insurance, and pension schemes (Sampath 2015). However, none of these new insurance schemes offer legal entitlement, which distinguished the National Social Assistance Programme (NSAP), Rashtriya Swasthya Bima Yojna (RSBY) and Aam Aadmi Bima Yojana, which had emerged from the 2008 Unorganised Workers' Social Security Act (Ruparelia 2015).

The distinctive feature of some of these welfare schemes is that they demand investment not from the state, but from the proposed beneficiaries and government support comes in the form of loans to prospective entrepreneurs. The intention behind these yojanas seems to be to disavow any responsibility on the part of the state for the socio-economically vulnerable. The presumption that the poor should contribute to the betterment of their lives, or of that of their families after death, is both implausible and unrealistic. None of these schemes are rights-based, which means they can be wound up at any time, or the benefits denied on technical grounds. In short, as Sanjay Ruparelia notes: "The government had taken an increasingly neoliberal approach to welfare services, encouraging individual households to rely on personal resources and market dynamics rather than legal entitlements to government programmes in order to enhance human capabilities and social protection" (Ibid.).

In addition to the Pradhan Mantri Jan Dhan Yojana, the Modi government has launched, or re-launched, flagship schemes in key areas of sanitation (Swachh Bharat Abhiyan), cooking fuel (Pradhan Mantri Ujjwala Yojana), skills (Pradhan Mantri Kasushal Vikas Yojana or PMKVY), and rural electrification (Deen Dayal Upadhyaya Gram Jyoti Yojana or DDUGJY). The Ujjwala scheme has raised the number of households with LPG connections but its impact on LPG consumption has been far less. Recent data on the Swachh Bharat Abhiyan (2017–18) shows a rapid rise in rural toilets, however, several experts have raised questions on the numbers, especially those relating to usage (Kundu 2018). Job placements under the skills initiative, PMKVY has been poor even as the scheme ended up enriching private institutes which offered, or claimed to offer, vocational training to youth (Ibid).

Social spending on education, health care and social security has witnessed a contraction with no significant increase in budgetary outlays for the social sector (Ghosh 2017).[2] The overall public spending on primary education and health sector has been reduced. The allocations for the Sarva Shiksha Abhiyan (SSA), the Rashtriya Madhyamik Shiksha Abhiyan (RMSA), the Teacher Training and Sakshar Bharat initiatives, and the Kendriya and Navodaya Vidyalayas have fallen. Overall the share of education has declined from 0.27 per cent of the GDP to 0.21 per cent as share of the gross domestic product (GDP), but also in real terms, counting for inflation (Ibid.). The Central government's health care spending is only 0.3 per cent of the GDP, out of a total of 1.3 per cent of the GDP spent by the states and the Centre together. It is nowhere near the 3 per cent of the GDP that is widely accepted to be the minimum level required to achieve reasonable universal health care coverage (Ibid.). The money allocated for key centrally sponsored social schemes – Integrated Child Development Services (ICDS) stands at Rs.100 billion, which is actually lower than what the UPA government spent on this in 2013–14, which was Rs.109.18 billion (Ibid.).

It's worth noting that there is almost no civil society consultation or participation in the policymaking process under the Modi government. The government is suspicious of civil society which is evident from the Modi government cracking down on NGOs. It has suspended the Foreign Contributions Regulation Act (FCRA) registration of hundreds of NGOs, preventing it from receiving any foreign funds. At base, the issue is one of political control. This is not entirely new. Past governments have harassed inconvenient NGOs by denying them FCRA clearance. Yet, it's clear the Modi government has gone much further in targeting NGOs and has done so with a renewed vigor. This government is not willing to listen to civil society organisations and those who say that something needs to be done about rampant poverty, deprivation, and lack of health facilities etc. The attitude towards civil society reflects the limits of people's participation under this government resulting in constraints on the space for dissent and public opposition. Arguably, it restricts the possibility for public pressure and public action essential for the promotion of social welfare in a democratic society.

Providing social protection requires taxing the rich and using the resources for welfare schemes for the poor, implementing higher minimum wages, regulating companies to ensure sustainable production, moving away from a focus on high growth to focusing on social sector policy for improving the basic living conditions of the masses. This government is unlikely to muster the political resolve required to put such a redistributive agenda into practice.

Conclusion

As noted, rising inequality has emerged as one of the most important problems confronting societies across the world. Inequality is a hot button issue globally and a key issue in India as well but there is no urgency about it in the public debate or in the political discourse in this country. Decades of political influence have tilted the economic scales in favour of the elite and the wealthy. Public policies can impact the distribution of wealth, but redistributive efforts have not gone very far not least because no one wants to promote policies which might hurt the corporate-financial elite and the middle classes. The right wing political regime offers little hope for improvement in this regard.

A major problem lies with the political class whose main preoccupation is winning elections and the bureaucracy whose most important responsibility is maintaining high rates of economic growth. None of India's foremost political parties and the governments they control have a coherent policy framework of how to genuinely incorporate 400 million very poor Indians into a dynamic and coherent political economy. India's political class has no clear views on how to tackle issues related to concentration of wealth, crony capitalism, jobless growth, and crisis of peasant economy, etc. Over the past few years, demands for change have been getting louder in India. Yet, much of the discontent is directed towards the incumbent government or against corruption or against under-representation in public institutions and not against inequalities, disparities and injustice per se. What we need is a political consensus, to act with urgency to reduce the huge levels of inequality, which results in conflict, and not only threatens our vision for sustainable development, but also threatens the stability of our democracy. We need to move the development discourse beyond the current discussion of outcomes and opportunities to reducing inequality which is central to the functioning of India's democracy. It requires civil society in India to demand more attention and engagement from our policy-makers towards addressing the structural causes of inequality and to push for a more inclusive growth. This can be achieved by promoting labour-intensive sectors that will create more jobs, investing more in agriculture and implementing fully social protection schemes and most importantly increasing public expenditures on health and education.

Notes

1 There are two types of inequality: vertical inequality defined as inequality of incomes and consumption between individuals and horizontal inequality defined in terms of inequality between groups.
2 For an analysis of the 'miserly treatment' given to crucial social sector areas such as education, health care and social security see Ghosh (2017).

References

Agarwal, Nisha. 2018. "Wealth of the Nation." *The Indian Express*, 23 January. Available at: https://indianexpress.com/article/opinion/columns/narendra-modi-davos-world-economic-forum-wealth-of-the-nation-5035177/

Bank, World. 2013. "The State of the Poor: Where are the Poor and Where are the Poorest?" *World Bank*. April 17. Available at: www.worldbank.org/content/dam/Worldbank/document/State_of_the_poor_paper_April17.pdf [Accessed July 12, 2016].

BusinessStandard. 2013. *India's ta-GDP ratio one of the Lowest*. March 26. Available at: www.business-standard.com/article/economy-policy/india-s-tax-gdp-ratio-one-of-the-lowest-113032500376_1.html [Accessed 2017].

———. 2014. "How Crony Capitalism Impacts India: RBI Governor Rajan Explains." *Business Standard*. August 2014. Available at: www.business-standard.com/article/economy-policy/how-crony-capitalism-impacts-india-rbi-governor-rajan-explains-114081400156_1.html [Accessed July 10, 2016].

Chancel, Lucas and Piketty, Thomas. 2017. "Indian Income Inequality 1922–2015: From British Raj to Billionaire Raj?, World Working Paper Series N° 2017/11." *World Inequality Database, World Inequality Lab*. Available at: wid.world/dev/document/chancelpiketty2017widworld/.

Chandrasekhar, C.P. and Ghosh, Jayati. 2014. "Is Rising Income Inequality Inevitable?" *MacroScan*. September 15. Available at: www.macroscan.org/fet/sep14/pdf/Inequality.pdf [Accessed October 15, 2015].

Chatterjee, Partha. 2012. "After Subaltern Studies." *Economic and Political Weekly*, XLVII (35).

Deaton, Angus. 2013. *The Great Escape: Health, Wealth and the Origins of Inequality*. New Jersey: Princeton University Press.

Dreze, Jean and Sen, Amartya. 2014. "Putting Growth in its Place." *Outlook*, November 14. Available at: www.outlookindia.com/magazine/story/putting-growth-in-its-place/278843.

Ghosh, Jayati. 2017. "Budget 2017: Worrying Failure." *Frontline,* March 3. Available at: www.frontline.in/economy/worrying-failure/article9541504.ece.

Hasan, Zoya. 2018. *Agitation to Legislation: Negotiating Equity and Justice in India*. New Delhi: Oxford University Press.

Idiculla, Mathew. 2013. "Rights Reconceived: India's New Approach." *OpenDemocracy*, September 3. Available at: www.opendemocracy.net/openglobalrights/mathew-idiculla/rights-reconceived-india%E2%80%99s-new-approach [Accessed April 25, 2016].

Kohli, Atul. 2007. "State and Redistributive Development in India." *Princeton*, October 3. Available at: www.princeton.edu/~kohli/docs/UNRISD.pdf [Accessed November 21, 2016].

Kundu, Tadit. 2018. "How Does the Narendra Modi Government Score on Welfare Schemes." *Livemint*, 23 May. Available at: https://www.livemint.com/Politics/3z36Ja NMpmhX68Kjc0BgfP/How-does-the-Narendra-Modi-govt-score-on-welfare-schemes.html

Mannuthukkaren, Nissim. 2015. "The Grand Delusion of Digital India." *The Hindu*, October 6. Available at: www.thehindu.com/opinion/op-ed/the-grand-delusion-of-digital-india/article7727159.ece [Accessed July 12, 2016].

Mohanty, Mritiunjoy. 2012. "The Growth Model Has Come Undone." *The Hindu*, 10 July. Available at: https://www.thehindu.com/opinion/lead/the-growth-model-has-come-undone/article3621241.ece

Oxfam. 2014. *Even it Up: Time to End Extreme Inequality*. Oxford: Oxfam International.

———. 2018. *The Widening Gaps. India Inequality Report 2018*. New Delhi: Oxfam India. Available at: www.oxfamindia.org/sites/.../himanshu_inequality_Inequality_report_2018.pdf.

Pandey, Piyush. 2016. "The Biggest Ever Fire Sale of Indian Corporate Assets has Begun, to Tide over Bad Loans Crisis." *The Hindu*, May 9. Available at: www.thehindu.com/business/Industry/the-biggestever-fire-sale-of-indian-corporate-assets-has-begun-to-tide-over-bad-loans-crisis/article8573163.ece [Accessed July 5, 2016].

Patnaik, Prabhat. 2018. "Why is India's Wealth Inequauliity Growing so Rapidly?" *Al Jazeera*, January 26. Available at: www.aljazeera.com/.../india-wealth-inequality-growing-rapidly-180125084201 [Accessed May 30, 2018].

Piketty, Thomas and Qian, Nancy. 2009. "Income Inequality and Progressive Income Taxation in China and India, 1986–2015." *American Economic Journal: Applied Economics,* 1(2): 53–63.

PRS. 2015. "Profile of the 16th Lok Sabha." *PRS Legislative Research*. Available at: www.prsindia.org/media/media-updates/profile-of-the-16th-lok-sabha-3276/ [Accessed September 18, 2015].

Rajan, Raghuram. 2014. "Crony Capitalism is a Big Threat to Countries like India, RBI Chief Raghuram Rajan Says." *The Times of India*, August 12.

Rukmini, S. 2014. "16th Lok Sabha Will Be Richest, Have Most MPs with Criminal Charges." *The Hindu*, 18 May. Available at: https://www.thehindu.com/news/national/16th-lok-sabha-will-be-richest-have-most-mps-with-criminal-charges/article6022513.ece

Ruparelia, Sanjay. 2013. "India's New Rights Agenda: Genesis, Promises, Risks." *Pacific Affairs,* 66(3).

———. 2015. "'Minimum Government, Maximum Governance': The Restructuring of Power in Modi's India." *South Asia Journal of South Asian Studies,* 38(4): 755–775.

Saha, Devanik. 2016. "Only 3.81% Indians Pay Income Tax." *FirstSpot*, May 4. Available at: www.firstpost.com/business/only-3-81-indians-pay-income-tax-maharashtra-delhi-pay-53-2761510.html [Accessed February 16, 2017].

Sampath, G. 2015. "Mr. Modi's War on Welfare." *The Hindu,* May 26. Available at: www.thehindu.com/opinion/op-ed/modi-government-is-determined-to-dismantle-the-twopronged-welfare-paradigm/article7244983.ece [Accessed April 18, 2016].

Save the Children. 2013. *Reducing Inequality: Learning Lessons for the Post-2015 Agenda – India Case Study.* New Delhi: Save the Children.

Sen, Kunal. 2014. "It's the Economy, Stupid: How the Poor Economic Performance of the UPA Regime is a Key Issue in the Indian Elections'. [Blog]." *University of Nottingham Blogpost,* May 8.

Shorrocks, Anthony, Davies, James B., Lluberas, Rodrigo and Koutsoukis, Antonios. 2016. *Global Wealth Report 2016.* Zurich, Switzerland: Credit Suisse AG.

The Times of India. 2011. "India's Income Inequality has Doubled in 20 Years." *The Times of India,* December 7. Available at: http://timesofindia.indiatimes.com/india/Indias-income-inequality-has-doubled-in-20-years/articleshow/11012855.cms [Accessed October 28, 2016].

Venu, M.K. 2016. "Saving Crony Capitalists From Raghuram Rajan." *The Wire,* June 20. Available at: https://thewire.in/44003/saving-crony-capitalists-from-raghuram-rajan/ [Accessed July 5, 2016].

WIRE. 2017. "Modi Government's Budgetary Allocation for MNREGA is Barely an Increase." *The Wire,* February 1. Available at: https://thewire.in/104882/modi-government-budget-mnrega/ [Accessed February 14, 2017].

15
THINKING *SAMATA* AT THE SDG MOMENT

Manoranjan Mohanty

Samata! What is that?

The context of increasing inequalities and increasing violence

Anand Teltumbde, a leading thinker and social activist of India has an interesting subtitle to his monumental work, *Republic of Caste: Thinking Equality in the Time of Neoliberal Hindutva* (Teltumbde 2018). I have framed the title of this chapter echoing his formulation partly to support his thesis, but mainly to extend the discourse on equality to ask as to why equality as a value has receded to the background. Some people seem to ask: *Samata! What is that?* They are more concerned with achieving growth targets or at best tackling concrete livelihood problems. Both these objectives may be laudable in themselves. The former creates wealth and resources needed for distribution. The latter is very important to alleviate immediate scarcities and deprivations. But the question is in what direction was a society moving as a result of those policies. The attention of policymakers was shifting away from equality exactly when people everywhere in the world were more conscious of their dignity as individuals and groups and demanding equal respect and equal rights. It is therefore important to address some of the new challenges in this context that we face in contemporary times. I share Teltumbde's thesis that unless class and caste issues were addressed together as a programme of democratic revolution, the egalitarian agenda will continue to elude us, and rulers would continue to maintain multiple dominations through a variety of political strategies of governance. But it is also important to understand why that goal of integrating the struggle for annihilation of caste and the struggle to end class exploitation has remained distant in Indian politics and political mobilisation on caste and class lines went on separate, and often on conflicting routes in India. We must ask why these struggles were overwhelmed by new forces which Teltumbde rightly calls "neoliberal Hindutva". My hypothesis is that because the centrality of political power in the struggle for equality has not been emphasised either in state policy or in the programmes of the social movements and also in the global agenda, the deprived groups continued to remain in unequal conditions. Here political power is not to be understood as only formal representation in institutions. It means that the political, economic, social and cultural sources of power which are unequal, needed to be altered so that the cumulative power relationships become increasingly equal. While Teltumbde restores the focus on structural roots of inequality, the interdependence of the multiple dimensions shaping power relations need further emphasis. In my view, globalisation and aggressive assertion of religious and cultural claims of the dominant elite is a governance response of the rulers to the growing challenge from oppressed groups in course of their struggle for equality.

The SDG presents a cluster of goals which are presented as concrete targets accompanied by even more concrete objectives seen as practical ways of achieving the goals. They are in a mould of measurable characteristics and countries are expected to present to the United Nations (UN) annual track records. In turn state governments and district authorities are supposed to monitor the progress on each target and report to the higher authorities. In India, the NITI Aayog oversees this entire process. This impressive arrangement of implementing a programme with the aura of the UN having proclaimed them as representing a global consensus prompts us to hail this effort as the SDG Moment! But because it is not grounded in basic premises of egalitarian transformation, the SDG turns out to be no more than a neoliberal adjunct. Even though no one can object to any of the specific goals and every effort must be made to fulfil them, it is important to recognise the nature of the political economy of the overall process of globalisation which has led to greater inequalities and consequent disquiet and violence in the contemporary society and the world.

In this essay we shall present some evidence on how inequality persists in India and the world and new forms of inequality were growing. Then we indicate the trends of violence and conflicts which we believe are the results of persisting inequalities. After that we discuss a few issues of theory and policy to argue that unless the drive for equality is given the central place in policy and politics, prospects of building a democratic society with ecological sustainability as well as peace, freedom and prosperity for all will not be possible. If the present trend of increasing inequalities persists, then more violence and alienation will be the norm. I argue that policies for promoting equality are not only normative ideals for building a society but a practical condition for peace, freedom and sustainability. In other words, it is a value that both idealists and pragmatists would have a stake in.

This is especially important at the time of neoliberal Hindutva which continued its expansive journey as the 2019 elections in India showed. In the 2019 Lok Sabha elections none of the political parties had any promise of reducing inequality among groups in their election manifestoes. All of them had a plethora of welfare support programmes for various categories. The Bharatiya Janata Party (BJP) which won the elections with increased seats in the Parliament and higher vote share had campaigned on the platform of its success in strengthening national security. Appealing to Hindu religious identity it promoted consolidation of Hindu votes. The prime minister's Kisan Yojana aimed at providing an annual grant of Rs.6000/- to the poor and marginal farmers was extended to all farmers by the Modi government at the first cabinet meeting after taking oath. It also did the same to the pension schemes for the senior citizens and unorganised workers. Congress's announcement of a minimum income guarantee scheme, Nyuntam Aay Yojana (NYAY) was a form of welfare support to the poor by promising to deposit a cash amount of Rs.21,000/- annually to the bank account of the poor households. In Odisha the Naveen Patnaik government had introduced a farmer support scheme called KALIA (Krushak Assistance for Livelihood and Income Augmentation) before the elections for the poor and marginal farmers, share croppers and agricultural labourers whose scope was enlarged to cover nearly 90 per cent of the agricultural households. Similar measures were announced in other states too. But they were all livelihood sustenance measures rather than serious capacity building for self-development that would help in reducing inequalities. Neither of them pledged any structural measures such as land reforms, substantial rise in investment in education, health and employment generation. The National Democratic Alliance (NDA) government led by Narendra Modi, after coming to power first in 2014 had abolished the Planning Commission which used to frame Five Year Plans (FYP) setting up specific goals for attainment and put in its place NITI Aayog (National Institution for Transforming India), something like a think tank to advise the central government. Growth with Equity was a goal for many FYPs which at least kept the commitment to the Constitutional goal of equality alive.

In fact, the indifference to the goal of equality did not start with the NDA regime. It was inherent in the neoliberal agenda of economic reforms which started in 1991 with P V Narasimha Rao as Prime Minister and Manmohan Singh as Finance Minister. As a part of the neoliberal discourse a whole set of new vocabulary came into vogue that replaced many conventional terms. A notable concept in the context of the "changing terms of discourse" was the term "inclusion" which took the place of equality (Mohanty 2004). The Eleventh FYP had the title, *Inclusive Growth*, while the Twelfth and the last FYP was titled *Faster, More Inclusive and Sustainable Growth*, adding extra adjectives. Neoliberal economy was now fully focused on achieving higher rate of growth relegating other values to the background. During the Congress-led regime of the United Progressive Alliance (UPA) which was in power during 2004–14 while pursuing the neoliberal growth strategy there were some important initiatives to address the problems of the poor. Many right-based laws were passed introducing programmes such as guaranteed rural employment, food security, education, forest rights which were certainly helpful to the marginalised sections of society. But they did not change the focus on growth. They were mainly livelihood sustenance programmes rather than promoting conditions for reducing inequalities.

Increasing inequalities

The Oxfam report to the World Economic Forum in Davos in January 2019 gave some startling figures depicting the state of inequality in the world and India. Here are some statements from the Oxfam Report (Oxfam International 2019):

> The rate at which extreme poverty is reducing has halved, and it is increasing in sub-Saharan Africa. In the 10 years since the financial crisis, the number of billionaires has nearly doubled. The wealth of the world's billionaires had increased by $900 billion in 2018, or $2.5 billion a day. Meanwhile the wealth of the poorest half of humanity, 3.8 billion people fell by 11 per cent. Wealth is becoming even more concentrated – in 2018, 26 people owned the same as the 3.8 billion people who make up the poorest half of humanity, down from 43 people the year before. The World Inequality Report 2018 showed that between 1980 and 2016, the poorest 50 per cent of people only received 12 cents in every dollar of global income growth (Alvaredo et al. 2017). By contrast, the richest 1 per cent received 27 cents of every dollar. Globally, women earn 23 per cent less than men. Unless growth benefits the poorest people more between now and 2030, the first Sustainable Development Goal (SDG) – to eliminate extreme poverty – will be missed.

These findings are culled from studies by professional experts and organisations and put together by Oxfam to create awareness among the business community and world leaders who assemble in Davos every year to take stock of the world economy and plan initiatives. The Oxfam report also highlights what consequences would follow from situations of gross inequalities. Some of the observations are worth quoting:

> Government economic decisions, especially on taxation on spending have a big impact on gender inequality. Inequality is destabilizing. For instance, in recent years we have seen a rise in authoritarianism by governments worldwide, with crackdowns on freedom of speech and democracy. We have also seen a rise in popularity for right-wing, racist, sexist views and authoritarian politicians who support them. Many have pointed to the link between this global trend and high levels of inequality. Inequality undermines our societies. It is bad for everyone, not just the poorest people. In more unequal countries, trust is lower and crime higher. Unequal societies are more stressed, less happy and have poorer mental health. Inequality makes the fight to save our planet from climate breakdown even harder. To get us to a situation where everyone on earth is living on more than $5 a day with current levels of inequality would require the global economy to be 175 times bigger than it is today, which would destroy our planet. The only way we can beat poverty while saving our planet is to tackle inequality. Inequality also has profound implications for the future of our children and the opportunities they will

have to live a better life. And perhaps the most powerful, uncomfortable and undeniable outcome of inequality is its impact on how long we can expect to live.

This being the global trend, what we find happening in India is even more disturbing. That inequalities are growing in India and the dalits, adivasis, minorities, unorganised workers and women are the worst sufferers have been documented by many reports, especially by the Centre for Equity Studies, Delhi in its India Exclusion Report and the many reports by civil liberty and democratic rights organisations (Centre for Equity Studies 2018; CPDR n.d.; CPDR 2017a, 2017b; Singh and Chauhan 2012; Tandon and Basu 2016a, 2016b). In this volume itself, many chapters give detailed accounts of this scenario. For our purpose a few telling instances of the condition of inequality at the time of rising growth rates will help in seeing its social and political consequences. These are clearly highlighted in the special report on India produced by Oxfam (Oxfam, India Story 2019). Following are some highlights from this report:

> The top 1 per cent of the population possesses 51.53 per cent of the national wealth and the top 10 per cent holds 77.4 per cent. The bottom 60 per cent, the majority of the population, own merely 4.8 per cent of the national wealth. Wealth of top nine billionaires is equivalent to the wealth of the bottom 50 per cent of the population. As for the gender dimension of inequality, in 2018, India was 108th on the World Economic Forum's Global Gender Gap Index, 10 notches less than in 2006. Forty-two per cent of India's tribal children are underweight, 1.5 times higher than non-tribal children. Children from poor families in India are three times more likely to die before their first birthday than children from rich families. A Dalit woman can expect to live almost 14.6 years less than one from a high-caste. While the literacy rate in Kerala, Mizoram and the union territory of Lakshadweep is over 90 per cent, it is just little above 60 per cent in Bihar. The percentage of children and young people who were never enrolled in school (age group 5–29) in rural areas is double than that of urban areas. Female labour force participation rates declined from 34.1 per cent in 1999–00 to 27.67 per cent in 2011–12.
>
> *(Oxfam India 2019)*

Inequality and violence

Whereas the outbreak of violence may have many causes, the trend of increasing inequality is a major underlying factor. Researches have shown that alienated ethnic and religious groups who have suffered from horizontal inequalities have often rebelled against their condition. The phenomenon of Islamic youth protesting against Western domination is a part of this trend. Actual or perceived discrimination against minorities that denies equality of status to their religion has been an important cause of many violent attacks in the recent decades. This has produced retaliations from extremist sections among the minority. The global situation since 9/11 attacks by Al Qaeda on the World Trade Centre in New York in 2001 provides many instances of this phenomenon. Many of these conflicts can be traced back to colonial regimes whose policies of divide and rule sowed the seeds of such confrontation and the Partition of India was one such example. Policies of migration and settlement of ethnic population also led to unequal privileges. In the post-colonial world, migration both voluntary and involuntary has gone on especially from the less developed regions of Africa, Latin America and Asia to Europe and North America. The incidents of terrorist attacks in many parts of the world in recent years have to be understood in this context of rising inequality. The terrorist attacks have been planned and perpetrated either by Islamic groups or by white supremacist groups who have resented the growth of non-white presence in what they perceived as their habitats. Sometimes it has been a series of possible reactions and retaliations by racially or religiously motivated groups or individuals. Some recent examples that shook the conscience of people all over the world were the attack on the Mosque in Christchurch in New Zealand on 15 March 2019 in which 51 people were killed and the attacks on three Churches and three luxury hotels in Sri Lanka on the Easter Sunday on 21 April 2019 in which 258 persons lost their lives. The terrorist attacks in Europe and the United States (US) in the recent years also show similar trends. Terrorist groups conspire and perpetrate violent actions. In the debate over causes and patterns of terrorist violence two lines of argument are prominent. One is that there are socio-political roots of alienation which are put in religious and cultural frameworks. The other is to see terrorist violence mainly as a governance problem that is to be tackled by counter force. The US regimes since the time of President George W Bush have followed the latter approach followed by rulers of many countries. That this approach has failed to contain terrorist violence in the world is demonstrated by the occurrence of many such incidents. The first perspective, on the other hand, looks at the sources of alienation of youth or communities which give rise to a situation of such confrontation. This is where the condition of inequality becomes relevant. The rebels may have religious visions to frame the nature of their struggle invoking scriptures and their past traditions. Juergensmeyer has investigated this phenomenon in depth and points out the multiple sources of alienation put by the rebels in the idiom of cosmic struggle (Juergensmeyer 2000). Therefore, socio-political basis of terrorism and in fact all forms of violence needed to be comprehended.

Referring to contemporary sources of horizontal inequality, Frances Stewart who has done extensive work on the subject lists the following: "geographic advantages and disadvantages; migration and its consequences; government policies which are often a reflection of political horizontal inequalities; and environmental degradations" (Stewart 2018, p. 81). To alleviate inequalities of caste, ethnicity, race and gender in modern era, legal and constitutional measures have been taken by many governments all over the world to provide "protective discrimination" to the under-privileged groups through "affirmative action" or "reservation" in employment, education and representative institutions. Sometimes there is a backlash from the sections who feel threatened by such measures. Atrocities against the dalits have continued in India and with greater intensity and revengefulness as documented by many scholars (Teltumbde 2018; Mohanty 2007). As for class inequality or what is conceptualised by some theorists as vertical inequalities, the historical examples of revolutionary movements are many. But only when communist parties provide leadership, organisation and follow appropriate strategy to respond to the concrete environment of contradictions there are some successes for the oppressed people (Mohanty 2010). In other words, the inequality condition does not automatically produce revolutionary movements. And often it has been seen in history that only when class issues are connected with caste, nationality and such other categories of social and political inequality we see a process of political transformation. Studies of Indian communist movement, especially of the Maoist movement in central India have given much evidence on this. This is where the Teltumbde thesis gets additional evidence as the failure of the Maoist movement to maintain its strength vis-à-vis the state is attributed to the lack of integration of class, caste and ethnic issues of conflict. The relationship between the phenomenon of inequality and the outbreak of various forms of violence is complex and needs to be problematised. But at least one thing can be accepted that no solution to address the trend of increasing violence can hold for long unless the problem of inequality is tackled.

Thus in the context of rising inequalities and increasing trends of violence the question that needs to be addressed is why there is a failure on the part of regimes and civil society organisations to contain these trends and redirect the process to move in the direction of peace, freedom and equality. What is more the goal of sustainability, especially ecological sustainability cannot be pursued in an unequal world where profit motive drives the growth process and where the stake of common people in saving the natural resources and promoting greater interdependence between humans and nature is not ensured. The answer may be that it is because the concept of inequality and the measures to reduce inequalities have missed the focus on political power, the present scenario of tensions continues. How to act on multiple fronts to ensure that social, cultural, economic power is shared by altering political domination over those domains is the central task for promoting equality. This task becomes very difficult under the current SDG framework which is steeped in the neoliberal ideology of growth with little regard for its disequalising effects.

SDG Moment vs the samata moment

At the time of India's Independence the idea of equality was a central goal and it was reflected in the Preamble of the Constitution and the Fundamental Rights. There were false assumptions of racial and cultural superiority at the root of Western colonial rule and affirmation of equality of races, cultures and languages was the guiding principle underlying the anti-colonial struggle. Under the Indian Constitution universal adult franchise replaced the system of limited franchise based on property, education and so on provided under the Government of India Act of 1935. This acknowledgement of political equality of citizens irrespective of caste, race, religion, sex or place of birth was a great democratic step for citizens of India. Equality before law under Article 14 and Prohibition of discrimination under articles 15 and 16 further strengthened this effort reaffirming the commitment to the value of equality. But that the task was complicated and involved multidimensional struggles was pointed out by no less a leader than Babasaheb Ambedkar himself. The statement of Ambedkar, the social revolutionary and the Chair of the Drafting Committee of the Indian constitution while introducing the bill to adopt the Constitution of India on 25 November 1949 acquires even greater significance for India and the whole world:

> In politics we will have equality and in social and economic life we will have inequality. In politics we will be recognising the principle of one man one vote and one vote one value. In our social and economic life, we shall, by reason of our social and economic structure, continue to deny the principle of one man one value. How long shall we continue to live this life of contradictions?
>
> *(Ambedkar 1949)*

Having recognised the political equality of all citizens the agenda was to work towards social and economic equality. Therefore the 1950s was evolving as the Samata Moment born out of and as a part of the Swaraj Moment. The transfer of power from the British to Indian rulers had made India Independent though, as Mahatma Gandhi had said as early as 1909 in Hind Swaraj, it was to be more than the "brown man replacing the white man". Equality, dignity, freedom, self-government for each Individual, village, town, group, region and nation was the agenda of swaraj. Indian constitution had already given equal status to all the major languages of India by listing them under Schedule VIII and the list continued to get extended. Minority religions and communities were assured cultural and religious rights under articles 25–27. Women acquired voting rights from the beginning of the republic whereas in Europe and US they had to struggle for long to achieve this right. Lower castes had the same voting right as the upper castes. Voting rights of the poor and the rich had equal value. Several such provisions reflected the new global environment of equality of nations and humans acknowledged in the United Nations Charter in 1945 and the Universal Declaration of Human rights in 1948. But as Ambedkar pointed out this was all in the realm of formal declarations. In reality, in each of these arenas there was substantive inequality and that was to be addressed. Class inequality persisted as a major phenomenon while regimes had settled for alleviating poverty and providing livelihood support to avoid destitution. Caste discrimination, inequality in multiple spheres continued despite some legal initiatives. Even atrocities on dalits were frequent almost in all parts of the country (Mohanty 2007; Teltumbde 2011). Gender injustice, oppression of women and sexual violence remained a major problem and some incidents such as the Nirbhaya rape and murder in 2012 and the "me too" exposures in 2018 dramatically brought attention to the persistence of gender inequality in India. In other words, progressive movement towards *samata* among groups reducing domination in every sphere by producing and distributing material, cultural and political conditions in such a way as to help individuals in every group to achieve their creative potentiality was the logical agenda of realising swaraj in free India. But gradually the *samata* agenda got disrupted first by redefinition of nation-building as maintaining unity, integrity and stability, then by neoliberal economic reforms through globalisation and more recently putting the two together by a new stress on Hindutva-led national security.

That the *samata* agenda was alive and challenging all political forces was visible conspicuously time and again. The rural unrest in India from time to time both in the form of farmers movement led by organisations such as the Shetkari Sanghatana, Bharatiya Kisan Union and Kisan Samanvaya Samiti during the past few decades and the armed struggle by Maoists in central India has brought the rural-urban inequality and especially the sufferings of the agricultural labour and poor farmers in focus. In 1990 after the V P Singh regime implemented the Mandal Commission recommendation (Government of India 1980) for reservation for the OBCs (Other Backward Classes) in services, the agenda of "social justice" came to the centre stage of Indian politics. Thereafter, serious debates over the issue of caste inequality and nature and adequacy of reservation started in a big way in India. The revival of interest in Ambedkar's political thought that began at this moment continued to acquire more and more salience in thinking and policy at all levels. It was at this time that all political parties pledged support for reservation for not only SC and ST, but also for OBC. Some political parties were born with the specific agenda of representing OBCs, (Samajwadi party in Uttar Pradesh and Rashtriya Janata Dal in Bihar) and dalits (Bahujan Samaj Party in Uttar Pradesh). There was even a political party named Samata Party led by George Fernandes in the 1990s which later merged with Janata Dal (United). The reaction to reservation for OBCs produced a counter trend of upper caste youth, especially the economically poor among them demanding reservation for them as well. A conspicuous group at All India Institute of Medical Sciences (AIIMS) in New Delhi called "Youth for Equality" spearheaded this drive. Both Congress and BJP tried the balancing act of defending reservation for the OBCs and responding to the demands of the upper castes. In 2004 the UPA regime formed an Equal Opportunities Commission to consider how to protect the interest of the poor among the upper castes (Government of India 2008). Finally the Modi-led NDA government passed a law just before the 2019 elections giving ten per cent reservation for the economically backward among the "general castes" – read upper castes. That equality was prominently present in the Indian political agenda was also pronounced when the UPA regime appointed the Sachhar Commission (Government of India 2006) to go into the socio-economic conditions of the Muslims whose recommendations had included a permanent Equal Opportunities Commission to monitor and suggest measures to promote equality across communities (Hasan 2009).

Economic reforms under globalisation launched in 1991 seriously upset this agenda. In less than two decades it became clear that globalisation had generated massive "discontent". Scholars such as Joseph Stiglitz, neoliberals themselves and those committed to promotion of capitalism in the world explained how globalisation had produced inequalities and how that could be contained (Stiglitz 2012). It is in this context that the global powers conceived first the Millennium Development Goals (MDGs) in 2000 and the Sustainable Development Goals (SDGs) in 2015.

> I would like to reiterate what I had said recently in my paper on "Inequality from the Perspective of the Global South" in the Oxford Handbook of Global Studies (Mohanty 2018a): No doubt when the UN General Assembly adopted the SDGs (Sustainable Development Goals for 2015–2030) replacing the MDGs it was yet another landmark declaration in contemporary history. The seventeen global goals with 169 targets seemed to have only a marginal interest in reducing inequality. Besides a commitment to the promotion of gender inequality under item five it declared a commitment to work for "reducing income inequality within and among countries" (goal 10). All the goals were certainly laudable and were necessary for human development and they would also impact on reducing inequality (Sachs 2015). But the thrust on the specific welfare programmes did not have a coherent focus on the burning issues of the age, namely the demand for equality and freedom for the struggling people. That income inequality was a part of the problem of cumulative inequalities was hardly appreciated. Reduction of arithmetic inequality or quantitative trends in raising income of the lower strata was only one aspect while many other dimensions of discrimination and oppression remained active. From that viewpoint, the SDGs seem to be meant to service the globalisation agenda of the dominant global elite which also included the elites of the global south. These goals were meant to manage the tensions generated by the expansion of free market economy and aid the economic growth agenda. Hence the SDG moment represented the historic acquiescence with prevailing inequalities in the contemporary world. While the anticolonial era upheld the movement for *swaraj* and *jiefang* and the post-colonial global society stressed the vision of *Samata* and *Ubuntu* the globalisation diffused and redirected historical processes towards a new version of the unequal world. The SDGs embodied that. But forces unleashed by the movements for *swaraj, jiefang, samata and Ubuntu* in the global south had encompassed global north as well. Therefore, struggles for equality were bound to continue even when the global elites sought to dilute the equality movement to promote their agenda of economic growth driven by the free market. Buddha's challenge thrown over 2000 years ago continues to confront twenty first century elites in the global south as well as in the global north who are preoccupied with economic growth and political stability.

Clearly they were meant to address the tensions, inequalities among groups, regions and nations and carry on the globalisation process from one stage to another. In this process, economic reforms to achieve high levels of growth using global capital, globally available modern technology, especially information and communication technology and global market with competing entrepreneurs as the drivers of the growth story became the norm in India and other countries too. The UN sought to promote the SDG vigorously and hence the effort to link the state and NGO initiatives to achieve the specific goal makes it appear as activities of the SDG Moment. But the historical process of humankind from Buddha till today is a struggle for *Samata* and the Indian discourse was constructed around it. In the West the French Revolution and the Bill of Rights in the US affirmed this commitment to "liberty, equality and fraternity" – fraternity to be understood as solidarity in a gender-just framework. Thus the contradiction between the Samata Moment and the SDG Moment is clear and unless the premises of the political economy of globalisation are altered fundamentally to putting equality at its core serious tensions will persist. This contradiction is sharply evident when we critically examine the question of reducing caste inequality through reservation in contemporary India.

Affirmation of the right to equality is a worldwide trend. But is it formal equality in law or substantive equality in status and opportunities or is it more than both? All individuals, social groups irrespective of caste, race and gender and all regions, small or big and even more importantly nations, religions and cultures are asserting their claim to equal dignity in all parts of the world. All modern Constitutions proclaim the right to equality before law for all citizens and all states claim to strive for providing equal opportunities to all in real life. At the same time, as the Oxfam report indicated, inequality within and between countries and regions was growing. Inequality of incomes in countries such as the United States (US), India and China has continued to rise with slight fluctuations occasionally. Discrimination on the basis of caste in India, race in US and South Africa, ethnicity in China and many other countries and gender in all countries persisted even though law prohibited it (UN Human Rights 2016). Sexual violence, caste discrimination in general and atrocities on *dalits* – the former "untouchable" castes in India remained a troubling trend. The contradiction between formal political equality among citizens and actual inequality in society, economy and culture continued to create tensions all over the world (Mohanty 2018a).

The irony is the growing justification of prevailing inequalities by regimes in the name of achieving economic growth or stability of the system. And this was taken as given by the framers of the MDG and the SDG rather than the constitutional goals and the aspirations of people in course of the anti-colonial struggle. This was also the belief that guided the Indian economic reforms launched in 1991. The state provided incentives to globalised capital and the corporate sector by withdrawing support from the working poor (Patnaik 2016), though the authors of reforms thought otherwise (Ahluwalia 2016). China's reforms may have been a success story with vastly improved infrastructure and people's living conditions and making it the world's second largest economy in 2010 but it has landed itself in a "success trap" with increasing inequalities, regional disparities, social alienation and environmental degradation and finding it difficult to tackle it (Mohanty 2018b). India was on the same path and reducing inequality was not a top priority for any regime in the recent decades. There are adequate evidences to prove that inequalities had been sharpened during the past thirty years (Nayyar 2017). The de-emphasis on equality as a goal was clearly discernible in the past two decades with change in the terms of discourse by depoliticising them. Inequality is replaced by "exclusion" and oppressed groups are called "marginalised" and programmes of "inclusion" were meant for them (Mohanty 2015).

The post-Soviet era of globalisation saw a rising wave of capitalist free trade around the world. But soon debates raged around the crisis of capitalism that unfolded in 2008 and the climate change crisis acquiring alarming proportions drew attention to the challenges of the era of Anthropocene (Falk 2017). The cultural and religious crises and terrorist actions acquiring serious dimensions in the recent years gave rise to fresh reflections of causes of alienation of communities and regions leading to multiple cycles of violence and counter-violence (Juergensmeyer 2008). Many economists around the world pointed out the growing dangers of rising trends of inequality (Stiglitz 2012). Piketty's historical analysis based on statistical data on income and wealth taxes showed how concentration of wealth was a persisting trend and was likely to grow in the 21st century (Piketty 2014). Since these developments and debates were underlying the formulation of the Sustainable Development Goals (SDG) of the UN in 2015, we call it the SDG moment. Whereas equality and freedom in a multidimensional framework informed the *swaraj, jiefang, samata* and *Ubuntu* moments, the SDG moment recorded an acquiescence of prevailing inequality with dangerous consequences for global future (Mohanty 2018a).

A political theory of equality

Those who have abandoned the idea that movement towards equality was desirable and possible are of two types. Some claim to be pragmatists who are concerned with attending to immediate problems such as reducing poverty, giving employment, expanding facilities for health and education and so on. Pressed hard they would admit that "all men are not equal" and therefore equality cannot be a goal. We must note they play an important role in society and polity and their role should be recognised. But it has to be pointed to them that any benevolent king or dictator can also do these things and instances are galore. That is not a democratic agenda of promoting equality and freedom for all. The other type which is the dominant stream at present pledges its commitment to equality but insists that priority must be given to produce enough wealth in society only after which it can be shared equitably. These are smart people who run the entire edifice of the globalisation network. They actually behave in manners which give the impression of equality of status among the corporate owner and the ordinary workers. Both these viewpoints carry the single misconception that equality is a mathematical or quantitative sameness or as Aristotle put it "numerical equality". It is about a domination-free condition. The political theory of equality is centred on reducing the uneven power relationship which is the cumulative outcome of multiple sources including social, economic and cultural which in turn leads to more and more inequalities. Inequality is a cumulative condition and cannot be reduced to any one aspect even though some aspects may be more important than others in a specific context. Universal adult franchise, one of the most valued achievements of modern history, for example, provided political equality to all citizens as voters. But economic inequality, caste, gender, religion and racial discrimination severely limited even the "political equality" in real life. Therefore, centrality of power and multidimensionality of inequality have stood out as the crucial elements in the definition of inequality (Mohanty 1983; Mohanty 2018a).

Moving towards equality is not mechanically levelling conditions in a society. A political order that promotes equal respect for every human being and access to life conditions, considered necessary by a civilisation at a historical moment for the fulfilment of the creative potentiality of a human being is the central point in the concept of equality (Mohanty 1998). Each of the elements is broad and can be subjected to a variety of interpretations (Beteille 1977). Respect for a human being involves respecting his/her language, culture and religion, and potential worth. All religions of the world major and local, Eastern and Western, Abrahamic and non-Abrahamic have gone through phases of transformation ultimately affirming equality of humans. Even though they may still not concede equal rights and privileges to the same degree to others as they themselves enjoy. This is not unique to religions. It applies to races, caste groups and many other collectivities as well.

That equality is a multidimensional condition has also seen a complex history and this is what seems to be absent in the list of the 17 SDGs where goal no. 5 is Gender Equality and goal no. 10 is on Reducing Inequality. Even gender inequality is the result of social, economic, cultural and political inequality. The liberal democratic path focused on universal adult franchise and equality before law. But it was realised that disadvantaged sections historically placed lower in social structures because of inherited conditions needed opportunities to make up for their disadvantages. Hence came the concept, "equality of opportunity". Public school system, public health system and equal wages for equal work irrespective of caste, class and religion marked a great advance in this process. But, in India, it was realised that "equality of opportunity" operating in an unequal social order still favoured the privileged, better-off, powerful sections and unless special support was accorded to the more disadvantaged, inequality will persist. Hence the need was felt for "reservation" in countries such as India (Galanter 1984; Sheth 2004). The reservation experience in India, however, brings out major limitations in pursuing the samata agenda in the neoliberal era.

Reservation: a token safeguard, a necessary condition or an alibi of the ruling forces?

Anand Teltumbde presents a powerful critique of the way reservation had been conceptualised and implemented in India. While unequivocally condemning the detractors of reservation he calls it a "token safeguard" for the dalits against centuries of oppression. He says:

> It has to be kept in mind that reservations are not reparations that the dalits are asking for, for wrongs done to them over millennia, but a token safeguard extended to the victims of an ongoing racism. . . . Reservations are simply a mechanism to ensure dalit participation, not a measure of justice.
> (Teltumbde 2018, p. 59)

The most important point he makes assessing the reservation experience in India is that rather than "moving in the direction of 'Annihilation of Caste'", which was the goal set by Ambedkar, this policy in effect has prolonged the life and dynamics of the institution of caste as a hierarchical order. In the services a small elite from the SC and ST had come up who identify more with the upper caste than with the dalits. In the major political parties they play the role of the stooges of the upper caste leaders or their dependable seconds even though they get statutorily elected from the reserved seats. Dalit political parties like the BSP and the Republican Party struggled for political space in their respective regions, but did not pose enough of a challenge to the national parties. Reservation does not extend to the private sector and in the neoliberal economy public employment continued to shrink in quantity and criticality. As privatisation spreads to more and more sectors the opportunities for employment for the dalits continue to decline. Teltumbde and some others have felt that the Poona Pact of 1932 in which Ambedkar gave up his demand for separate electorate for the dalits and accepted Gandhi's formula that went into the Indian Constitution and operates even today was a mistake. In my view a separate electorate also would have been inadequate to achieve a momentum for "annihilation of caste". Electoral democracy which put majoritarianism in command and the economic policies which unfolded in the recent decades would still have kept the caste hierarchy in place with some minor modification. Caste acquired modern electoral character and became a functional tool for parties (Kothari 1973).

As I have analysed in a recent paper in the Oxford Handbook of Global Studies (Mohanty 2018a), the Indian experiment in reservation has exposed some important dimensions of the prevailing approaches to promoting equality. The liberal democratic approach values equality of opportunity and insists on the principle of fair competition for various positions. Therefore, the insistence on the principle of merit is a common principle. This is where two lines of action emerge. One is to take "affirmative action" by giving support for the weaker sections as is the case in US. But in India that is considered inadequate and hence the need for the second, namely reservation. The elites invariably claimed that by supporting affirmative action and reservation they had done enough to promote equality. In reality however, this had become an alibi for not taking some fundamental measures to address longstanding inequalities of caste, race and gender. Because such inequalities had a strong basis in economy and culture, it needed a comprehensive programme of action. In the cultural realm, attitudes towards *dalits* and *adivasis* (tribal people) have remained prejudiced. The idea that all humans irrespective of identities deserved equal respect was still not imparted either in early education or in early childhood socialisation in family and society. Debates on continuing cultural degradation and humiliation of the oppressed groups, especially the *dalits* in India signify the serious magnitude of this phenomenon (Ilaiah 2009; Guru 2011; Mohanty 2018a). Thus, the perspective of reservation and affirmative action has been grossly inadequate in reducing inequality. What was needed was a perspective of "structural affirmation" involving economic, cultural and political measures that addressed the roots of longstanding inequalities.

Politics of structural affirmation

Affirmative steps to transform the unequal structures in economic, social, cultural spheres accompanied by adequate representation in decision-making institutions at every level constitute politics of structural affirmation. Property relations, especially in land, forest, water and industry continue to be dominated by upper caste, upper class dominant forces. But unless these relations change along with the cultural practices and attitudes, structural affirmation would be incomplete. This is where Anand Teltumbde is right when he says, "Contrary to the prevailing understanding of both dalit and the left movements, I see both caste and class intertwined. Without annihilation of caste there can be no revolution in India, and at the same time, without a revolution there can be no annihilation of caste" (Teltumbde 2018, p. 19). I would go a step further to say that beyond class and caste there are other significant contradictions including gender, religion, ethnicity and aspects of culture, knowledge and environment where inequalities, injustices, oppression pervade. The challenge is to weave these contradictions together and confront the neoliberal state and global capital. Only then politics of structural affirmation can pursue samata agenda beyond the SDG Moment.

References

Ahluwalia, Montek S. 2016. "The 1991 Reforms: How Home-grown were they?" *Economic and Political Weekly*, 51(29): 39–46.

Alvaredo, F., Chancel, L., Piketty, T., Saez, E., and Zucman, Gabriel. 2017. *The World Inequality Report 2018,* World Inequality Lab. Available at: https://wir2018.wid.world/files/download/wir2018-full-report-english.pdf

Ambedkar, B.R. 1949. "Speech Moving the Resolution for Adoption of the Constitution of India." Available at: www.parliament ofindia.nic.in/ls/debatesvol11p11.htm [Accessed October 5, 2017].

Beteille, Andre. 1977. *Inequality Among Men*. London: Basil Blackwell.

Centre for Equity Studies. 2018. *India Exclusion Report 2017–18*. New Delhi: Yoda Press.

CPDR. n.d. *How Secular Is the Indian State – Theme Paper*. Mumbai: Committee for Protection of Democratic Rights. Available at: www.unipune.ac.in/snc/cssh/HumanRights/03%20STATE%20AND%20MINORITIES/19.pdf [Accessed June 19, 2019].

———. 2017a. *Fact Finding Team's Report on Garib Nagar (Bandra East) Fire and Demolitions*. Mumbai: Committee for Protection of Democratic Rights. Available at: https://countercurrents.org/wp-content/uploads/2017/05/demolitions-Ambedkar-Nagar.pdf [Accessed June 19, 2019].

———. 2017b. *Fact Finding Team's Report on Ambedkar Nagar Demolition*. Mumbai: Committee for Protection of Democratic Rights. Available at: https://countercurrents.org/wp-content/uploads/2017/11/Garib-nagar-fact-finding-CPDR.pdf [Accessed June 19, 2019].

Falk, Richard. 2017. "The World Ahead: Entering the Anthropocene?" In Falk, Richard, Manoranjan Mohanty, and Victor Faessel (eds.). *Exploring Emergent Global Thresholds: Towards 2030*, pp. 19–47. New Delhi: Orient Black Swan.

Galanter, Marc. 1984. *Competing Equalities: Law and the Backward Classes in India*. Berkeley, Ca: University of California Press.

Government of India. 1980. *Report of the Backward Classes Commission*. New Delhi: National Commission for Backward Classes.

———. 2006. *Social, Economic and Educational Status of the Muslim Community of India: A Report*. New Delhi: Prime Minister's High Level Committee, Cabinet Secretariat.

———. 2008. *Equal Opportunity Commission: What, Why and How?* New Delhi: Ministry of Minority Affairs.

Guru, Gopal. (ed.). 2011. *Humiliation: Claims and Context*. New Delhi: Oxford University Press.

Hasan, Zoya. 2009. *Politics of Inclusion: Caste, Minorities and Affirmative Action*. New Delhi: Oxford University Press.

Ilaiah, Kancha. 2009. *Post-Hindu India*. New Delhi: Sage.

Juergensmeyer, Mark. 2000. *Terror in the Mind of God: The Global Rise of Religious Violence*. Berkeley: University of California Press.

———. 2008. *Global Rebellion: Religious Challenges to the Secular State, from Christian Militias to al Qaeda*. Berkeley: University of California Press.

Kothari, Rajni. (ed.). 1973. *Caste in Indian Politics*. Hyderabad: Orient Longman.

Mohanty, Manoranjan. 1983. "Towards a Political Theory of Inequality." In Beteille, Andre (ed.). *Equality and Inequality*. New Delhi: Oxford University Press.

———. 1998. "Social Movements in Creative Society." In Mohanty, Manoranjan and Mukherji, Partha Nath, and Olle Tornquist (eds.). *People's Rights: Social Movements and the State in the Third World*. New Delhi: Sage.

———. (ed.). 2004. *Class, Caste, Gender: Readings in Indian Politics (Readings in Indian Government and Politics Series)*. New Delhi: Sage.

———. 2007. "Kilvenmani, Karamchedu to Khairlanji: Why Atrocities Against Dalits Persist." *Paper at World Safety Congress at Mareda, Mexico*. Available at: www.boellindia.org/download-en/mohanty [Accessed October 22, 2018].

———. (ed.). 2010. *The Social Development Report 2010: The Land Question and the Marginalised*. New Delhi: Oxford University Press.

———. 2015. "Reconceptualising Social Development." In Roy, AshNarain and Mathew, George (eds.). *Development, Decentralisation and Democracy*. New Delhi: Orient Blakswan.

———. 2018a. "Inequality from the Perspective of the Global South." In Juergensmeyer, Mark, Sassen, Saskia, Steger, Manfred B., and Victor Faessel (eds.). *The Oxford Handbook of Global Studies*. New York: Oxford University Press.

———. 2018b. *China's Transformation: The Success Story and the Success Trap*. New Delhi: Sage.

Nayyar, Deepak. 2017. *Employment, Growth and Development: Essays on a Changing World Economy*. London: Routledge.

Oxfam India. 2019. *Public Good or Private Wealth? Oxfam Inequality Report: The India Story*. New Delhi: Oxfam India. Available at: www.oxfamindia.org/sites/default/files/Davos-India_Supplement.pdf [Accessed June 19, 2019].

Oxfam International. 2019. *Public Good or Private Wealth*. Oxford: Oxfam International.

Patnaik, Prabhat. 2016. "Capitalism and its Current Crisis." *Monthly Review*, 67(8): 1–13.

Piketty, Thomas. 2014. *Capital in the Twenty First Century*. London: The Belknap Press of Harvard University Press.

Sachs, Jeffrey D. 2015. *The Age of Sustainable Development*. New York: Columbia University Press.

Sheth, D.L. 2004. "Reservation Policy Revisited." In Mohanty, Manoranjan (ed.). *Class, Caste, Gender: Readings in Indian Politics (Readings in Indian Government and Politics Series)*. New Delhi: Sage.

Singh, Paramjeet and Chauhan, Preeti. 2012. *How Many Protests will it Take? The Bhagana Dalits in Delhi*. New Delhi: Peoples Union for Democratic Rights. Available at: www.pudr.org/how-many-protests-will-it-take-bhagana-dalits-delhi, [Accessed June 19, 2019].

Stewart, Frances. 2018. "Inequality and Conflict: Global Drivers and Interventions." In Ghosh Dastidar, Ananya et al. (eds.). *Economic Theory and Policy amidst Global Discontent*. London: Routledge: 78–97.

Stiglitz, Joseph. 2012. *The Price Inequality*. London: Allen Lane.

Tandon, Deepika and Basu, Moushumi. 2016a. *Manual Scavenging must End*. New Delhi: Peoples Union for Democratic Rights. Available at: www.pudr.org/manual-scavenging-must-end [Accessed June 19, 2019].

———. 2016b. *Holy Cow, Unholy Carcass and Dalits*. New Delhi: Peoples Union for Democratic Rights. Available at: www.pudr.org/holy-cow-unholy-carcass-and-dalits [Accessed June 19, 2019].

Teltumbde, Anand. 2011. *The Persistence of Caste: The Khairlanji Murders & India's Hidden Apartheid*. New Delhi: Navayana.

———. 2018. *Republic of Caste: Thinking Equality in the Time of Neoliberal Hindutva*. New Delhi: Navayana.

United Nations Human Rights. 2016. *Human Rights*. Geneva: United Nations Human Rights Office of the High Commissioner.

PART VII
Conclusion

16
MAKING INDIA'S DEVELOPMENT INCLUSIVE
Centrality of education and health

Muchkund Dubey

Towards inclusive development

Inclusion in the process of development has two broad dimensions, economic and social. These are mutually reinforcing. In its economic dimension, inclusive development is achieved mainly by means of reducing income poverty. Reduction in income poverty no doubt makes growth more inclusive than will be the case otherwise, but inclusive growth in the real sense of the term must be accompanied by lower income inequality. This can be brought about by a substantially larger increase in the income of the lower income groups as compared to the increase in the income of the population in general.

Inclusive development is a somewhat broader concept than inclusive growth. The former includes several other dimensions of wellbeing than that brought about by income growth. Development refers to changes in social, economic and production structures, improvements in social indicators like education and health, and improvements in the living conditions of the poor and the marginalised. In the Indian situation, the last mentioned category refers mainly to the Scheduled Castes, Scheduled Tribes, Other Backward Classes, Minorities and Women.

There are economists who raise the question: "Why Inclusive Growth? Those who raise this question believe that a measure of inequality is necessary for accelerating growth as it increases the rate of savings. This is because the higher income groups have greater propensity to save whereas the lower income groups have higher propensity to consume because of the bulk of the addition to national income by the lower income group is in the form of wages which is used for consuming goods and services and not producing them. Joseph Stiglitz (2016) has contested this argument mainly on two grounds. Firstly, an increase in savings is unlikely to make much difference to the present sluggish world economy. For, there is a global savings glut. Secondly, there are better ways of encouraging savings than by perpetuating or increasing inequality. The most effective way is progressive taxation on the incomes and the wealth of the rich. Stiglitz (2016) quoting an IMF Research paper points out that inequality is associated with economic instability as witnessed in the form of global economic crises of different intensity occurring from time to time in the past four decades (Berg and Ostry, 2011). He also refers to an OECD study which found that income inequality had negative effect on medium term growth (Cingano, 2014). According to this study, in countries like the United Sates, the United Kingdom and Italy, overall economic growth would have been 6 to 9 percentage points higher in the past two decades, had there been no increase in inequality in these countries. Inequality hampers economic growth mainly by way of leading to weak aggregate demand. Besides, inequality of outcomes is associated with inequalities of opportunities. Stiglitz also argues that societies with greater inequality are less likely to make public investments in infrastructure, health, education and technology, which enhance productivity. Empirical studies show that public investments in countries with higher inequality have been steadily going down (Stiglitz 2016).

Economic growth and inclusive social order

Making a transition from economic inclusion to social inclusion, an inclusive social order can be understood better in terms of what it is not than what it is. The concept of social exclusion is a recent one starting from the decade of the 70s of the last century. The concept was first propounded by European social scientists. The authorship of the term is attributed to the French scholar Rene Lenoir (1974) who spoke of the excluded in the French society. According to him, one-tenth of the total population of France were "excluded" who consisted of:

> mentally and physically handicapped; suicidal people; aged and invalids; abused children; substance users; single parents; multi-problem households; marginal and asocial persons; and other social misfits.

This characterisation of the "excluded" was vastly expanded by authors who wrote on the subject later. Writing in 1995, Hillary Silver stated:

> People may be excluded from a livelihood; secure permanent employment; property; credit or land; housing; minimal or prevailing consumption levels; education, skills and cultural capital; the welfare state; citizenship and legal equality; democratic participation; public goods; the nation or the dominant race; family and sociability; respect, fulfilment and understanding.

In the United States, the term "underclass" was used in place of "socially excluded". "Underclass" carried the implication that those included in this category were themselves responsible for their plight. In contrast, the socially excluded, as understood by the Europeans, were generally the exploited by the society or the victims of injustice.

An aspect of social inclusion which has acquired salience and general acceptability recently is that it is a relative concept. David Byrne in his book "Social Exclusion", points out: "Exclusion is something that is done by some people to other people". It is "about the character of the social system and about the dynamic development of social structure. At the same time, it has implications for social agency" (Byrne 2000). Another defining feature of social inclusion is its multi-dimensional character, embracing inclusion in social, economic and political spheres. Elaborating this aspect, David Byrne refers to the process of participation in decision-making, access to employment and material resources, and integration into common cultural processes, as some of the factors constituting the multi-dimensional process of inclusion.

Amartya Sen has made his own contribution to the idea of social exclusion in the broad framework of his concept of development. He has tried to establish a conceptual connection between this idea and well established notions in the literature on poverty and deprivation. In his paper, Social Exclusion, Sen analyses the process mainly in terms of deprivation. In this connection, he makes a distinction between what he calls "constitutive" and "instrumental" social exclusion (Sen 2000). An example of constitutive social exclusion is not being able to take part in the life of the community which directly impoverishes a person's life. Here, he quotes from Adam Smith who saw deprivation involved in not "being able to appear in public without shame". On the other hand, instrumental social exclusion is itself not a form of deprivation, but can lead to deprivation. The example cited by Sen of this category of social exclusion, is not having access to the credit market. Sen regards landlessness as an example of both constitutive and instrumental social exclusion. Landlessness itself carries a social stigma, in addition to being a source of multipurpose deprivations like livelihood, income etc.

It is difficult to establish a hierarchy among various forms of exclusions, in terms of what is more degrading or debilitating and what is less so. However, in the Indian context, it can be said safely that the Hindu caste system is one of the worst forms of social exclusion because it acts in a vicious multi-prong way and is distinctly designed to perpetuate exclusion. It was, therefore, not surprising that Dr B. R. Ambedkar in his celebrated monograph, "Annihilation of the Caste" wrote that what was needed was to do away with the Hindu caste system altogether; any attempt to reform it would be infructuous (Ambedkar 1936).

At the global macro level, market exclusion has acquired new salience in recent years, particularly after the world wide pursuit of the policy of liberalisation and globalisation. Because of its imperfections, the market in its operation, excludes a whole mass, cutting across castes, religions, class and gender. Moreover, unless properly moderated, the market generally excludes those who are in the periphery and makes the plight of those already excluded, more miserable than before. Therefore, in the past, states all over the world, including India, regarded it their duty to provide social and economic protection to the poor and those bypassed in the development process. Economic policies were devised to give preferential treatment and fiscal and financial compensation to socially disadvantaged groups and poor households. Social measures were also adopted to improve the access of the socially disadvantaged to social services like health and nutrition.

Indian constitution and vision of an inclusive society

The vision of the leaders of India's independent movement of an inclusive society for the country was best reflected in the Constitution of India. In the Preamble to the Constitution, "We, the people of India", resolve to secure for all the citizens of the country, social, economic and political justice and equality of status and opportunity, and fraternity assuring the dignity of an individual. Article 14 of the Constitution covers non-discrimination in the broadest sense of the term. It provides that "the State shall not deny to any person equality before law or the equal protection of law". Article 15 specifically prohibits discrimination on grounds of religion, race, caste, sex and place of birth. At the same time, it leaves scope for affirmative action by stating that nothing in this Article, "shall prevent the state from making any special provision for women and children" or for "the advancement of any socially and educationally backward classes of citizens". Article 16 provides for equality of opportunity in matters of public employment. It specifically prohibits discrimination on the grounds of religion, race, caste, sex, place of birth, with respect to any employment to office under the state. This article also leaves scope for affirmative action in favour of the backward class of citizens. Article 17 abolishes untouchability and its practice in any form. Article 21 on Right to Life has in recent years been extended through creative judicial interpretations to include right to quality education, right to livelihood and right to food. Article 23 prohibits forced labour. Article 24 prohibits the employment of children to work in a factory or mine or engage in any other hazardous activity.

The Articles are in the Chapter on Fundamental Rights and hence justiciable. On the other hand, the Chapter that follows and is titled "Directive Principles of State Policy" contains provisions which are not justiciable but "are fundamental in the governance of the country". In this Chapter, the Constitution, among others, lays down that state shall ensure social justice and social inclusion, equal pay for equal work for both men and women; secure right to work and provide public assistance in cases of public unemployment, old age sickness and disability; to secure to all workers a living wages and conditions of work ensuring decent standard of living and provide within a period of 10 years after the commencement of the Constitution, free and compulsory education for all the children up to the age of 14 years.

The Government has adopted a series of measures to give effect to those provisions of the Constitution. These relate to elimination of specific types of discrimination and specific forms of exploitation, affirmative action including reservation in posts in government services and in public educational institutions and specific measures for the upliftment and empowerment of the weaker sections of the society, particularly the Scheduled Castes, Scheduled Tribes and Other Backward Classes. There has been a Special Component Plan for Scheduled Castes and Tribal Sub-Plan in the Five Year Plans of the later vintage. Special Finance and Development Corporations were set up for these and other under privileged sections of the population. However, the Special Component Plans and Sub-Plans have suffered from inadequacy of resources and poor implementation. The financial institutions set up for the benefit of the marginalised sections of the population have persistently suffered from paucity of resources.

Advent of liberalisation and increasing inequality

There is a vast amount of literature providing evidence that economic growth witnessed in large tracts of developing countries has been accompanied by increasing income disparities which is mainly due to vastly unequal access to resources and basic services across income strata. It was, therefore, not surprising that from the beginning of the present millennium, inclusive development became the focus of the development strategy adopted at the national level and advocated at the international level. In India, this phase started with the 11th Five Year Plan (2007–12), the central vision of which was to realise the objective of inclusive growth which was defined in the plan document as "a process that yields broad-based benefits and ensures equality of opportunity for all" (Government of India 2008). Adopting a similar approach, UNDP characterised inclusive growth as an outcome that should be "measured by equity of access and contribution to the benefits of economic growth" (UNDP 2011). A Report of the Eminent Persons Group set up by the President of the Asians Development Bank in 2006 recognised that "while markets are central to generating growth, an inclusive growth strategy incorporates economic policies and government programmes that address 'market failures', and permits all segments of the society to participate more fully in the new opportunities" (ADB 2007).

There are several indications providing evidence of increasing income disparities in India. The first and the most obvious manifestation has been the high incidence of poverty. Earlier estimates of poverty had shown that the share of the country's population below the poverty line (approximately Rs.12 per day per capita consumption at 2004–5 prices) was decreasing during the period of high growth. According to an estimate made by the Planning Commission in 2009, the share of the country's population below the poverty line came down from almost 36 per cent in 1993–94 to 26.75 per cent in 2004–05. The poverty ratio for the rural area was estimated to be 28.3 per cent while for the urban area the corresponding figure was 27.54 per cent. However, a new set of estimates provided by an expert group headed by Suresh Tendulkar showed that the problem of poverty was considerably greater than what the earlier estimates had indicated. According to the Tendulkar Committee, more than 41.8 per cent of the country's rural population was below the poverty line in 2004–5; for the country as a whole, the poverty ratio was 37 per cent (Government of India 2010, p. 24). The National Commission for Enterprises in the Unorganised Sector estimated that the share of country's population stuck below an average expenditure of Rs.20 per day per capita, a group that the Commission had termed as "Poor and Vulnerable" was 77 per cent (NCEUS 2009).

The increase in income disparities in India is also reflected in the lower growth rate of employment in the country. Estimates show that the annual rate of employment growth declined from 2.03 per cent in 1983 to1.85 per cent during 1993–94 to 2004–5. Further, the net growth of employment in the five year period from 1999–2000 to 2004–5 took place largely in the informal sector which accounted for 93 per cent of the total industrial sector. This suggests an increase in the informalisation of the workforce resulting in an increase in its vulnerabilities. Informal sector enterprises faced formidable difficulties for lack of credit, marketing skills, incentives and infusion of technology.

There is an unmistakeable trend of an increase in inequality in India since the introduction in the early 1990s, of the policy of full-fledged liberalisation. The performance of the Indian economy since the early 1940s in terms of its success or otherwise in reducing inequality is very well summed up in a paper prepared by Lucas Chancel and Thomas Piketty (July 2017). According to them: (a) There was a marked decrease in inequality in the early 1940s; (b) There was even a stronger reduction in inequality during the period 1950–1980. This was mainly because of strong government control of the economy, policy of nationalisation, strong market regulations and high progressive taxation; and (c) There was a significant increase in inequality from the mid-1980s after the introduction of the policy of liberalisation. As brought out in this chapter, the share of national income accruing to the top 1 per cent of income earners in India is today at the highest level since the creation of the system of Indian Income Tax in 1922. The top one per cent of the population accounted for 21 per cent of the national income in the 1930s, 6 per cent in the early 1980s, but 22 per cent today. During the 1980–2014 period, the top 0.1 per cent of the income earners captured a higher share (12 per cent) of the total income growth than the bottom 15 per cent (11 per cent).

The share of the income accruing to the top one per cent of the income earners shrank substantially from the mid-1950s to mid-1980s – from 13 per cent of the total income to less than 5 per cent. This trend was reversed after the mid-1980s, when pro-business and market deregulation policies were introduced. The bottom 15 per cent of the income earners grew at a substantially lower rate than the average growth (Ibid.).

The wealth of the richest Indians reported in the Forbes India Rich List, amounted to less than two per cent of national income in the 1990s, but reached 10 per cent in 2015. The peak was 27 per cent just before the 2008–09 financial crises. India today has the fourth largest number of dollar billionaires in the world. Thus the high growth in the Indian economy since the advent of liberalisation resulted in an unequal and lopsided impact on the standard of living of the people. Benefits accrued disproportionately to those at the higher income level, mostly with higher education and skill levels. Similarly benefits flowed to those in the organised and formal sectors and service industry, followed by manufacturing.

Regarding inter-state disparity, some state governments succeeded in reducing substantially the size of their population below the poverty line. States with better initial conditions – such as a relatively higher-level modern industrial base, greater degree of urbanisation, higher educational achievements and a higher inflow of remittances from abroad – benefitted more from the economic growth. Reductions in poverty took place in as many as 12 states ranging from a 10 percentage point reduction in Gujarat, Rajasthan, Andhra Pradesh, Himachal Pradesh and West Bengal to as high as 18 percentage reduction in Uttarakhand. According to a forecast, eight high performing states will account for 52 per cent of India's incremental GDP growth from 2012 to 2025. However, this reduction in poverty was the fall out of not only the high rate of growth but also of the initiatives taken by some of these states for adopting pro-poor programmes. The most outstanding case of success in this category was that of Kerala which already had headlong start with some of its flagship pro-poor programmes such as early introduction of Public Distribution System (PDS), establishment of a Welfare Fund for the Unorganised Workers and strengthening of the emerging organisations of women from the poor and vulnerable classes. At the same time, the states with the highest instance of poverty mainly Bihar, Chhattisgarh, Madhya Pradesh, Uttar Pradesh, Jharkhand and Assam, witnessed slower reductions in poverty in the post-liberalisation period. While in 1993–94, 41 per cent of India's poor lived in these poorer states, this proportion increased to 57 per cent in 2011–12 (Kannan 2012; Radhakrishna 2014).

Empirical studies indicate that initial inequality matter a great deal when it comes to poverty reduction. Decline in poverty tends to be less for the poor sections of the community in a situation where initial inequality is high. Inequalities caused by social exclusion and constraints on human development particularly limit the prospect of poverty reduction among the excluded group. Therefore, non-discriminatory participation in the growth process and the policies specifically designed to reduce initial disadvantage are a necessary pre-condition for inclusive growth. In the hierarchical structure of Indian population there are certain groups that lag behind on a range of development outcomes. Any strategy for inclusive development must ensure disproportionate gains from development for the excluded groups. Throat and Dubey (2012) in their study on progress in the reduction of poverty and inequality in the post-liberalisation period in India have brought out that rural poverty declined during 1993–2010 by two per cent annually and during 2005–10 by four per cent annually. However, during the latter five year period, Scheduled Caste communities did not gain as much as the other social categories.

Hanumantha Rao (2009) makes the same point when he states that populations belonging to the socially and economically disadvantaged sections like Scheduled Castes, Scheduled Tribes, OBCs, women and children, benefited the least from the growth and rising prosperity in the post-liberalisation period. There was growing inequality in the phase of higher growth. Rural-urban disparity, regional divide and the rich-poor divide became glaring. Those who took advantage of the prosperity brought about by liberalisation were generally adequately endowed with infrastructure resources, skill, power and influence. They were also concentrated in states and regions that were well developed. The government failed to counter the initial adverse conditions of the disadvantaged by according greater priority to public investments in infrastructure, agriculture and social sector because of their misplaced faith in the trickle-down theory and in the private sector to fill the public space. Economic polarisation was the logical corollary of such a policy.

In China, on the other hand, there was rapid reduction in poverty as a result of high growth following the economic reforms starting from 1976. Poverty rate in China, set at $1 per day measured in purchasing power parity, declined from 63 per cent of the population in 1981 to 10 per cent in 2004. About 500 million people climbed out of poverty during this period (Ravallion and Chen 2007). This was mainly because the initial condition had been taken care of during the pre-reform period. The process of land reform was completed along with the completion of the Communist revolution. There was massive investment in infrastructure, at least in some regions even before the economic reforms started. Basic education and health services had also been universalised soon after the Communist Revolution.

Economic growth and human development

During the last four years, we have been subjected to a great deal of self-praise about India being the fastest growing country in the world, even overtaking China in the process. This is factually incorrect as there are countries growing faster than India such as Ethiopia (8.30 per cent in 2017), Uzbekistan (7.60 per cent in 2017) and in our neighbourhood Nepal (7.50 per cent in the same year) (Gray 2017). As per World Bank data, Ivory Coast and Ethiopia grew by rates higher than that of India every year during the five year period 2012–16. But more importantly, in order to get an accurate picture of a country's socio-economic situation, the reference should not be the rate of growth, but success in poverty reduction, bridging the economic gap between the rich and the poor, achieving progress in human development and ameliorating the living conditions of the common people. On the human development front, China's index valued at 0.66, which was 28 percentages point higher than that of India (2012 figure). In most dimensions of human development and in terms of reductions in human deprivations, India is far behind not only China but also smaller countries like Vietnam, Sri Lanka and Bangladesh.

UNDP's Human Development Report, 2010, indicated that on most health and education indicators, India's position was worse than that of China and even a small developing country like Sri Lanka. Infant mortality rate in India, at 50, was three times more than that in China and four times more than that in Sri Lanka. Maternal Mortality Rate (MMR), at 450, was ten times more than that in China and Sri Lanka (UNDP 2010). Life expectancy in India has indeed improved and stood at 65 years in 2010 but it was still ten years less than that in China and Sri Lanka. Mean years of schooling of adults in India was 4.4 years, which was half that of China and Sri Lanka. Bangladesh which has less than half of India's per capita income, reported better outcome in terms of education, higher life expectancy at birth, higher mean year of schooling and lower gender inequality than India (Sen 2011). India is ranked at 154 out of 195 countries, in terms of access to health care. India has the largest number of malnourished children, the largest number of children out of school and the largest number of child labour in the world.

Data collected for National Family Health Survey (NFHS)-3 (2005–06) and Household Survey of Reproductive Health in 2002–05 bring out that as high as 45 per cent of children under three years of age in India suffered from malnutrition, 79 per cent of children in the age group 6 to 35 months suffered from anaemia, 56 per cent of children were not fully immunised and 79 per cent of them did not receive Vitamin-A dose in the last six months of the survey (IIPS and Macro International 2007). These surveys further indicate that 35 per cent of ever-married women suffered from chronic energy deficiency, 58 per cent from anaemia and 59 per cent deliveries were not in institutions providing such services. According to a UNICEF Report, India contributed a quarter of global maternal deaths (UNICEF 2013).

In India, inclusive development is needed not only for imparting speed and sustainability to growth, not only for alleviating a substantial part of the current distress and deprivation but also for the very survival of the nation with all its diversity and plurality. For, the centrality of inclusion grows out of the need to weld a diverse people into a modern nation and to overcome the deeply entrenched and long established injustices and hierarchies in Indian society.

India's most defining characteristic has been diversity. An explicit recognition of this fact is crucial for understanding its social and economic dynamics. Inclusion is central to the political and economic process in a richly diverse country that India is. Inclusion is indispensable for the nation building project, for holding the country together and preserving its democratic institutions.

In his celebrated speech in the Constituent Assembly delivered while introducing the final version of the draft Constitution of India, Dr B.R. Ambedkar, the architect of the Indian Constitution, had prophesied:

> On the 26th of January 1950, we are going to enter into a life of contradictions. In politics, we will have equality and in social and economic life we will have inequality. In politics, we will be recognizing the principle of one man one vote and one vote one value. In our social and economic life, we shall, by reasons of our social and economic structure, continue to deny the principle of one man one value. How long shall we continue to live this life of contradictions? How long shall we continue to deny equality in our social and economic life? If we continue to deny it for long, we shall do so only by putting our political democracy in peril. We must remove this contradiction at the earliest possible moment or else those who suffer from inequality, will blow up the structure of political democracy which this Assembly has so laboriously built up.
>
> *(Ambedkar 1949)*

Centrality of education and health

Social sectors play a crucial role not only in promoting development but also making it inclusive and sustainable. Among these, education and health take the pride of place. These two sectors are the foundations on which an inclusive society can be built in India. Centrality of education in the development process has been underlined by eminent economists at successive stages in the growth of development theory and practice. Here we quote from three Nobel Laureates in Economic Science. The 1979 Nobel Prize Winner Sir Arthur Lewis pointed out: "Education is not invented in order to enable men to produce more goods and services. The purpose of education is to enable them to understand better the world in which they live so that they can more fully expand their potential capacity" (Lewis 1961). Jan Tinbergen who got the Nobel Prize in 1969 regarded human capital as a key instrument for reducing inequality in the process of development (Tinbergen 1975). Theodore Schultz, who got the Nobel Prize jointly with Arthur Lewis, pioneered the Human Capital Theory (Schultz 1961). He demonstrated the critical contributions that investment in education and health make to development. According to Schultz, while education contributes to the augmentation of production of goods and services and enhancement of individual incomes, health ensures that the educated people keep on producing. It also helps in preserving their size and imparting sustainability to their contribution.

In India, education and health constitute the biggest constraints to development in general and inclusive development in particular. Most of the development schemes that the Government has launched in recent years with great fanfare after coming to power in 2014 are unlikely to succeed in the prevailing conditions of health and education in the country. For example, an uneducated or poorly educated India cannot be 'Skilled India'. Skills of the required quality can be acquired only on the foundation of good quality basic education. For instance, we cannot train nurses unless the candidates to be trained have acquired thorough school education, minimum necessary knowledge of chemistry, physiology and biology.

According to the data obtained from the National Skill Development Corporation (NSDC), just half of the candidates landed a job after getting training under Skill India Mission. For example, in 2016–17, out of 800,145 candidates trained, just 48.4 per cent (387,762) got jobs (Surabhi and Nigam 2018). This is mainly because most of those who got certificates of training did not have the knowledge of basic sciences which are acquired through school education. Similarly, we cannot achieve the goal of "Clean India" by merely mounting well-advertised cleanliness drives from time to time. Cleanliness is a habit cultivated in the childhood, first and foremost at home and the next in schools where lessons on cleanliness should be included as an integral part in the syllabus.

The Government is in the process of developing and promulgating a new national industrial policy. However, such a policy is unlikely to yield the desired results unless it is underpinned by good quality education and health. For, the success of an industrial policy is critically dependent upon the availability of educated and healthy labour force. The same fate awaits, if the governments tries to launch an employment policy without ensuring that persons for whom employment is to be provided, are educated and healthy.

The Government has also been laying a great deal of emphasis on "Ease-of doing-business" and is taking credit for putting India higher up in the global index of "ease-of-doing business". The Government has also claimed that the recent increase in the inflow of private foreign capital which according to the latest figure is a little above $60 billion US per annum, is due to the success of its policy of improving "ease-of-doing-business". In this connection, it should, first, be recognised that an addition of $60 billion US per annum by way of inflow of foreign capital, cannot make any significant contribution to improving the currently declining investment ratio. The investment ratio came down from 38.6 per cent in 2007–08 to 30.8 per cent in 2011–12 and the trend of decline has continued since then. Moreover, beyond a limit which cannot be set too high, the inflow of private foreign capital into a country depends critically on the availability of educated labour force.

Progress in education and health in India has been very poor both in absolute terms and relative to that achieved by other newly independent countries and emerging economies. In the discussion during the pre-independent period on policy measures for India's development, education was regarded as a pre-requisite for nation building and stable economic growth. As early as in the early 1920s, the great Indian engineer Visvesvaraya, in his book *Reconstructing India*, published in 1920, gave primacy to education in his vision of reconstructing India. According to him, education provided the foundation for inclusion in the political and economic spheres (Visvesvaraya 1920). Moreover, it was a spur to growth, a pre-requisite for development and indispensable means of nation building. The leaders of our independence movement particularly, Mahatma Gandhi and Jawaharlal Nehru also laid emphasis on education as an important means for laying the foundations for India's development and establishing an inclusive society. There was, thus, continuity in the thinking of the early planners of India's development on the importance of education. However, while education remained salient in the post-independence economic and social rhetoric, India lost the ground in this respect to both centrally planned economies and to the dynamic economies of East Asia, because of the neglect of primary and secondary education (Mody 2005). Development planners departed from the prescriptions of their predecessors and placed emphasis on growth over the goal of reducing poverty and inequality and universalising quality education.

The result of the neglect of education has been that even more than 70 years after our independence we have not been able to provide quality education to all our children even at the elementary level. Universalisation of secondary education has been consigned to the category of a distant goal left to the mercy of the market force and the rent-seeking private sector. The quality of school education at each level as well as of higher education, is abysmally poor so much so that a large proportion of the Indian graduates – some put the figure at above 80 per cent – are regarded unemployable.

Finally, the Indian school education system is among the most discriminatory in the world. There are varieties and hierarchies of schools, each designed to cater to the needs of the children of parents belonging to particular class, religion and profession. This inequality is primarily inherited and has also been accentuated in the post-independence period. It has also worked relentlessly to perpetuate and aggravate economic and social inequality.

There has been frequent reference in the country beginning from the highest level of political leadership to members of the media, academia and in public discourse, about the goal of India becoming a developed country. There is, however, no example in history where a country has become developed without having a school education system which provides education to all the children without discrimination, which applies a set of norms to ensure both quality and equality, and which is financed and administered by the state. Therefore, the essential and indispensable pre-requisite for India to become a developed country is to make education and health the linchpin of its national development project, accord to these sectors the priority that has been denied to them and earmark the resources and deploy the manpower needed for universalising quality school education and basic health care within a finite period.

References

ADB. 2007. *Toward a New Asian Development Bank in a New Asia*. Manila: Asian Development Bank.

Ambedkar, B.R. 1936. "Annihilation of Caste", Undelivered Speech Prepared for the Annual Conference of the Jat-Pat-Todak Mandal of Lahore.

Ambedkar, B.R. 1949. *Constituent Assembly of India Debates – Volume XI*. Available at: http://164.100.47.194/Loksabha/Debates/cadebadvsearch.aspx [Accessed June 12, 2018].

Berg, A and Ostry, J.D. 2011. "Inequality and Unsustainable Growth: Two Sides of the Same Coin?" IMF Staff Discussion Note 11/08, Washington: International Monetary Fund.

Byrne, David. 2000. *Social Exclusion*. Buckingham: Open University Press.

Cingano, F. 2014. "Trends in Income Inequality and Its Impact on Economic Growth", *OECD Social, Employment and Migration Working Papers*, No.163. Paris: OECD Publishing.

Chancel, Lucas and Piketty, Thomas. 2017. "Indian Income Inequality, 1922–2014: From British Raj to Billionaire Raj?" *WID World Working Paper Series No. 2017/11*. Available at: http://wid.world/wp content/uploads/2017/08/ChancelPiketty2017WIDworld.pdf [Accessed June 16, 2017].

Government of India. 2008. *Eleventh Five Year Plan 2007–2012: Volume II – Social Sector*. New Delhi: Planning Commission, Government of India.

Government of India. 2010. *Economic Survey 2009–10*. New Delhi: Ministry of Finance.

Gray, A. 2017. June 9. *Future of Economic Progress*. Available at: www.weforum.org/agenda/2017/06/these-are-the-world-s-fastest-growing-economies-in-2017-2/ [Accessed June 13, 2018].

IIPS and Macro International. 2007. *National Family Health Survey (NFHS-3), 2005–06: India Volume I*. Mumbai: International Institute for Population Sciences.

Kannan, K.P. 2012. "How Inclusive is Inclusive Growth in India?" *Working Paper No. 03/2012*. New Delhi: Institute of Human Development.

Lenoir, Rene. 1974. *Les Exclus: Un Francais sur Dix*. Paris: Editions du Seuil, cited in Sen, Amartya. 2000. "Social Exclusion: Concept, Application and Scrutiny." *Social Development Paper No. 1*. Manila: Asian Development Bank.

Lewis, A.W. 1961. "Education and Economic Development." *Social and Economic Studies*, 10(2). 113–127.

Mody, Ashoka. 2005. "Quest for Inclusive Growth: Continuity and Constraints in Indian Economic Policies." *Economic and Political Weekly*, 40(37): 4052–4061.

NCEUS. 2009. *The Challenge of Employment in India: An Informal Economy Perspective – Volume 1-Main Report*. New Delhi: National Commission for Enterprises in the Unorganised Sector.

Radhakrishna, R. 2014. "Performance of Indian Economy in the Post-Reform Period." *Indian Journal of Human Development*, 8(1): 5–27.

Rao, Hanumantha. 2009. 'Inclusive Growth: Recent Experience and Challenges Ahead', *Economic and Political Weekly*, 44(13): 16–21.

Ravallion, M. and Chen, S. 2007. "China's (Uneven) Progress against Poverty." *Journal of Development Economics*, 82(1): 1–42.

Schultz, T.W. 1961. "Investment in Human Capital." *The American Economic Review*, 51(1): 1–17.

Sen, Amartya. 2000. "Social Exclusion: Concept, Application and Scrutiny." *Social Development Paper No. 1*. Manila: Asian Development Bank.

———. 2011. "Growth and Other Concerns." *The Hindu*, February 4, 2011. Retrieved June 12, 2018, from The Hindu: www.thehindu.com/opinion/op-ed/Growth-and-other-concerns/article15444092.ece

Silver, Hilary. 1995. "Reconceptualizing Social Disadvantage: Three Paradigms of Social Exclusion." In Rodgers, Gerry, Gore, Charles, and Figueiredo, Jose (eds.). *Social Exclusion: Rhetoric, Reality. Responses*. Geneva: International Institute for Labour Studies.

Stiglitz, Joseph E. 2016. "Inequality and Economic Growth." *Political Quarterly*, 86(51): 134–155.

Surabhi, and Nigam, A. 2018, March 9. "Just About Half The Candidates Who Get Skilled Land Jobs." *The Hindu Business Line*. Available at: www.thehindubusinessline.com/economy/policy/just-about-half-the-candidates-who-get-skilled-land-jobs/article9578024.ece

Throat, Sukhadeo and Dubey, Amaresh. 2012. "Has Growth Been Socially Inclusive during 1993-94-2009-10?" *Economic and Political Weekly*, 47(10): 43–54.

Tinbergen, J. 1975. *Income Distribution: Analyses and Policies*. Amsterdam: North-Holland Publishing Co.

UNDP. 2010. *Human Development Report 2010 – The Real Wealth of Nations: Pathways to Human Development*. New York: United Nations Development Programme.

———. 2011. *Human Development Report 2011 – Sustainability and Equity: A Better Future for All*. New York: United Nations Development Programme.

UNICEF. 2013. *Maternal Health*. Available at: http://unicef.in/Whatwedo/1/Maternal-Health [Accessed June 12, 2018].

Visvesvaraya, M. 1920. *Reconstructing India*. London: P. S. King & Son Ltd.

INDEX

access to justice 6, 66, 67, 218
adivasi 35, 80, 215, 300, 310
adult literacy rate 21, 22, 55, 80, 82; *see also* literacy
affirmative action 129, 301, 309, 310, 318
agriculture 41, 49, 98, 167, 182–83, 195–98, 240, 250–52, 258, 260, 280; agricultural policy 167; agriculture based economy 187; organic farming 193; sustainable agriculture 182, 192
Ahluwalia, Montek S. 263, 306
Alvaredo, F. 50, 52, 299
Ambedkar, B.R. 303, 304, 309, 317, 323
anganwadi 40, 84, 86, 92, 95, 187, 235
Annan, Kofi A. 206
annihilation of caste 296, 309, 317
Annual status of education report (ASER) 94, 114
antenatal care 158, 184, 234
anti-discrimination law 211
Auxiliary nurses & Midwives (ANMs) 40, 41, 189

Bandopadhyay, M. 35, 43, 94
below poverty line 47, 48, 174
Beteille, Andre 308
budget 12, 16, 28, 29, 31, 36, 57n8, 132, 133, 143, 148, 158–60, 197, 198, 203, 210, 212, 216–18, 229, 238, 288, 290, 291

capability 46, 79, 187, 278
cash transfer 38, 159, 242; conditional cash transfer 241, 242

centrally sponsored schemes 14, 15, 217, 241, 291
Chancel, Lucas 285, 320
Chandrasekhar, C.P. 48, 231, 253, 271, 284
child development 40, 235, 237, 238; early childhood care 84, 85, 187, 310
child malnutrition 4, 22, 25
child under nutrition 39, 174, 175
civil and political rights 67, 72, 222n23
civil society 13 38, 45, 68, 73, 130, 159, 217, 289, 292, 302 civil society activism 12; civil society organization 34, 42, 44, 55, 66, 205, 206, 220, 235
climate change 6, 7, 66, 74, 192, 208, 307
community based organisations 121
community health centre 41, 189
compound annual growth rate (CAGR) 151, 159, 267, 274
Constituent assembly 13, 323
Constitution: Constitutional amendment 13; Constitutional commitment 5, 51, 143; constitutional democracy 10, 54; Indian Constitution 4, 302, 303, 309, 318, 323
constitutive social exclusion 317
corporate social responsibility *see* CSR
corruption 55, 66, 152, 287, 288, 293
cost of schooling 84, 86, 93
crony capitalism 285–87, 292
crop diversification 183, 193, 198
crop yield 183, 184, 192
CSR 115, 148, 154, 158, 159

dalit 35, 80, 215, 300, 302, 303, 309, 310
Deaton, Angus 169, 185, 284

Index

decent work for all 6, 48, 119
decentralisation 146, 286
deprivation 4, 23–50, 74, 84, 178, 232–35, 260, 292, 296, 317–23
deregulation policies 50, 320
developing countries 33, 38, 65–75, 98, 120, 135, 137, 159, 161, 204, 206, 208, 259–61, 319, 322
development 3–11, 17, 52–56, 66, 73, 74, 129, 142, 161, 206–10, 228, 231, 237, 250, 258, 287, 315–19, 324–26; development agenda 7, 41, 207, 210, 228, 285; development programmes 15, 16
development planning 3, 5, 52
developmental policies 52, 54, 56, 210
Digital India 216, 251
discrimination: caste discrimination 303, 306; protective discrimination 301
disguised unemployment 48, 253, 260
disparity: income disparities 319; inter-state disparity 321
Doha Declaration 67, 131–35
Dorling, D. 50, 51
Dreze, Jean 46, 48, 50, 54, 55, 185, 284
drinking water: access to safe drinking water 34, 71, 189, 190, 198
dropout 80, 90–95, 113, 187

ease-of doing-business 258, 325
economic distress 44, 100
economic growth 52, 66, 74, 97, 98, 113–23, 138, 211–12, 231, 243, 249, 264–80, 284, 288, 292, 305, 316–26; growth with equity 266; long term rates of growth (LTGR) 266
economic inequality *see* inequality
economic liberalisation 11, 14, 249, 262, 284, 285, 287
education 109; adult literacy rate 80; District Primary Education Programme (DPEP) 12, 79; Education Attainment Index (EAI) 270–76; education for sustainable development (ESD) 97; Education Guarantee Scheme (EGS) 12; educational exclusion 80; literacy rate 80; youth literacy rate 80
education for all 5, 14, 54, 93, 101, 318
educational expenditure 88–90
elementary education 13, 15, 79
elite 35, 51, 54, 153, 286
elite capture 51–54, 283–86
elite dominance 51, 283
employability skills 105, 109, 114, 119, 121, 123n4

Employment: Employment Quality 266–79; global employment gap 99; National Rural Employment Programme (NREP) 13
employment quality 266, 270–72, 276–79
empowerment 41, 42, 44, 45, 203, 205, 206, 208, 209, 212, 213, 216, 217, 221nn5, 7, 8, 10, 16; 229, 243, 318
empowerment of women 41–45, 203–17, 221, 243
enrolment: gross enrolment rate 35, 113; net enrolment rate 35, 113
environmental degradation 52, 183, 301, 306
environmental sustainability 7, 8, 123, 206, 208
equality 308; drive for equality 297; economic equality 303; gender equality 41, 66, 203–04, 219–21, 228–38, 254, 308; idea of equality 302; political equality 283, 302–08; principles of equality 68; social equality 303; substantive equality 306
equality of opportunity 84, 238, 308, 309, 318, 319

feminization: of poverty 230; of survival 230; of the labour force 230
Five year plan 9–13, 15, 37, 42, 106, 118, 132, 133, 142, 145–47, 192, 250, 278, 298, 319
food: accessibility of food 184; availability of food 168, 182–85; public distribution system (PDS) 15, 184, 186, 187, 198, 321
food insecurity 39, 169, 174, 176, 179
food security 6, 12, 15, 29, 33, 37, 38, 41, 129, 143, 144, 167, 168, 171, 179, 182, 183, 185–87, 197, 217, 237, 240, 298
food security act 12, 29, 38, 217, 240
foreign direct investment 138, 258
free and compulsory education 13, 79, 318
Fukuda-Parr, Sakiko 66, 75, 208
fundamental right 13, 14, 79, 302, 318

Gates Foundation 134, 136, 138
gender: development index 22, 25; discrimination 39, 160; disparity 8, 66, 113, 118, 122; equality *see* equality; inequality *see* inequality; inequality index 22, 25, 42
gender norm 43, 205, 212
gender parity 9, 95, 104, 113, 177, 205
generic skill 114, 122, 123, 123n4

Index

Ghosh, Jayati 48, 231, 252, 253, 271, 284, 290, 291
global economy 73, 97, 260–62, 299
global partnership 6, 8, 67, 72
globalisation 5, 11, 49, 98, 99, 208, 230, 261, 297, 304–07, 317
goals and targets 7, 9, 37, 43, 56, 65, 66, 70, 206
Govinda, R. 12, 35, 94
gross domestic product (GDP) 19, 26, 28, 29–32, 37, 46, 49, 116, 120, 132, 136, 138, 143, 148, 149, 152, 158–60, 182, 189, 197, 198, 213, 230, 231, 251–53, 256, 257, 260, 261, 262, 271, 284, 288, 291
Guru, Gopal 310

Haddad, Lawrence 39, 236
harassment 213, 215
Hawkes, Sarah 66, 70
health 132; access to health care 188; health care 142; health care sector 150; health policy 139, 143, 162; health sector reform (HSR) 137, 143, 144; health workforce 135; maternal health services 234; primary health care 145; primary health centres 189; public health 38, 142–43, 162
Health for All Declaration of Alma Ata 130, 136, 139, 142
health insurance 38, 134, 135, 145, 147, 151, 162
health management and information systems (HMIS) 145, 152
higher education 33–36, 97, 100–09, 115–16, 177, 265–66, 278–79, 320–21, 325; National Higher Education Qualification Framework (NHEQF) 107
HLEG 40, 147, 156–59
Hulme, David 75
human capabilities 74, 291
human capital market 265
human capital theory 264, 324
human development 4, 5, 8, 18, 21, 25, 36, 37, 74, 79, 129, 176, 192, 198, 265, 284, 305, 321, 322; human development indicators 176, 192, 284; Human Development Report (HDR) 18, 284, 322
human rights 42, 43, 67, 68, 71, 75, 139, 142, 203, 204, 206–10, 215, 216, 222n17, 238, 303, 306
hunger 6–8, 37–38, 67–70, 215, 217; global hunger index 185

inclusion 13, 42, 53, 69, 71, 72, 75n1, 79, 143, 203, 206, 209, 215, 221n6, 298, 307, 315, 316, 317, 323, 325
inclusive development 19, 33, 52–54, 143, 146, 204, 206, 211, 265, 284, 315–24
inclusive growth 298, 315, 318, 324
inclusive social order 316, 317
Indira Gandhi Matritva Sahyog Yojana (IGMSY) 241
industrial training institute (ITI) 112, 117
inequality 98, 182, 265, 283; caste inequality 304; class inequality 302, 303; economic inequality 51, 265, 308; education inequalities 35, 50, 102, 269, 271; gender inequality 95, 208, 211, 299, 303, 305, 308, 323; horizontal inequality 284, 301; income inequality 98, 276, 285, 305, 315, 316; inequality in higher education 104; social inequality 15; substantive inequality 303; vertical inequalities 284, 302; wealth inequalities 285
inequity: gender inequity 113, 237
informal employment 99, 230, 256
informal learning 36, 120, 124n5
information and communication technology 3, 262, 306
injustice: distributive injustice 144; gender injustice 303; structural injustice 144
institutional reform *see* reform
institutions: private higher education institutions 104; public sector institution 144
institutions of political governance 51
instrumental social exclusion 317
Integrated Child Development Scheme (ICDS) 15, 160, 184–98, 217, 235, 291
International labour organisation 29, 238, 239
Izhar, Alam Md. 152, 157

Janani Suraksha Yojana 241
Jha, Praveen 48, 49, 56, 253, 271
John, T.J. 13, 162
Juergensmeyer, Mark 301, 307

Kabeer, Naila 206, 228, 231
Kanchi, A. 232, 239
Kapoor, A. 19, 20
Khare, Mona 105, 269
Khor, Marti 73, 74
Krishnan, Vidya 158, 159
Krushak Assistance for Livelihood and Income Augmentation (KALIA) 298
Kundu, Amitabh 50, 103, 268

labour 23–30, 43, 46–49, 72, 90, 98, 99, 113, 116–19, 194, 212, 229, 253, 260, 278, 285, 325; labour force participation 100, 114, 116, 213, 229, 230, 231, 235, 243, 300; labour market 106, 107, 112, 114–17, 120, 212, 229, 231, 232, 240, 243, 252, 264, 265, 269, 270, 278, 279; participation of women 231
labour market 31, 36, 43, 44, 48, 49, 90, 99, 105, 106, 107, 112, 114–18, 120, 123n1, 212, 228, 229, 231, 232, 240, 243, 249, 252, 262–65, 269–71, 278, 279
learning outcomes 107, 113, 117
LGBTIQ 205, 209, 215, 219
life expectancy at birth 3, 18, 22, 24–25, 55, 189, 322–23
lifelong learning 80, 107, 116, 122
Lingam, Lakshmi 232, 239, 242,
literacy 15, 21, 22, 43, 55, 80, 81, 121, 211, 230, 232, 300; female literacy rate 176
literacy rate *see* education
livelihood 4, 5, 26, 47, 162, 179, 182, 213, 214, 240, 250, 257, 296, 298, 303, 316–18
local self government 41, 55
Lucas, Robert E. 269

macro-economic policy 49, 208, 209, 249, 250, 258, 259, 262
Madheswaran, S. 101–03
Mahatma Gandhi National Rural Employment Guarantee Scheme (MGNREGS) 11, 16, 47, 179
Make in India 216, 258, 259, 263n5
malnutrition 4, 12, 13, 22, 25, 37, 40, 41, 57nn10, 11; 168, 169, 171, 184–88, 192, 198, 236, 237, 323
manufacturing sector 250–53, 255–58, 262, 263n5
marginalised 6, 9, 11, 35, 41, 42, 51, 80, 122, 129, 154, 203, 215, 223, 236, 286, 298, 307, 315, 319
market 53, 56, 118, 120, 121, 137–39, 143, 148, 149, 150, 169, 178, 179n1, 194, 249, 278, 284, 286, 305, 317; elite market 153; free market choice 139; market dynamics 291; market exclusion 317; market failures 145, 319; market force 35, 98, 117, 325; market fundamentalism 259; market imperfection 264, 279
maternal health 8, 40, 44, 207, 229, 234, 237, 243
maternal health service 229, 234, 243
maternal mortality rate 5, 9, 19, 44, 192, 211, 236, 322

maternity: maternity benefit schemes 241; maternity benefits 240; Punjab Maternity Benefit Act (1943) 239
maternity protection 44, 229, 231, 238, 239, 243n1
Mayer-Foulkes, David 265
McPake, B. 137, 138
means of implementation (MoI) 67, 70, 71, 75
medical: medical care system 152; medical industry 152; medical tourism 151; mobile medical units (MMU) 189
Mehrotra, Santosh 106, 108, 112–17, 120
mid-day meal scheme 40, 94, 184, 188, 189
millennium declaration 42, 71, 206, 221n9
Millennium development goals (MDG) 5–9, 33–34, 42, 46, 65–72, 129–32, 137, 146, 162, 206–08, 211, 214, 305–06
Mills, A. 137, 138
Minimum Needs Programme 10–12
minimum wage 47, 48, 290, 292
minority 16, 215, 242, 303
mixed economy 143, 249
Mohan, Ghosh Sourindra 148, 160
Mohanty, Manoranjan 4, 51, 298, 302, 303, 305–10
mortality 5, 24–25, 130–31, 136, 162; child mortality 8, 236; infant mortality 9, 211, 322; infant mortality rate 19; maternal mortality ratio 8, 19, 322
movement: jiefang 305; Maoist movement 301; samata 305; swaraj 305; Ubuntu 305
Muchhala, Bhumika 67, 70–74
Mukherjee, Sharmistha 207, 214
Muslim 35, 80–82, 84, 91, 95, 101, 304

National Democratic alliance (NDA) 258, 298
National occupational standard (NOS) 115, 117, 123
National rural health mission (NRHM) 147, 148, 189
Nayyar, Deepak 75, 307
neoliberal 74, 204, 251, 261, 285, 291, 297, 298, 308, 310; neoliberal economic reforms 252, 304; neoliberal economy 298; neoliberal Hindutva 296–97; neoliberal policies 249; neoliberalisation 204
NITI aayog 15, 37, 144, 158–61, 216, 297, 298
Non-communicable diseases 69, 131, 152, 161, 189
non-discrimination 45, 68, 95, 206, 210, 211, 318
non-timber forest produce (NTFP) 177, 178

Nurkse, Ragnar 264
nutrition 4, 6, 7, 10, 16, 19–22, 25, 26, 36–41, 84, 86, 129, 144, 155, 167, 169, 177–79, 182, 206, 229, 318; child nutrition 39, 44, 236–43; under-nutrition 38, 161, 162, 176; underweight 176
nutritional status 39, 40, 144, 148, 173, 176–79, 186, 188
Nyuntam Aay Yojana (NYAY) 298

OOPE 146, 152, 156–58, 160
organic farming *see* agriculture
out of pocket (OOP) payments 189
out-of-school children 4, 91, 92, 94–95, 115, 205, 323

panchayati raj institutions 41, 45, 55
participation: labour force participation 243; participation of women 231; private sector participation 146
partnership 34, 45, 65, 72–75, 119, 123, 143, 147–52, 156, 157, 159, 204, 205, 219, 220, 263n5,
Patnaik, Prabhat 284, 285, 306
Patnaik, Utsa 46, 185
Pharmaceuticals 135, 256
Piketty, Thomas 285, 288, 307, 320
Pilz, Matthias 117
Planning commission 9, 10, 15, 132, 158, 159, 298, 319
pluralism 53, 290
Pogge, Thomas 71, 74
policy of liberalisation 317, 320
political equality 283, 302, 303, 306, 308, 309
political leadership 14, 46, 51, 326
political power 51, 54, 286, 297, 302
political process 211, 283, 287
political rights 67, 72, 207, 222n23
poverty 317; absolute poverty 142; capability poverty 46; income poverty 46; poverty ratio 175; relative poverty 50, 142
poverty eradication 7, 46, 47, 206
Pradhan Mantri Matru Vandana Yojana (PMMVY) 242
pregnant and lactating women 37, 217, 241
primary education 8, 11, 12, 21, 42, 67, 178, 182, 206, 291
Primary Health Care *see* health
privatisation 50, 74, 104, 139, 146, 231, 309
productive employment 6, 43, 48, 97, 119, 276
Public Distribution System (PDS) *see* food
public health *see* health

public policy 47, 239, 240, 286
public services 38, 55, 133–39, 145, 158, 212
public spending 29, 155, 156, 159, 288, 291
public-private partnership (PPP) 11, 13, 23, 74, 118, 119, 134, 135–38, 146–48, 152, 155, 158, 260

Qadeer, Imrana 142, 148, 160
qualification framework 106, 107, 109, 114
qualification pack 115
quality education 6, 16, 21, 42, 79, 80, 90, 94, 95, 102, 114, 118, 206, 264, 318, 324, 325
quality of life 3, 5, 16, 18, 25, 26, 34, 52–53, 114

Radhakrishna, R. 178, 321
Rajan, Raghuram 286
Rao, Hanumantha 321
Rapid Survey on Children (RSoC) 40
Rashtriya suraksha bima yojana (RSBY) 148, 160, 189, 291
Ravallion, Martin 266, 322
recognition of prior learning (RPL) 36, 107, 120–23
reform: health sector reform (HSR) 37, 137, 138, 143–44; institutional reform 74, 75, 211; land reform 322; market oriented reform 12; neoliberal reform 252, 304; structural reform 11
Regulatory mechanism 144, 148, 151, 152
Reich, R.B. 51, 52
reproductive and child health 37, 133
reproductive health 70, 131, 137, 207, 323
right based approach 68; right based framework 45, 79, 204; right based laws 298
right to development 67, 72
right to education (RTE) 13, 29, 68
right to food 12, 13, 197, 289, 318
right to work 44, 238, 318
rule of law 53
Ruparelia, Sanjay 68, 289
rural development 16, 26, 47, 98, 197, 198
Rural Landless Employment Guarantee Programme (RLEGP) 13

Sachs, Jeffrey D. 305
Samata 296, 305, 306; *samata* agenda 304, 308, 310; *samata* moment 302, 303, 306
sanitation 6–9, 19, 27, 40, 66, 145, 147, 160, 182, 190, 198, 211–12, 291
scheduled caste (SC) 4, 15, 45, 48, 92, 104, 217, 231, 232, 315, 319, 321
scheduled tribe (ST) 4, 15, 95, 104, 169, 217, 231, 232, 315, 319, 321

school education 15, 16, 34, 35, 79, 80, 86, 88, 96, 324–26; net attendance ratio 81; preschool education 79, 80, 84, 187; School attendance 81
Schultz, T.W. 264, 324
Sector: agricultural sector 183, 214, 240, 250; corporate sector 148, 154, 157, 210, 258, 288, 306; economic sector 182; education sector 11, 34–35, 103, 106; health sector 11–12, 19, 28, 37, 129, 131, 134–35, 139, 142–43, 149, 156, 159; informal sector 43, 115, 147, 161, 212, 230, 255, 320; multi-sector development programme 16, 229; non-agricultural sector 250–51, 255, 260; organised sector 119, 230, 239, 240, 255, 275; private sector 8, 45, 73, 105, 114, 118, 119, 134, 138, 143–49, 151–60, 219, 251, 253, 278, 301, 322, 325; public sector 41, 134, 136, 145, 148, 157, 159, 230, 240; service sector 11, 13, 113, 138, 230, 255; social sector 9, 11, 14, 16, 26–29, 52, 160, 197–98, 231, 288–92, 322, 324; social sector concerns 10, 53, 68; social sector development 11, 17, 26–29, 33, 54, 65–66, social sector expenditure 26, 29, 31; social sector goals 9, 52, 53; social sector policies 10, 68; social sector programmes 14; unorganised sector 36, 44, 108, 120, 229–30, 239–41, 255, 329; welfare sector 147
sector skill council (SSC) 115, 119
Sen, Amartya 4, 46, 48, 50, 53–55, 74, 187, 284, 317, 323
Sen, Gita 130, 207
Sengupta, Mitu 71–74
shadow economy 230
Sinha, Dipa 84, 229, 242
skill development 16, 34, 36, 106–09, 112–16, 119, 122–23, 216, 324; National policy on skill development 115; National Quality Assurance Framework (NQAF) 115; National Skill Development Corporation (NSDC) 114, 119, 324; National Skills Qualification Framework (NSQF) 107–18
skill India 106, 109, 324
skill training 106, 108, 112, 113, 115, 214, 230
social development 3, 5, 7, 10, 12, 14, 16–18, 25, 33, 34, 66, 68, 98, 161; social progress 17, 53; Social Progress Index (SPI) 19; social security 99; social services 10
social development indicators 3, 5, 8

social exclusion 39, 182, 243, 316, 317, 321; constitutive social exclusion 317; instrumental social exclusion 317
social insurance 31, 156, 158
social movements 55, 289, 297
social protection 1, 29, 33, 44, 53, 67, 121, 129, 209, 212, 240, 243, 288, 291–93
Stewart, Frances 301
Stiglitz, Joseph 18, 307
structural affirmation 310
structural reform 11, 71, 143, 249
stunting 22, 25, 37, 39, 57n10, 162, 171, 174, 175, 236, 238
Sundararaman, T. 132, 135
sustainable development 6, 8, 42, 57nn1, 17, 65, 73, 74, 95, 97, 113, 116, 118, 120, 122, 123, 139, 182, 207, 264, 293; sustainable development concerns 10, 66, 69
sustainable development goals (SDG) 5–7, 9, 10, 33, 34, 37, 38, 42–46, 49, 52, 56, 65–75, 79, 84, 92, 95, 97, 113, 114, 117–22, 129–39, 162, 167, 179, 182, 198, 203, 204–20, 221nn12–14, 222nn15, 24; 228, 229, 236, 243, 296–99, 302, 305, 307, 310; SDG framework 7, 9, 33, 48, 204, 228, 302
sustainable economic growth 6, 74, 97, 118, 265
sustainable growth 251, 265, 280, 298
Swaminathan, M.S. 182

targets 7–9, 15, 16, 33, 34, 37–43, 46, 56, 65–72, 79, 113, 114, 117, 118, 122, 129–39, 167, 182, 192, 198, 206–11, 216, 217, 228, 296, 297, 305
technical and vocational education training (TVET) 116–19
technical education 100, 106, 112, 115
technology transfer 73, 75
Teltumbde, Anand 296, 297, 302, 303, 308–10
Tendulkar, Suresh 56, 57n15, 169, 184, 319
Tilak, J.B.G. 86, 105
trafficking 42, 208, 216, 218, 230
Training: TVET 117–19; vocational education and training 112
training institution 108, 109, 112, 122
transparency and accountability 53–55
tribal population 39, 104, 161, 168–70, 176

UN Beijing Platform for Action (BPfA) 203–07, 209–11, 220nn1, 2, 3, 4, 6
under employment 48, 253, 270
undernourishment 4, 34, 39, 71, 72, 173–75, 182, 185

undernutrition 40, 171, 172, 174–77, 236
underweight 4, 171–78, 220nn1, 2, 3, 4, 6; 211, 300
unemployment rate 101, 109
United Progressive Alliance (UPA) 251, 257, 298
universal health care 143
universal health coverage (UHC) 37, 132, 133, 134, 143
USAID 133, 134, 136, 138
Uttar Pradesh Basic Education Programme (UPBEP) 12

Varghese, N.V 101, 103, 109
Verma, Justice, J.S. 211
viability gap funding (VGF) 154
violence against women (VAW) 23, 42, 43, 203–06, 208, 212, 214, 219, 220
virtuous growth cycle 277, 279
Visvesvaraya, M. 325
voucher 38, 115, 159

vulnerability 39, 44, 56, 179, 183, 198, 230, 234, 236, 243, 256
vulnerable employment 23, 44, 99, 231

Wage employment 9, 177, 211
Waldorf, Lee 207
wasting 37, 57n11, 171, 174, 175
welfare policies 142, 290
well-being: 4, 9, 34, 41, 97, 261, 283, 284; human well-being 3, 53; subjective wellbeing 17
women's autonomy 206, 236, 243
Women's empowerment 41–45, 205, 206, 208, 212, 213, 216, 217, 221nn5, 7, 8, 10; 222n16, 243; economic empowerment of women 203, 209
women's movement 203, 204, 208, 210, 220
World Bank 11, 12, 98, 121, 133, 134, 136, 149, 322

youth literacy rate 22, 80–82, 95, 211
youth participation 118